D0794316

CONVICTIONS

CONVICTIONS

SIDNEY HOOK

Introduction by
PAUL KURTZ

Prometheus Books
Buffalo, New York

Published 1990 by Prometheus Books
700 East Amherst Street, Buffalo, New York 14215

Library of Congress Cataloging-in-Publication Data

Hook, Sidney, 1902-1989
Convictions / by Sidney Hook.
p. cm.
ISBN 0-87975-473-7
1. Philosophy. 2. Education. 3. Political science. 4. Social ethics. I. Title.
B945.H683C66 1990
191—dc19 89-3676
CIP

Contents

Introduction *by Paul Kurtz* 7

PART ONE: PERSONAL AND PHILOSOPHICAL

1. Convictions 15
2. The Uses of Death 23
3. In Defense of Voluntary Euthanasia 33
4. The Ethics of Suicide 36
5. Reflections on the Jewish Question 47
6. Toward Greater Equality 63

PART TWO: ON EDUCATION

7. Minimum Indispensables of a Liberal Education 73
8. John Dewey's Philosophy of Education 82
9. Education in Defense of a Free Society 94
10. The Principles and Problems of Academic Freedom 105
11. Allan Bloom's Critique of American Education: A Noble Failure 117

PART THREE: IN DEFENSE OF WESTERN CULTURE

12. An Open Letter to the Stanford Faculty 133
13. The Attack on Western Civilization: An Interim Report 139
14. Educational Disaster at Stanford University? 148
15. The Academic-Brawley Cases 157
16. "Diversity": A New Code Word? 163
17. The Mischief Makers 167
18. The Politics of Curriculum Building 170
19. In Defense of the Humanities 182

PART FOUR: POLITICAL AND POLEMICAL

20. The Faiths of Whittaker Chambers 193
21. The Rationale of a Non-Partisan Welfare State 200
22. How Democratic Is America?
Howard Zinn 217
23. How Democratic Is America?
A Response to Howard Zinn 231
24. Rebuttal to Sidney Hook
Howard Zinn 245
25. Rejoinder to Howard Zinn 250
26. Can American Universities Be Depoliticized?
Henry David Aiken 253
27. From the Platitudinous to the Absurd
(A Response to H. D. Aiken) 268
28. Myths and Realities: McCarthyism and Communism 276
29. A Philosophical Perspective 299

Introduction

Sidney Hook (1902–1989)

I

Sidney Hook played a unique role in contemporary philosophy. He was among the chief heirs in the later part of the twentieth century to the pragmatic tradition in American thought. A student of John Dewey, Hook illustrated, perhaps better than any other contemporary philosopher, the application of pragmatic intelligence to ethical, social, and political issues. His main contribution has been his use of analytic methods in dealing with concrete problems of praxis. Hook's basic interest was normative: he constantly sought to test ideas experimentally by reference to their observed consequences in behavior.

Influenced by his early reading of Marx, he attempted to reinterpret Marxism in pragmatic terms. Indeed, Hook was one of the first in America to treat Marx in a serious scholarly vein, as his early books—*Towards the Understanding of Karl Marx* and *From Hegel to Marx*—testify. He dealt at length with the practical results of Marxist theory in real life, and was a leading critic of the contradictions and failures of totalitarian forms of Marxism, e.g., Leninism, Stalinism, and latter-day varieties of the New Left. Fortunately, Hook lived to see his criticism vindicated. He is today recognized as one of the earliest and most powerful critics of totalitarianism. He helped turn the tide of intellectual opinion from an earlier defense of Marxism to an appreciation of the true nature of Stalinist repression.

Democracy plays a central role in Hook's normative position. Calling himself a democratic socialist (or social democrat), he consistently defended freedom as a basic value. Democracy is grounded, he said, upon the ethical principle of "equality of concern." This principle is not a description of fact about human nature but a prescription of how to treat others. It states that individuals should be provided with opportunities to fulfill their own unique dimensions of freedom and growth; and, where necessary and available, the means to satisfy their basic economic and cultural needs should be supplied.

Political democracy, including civil liberties and majority rule, are necessary preconditions of any viable democracy and cannot be sacrificed at the altar of egalitarian ends. Hook believed that democracy is empirically justified by its benefit to the common man and is in no way derived from any metaphysical premises or natural rights doctrine. For democracy achieves more freedom, security, economic well-being, cooperative diversity, and voluntary creativity than alternative systems.

Hook, like Dewey, argued that a key goal of education in a democracy is the development of critical intelligence and an appreciation of the art of negotiation. He consistently defended the important role public schools have played in achieving a democratic society. Hook has devoted much attention to defining academic freedom and integrity in the universities and colleges. Indeed, in his later years Hook founded the University Centers for Rational Alternatives, a faculty group concerned with defending such ideals as essential to the academic process. We must resist any efforts, he said, to politicize institutions of higher education or lower their qualitative standards of excellence by introducing extraneous political criteria, such as quotas of admissions and employment. These detract from the primary function of the university: teaching and the search for truth.

Hook defended a form of naturalistic ethics, arguing that ethical principles, norms, and values grow out of individual and social reflection and must be tested by their consequences in conduct. Although relative to human interests and needs, these values entail some rational criteria of scientific objectivity and need not be subjective. Factual knowledge pertaining to situations helps to shed light on alternative courses of action; our principles need to be constantly modified in the crucible of experience.

Hook was a secular humanist. A critic of theology, he argued that there is insufficient evidence for the existence of God or a divine purpose to reality. In *The Quest for Being,* he was skeptical concerning the search for ultimate Being or the development of an existential ontology. Even those who are humanists do not escape his skeptical eye. For he was also critical of Dewey and Tillich for misusing language and for attempting to redefine the term "God" in naturalistic terms. Hook criticized any effort to derive ethical conclusions from theological premises. From the fatherhood of God different moral and political prescriptions can and have been drawn. Humanism for Hook is primarily an ethical position, in the sense that ethical judgments are autonomous, growing out of human experience and reflection, and do not need any reference to ultimate first principles for their validation.

A scientific naturalist, Hook maintained that the method of science is the most reliable method for establishing truth claims, but this is continuous with the use of critical intelligence in ordinary life. He held that we should draw upon the sciences for our understanding of the universe and humanity's place within it. Although materialistic in foundation, Hook was a non-reductionist; for he allowed that there are various qualitative dimensions of nature as revealed by art, culture, history, and other forms of human experience.

In *Pragmatism and the Tragic Sense of Life* Hook criticized any pessimistic retreat from the world. Pragmatism, he said, is not insensitive to the tragic, which arises primarily from the conflict of moral ideas, goods, rights, and duties. Pragmatism is for Hook "the theory and practice of enlarging human freedom in a precarious and tragic world by the arts of intelligence and social control." The great challenge for human beings is to use their creative intelligence in order to resolve problems, not seek to escape into a world of theological salvation or an ideology of messianic utopianism. Hook believed that with the cultivation of the humanist virtues of intelligence and courage, and the development of a free, democratic, and open society, it is possible for humans to resolve many, if not all, of their problems and achieve a better life.

II

Several years ago, Sidney Hook proposed that Prometheus Books publish what he called his "Fugitive Essays," many of which had been published in scholarly journals and magazines and were inaccessible to the general reader. These he thought should be collected in one volume—all under the title *Convictions,* for they expressed some of his deepest convictions about a wide range of topics. We were enthusiastic about the book and proceeded with plans to publish it. Hook had been working on this collection of his writings when ill health forced a delay in publication. Although *Convictions* had been announced the previous year, he was unable to complete it. Hook had selected the papers for the volume and determined the order in which they should appear. These essays, except for Part Three, were being edited, and Hook had still to complete his Introduction, which, unfortunately, he was unable to do because of his death.

Another reason for delay in publication was that Hook became involved in a new controversy: a dispute about the courses in Western culture that were being taught in many colleges and universities. Critics, particularly at Stanford University, sharply attacked these courses and insisted that books from non-Western cultures and authored by women and Third World writers should be included. Hook differed with these critics. Since he spent his later years at the Hoover Institution for War and Peace in Palo Alto, Hook was well-versed in the controversy at Stanford and he had already published several essays about it.

Several months before his death, Hook contacted me saying that he proposed to publish still another book, which would include his writings critical of the radical revisionists of Western civilization courses. This he wished to call *In Defense of Western Culture.* He indicated to me that he had received a tremendous amount of support from people who urged him to publish these essays in book form. He sent me his manuscript and asked whether Prometheus was interested. Our answer was in the affirmative. Unfortunately, his death also cut short this project.

Since *Convictions* was already in press, we have decided to combine both projects and to include "In Defense of Western Culture" as a special section of *Convictions.*

Part One of *Convictions,* titled "Personal and Philosophical," presents Sidney Hook's views on suicide, voluntary euthanasia, and death. These essays express Hook's deep-seated convictions, published over his lifetime, about the right of free persons to choose the time of their own death. His defense of euthanasia and the right to die with dignity was based on his own encounter with death several years earlier, which he survived. This essay, he said, brought forth more positive letters than anything he had ever written. Part One begins with Hook's own autobiographical account of his philosophical outlook and ends with essays on the Jewish question and equality.

Part Two, "On Education," provides Hook's reflections on a topic dear to his heart; for he profoundly believed that a liberal education was essential to a vital democratic society. Education for democracy attempted to cultivate the arts of intelligence and share them widely among all men and women in society. Liberal education also presupposes that academic freedom will be defended from those who attempt to undermine the integrity of the university. This section concludes with an analysis of Allan Bloom's popular book, *The Closing of the American Mind.* Although Hook agreed with a good deal of Bloom's critique of the state of American education today, he disagreed with Bloom's own philosophical premises and his elitist agenda for education.

Part Three, "In Defense of Western Culture," presents, as we have indicated, Hook's defense of the classics of Western civilization in the curriculum. These courses, he argues, should be taught without watering them down because of the demands of ideological power blocs on campus. These books offer a range of thought and qualitative excellence unparalleled in human history and they deserve a central place in liberal colleges and universities as the heritage of all of world civilization.

Part Four, "Political and Polemical," presents some of the debates that Hook had with left-wing intellectual figures. We are grateful for permission to publish their essays. Hook was no doubt one of the leading polemicists of his time. These papers vividly illustrate his devotion to and his uncompromising defense of the ideals of Western democracy.

Convictions demonstrates anew that Sidney Hook is the preeminent Socratic figure America has thus far produced. Always prepared to use critical inquiry to challenge the popular assumptions of the day, Hook exemplifies the commitment to reason and freedom as basic values. Rather than being out of step with the times, as his autobiography suggested, Hook was usually one step ahead, able to identify issues and options on the horizon before anyone else.

Although written over many decades, the essays in this volume present the deep convictions about basic ideas and values of one of America's leading philosophical minds.

Paul Kurtz
March, 1990

Part One

PERSONAL AND PHILOSOPHICAL

1

Convictions

As I write these words I am of an age older than most of those who have taught me, and of almost all of those who will read me. But although considered, and sometimes referred to, as an old man, I feel no different from the days when I set out on my career or from the earlier days when I resolved to add to the store of truth or beauty that inspired me when young. I have been mistaken about many things, some of great importance, and I have modified my views accordingly. But I am not aware of having abandoned any of the ideals that motivated me to run risks, to throw myself into the political movement of my time, to do some rash and foolish things from whose consequences I escaped I know not how, to endure long years of unpopularity, to pit myself against powers and movements that could have easily crushed me.

When I try to explain myself to myself I find one trait that may account in part for some of my beliefs. I have always been unduly sensitive to the sight and thought of human suffering. Sardonic critics may dismiss this as just a case of weak nerves. But I can endure prolonged physical suffering and pain and have had several occasions to do so. A few years ago when I lay at death's door in the throes of agony, drowning in a sea of slime, I asked my doctors to cut off my life-support services. I was skeptical about their judgment that my request was premature. I persisted in my request, in vain as it turned out, because of the thought that even if I recovered, the likelihood of going through the same or similar experience again, and imposing once more the burdens and grief of "the last days" on those I loved, could hardly be compensated for by the satisfactions of the uncertain period ahead. I had paid my dues to death. Once was enough. Long before this, the sight of hundreds of persons living on mattress graves in the home of

---

From *The Courage of Conviction,* edited by Phillip L. Brown (New York: Dodd, Mead, 1985), pp. 98–106. Reprinted by permission of the publisher.

the disabled and incurable in which my father took twenty-five years to die had made me a fevent believer in voluntary euthanasia.

I can reconcile myself to the sight of suffering and pain when they are necessary for treatment. One of my most gruesome memories is of the time when I held my three-year-old daughter in my arms when her wound, caused by the bite of an animal suspected of having rabies, was being cauterized with fuming sulphuric acid. But I cannot reconcile myself to cruelty—to the deliberate imposition of gratuitous suffering on sentient creatures, especially human beings. Cruelty has always enraged me and sickened me. Some of my own actions, which have verged on the immoral, have been those in which I have reacted to cruelty in the spirit of Shakespeare's lines: "The villainy you teach me I shall execute. And it shall go hard: but I will better the instruction." I am no Christian, but I can honor and admire a man who can forgive someone who has abused and tortured him, who in his personal life can live by the Sermon on the Mount. But any man who can forgive, no less cherish or love, those who have abused or tortured others including his loved ones, must be more than man—or far less.

These autobiographical details may be considered irrelevant but in my case perhaps they throw some light on some of my basic beliefs with respect to religion and society. At the age of twelve I discovered the problem of evil—the age old problem of reconciling the existence of an all-powerful and all-loving God with a world He created and controlled in which so many of the innocent suffer and so many of the wicked prosper. I was unaware that theologians had choked over this problem from time immemorial and that the bone was still choking them. I refused to go through the ritual of confirmation—the Bar Mitzvah ceremony, when a Jewish child takes responsibility for his own sins. My rabbi was affronted, my parents distressed. In trying to persuade me, my father, an autodidact but an intelligent man, rediscovered Pascal's argument although he had never heard of Pascal. "What are we asking you to do?" he pleaded. "To say a few prayers, to attend the synagogue occasionally. Suppose it turns out there is no God. What will you have lost? A little time at most. But suppose there is a God, and you refuse to obey His Commandments? You will suffer forever in the fires of Gehenna. Why take the chance? You are investing a few hours to insure yourself against an eternity of pain." My mother, whose first-born child had been scalded to death in an accident, seemed more sympathetic to me but quietly said that if she could live with her pain and still have faith, I could try.

I had wit enough to retort to my father that if God did indeed exist and was all-knowing, he would hardly approve of the grounds of my piety and give me any credit for it. In the end I capitulated not because of any arguments but out of social consideration to avoid the scandal to my family of community disapproval. But my faith was gone, and I soon realized that to someone like myself there was not the problem of evil but only problems of evils—some remediable, some not. I could not accept any of the multiple explanations that I later read about. William James's view that God was finite in power and needed our help, a good angel, so to speak, summoning good men for the good fight, seemed quaint and charming. It made as much sense as to postulate the existence of a finite bad angel. Zoroastrianism was more consistent but no less credible. The Hindu views of *karma* and *samsara,* which taught that every evil or suffering experienced in this life was the justified punishment for an evil action committed in a previous life, and that no matter how desperate one's plight, there was the redeeming hope that one could advance in the scale of being by adhering strictly to the rules of the caste system in this existence—all these beliefs shattered on the elementary facts of the sciences. It was an illuminating explanation of why India, locked in the grip of these beliefs, had no genuine social revolution, as Karl Marx claimed, until the British came.

It has always amazed me that intelligent and sensitive thinkers could ever have convinced themselves that every case of evil or suffering in the world is a necessary part of the good of the whole. Since dissonance is sometimes a necessary element in the harmony of a whole symphony, the agony of a tortured child is a necessary part of the structure of existence. Since the *concept* of good has no meaning unless contrasted with the *concept* of evil, good *things* cannot exist unless evil *things* necessarily exist. All of these views seem to me to betray a willful refusal to accept the stark facts of unnecessary cruelty in nature and social life. Ultimately it presupposes the view that all is well with the world, that evil is an illusion of perception or perspective. To believe this seems to me an intellectual mask for cruelty. I could never take Emerson seriously as a thinker after reading his essay on *Compensation* in which he argues that there is always a compensating good for any and every evil, that if a man loses his legs, the muscles of his arms, as a compensating blessing, become stronger, and if he loses his sight, his other senses become more acute. First of all, this is not always true; and secondly, even if true, it certainly is not a sufficient compensation. It is comparable to the Hebrew prayer in times of calamity, in which one thanks God, if he has been struck blind in one eye, that he has not been stricken blind in both. The last person or power to whom such a prayer should be addressed is the all-powerful architect of the universe—if there is one. The response of Job's wife to the gratuitous persecutions to which Job was subject seems more appropriate than his unwavering faith.

At the age of fourteen I read Heinrich Graetz's *History of the Jews.* I never recovered from the consequences. It left me reeling with horror at the periodic and prolonged waves of savage persecutions, which were visited on the unarmed, peaceful, and inoffensive communities of European Jews.

There was not the slightest justification for the autos-da-fé, pogroms, exiles, tortures, and holocausts they suffered at the hands of their neighbors. My opposition to organized religion was rooted in the shock of that searing experience of reading Graetz, and it was reinforced in subsequent years by my reading of Lecky, Henry C. Lea, Gibbons, and Coulton. It built up in me the lasting impression that all peoples obsessed by fanatical dogmas are capable of lapsing into the unspeakable barbarities of the past.

Although as a secular humanist I reject all religious faiths, I nonetheless recognize and respect the role of religion in *personal* human experience. Religion is and should be a private matter. Freedom of worship (including not to worship) is central to our Bill of Rights. I would never dream of disputing or trying to deprive anyone of his or her religious faith. My arguments with religionists have been only with those theologians or representatives of organized churches who have attacked my views or who have sought to convert me or to invoke religious dogmas to support dubious social proposals. This they have every right to do, as I have to make a critical response to them.

Even in my salad days as a Marxist I realized that Marx's philosophy of religion was shallow compared to the profound views of Feuerbach from whom he had originally taken this point of departure. Both were unbelievers. Marx accepted Feuerbach's analysis that religious beliefs and emotions were projections of man's emotional needs. Yet he saw in the succession of religious ideologies and myths nothing but the systematic exploitation of human and emotional needs in order to keep the masses in subjection. By promising the masses enjoyment of a heavenly estate, religion kept them from rebelling against their miserable earthly estate. Feuerbach, on the other hand, anticipted Max Weber's insight that the great religions were interpretations that tried to make sense of the meaningless suffering in human life. He, too, believed in science and socialism and that man's moral vocation was, within the limits of his capacity, to remake and reform the world in the light of consciously held moral ideals whose appeal, as distinct from their validity, could be enhanced by symbols and rituals. He called atheism a religion—to the disgust of Marx and his followers. He believed religion had a sustaining and consolatory function in helping human beings to face evils that did not necessarily flow from economic deprivation but from the experiences of death, failure, and tragedy.

It may be hard to separate the existence of organized religion from personal religious experience, but it is possible to distinguish them. It is only the first with which I have been polemically involved. In a statement made long ago, which still expresses my considered view, I wrote:

> So long as religion is freed from authoritarian institutional forms, and conceived in personal terms, so long as overbeliefs are a source of innocent joy, a way of overcoming cosmic loneliness, a discipline of living with pain or evil, otherwise

> unendurable or irremediable, so long as what functions as a vital illusion, or poetic myth is not represented as a public truth to whose existence the once-born are blind, so long as religion does not paralyze the desire and the will to struggle against unnecessary cruelties of experience, it seems to me to fall in an area of choice, in which rational criticism may be suspended. In this sense a man's personal religion justifies itself to him in the way his love does. Why should he want to make a public cult of it? And why should we demand that he prove that the object of his love is, as he believes, the most beautiful creature in the world? Nonetheless, it still remains true that as a set of cognitive beliefs about the existence of God in any recognizable sense continuous with the great systems of the past, religious doctrines constitute a speculative hypothesis of an extremely low order of probability.

With such views about religion, it is not surprising that I immersed myself in the socialist movement in order to modify social and economic institutions and to improve the lot of the working masses. I never shared the Utopian illusions of many of my comrades who, having lost their traditional religious faith, found a substitute faith in the Socialist revolution that would solve all human problems, and introduce on earth a secular equivalent to the kingdom of heaven. To me socialism was a set of institutions, which I hoped would realize two things: the elimination of material want and the resultant suffering of all persons able and willing to work, and secondly, the extension of freedom of opportunity based on the acceptance of the moral equality of all members of the human community. Today I would sum it up as a commitment to democracy, in John Dewey's words, as "a way of life." The first approximation to democracy as a way of life is the establishment of a genuine welfare state free of the waywardness and abuses that infect some of its exemplifications at home and abroad. The transformation of the socialist dream into a totalitarian nightmare in the Soviet Union and other Communist countries does not invalidate the premises of a democratic welfare state.

One of the great and abiding problems of a democratic welfare state is to avoid the generation of a welfare *class*. The members of this class gradually lose the incentives to engage in the productive labor necessary to sustain growth. One must provide the means that enable the community to erect the safety net or minimum adequate standard of living beneath which human beings should not be permitted to sink. This should be one of the primary tasks of our educational system.

Certain misconceptions about the nature and place of equality in a democratic society sometimes have mischievous effects. A democratic society, indeed any society, cannot reasonably be based on the assumption that all its citizens are physically or intellectually equal or that they are equally gifted in every or any respect. It recognizes and cherishes individual differences that are the basis of the diversity of personalities that distinguish truly human communities from animal and insect societies. As we have said, in a free and open democratic society, citizens enjoy a *moral* and *legal* equality, and therefore, as far as the times and resources permit, the institutions of such a society should seek to provide an equal opportunity to all its citizens to develop themselves to their full potential.

There cannot, of course, be absolute equality of opportunities for all children since they are brought up by parents of different degrees of emotional and intellectual maturity in homes that reflect different levels of cultural achievement and appreciation. Nonetheless, despite this and all the drawbacks of the family system elaborated upon by thinkers from Plato to Freud, the compensations of family life more than make up for them. The family as a rule provides the emotional security and support obtainable in no other way. If the esteem and affection necessary for growth depended only on our beauty, intelligence, congeniality, or other virtues and talents, the world would be a cold place for most of us. The family accepts us and cherishes us for what we are regardless of our merit or achievement. Home is the place we return to after all and everyone has failed us.

The belief in moral equality does not require that all individuals be treated identically in every respect or that equal treatment entails, or can be measured by, equality of outcome or result. It requires that there should be no invidious discrimination against or in behalf of anyone on the basis of race, color, religion, sex, or national origin. For example, every citizen should have a right to equal access to an education appropriate to his talents, interests, and special needs. That does not mean that all persons necessarily will have the same education on every level or even that they should have the same amount of the same schooling regardless of their capacities. Equal access is no guarantee of equal achievement. Where resources make it possible, I believe that all citizens should have an equal right to health care and medical treatment. But only a quack or ideological fanatic would insist that all individuals should have the same medical regimen no matter what ails them. This would truly be putting all human beings in the bed of Procrustes.

It cannot be too strongly emphasized that moral equality is perfectly compatible with the intelligent recognition of human inequalities and relevant ways of treating these inequalities, without invidious discrimination, to further both the individual and common good. After all, intelligent and loving parents are equally concerned with the welfare of all their children. Yet precisely because they are concerned, they may take measures to provide different specific strategies in health care, education, environmental stimulus, and intellectual and psychological motivation, to elicit the best in all of them.

More broadly speaking, if all human beings able and willing to work receive adequate compensation for their labor, there is nothing morally wrong if some receive more, even much more, for their efforts. In other words, when everyone has enough, there is nothing wrong if some receive more than enough because of some service they perform. A great deal of nonsense is written by some philosophers who assert that a good society must make up for the injustices of nature or life. They hold that society must redress the imbalance resulting from the fact that some people are born more beautiful or more intelligent or more energetic or more musical and artistic than others, and that they, in virtue of their unearned gifts of nature, receive more than others. Hegel answered these philosophers with his tart observation that neither nature nor life can be just. Only human beings can be just or unjust to other human beings.

I have always maintained that a reliable sign of whether a human being has found life on the whole worth living is whether he or she would be willing to accept another incarnation—another chance to live—if it were in his or her power to make the decision. By this criterion I have had a life very well worth living. This is not the same as a desire for immortality. Extinction has no terror for me, and I can very well imagine a time at which I would tire of being myself.

Nonetheless, aside from one thing, I shall have a few regrets at leaving the world as it is presently constituted. I shall feel remiss in not being able to continue the struggle in defense of a free and open society. The fear that civilization will be destroyed in a nuclear holocaust, which is fed by horror stories in all the media, seems to me to be an expression of paranoia that weakens the will to resist aggressive and expanding totalitarian systems. There will be no world-wide nuclear war unless the Kremlin is certain to win it, and the Western world can easily keep a posture of deterrent defense that can keep its enemies guessing.

Even if Western Europe and North America survive as free communities, the remaining world will remain predominantly one of squalor and tyranny. In the relatively free areas of the world, eroding its vitality and the health of its institutions, we can observe the growing abandonment of the sense of moral responsibility, the proliferation of noisy demands for all kinds of rights and entitlements without the willingness to accept correlative duties and obligations. The quality of human relationships between the sexes has deteriorated. The obligation to help those who are weaker and more vulnerable is rooted in the fact of interdependence, in the recognition of the community and its traditions as the source and support of our intellectual achievements. We owe more to the heritage of the past than we can ever repay.

Not everyone can do everything well, and so long as individuals make uncoerced choices of careers and vocations they should be judged by their achievements and not by their race, religion, or sex. The woman who freely chooses to fulfill the role of wife and mother is as worthy as the woman who forswears that role for others hitherto pursued by men. The male chauvinist who decries the career woman and the militant feminist who scorns the housewife are equally miscreant proponents of the democratic ethics. The traditional chivalry of men toward weakness and vulnerability, both in men and women, has been undermined by false conceptions of equality that overlook biological differences that transcend social and cultural forces. Such a false view absolves many men of a sense of responsibility.

It is sheer sentimentalism to deny the fact that men, as a rule, are more brutal to children than women. We rarely hear of bestial crimes, especially sexual crimes, committed against children by women. Men are more likely than women to abandon children to whom they owe responsibility. In the general erosion of the sense of individual responsibility, often facilitated by the rationalizations about the misconceptions of the meaning of equality, children suffer most.

When I reflect on first and last things, I find myself believing that we value life and fear death too much. Unless we recognize that there are some things more valuable than life itself, life is not worth living. It may be puzzling but it is true: to be ready to die with dignity and courage not only enhances the quality of human life, sometimes it prolongs our life. When it does not, we may go down fighting in a good cause. But so long as we do not strike our own colors, so long as we resist with integrity and dignity, failure does not spell defeat.

2

The Uses of Death

A wise man, according to Spinoza, does not think about death. In our day, however, he would be regarded as very unwise if his failure to think about death led him to neglect making provisions for his family by leaving a proper will, arranging adequate insurance, and in some metropolitan centers even choosing where to live. Modern society, at least American society, confronts a problem, a whole series of problems, resulting from increasing longevity, changes in the pattern of family life, and a greater concern about the quality of life of the aged. Scientific medicine has been able not to renew life but only to prolong it. In a world of finite resources, physical and human, the public costs of prolonging life at some point become disproportionate to the social benefits. This is especially so when choices must be made about the investment of research funds and medical services for different age groups in the population, and for the study and treatment of different ailments.

Most human beings take for granted that since life is a good, if not an intrinsic good, then at least as a necessary condition for any other experienced good its preservation and extension are always a good. This assumption also seems to be behind the unsophisticated desire for immortality.

For many years, when I would ask my classes whether they would accept the gift of immortality, students would invariably respond that they would, until I reminded them of the Greek myth about the goddess Eos or Aurora, who fell in love with the mortal Tithonus. Eos besought the gods to make her lover immortal. They refused, but to console her they bestowed on Tithonus never-ending life. Not until Tithonus had become aged and feeble but could not die did the goddess and her lover discover what a poisonous gift they had accepted.

Review of *Setting Limits: Medical Goals in an Aging Society* by Daniel Callahan (New York: Simon and Schuster, 1988). Reprinted with permission from *The New York Review of Books*.

It is clear not only after a moment's reflection but from a study of the representations of immortality in all ages and in virtually all the visual arts that when human beings desire immortality it is not eternal life they seek or yearn for but eternal youth. William Blake's *Reunion in Heaven* shows a man and his wife in the prime of life, their small children, and even the family cat. The denizens of Heaven in all paintings I have seen seem hale and hearty even when gray-bearded, never in the last stages of doddering decay.

The progress of scientific medicine and industrial society has led to a changing conception of old age and of its place in society. It is still true that biology sets limits on what can be done, yet it is not biology but society that determines the place of old age in a culture, its authority, what is to be regarded as appropriate for the elderly, and the time and degree of retirement from active life because of old age. Regardless of what we deem desirable for the aged in our society, we must take our point of departure from the fact that until the last century or so average life expectancy was approximately thirty years but that today in the United States it is close to two and a half times as much and rising. The fastest growing age group in the population is made up of those who are over eighty-five, and in a couple of generations it is anticipated that 24 percent of the population will be sixty-five and older. At present, those over sixty-five, who constitute 11 percent of our population, account for more than 31 percent of total medical expenditures.

These figures and a discussion of the numerous problems arising from the health costs of providing decent medical care for the aged are contained in a thought-provoking, in some ways profound, work by Daniel Callahan, former editor of *Commonweal,* founder of the Institute of Social Ethics and the Life Sciences (The Hastings Center), and author of *The Catholic Case for Contraception.* His is a morally courageous book, challenging current widespread assumptions that we should prolong life by increasing medical care even if the result is worsening health throughout the United States.

Callahan argues in language more circumspect and sensitive than that of former Colorado Governor Lamm a few years ago that it is possible to limit care for the aged without any diminution of respect and concern or lack of appreciation for their worth to society. Callahan offers three principles to guide us in the medical treatment of the aged. "After a person has lived out a natural life span, medical care should no longer be oriented to resisting death." By a "natural life span" he means a life whose opportunities "on the whole" have been fulfilled. He explains that he means by this "something very simple: that most of those opportunities which life affords people will have been achieved by that point." These include "work, love, the procreating and raising of a family, life with others, the pursuit of moral and other ideals, the experience of beauty, travel, and knowledge, among others." He does not deny that new "opportunities" may arise later in life, only that this is not "what occurs ordinarily."

He admits that we cannot be very specific about the idea of a natural life span; it will vary from case to case and embrace personal as well as objective factors. But Callahan believes substantial agreement can be established when it has been reached in particular cases by the disinterested inquiry of responsible physicians. There is to be sure something inherently vague in Callahan's first principle. He does not adequately define what an "opportunity" is, nor does he clarify how opportunities are "afforded" us by "life"; it seems instead that the kind of opportunities we have depend upon the kind of society we live in—on its political organization and its level of technological and economic development. The obscurity of Callahan's notion of "opportunities" extends to that of a "natural life span."*

Determining when a "natural life span" has been reached, or when an "opportunity" has been fulfilled and when it is open, is admittedly difficult if not impossible to do by any formula or rule. Callahan, I presume, would agree that we can only decide case by case, but he does not present clearly the kinds of considerations that should be taken into account in making such decisions. My guess is that even those who rule out anything except age and medical condition as relevant would in most cases make the same decision.

Of course, one may argue that living under any conditions, costs, and consequences is worthwhile in itself no matter what. This does not seem to me to be true. I believe I can convince anyone of a sound mind, even if he doesn't care a fig about honor or moral decency, that sometimes it is better not to be than to be.

Callahan's second principle is that "provision of medical care for those who have lived out a natural life span will be limited to the relief of suffering." But suppose the temporary relief of suffering prolongs life without generally alleviating a person's suffering. Suppose pain cannot be relieved. Suppose we are dealing with the current California case in which a man who has been permanently unconscious for five years as a result of a car accident can be maintained indefinitely by a nasogastric feeding tube. Under no circumstances would Callahan approve of active intervention to end life. At most he would approve of hospitals forgoing heroic measures such as the use of mechanical ventilators or expensive forms of intravenous nutrition to sustain life; but, surprisingly, he is resolutely opposed to voluntary euthanasia and medically

---

*The notion is even frightening if it is interpreted to mean that access to medical treatment depends on whether one is held to have completed his life span. But as I understand Callahan he is not urging denial of medical care but only of the continued, indefinitely prolonged care "oriented to resisting death" and all the heroic measures and mobilization of resources that this involves.

assisted suicide even in cases of prolonged agony that can be terminated only by death. (He does not give an extensive account of his reasons for opposing euthanasia. He writes that "a sanctioning of mercy killing and assisted suicide for the elderly would offer them little practical help and would serve as a threatening symbol of devaluation of old age.")

The third of his principles forbids the mandatory use of medical technologies to extend life for the elderly who have outlived their natural life span. Presumably this would apply to all, the elderly poor and rich alike.

Callahan's position in some respects is not as radical as it sounds and is not far removed from attitudes and actual practices in some parts of the country. One does not have to agree with his views about the "natural life span" of individuals to agree with him that since our social resources are limited, we cannot regard medical research, treatment, and care as unlimited.

Preventive medicine is preferable, if successful, to any other kind, but without a sense of proportion the community can bankrupt itself by its programs of preventive medicine. The financial cost of prolonging the lives of the aged beyond the shifting natural life span is a relevant consideration not simply because so much money and effort are involved but because the cost may prevent us from using our resources to save and prolong the lives of those who have not had the opportunity to live out their natural span. The current allocation of public funds for safeguarding the health of different groups of the population, and for engaging in research to overcome the diseases that afflict them, can often be explained by the fact that old people vote, are well organized, and have well-paid and outspoken lobbyists, whereas children do not.

The Association for Retired Persons, for example, lobbies extensively for increased allocation of funds to scientific research designed to cure or control the diseases of the elderly. Other groups, such as the Gray Panthers and the National Association of Mature People, promote legislation that will protect the right of older people to work and to freedom from discrimination. It cannot reasonably be denied that longer lives increase the prospects of chronic illness, such as degenerative joint disease (osteoarthritis), Alzheimer's, and senility secondary to cerebral atherosclerosis, which entails heavier medical costs.

Some policy to limit the kind and nature of medical treatment seems warranted. Just how such a limitation should be applied Callahan does not say precisely; but it is not difficult to conceive of a system by which a medical board would withhold various kinds of expensive treatment, including such procedures as kidney dialysis and administration of prolonged intravenous treatment, from very old patients whose conditions had already deteriorated. That a man has the money to pay for all the medical care and skill available does not necessarily entitle him to them, because what his money buys is not merely a private good but a form of social capital cumulatively built up over generations that someone without much money but in greater need may require.

Because Callahan writes with sensitivity and common sense, I find surprising his opposition to euthanasia and assisted suicide. The reason he offers seem to be inconsistent with his other views. We are dealing here with a matter not of money but primarily of compassion for the suffering of the terminally ill, the agonies of the irremediably stricken that may last for years, and their right to die with dignity, which should extend to those lying comatose and paralyzed, unable to control their natural functions. We do not know the relative number of people in these conditions, but in absolute figures they run into many thousands. Every nursing home has a few.

A *New York Times* article of several hundred words that I wrote in defense of voluntary euthanasia brought a greater outpouring of letters than anything else I have published during my lifetime. Many of the letters were poignant expressions of grief and despair at the suffering of a beloved parent, ill beyond recovery, in torment of lying in a coma unaware of anything. Some revealed a sense of guilt and shame over their hope for an early death of those they loved. A few mentioned the drain of family resources that would have been cheerfully accepted if there was any hope of recovery but that was impoverishing the family and blasting the life plans of its younger members. Most were sympathetic to the various proposals to legalize voluntary euthanasia.

Under some of these proposals a patient, whether suffering or not, would have to ask to die on grounds that his or her condition was hopeless and intolerable; and a doctor would have to certify that the patient's physical condition justified his demand. The doctor would either allow the patient to die by withholding medical treatment or would intervene to cut short his life. In other cases, in which patients are incapable of making a request—because they are in a coma, for example—some advocates of euthanasia believe the patients' families should be allowed to make the request.

As Callahan notes, "the traditional basis for a claimed right to euthanasia" is that people have "absolute dominion over their own bodies. If their death will not do harm to others, then they have a right to will their own death and to seek the means necessary to achieve it."

In rejecting such arguments and proposals, Callahan asks:

> What larger significance might the elderly in general draw from the new situation? It would be perfectly plausible for them to interpret it as the granting of a new freedom. It would be no less plausible for them to interpret it as a societal concession to the view that old age can have no meaning and significance if accompanied by decline, pain, and despair. It would be to come close to saying officially that old age can be empty and pointless and that society must give up on elderly

> people. For the young it could convey the message that pain is not to be endured, that community cannot be found for many of the old, and that a life not marked by good health, by hope and vitality, is not a life worth living.

Legalizing voluntary euthanasia would not convey anything of the sort. What Mr. Callahan deems in the above passage "no less plausible" is in my view sheer fantasy. We are not here discussing voluntary euthanasia for old people—or people of any age—whose lives are marked merely by decline, pain, and despair. The proposals for voluntary euthanasia concern only those people who are in an acutely painful or hopeless condition that can terminate only in death, and who have expressed a strong desire to be free from their racking pain and total dependence on others, and who are in despair that the mercy shown to a suffering animal is denied them. To advocate legal and voluntary euthanasia is not to say that society must give up on elderly people, only that elderly people should be free to have surcease from further treatment when the insults to their body and mind degrade and dehumanize them.

I venture the opinion that Mr. Callahan does not know what very many old people actually fear. Probably most of those who are medically knowledgeable fear that they may be stricken by a catastrophic and lingering illness, with their vital and natural functions impaired, that will result in a painful death, and that they will be utterly dependent on the attentions of strangers. The lessons Callahan sees conveyed to the young—for example that "community cannot be found" for many old people—presuppose that they are extraordinary stupid. We are speaking here only of voluntary euthanasia for those who do not want to endure a life in which "community" is literally impossible. I doubt that any intelligent young man or woman who learns that someone suffering from terminal cancer has the legal right to terminate a life he deems not worth living would conclude that pain from a headache or toothache or even a heartache is "not to be endured." I doubt that anyone old or young who witnessed the final scene of the televised version of Warwick Deeping's novel of 1925, *Sorrel and Son,* where the son relieves the agony of his father in the last stages of cancer, felt that his was anything but an appropriate act of filial affection. When I was young I was told that kindly family physicians in extreme situations of terminal illness discreetly helped their patients "to pass over." But in our litigious age, the practice has largely died out.

A recent Chicago case of medical intervention reported in the *Journal of the American Medical Association (JAMA)* is so bizarre as to raise doubts about its authenticity. According to the report, a resident gynecologist—tired, exhausted, and irritable at the end of a long day in a large private hospital—was awakened by a call that a patient was in distress. Rushing off sleepily to do his duty, he learned that the patient, whom he had never seen before, was suffering severely from ovarian cancer. Moved by her plight and her request: "Let's get this over with," he administered a fatal dose of morphine "to give her a rest."

I do not know of any advocate of voluntary euthanasia who would approve of this irresponsible action. The resident didn't know the patient's history, made no effort to reach the physician in whose primary case she was, and by his own admission was in no fit state to make a judgment. For all he knew, he may not even have understood her properly. No one proposes that a decision of this kind should be made by a single physician. Any legislation providing for medically assisted termination of life would require cautionary and checking procedures that could not be disregarded without risking criminal sanctions. That the gynecologist publicized an act that would have made him criminally liable, and did so in language that made him seem crude in thought and feeling, suggests the possibility that the report was a scam by a prolifer seeking to discredit the movement for humane voluntary euthanasia.

The irony of Callahan's words is that his objection to legally approved euthanasia applies far more strongly to his own view that medical treatment to prevent death should be discontinued for *all* the aged after they have lived beyond their natural life span. Even so, the objection would be invalid. I have a half-suspicion that Callahan has taken his stand against euthanasia and legally assisted suicide to divert attention from the less dramatic but far broader sweep of his own recommendations to limit the medical treatment of large numbers of old people. I hazard the guess that the latter are more likely to win public acceptance only after state legislatures enact laws for the special class of aged that would be affected by the practice of voluntary euthanasia.

Callahan is very much concerned with the symbolic importance of accepting the practice of euthanasia. But his reading of its symbolic significance seems to me arbitrary and his eloquent sentences paying tribute to the elderly when he discusses the issue end in a flat *non sequitur.* "If one believes," he writes, "that the old should not be rejected, that old age is worthy of respect, that the old have as valid a social place as any other age group, and that the old are as diverse in their temperaments and outlooks as any other age group, an endorsement of a special need for euthanasia for the old seems to belie all those commitments." But why? On the contrary, it recognizes that the old suffer from greater hazards than others, that we respect the diversity and freedom of their choices, that we are not imposing a mandatory medical regimen on them from which they cannot escape, regardless of the degree of their torment and physical (or mental) degeneration.

Callahan is careful not to imply that the symbolic significance of the practice of euthanasia is to encourage community insensitivity to the medical needs of other and younger groups of the community. For if that were true, it would hold all the more for his own recommendations. But there are others who invoke the argument of the slippery slope and assert that the practices of euthanasia would necessarily coarsen our sensitivity to the medical needs of those who are not terminally ill, particularly old people, and lead to the slackening of our moral responsibility to anyone gravely ill. The ultimate result, they claim, would be the abandonment of the rights of infants who are ailing or handicapped to the special care required for them to survive.

The argument from the slippery slope is rarely a valid one. Any policy may be abused under some conditions. To the inevitable question: where will you stop? the answer always should be: where our intelligence and sense of proportion tell us to stop. There are special problems concerned with the attitude of society toward infants born without necessary organs or doomed to a life of pain, but how they are resolved is not related to any decision we make about voluntary euthanasia, which would be chosen principally by old people. It seems to me extraordinary that anyone can believe that the adoption of such a policy would even indirectly erode the customary attitude of parents toward their newborn infants. After all, we cannot reasonably assume that women as a rule are looking for an opportunity to get rid of or dispose of their children. If a child is born seriously ill or crippled it seems to evoke more intense protective feelings on the part of many parents.

On the whole, old age has been honored and revered more in Oriental, especially Chinese, civilization than in Western civilization. At a meeting of the East-West Philosophers Conference in the late 1950s a group of Chinese scholars, mostly Confucian, but not from the mainland, proposed that reverence for age be a cardinal principle in unifying world civilizations. When I made a counter-proposal that without disparaging the elderly in any way we would have a greater likelihood of agreement if we stressed the needs of children, they delicately implied that this was the outlook of young barbaric peoples. There have certainly been shifts in the attitude toward old age and, in recent years, especially in the United States, a growing increase in awareness that age by itself is not incapacitating, and that the elderly have the right to be judged by the same criteria of performance and excellence as other groups. It would be foolish, however, to pretend that there is no natural decline in physical and intellectual energy with advanced years. It would be equally foolish to claim that certain precautions—for example, in approving driving licenses—that are intended to safeguard us against dangers arising from the natural tendency of the old not to recognize the effects of age are invidiously discriminatory.

It is one thing to accept old age and ultimately death with serenity and to make life, as long as it lasts, comfortable, with as little pain as possible. It is something else to glorify it. "Grow old along with me/The best is yet to be," addressed to a youth on the threshold of his career makes stirring sense. It would be a mockery addressed to a person of advanced years, as if life were without limits or possessed perpetually expanding frontiers, not only for the human race but for the individual. I still recall Bertrand Russell, who said he deliberately lied only once in his life (in the hope of mitigating the death sentence of a mathematician in Horthy's regime), turning to me and saying, long before he died, "Hook, don't let anyone tell you about the great satisfactions of old age!" He himself strove gallantly to live to the top of his form but because he refused to recognize no limits succumbed to the foolishness of old age.

These days institutions and individuals are being charged not only with racism and sexism but with "agism." Like the charge of racism and sexism, the term is used too loosely. It would be absurd to demand an affirmative action program for the aged with numerical goals and time-period objectives. Where there are no rational grounds for making age a general criterion for a policy, it is ethically if not legally wrong to discriminate against the elderly. But sometimes there are situations in which desirable social policy is affected adversely by the denial that age is relevant. I wish briefly to consider two of them.

In the near future, according to federal law, as I understand it, most mandatory retirement laws based on age are to be abolished, with only a few exceptions. In 1978, the upper age limit was raised from sixty-five to seventy for most nonfederal workers and any such limit was abolished for most federal civilian workers. As a result of recent legislation, the upper age limit of seventy will be abolished for most nonfederal employees as well; but there will be seven-year exemptions for civilian public safety workers, such as prison guards, and for tenured professors, so that studies can be made to determine whether a required age of retirement for these occupations is justified.

A decision to abolish mandatory retirement for university professors would seem to me unfortunate. Most professors at the conventional retirement age of sixty-five or sixty-eight or seventy have reached the height of their earning power. Their pensions and social security income are usually sufficient to sustain them and their wives. Their children are no longer dependent upon them. In the past, mandatory retirement applied to everyone, the gifted as well as the ungifted, the productive and the unproductive. As a matter of fact, only a very small percentage of tenured faculty continue fruitful research, and the percentage declines with age. In most universities mandatory retirement is the only way of getting rid of dead wood, of correcting mistakes in faculty appointments for which students are the main sufferers. It would be insidious to dismiss some professors and retain others, even though there may be a consensus in the university community on who is first-rate and who is not. Outside of the sciences, faculties are more divided on ideological issues.

A mandatory age retirement for all is not discriminatory. On retirement, nearly any first-rate scholar or teacher, if willing, can teach for years as a visiting professor elsewhere. There need not be any loss to the discipline or its students. The philosopher Brand Blanshard after his retirement from Yale had more invitations to teach at other institutions than he could accept. Even professors who are not of Blanshard's stature but are competent scholars and teachers have many opportunities to work elsewhere. The abolition of mandatory retirement in universities would lead to an over-tenured faculty, and delay or denial of opportunity to younger scholars, especially to those who are not women or members of minorities. Such delay or denial is not in the public interest.

It is easy to suggest that the situation be met by the abolition of tenure or by its periodic renewal. But anyone familiar with universities, and our courts are not, will realize that this is not feasible. Once the probationary period has been served and tenure won, the life plan of most people in the academy is set. When I was chairman of a department, I would take it for granted that young scholars at first-rate institutions normally would not get tenure when the rule "after six years—up or out" was first applied. But if a scholar has acquired tenure and is then, when he is up for renewal, dismissed as unfit to continue, I would be very suspicious of his qualifications for further employment. After twelve or fifteen or twenty years in a department, it is very unlikely that a professor's colleagues, with families and children all involved with one another in community life, would vote for dismissal. For it would be tantamount to a sentence of academic death, not only at his own university but at others as well. If someone hasn't made good after such a prolonged period, why should we assume he or she will prove more satisfactory at our own institution, which may not be as good as University X but will not regard itself as a dumping ground for University X's discards?

My second illustration of a field in which the policy of no mandatory retirement seems dubious is the airline industry, about which I confess to no competence. But even if I were assured that pilots of any age would still have to pass tests of competence, I would be uneasy. Even assuming that the criteria of competence would be rigorously enforced and not bent for the veterans of long service, age may affect judgment and energy in sudden emergencies. Recently one of the airlines paid a penalty for limiting the age of flight engineers eligible to fly in the cockpit to sixty years. But it is not only the knowledge of engineering that is necessary in an emergency. Anyone in the cockpit should be strong enough to help the passengers in extreme situations, and what people of sixty can do may be too much for those of seventy or more.

It seems to me to be unwise to apply mechanically the rule that age is irrelevant to performance or a host of other activities. It may be true for selling or editing or publishing, as this change in the federal law would reflect. It may not be true where physical performance affects the lives and safety of others.

3

In Defense of Voluntary Euthanasia

A few short years ago, I lay at the point of death. A congestive heart failure was treated for diagnostic purposes by an angiogram that triggered a stroke. Violent and painful hiccups, uninterrupted for several days and nights, prevented the ingestion of food. My left side and one of my vocal cords became paralyzed. Some form of pleurisy set in, and I felt I was drowning in a sea of slime. At one point, my heart stopped beating; just as I lost consciousness, it was thumped back into action again. In one of my lucid intervals during those days of agony, I asked my physician to discontinue all life-supporting services or show me how to do it. He refused and predicted that someday I would appreciate the unwisdom of my request.

A month later, I was discharged from the hospital. In six months, I regained the use of my limbs, and although my voice still lacks its old resonance and carrying power I no longer croak like a frog. There remain some minor disabilities and I am restricted to a rigorous, low sodium diet. I have resumed my writing and research.

My experience can be and has been cited as an argument against honoring requests of stricken patients to be gently eased out of their pain and life. I cannot agree. There are two main reasons. As an octogenarian, there is a reasonable likelihood that I may suffer another "cardiovascular accident" or worse. I may not even be in a position to ask for the surcease of pain. It seems to me that I have already paid my dues to death—indeed, although time has softened my memories they are vivid enough to justify my saying that I suffered enough to warrant dying several times over. Why run the risk of more?

Secondly, I dread imposing on my family and friends another grim round of misery similar to the one my first attack occasioned.

My wife and children endured enough for one lifetime. I know that for them the long days and nights of waiting, the disruption of their professional duties and their own familial responsibilities counted for nothing in their anxiety for me. In their joy at my recovery they have been forgotten. Nonetheless, to visit another prolonged spell of helpless suffering on them as my life ebbs away, or even worse, if I linger on into a comatose senility, seems altogether gratuitous.

But what, it may be asked, of the joy and satisfaction of living, of basking in the sunshine, listening to music, watching one's grandchildren growing into adolescence, following the news about the fate of freedom in a troubled world, playing with ideas, writing one's testament of wisdom and folly for prosperity? Is not all that one endured, together with the risk of its recurrence, an acceptable price for the multiple satisfactions that are still open even to a person of advanced years?

Apparently those who cling to life no matter what, think so. I do not.

The zest and intensity of these experiences are no longer what they used to be. I am not vain enough to delude myself that I can in the few remaining years make an important discovery useful for mankind or can lead a social movement or do anything that will be historically eventful, no less event-making. My autobiography, which describes a record of intellectual and political experiences of some historical value, already much too long, could be posthumously published. I have had my fill of joys and sorrows and am not greedy for more life. I have always thought that a test of whether one had found happiness in one's life is whether one would be willing to relive it—whether, if it were possible, one would accept the opportunity to be born again.

Having lived a full and relatively happy life, I would cheerfully accept the chance to be reborn, but certainly not to be reborn again as an infirm octogenarian. To some extent, my views reflect what I have seen happen to the aged and stricken who have been so unfortunate as to survive crippling paralysis. They suffer, and impose suffering on others, unable even to make a request that their torment be ended.

I am mindful too of the burdens placed upon the community, with its rapidly diminishing resources, to provide the adequate and costly services necessary to sustain the lives of those whose days and nights are spent on mattress graves of pain. A better use could be made of these resources to increase the opportunities and qualities of life for the young. I am not denying the moral obligation the community has to look after its disabled and aged. There are times, however, when an individual may find it pointless to insist on the fulfillment of a legal and moral right.

What is required is no great revolution in morals but an enlargement of imagination and an intelligent evaluation of alternative uses of community resources.

Long ago, Seneca observed that "the wise man will live as long as he ought, not as long as he can." One can envisage hypothetical circumstances in which one has a duty to prolong one's life despite its costs for the sake of others, but such circumstances are far removed from the ordinary prospects we are considering. If wisdom is rooted in knowledge of the alternatives of choice, it must be reliably informed of the state one is in and its likely outcome. Scientific medicine is not infallible, but it is the best we have. Should a rational person be willing to endure acute suffering merely on the chance that a miraculous cure might presently be at hand? Each one should be permitted to make his own choice—especially when no one else is harmed by it.

The responsibility for the decision, whether deemed wise or foolish, must be with the chooser.

4

The Ethics of Suicide

I

"I take it that no man is educated," wrote William James in one of his letters, "who has never dallied with the thought of suicide." Yet James was no modern Hegesias. His philosophy was an affirmation, not a deep-seated denial or questioning of life. He relied upon the sense of instinctive curiosity and pugnacity to make life worth living for those "who have cast away all metaphysics to get rid of hypochondria." Only in some of the sacred books of the East and the mystic novels of Russia is the message written clear-gray on black: that the highest assertion of personality of one who has not asked for his existence is suicide.

The problem of suicide has generally been approached from the sociological and theological aspects. The studies of Masaryk[1] and Durkheim,[2] who followed the pioneer work of Quetelet, have been in the main scholarly researches into the statistical correlations between the character of the climate, the variation in age, the purchasing power of wages, and other indexes of the tone of economic life, and the suicide rate. And from a molar point of view, the positive coefficients discovered to hold between these diverse social phenomena have been very illuminating. But, as is quite evident, these investigations leave the heart of the individual question entirely unaffected. This is not a criticism so much as a reminder of the self-confessed delimitation of all studies based on large numbers. Nor, on the other hand, has current theological doctrine been more discriminating in its consideration of the particular case. The teaching of Western religion since the time of Augustine has been a resolute condemnation of all forms of self-destruction, and the criminal legislation of various communities has reflected these sentiments. Not so many years ago the penal

From *International Journal of Ethics* 37 (January 1927): 173–188. Reprinted by permission of the University of Chicago Press.

code of the state of New York specified that any person guilty of an attempt upon his own life was guilty of a felony punishable by fine or imprisonment.[3] Only when it dawned upon our enlightened legislators that this statute was setting a premium upon truly effective attempts at suicide was the article repealed. It was practically saying to the hesitant: "Make a good job of it or you will be punished." To this day in many districts, a person whose complicity in such an unfortunate affair has been established may be tried for homicide.

There is another method of treating the problem, however, which is far more relevant and significant for the specific deed than either the absolute pronouncements of theology or the summaries and conclusions of sociology. It is the method of moral and philosophic analysis. From this standpoint, the individual suicide, just as any other individual act, is judged by a certain moral scale or standard. This is the only intelligent approach, for it is as clear that no knowledge of statistical tables will enable us to predict whether our friend who is trembling at the brink of destruction will take the plunge as it is that no moral judgment passed upon his act can be derived from a perusal of such figures. And it is also true that those who spell out with difficulty the letters of a supernatural revelation generally add moral support to their deliberate judgment. Now it is no exaggeration to say that traditional social morality in modern times has set its face sternly against suicide. Suicide has been interpreted as indicating a dry-rot of the soul, as a perverse and pernicious setting-at-nought of all human values, and finally as a cowardly flight from the duties and burdens to which human flesh is heir. This attitude is not confined to the great mass of people whose views, molded by press, school, and church, have been baked hard in the social crust. It is an attitude expressed everywhere by the official spokesmen of the official morality. Of forty-two French textbooks on moral education consulted by Bayet which treat of the question of suicide, forty condemn it outright, allowing no extenuating circumstances. And although some may see merely the wisdom of the ostrich displayed in the fact that of thirty-eight English and American texts examined by the present writer, thirty-two do not mention the subject at all (four express disapproval, two are noncommittal), it is the writer's impression that most of the authors who make no mention of the matter consider the question as closed beyond the need of discussion.

In the course of this paper, I shall try to show that any system of thought which absolutely refuses to countenance suicide as a rational possibility is either irresponsibly optimistic or utterly immoral. Admitting the right to take one's life under *some* circumstances, I shall attempt to sketch some of the cardinal doctrines of a theory of moral education designed to make suicide less prevalent in other trying moments and situations. To uphold a position of this kind has often required a great deal of temerity, for fools and obscurantists have not been loath to distort a particular justification into a wholesale recommendation. But that is the price we pay for not speaking out *plainly* rather than for speaking out at all.

Although the cult of suicide has been viewed as a psychical aberration peculiar to modern society and suicidal practices have multiplied many times over in the last century, reaching appalling figures in the last decade, hardly any modern philosopher has preached or advocated it as a way out. Almost all of the avowed pessimists more or less inconsistently have advised against it: Leopardi, Schopenhauer, von Hartmann, and Nietzsche.[4] On the other hand, ancient philosophy on the whole seems to have regarded a self-inflicted death as justified when committed by the wise man. Plato and Aristotle, it is true, objected to suicide on the ground that the state loses a citizen; but both allowed it in extreme cases. Epictetus, Marcus Aurelius, and the entire Stoic school enjoined suicide upon those who were unable to free themselves from dominating impulses of envy, cupidity, or debauchery. To snuff out the candle of one's life was also permitted in the face of extreme difficulties. Saint Augustine, the most uncompromising opponent of voluntary death in the history of thought, scornfully points out the root incompatibility between the voluntaristic psychology of Stoicism and its cosmic determinism.[5] If there are no ills in life, is it not passing strange that the *wise* man should seek to end all in death? It would be just as rational, Augustine might well have said, for a man who complained not of the burden of life but of its brevity to shorten his natural life-span. Augustine is more consistent but hardly therefore more profound when in consonance with an unmitigated theological determinism he denied to men and women—even to outraged virgins—the right to hand their souls back to God. Plotinos, from the point of view of cultural continuity the last of the Greek philosophers, taught that there was to be no withdrawal from the evils of this world so long as there was any hope of the soul's progress in an upward way. But his theodicy was not so cruelly optimistic as to hold that there was always room or ground for hope.

Bayet, whose eight-hundred-page thesis on suicide and morality represents almost a lifetime of research, has found that the literary currents of French cultural life reflect a reaction to suicide which is apparently more complex than what has been called the traditional point of view.[6] He contrasts the *morale simple,* which passes adverse judgment against all forms of self-destruction, and the *morale nuancée,* which evaluates the act by its motives and effects. The *morale simple* seems to be bound up with the social mores, the *morale nuancée* with social morality. Bayet finds that the arguments advanced against suicide fall under nine divisions.[7] These can really be reduced to five. Surprisingly enough, Bayet seems to be unacquainted with the simple yet effective argument propounded by Leopardi in his *Dialogue between Plotinos and Porphyry,* an imaginary conversation based on Porphyry's confession in his *Life of Plotinos* that Plotinos' intercession had saved him from doing violence to himself while wrestling with a stubborn mood of hypochondria.[8]

II

The major arguments advanced against suicide may be classified under the following heads:

1. *Suicide is a crime against society.*—This has been the chief objection leveled by rational morality. The resolution to cut the bonds that tie us to earth, it is argued, does not absolve us from the moral mandates we recognized as valid until that moment. The fact of our social existence implies the existence of certain social duties, the compelling power of which does not depend upon our acknowledgment of them, etc.

Now, it would be a very easy line of defense against this view to make detailed inquiries as to the exact nature of the duties which the individual owes society and whether these duties are morally compelling irrespective of the social status and opportunity of the person upon whom they are alleged to be binding. This would raise too big a problem to be thrashed out here, like so many other questions of rights and duties, it implies that each one has in certain respects an equal stake in society. And this, by no means is everyone willing to grant. But we may counter with a more direct and effective response. Far from being a crime against society, suicide may actually further the welfare of society. The logic of utilitarian ethics leads inevitably to this position, to the surprise of a number of its professed adherents. The greatest good or happiness of the greatest number may sometimes be attained by personal sacrifice, as the annals of heroism and martyrdom will attest. Unless it is maintained that life itself is worth living—a position that is tantamount to the repudiation of all morality—I cannot see how personal immolation in order to foster and further the ends that give meaning to life can be categorically condemned before an attempt is made to ascertain the impelling motives and weigh the derivative effects. And if it is true that we can readily think of situations not so far removed from our daily experiences in which suicide would be a legitimate means to attain our ends, often a praiseworthy means, and sometimes even an obligatory means, then it follows that we can flatly contradict the first argument and retort that it is not altogether inconceivable that sometimes refusal to commit suicide would constitute a crime against society.

2. *Suicide is cowardly.*—Aside from the line of defense taken above, which in essentials covers every objection, it is evident that if by cowardice is meant *physical* cowardice, then there is presumptive evidence against it in the *behavior* of a great many suicides. Sometimes the implication seems to be that were a self-inflicted death conceived and executed without any hesitancy whatever, less blame would attach to it. This is absurd, for, other things being equal, the greater the hesitation, the greater the probability that the reflective energies are engaged in tragic debate. If by cowardice is meant *moral* cowardice, the

shrinking and shirking from responsibilities and obligations personally incurred, then the particular suicide has really been prejudged, a fact which is disguised from us because of confusing phraseology. In this last case, significant judgment can be passed on the specific event only after an analysis has been carried out in the same terms of our ethical vocabulary as we use for other events.

3. *Suicide is a violation of our duty to God.*[9]—In the absence of specific biblical texts, it is a much mooted point whether the sixth commandment can be extended to cover suicide; but having confined ourselves to questions of ethics, we are excused from entering into considerations of pure theology.

4. *Suicide is unnatural.*—The word "unnatural" ought to be stricken from the pages of our ethical vocabulary. Too many proposals are dismissed with a word whose only intelligible meaning makes it irrelevant to ethical evaluation and whose promiscuous use, empty of any definite or concrete connotation, makes it positively pernicious, blinding those who mouth it to the fact that they have already passed judgment. If "unnatural" means "unusual," then courage, sacrifice, temperance, and every other good whose rarity is attested by the fact that it is regarded as an ethical ideal become unnatural. What else is meant by the word, save a definite indication of a vague disapproval, is difficult to say. Were it not for the platitudinous vacuity of so much ethical effusion on the subject, one would have to apologize for calling attention to the fact that the descent of the moth into the flame and the precipitate bolt of the rabbit into the jaws of the python are as natural as the self-preserving instincts of other creatures.

5. *Suicide is an insult to human dignity.*—The obvious retort is that we generally recognize certain kinds of life as much more insulting to human dignity than any suicide can possibly be. A political prisoner about to be tortured, fearing that a confession might be wrung from him in the throes of his agony, opens his veins. Another human being, helpless in the torment of an incurable, advanced stage of cancer, administers to himself an overdose of morphine. A third, subject to recurrent fits of insanity, in a lucid moment snuffs out the feverish flame of consciousness. Who will say that the lives these men fled were worthy of human beings, were conducive to noble, dignified living or complete personal expression? The medical tradition of enshrining the practice of keeping a patient alive as long as possible irrespective of prospects of recovery makes its grudging genuflections before the white cow of moral orthodoxy. Now, there may be adequate reasons for adopting this attitude in specific cases, but to erect reasons of occasion into inflexible principle of practice is too often prolonging the span of human life by degrading its level and diminishing its dimensions. Why should not the tenderness lavished upon a dumb, suffering dog be extended to an articulate human being who in the grip of a moral ailment asks to be relieved from a "mattress grave"? It requires a brazen optimism, unless one believes in miracles, to reply that there is always

room for hope. Such a reply, however, concedes the main point at issue, since it is tacitly admitted that it is not the sacredness of life but the hope of attaining a certain order of life which should determine the specific recommendation. In this connection we may recall that the lingering death urged by Schopenhauer upon all who would still the assertion of the will in themselves is a mode of suicide much more inhuman than a thousand direct measures could be.

6. *Suicide is cruel in that it inflicts pain upon one's friends and family.*— This last argument seems to be too simple and obvious to have much importance; but in the opinion of the writer, although far from being a conclusive argument against suicide, it is much more weighty than any of the others. It is the final and most effective argument that Leopardi puts into the mouth of Plotinos, "To reckon as nothing the grief and anguish of the home circle, intimate friends and companions, or to be incapable of feeling such grief, is not wisdom but barbarity." Unless one is imbued with the most implacable distrust of the deliverances of introspection, he cannot but be impressed, if people whom he knows are ever to be taken at their word, with the fact that consideration for the peace of mind of one's friends and family is the most powerful deterrent to suicide. It is the common confession of those who have just grazed the abyss of darkness and fought their way back to the light again. And it is not to be wondered at that in a mental crisis the sympathies and bonds formed in the course of one's lifetime should tighten. The cruelty of which we are guilty can be excused when it is the result of a close adherence to nobler ideals than love and friendship. For how many do nobler ideals exist?

Of course this argument has no absolute force, for it does not touch that individual whose spiritual roots are not strongly intertwined with those of his fellows. It also breeds a spirit of exclusive emphasis upon love and friendship, forgetting too often that in this world even these must sometimes be sacrificed. We shall see, however, that what is sound in this objection may be of significance in suggesting the possible place for emphasis in a system of moral education.

III

"When the *taedium vitae* attacks a man it can only be regretted, not censured," wrote Goethe to Zeltner, whose son had committed suicide. *Taedium vitae* may be a malady of the soul; it is also more than that, since it is as often the result of reflection as of the lack of it. Life-weariness is not always begotten of the satiety consequent upon excess. Nor is the accession of such a mood an unfailing index of a spiritless melancholia or a progressive paranoia. A short-sighted jurisprudence and medical theory has often regarded acts performed in these moments as unmotived, and the poignant declarations of the literary testaments as revealing attitudes of mind more in need of cure than of refutation. Yet the modern consciousness seems to be peculiarly subject to this spiritual lassitude. Wealth and station are no safeguards against it. The intricate web of disillusionment and despair in which the mind palpitating for vital experience is finally stilled has been subtly spun out for us in the modern novel—especially the Russian novel. In this section we shall make a brief excursion into the field of Russian literature in order to illustrate certain types of psychodramatic suicidal impulses, to lay bare their spiritual sources and tragic fulfillments.

Some years ago the novels of Dostoyevsky were used by Masaryk as source books in his courses in abnormal psychology at the University of Prague. They are even richer in their bearing on the phenomenology of the ethical and religious consciousness. The rapt religious soul—more than a little warped—is as much reflected in the moral dyspepsia of the character in *Notes from Underground* who begins his splenetic confession with "I am a sick man. . . . I am a spiteful man," as in the cosmic mutiny of Ivan Karamazov, whose pitiful "Euclidean understanding" cannot make out how the polar parallels of good and evil ever can meet at infinity—at some remote moment of eternal harmony. The feverish romanticism of the unnamed character writing from an underground hole arises from his revolt against the insufferable certainty of mathematical and physical necessities. His failure to suppress or control his own spiteful impulses, to transform the world by a gesture, is expressed in a venomous perversity that takes a masochistic delight in ferreting out ugly motives in himself and others. No promise of a beatific harmony can console Ivan for the tears of one tortured child; and refusing to regard the presence of evil as one of the major perfections of the universe, he hastens "to return his entrance-ticket to God." Dostoyevsky believed that he who rejected the God-man of Christianity for the man-god of positivism and socialism was driven by the logic of his position to commit either suicide or murder. This startling deduction was achieved not so much by reasoning as by those imaginative flights to which contemporary God-seeking spirits are given.[10] But the periodic crises and waves of startling conversions and hypostases which welled up after Dostoyevsky hurled his stone into the muddy stream of Russian life are symptomatic of the absolute antinomies which pervade Russian thought and politics. Raskolnikoff in *Crime and Punishment* is torn by the fancied dilemma of always killing or never killing. Kirillov in *The Possessed* believes that to recognize that there is no God, and not to recognize at the same instant that one is God one's self, is an absurdity. Identifying the attribute of godhead with self-will, he kills himself to establish his new terrible freedom. Stavrogin, having followed his senses and mind from one guidepost to another, is drowned in a sea of half-hearted negations. He ends it with a nail and soaped cord. Smerdyakov, whose heart and mind do not feel the living presence of God, seizes the casually uttered phrase of Ivan, "All things are justifiable," as a pretext to kill a dissolute wretch. Yet, even when he acts as his own hangman, he knows that he cannot expiate that death by his own.

The three generic problems which obsessed Dostoyevsky: (1) the existence of evil, (2) the validity of objective ethical standards as against ethical solipsism, and (3) the question of moral responsibility, were handed down to the next generation of Russian writers. They are the ideas which have set off the fuse to the powder magazine of more than one fervent soul. Soloviev follows Dostoyevsky in believing that morality can be founded only on the basis of a supernatural order, that atheism and moral anarchy are bedfellows.[11] Andrayev, dwelling upon the problem of evil, becomes preoccupied with death. Almost every line of his work is a variation of the same dismal theme. Merezkovski, a self-heralded disciple, having failed to erect a niche for Christ on Mount Olympus, has fallen a prey to intermittent moods of frenetic religiosity. To Dostoyevsky is indirectly due the long line of revolutionary Hamlets in Russian literature and life.[12]

After the abortive revolution of 1905, the spiritual currents of Russian life were at their ebb. The golden dreams and longings of the preparatory phase had become transmuted into a leaden despair. The sensitive-spirited sought an escape from the maddening horrors of an autocratic reaction. The three avenues of escape from themselves and an unendurable social milieu which opened up for them were suicide, mysticism, and sex.[13] In Artzibashev's *Sanine* the chief protagonist embodies the type of worldly-wise intelligence for whom all ideals and goals have the same status and relation among themselves as the natural equality of colors and sounds, and who openly proclaims the glorified egoism of a rapturous life of the senses. But the author, *malgré lui,* has cast others in a finer mold. Even Yourri, who had neither faith in life nor faith in death and who died by accident rather than by deliberate suicide, was above sneering at a man who lost his life in the wilderness in an attempt to save a friend. And then there is that timid creature Soloveitchik, who, sickened by the cruelty of man and nature, cannot blunder through, and creeps into a corner to die. Mystical fervor broke out in unexpected places. Vania in Ropshin's *Pale Horse* believes that it is wrong to kill, and yet he writes to his comrades from the prison cell in which he awaits execution for having assassinated the governor, "I did not feel in me the strength *to live* for the sake of love, and I understood that I could and ought *to die* for the sake of it." George, the hardened practitioner of propaganda by the deed, as a result of his brooding on Vania and the ethics of terrorism suffers a paralysis of his revolutionary will. Overwhelmed by the sense of the futility and vanity of all things, the flame of his revolutionary fire reduced to ash, he shakes off the lingering touch of the natural beauty around him and goes out into the autumn night—his revolver with him.

What can save these religious souls?

IV

In view of the foregoing, it may appear not a little anomalous to offer anything in the nature of a moral propaedeutic to make suicide less prevalent. Yet there is no inconsistency involved, for we have not retreated from our main position that suicide is sometimes ethically justifiable. It is admitted that for a great number of suicides there seems to be no ethical necessity and that for even a greater number, the fleeing of this life is a sign of moral surrender. Of course this commits the writer to a belief in the objectivity of moral values, that is to say, to a belief that they are not completely dependent upon *our* recognition of them. The only view which would make suicide altogether justifiable is a thoroughgoing ethical solipsism. But it is yet to be established how a theory of radical solipsism can posit an ethics, since on this view the word "justifiable," lacking an intelligible opposite, is empty of concrete content. Everything or anything becomes justifiable if it is an adequate means of gratifying a conscious desire. The apparently diametrically opposed views that suicide is always justifiable or never justifiable, just as the formulas "this is the best of all possible worlds," "this is the worst of all possible worlds," or "everything is mental," "everything is material," are really different ways of expressing the same thing—in the point at issue, the absence of any standard of what is right or wrong, good or bad. And it must not be forgotten that social *a*morality is social *im*morality.

If the sacredness of human life be invoked to furnish grounds against all forms of self-destruction, then we are duty bound in logic and in humanity to adopt the same attitude toward war and capital punishment. The converse, however, does not follow. The implications of an absolute interdiction of suicide resolutely carried out lead directly to the acceptance of a philosophy of nonresistance. The doctrine of nonresistance literally interpreted is self-defeating and contradictory. The only logically coherent derivative theory is one of *passive* resistance, which is not so much a religion as a social philosophy with a religious flavor.[14] It is insisted here that an absolute crime suicide can never be, for a moral crime consists only in the conscious surrender or betrayal of certain ideals involved in the specific act. For philosophers at any rate, it is not life itself, as Aristotle held forth long ago, that is worth living, but only the *good* life. We may define the good life differently, but no matter what our conception of the *good* life is, it presupposes a physical basis—a certain indispensable minimum of physical and social well-being—necessary for even a limited realization of that good life. Where that minimum is failing together with all rational probability of attaining it, to avoid a life that at its best can be only vegetative and at its worst run the entire gamut of degradation and obloquy, what high-minded person would refuse the call of the poet *"mourir entre les bras du sommeil"*? We must recognize no categorical imperative "to live," but to "live well."

From the above, two corollaries may be drawn significant for a theory of moral instruction: (1) No rational morality can compel us to perpetuate lives that are irretrievably blasted by accident or birth, or blighted by some horrible malady before which remedial measures are unavailing; and more important, (2) no social morality can be equally binding upon everyone unless a social reconstruction makes possible a more equable distribution of the necessities of life. The necessities of life are to be understood as functions of our material and cultural development. Specific recommendations, however, may be urged bearing more directly on suicide.

When life ceases to offer that which makes our activities meaningful and our purposes self-sustaining, the fatuity of bare living cannot but be poignantly brought home to the sensitive intelligence. Those who lose faith in a single exclusive ideal are sorely tempted to desperate measures. Precipitate action arising from too hasty conclusions concerning the futility of all things may to some extent be counteracted by presenting the moral life as an organization of specific, individual *goods* rather than as a holy quest for *the* good. We cannot, so to speak, live through one sense. Besides the possible depression which may attend the deprivation of stimuli, the danger with which all intense sense expression is fraught makes continued enjoyment of its exercise extremely precarious. Suicide is all too frequent among those who have lived for color only, or sound only, or love or power or fame only. The senses give out, the soul grows cold, and the world is too often refractory. Even the truth alone—be it austerely spelled as The Truth—does not save, for it is too easy to kill one's self by pressing on its sharp point. It is almost banal to repeat that the probability of succumbing to the feeling of *taedium vitae* is inversely proportional to the number of interests in which one is actively engaged. We should expect therefore that the aims of moral instruction should point toward (3) an ethical pluralism, a democracy of certain values, an emphasis not on the value of life but on the values of living, rather than toward an ethical monism or hierarchical scheme of values culminating in a *summum bonum.*

Leopardi's argument, together with the testimony of those whose tragic soliloquies have not eventuated into more tragic deeds, seems to show that there are certain goods which make the feeling of human kinship and kindness beat more strongly within our breast. These goods, which must have a place in every moral creed or practice, are (4) love and friendship. As social and personal ties, their very existence implies a capacity for tenderness and sacrifice which makes inevitable hardships more endurable. The more we live in the lives of others, the more certain do our own lives become.

For those romantic souls, angels in revolt, who are moved to cosmic mutiny at the sight of man's pitiful finitude, his helplessness before unavoidable frustration, disease, and death, who at the cry of a kitten are like "to hurl their souls back into the face of God with a curse," we can offer as a religion a kind of inverted Manichaeism in which the supreme power is regarded as the personification of all the forces of evil and destruction in the universe. Masaryk concludes his study of suicide with a plea for a new religion. Here is a religion which is a bond that unites mankind—for once transcending national boundaries—against a common enemy.

NOTES

1. *Der Selbstmord als sociale Massenerscheinung* (Vienna, 1881).
2. *Le Suicide* (Paris, 1897).
3. Compare in the *Digest* of Justinian: *Mori licet cui vivere non placet.* I am not unaware that legislation of the kind referred to above has often been motivated by a desire to insure the faithful performance of military service regarded as due from each subject. But it was not *this* particular kind of bad reasoning that influenced the state legislature.
4. An exception should be noted for Philip Mainlander (Baitz), for whom suicide is a way to salvation. Cf. *Philosophie der Erlösung* (Frankfurt, 1894), pp. 350–51.
5. *City of God.* Bk. XIX, chap. iv.
6. *Le Suicide et la Morale* (Paris, 1922).
7. Ibid., pp. 26–29.
8. Another surprising omission in Bayet's book arises form his apparent unfamiliarity with Dr. Binet-Sangle's *L'Art de mourir* (Paris, 1919). Dr. Binet-Sangle is the most ardent and outspoken defender of voluntary death in all Europe. Developing a suggestion in Thomas More's *Utopia,* he goes so far as to advocate the founding of *un institut d'euthanasie* to be operated by the state under the supervision of a board of philosophers and physicians and to which souls in distress may apply for a truly definitive treatment.
9. In the words of the edict of Louis XIV, *"un crime de lèse-majesté divin et humain."*
10. The distinction cannot be too sharply drawn between the modern mysticism which makes its leap to Nirvana at one bound and the mysticism of the type of Plotinos in which the beatific ecstasy crowns the dialectical ascent. There is nothing savoring of *Schwarmerei* in the latter variety.
11. *Justification of the Good,* p. xix.
12. *Vide* Masaryk, *The Spirit of Russia,* 2 vols. (London, 1919. Translated from the German.)
13. Lenin, who as leader of the extreme socialist element bitterly contested all three tendencies, bitingly remarks in his pamphlet on *The Infantile Sickness of "Leftism" in Communism* that after the revolution of 1905, "pornography took the place of politics."
14. For an elaboration of these theses see the writer's article on "The Philosophy of Non-Resistance" (*Open Court,* January 1922).

5

Reflections on the Jewish Question

Whatever Sartre's merit as a philosopher—not very considerable, in my opinion—his writings reveal a depth of psychological insight more rewarding than a library of tomes on scientific psychology. Why, despite these psychological gifts, Sartre writes such bad novels perhaps others can explain. Psychology, however, has its limitations when applied to historical themes, and all Jewish questions, except the definition of what constitutes a Jew, are historical. Sartre's "anti-Semite" and "Jew," authentic and inauthentic, are ideal psychological types based not on what most Jews and anti-Semites are but on the kind of Jews and anti-Semites literary people are interested in. In virtue of his phenomenological approach, all Sartre needs is just a few specimens to construct a timeless *essence* of Jewishness and anti-Semitism.

For all its historical limitations, Sartre's book, *Anti-Semite and Jew,* is unquestionably one of the most brilliant psychological analyses of the marginal Jew and the fanatical anti-Semite which has ever been published. That he has independently discovered conclusions which Kurt Lewin and Horace Kallen, who know infinitely more about the subject than he, reached many years ago, only adds to the measure of his achievement. Would only that he had kept to psychology. For when Sartre does discuss social and political matters he lapses into the most vulgar and sentimental kind of orthodox Marxism. Anti-Semitism is a "bourgeois" phenomenon—as if it were not found among peasants, in feudal society, among the nobility. It is a mythical representation of the class struggle. "It could not (*sic!*) exist in a classless society"—presumably by definition. Its presence in the Soviet Union (legally forbidden—to be sure) Sartre would probably explain as the result of capitalist encirclement and the existence of those terrible "cartels" which he regards as also responsible for the Marshall plan.[1]

In a curious way Sartre's book supplements the politically acute and psycho-

First appeared in *Partisan Review,* 16, No. 5 (1949).

logically obtuse study Marx wrote on the Jews a century ago. Marx argues against Bruno Bauer's demand that the German Jews give up their Jewishness as a precondition of being regarded as Germans and citizens. Sartre argues against French anti-Semites who insist that the Jews can never really become French because they can never cease being Jews. His answer is that the Jew can be just as good a Frenchman as the Gentile, and that after the social revolution, the Jews may assimilate themselves willingly, and become authentic Frenchmen. The naiveté of Marx's solution—"The emancipation of the Jews is the emancipation of society from Judaism" (which is commerce)—is mitigated by his assumption that what distinguished the Jews would automatically evaporate in the strong sun of the political enlightenment.[2] A century later, and after Hitler, too, this naiveté is a little too much.

Economic competition or distress exacerbates oppositions. It intensifies anti-Semitism but it does not create it. It explains why a scapegoat is sought but not why one particular group is *always* the scapegoat in the West whenever any profound social change or affliction takes place. Is capitalism the common causal factor in Russian, Polish, English, and Spanish anti-Semitism?

Even the radical movement is infected with anti-Semitism—conscious and unconscious. At the time of the Stalin-Trotsky feud most non-Jewish Stalinists used anti-Semitic arguments against the Trotskyists. On the West Coast I was asked by a Stalinist why all the Trotskyists were Jewish intellectuals. In the East during the period when Malcolm Cowley was writing literary criticism for the Stalinists in the pages of *The New Republic,* Communist Party fellow-travelers made no secret of their belief that the Trotskyists were a bunch of "neurotic New York Jews." Just about two years ago, Pierre Hervé wrote in *l'Humanité:* "It is not by accident that three quarters of the Trotskyist leaders are Jews."

I once asked a leading Communist who had broken with the Stalinists to explain as objectively as he could the source of this anti-Semitism. He groped haltingly for an explanation. "It's a matter of superficial cultural differences." He then exclaimed in a burst of honest confession: "I must admit that even I become irritated when I see people in the subway pull Jewish newspapers from their pockets. I feel that if they are living here they really ought to become part of the culture." "Do you feel the same way, " I asked him, "when people draw Greek, Russian, German or Italian newspapers from their pockets?" "Why, no," he replied wonderingly. "That's odd," he added, "I never thought about that before." He is still mystified.

Sartre is aware, however, that the causes of anti-Semitism are not to be found in the behavior of the Jews. That is why the theme of his book is more topical today than it was when it originally appeared. For since then, the actions and thought-ways, to some extent even the psychology, of many Jewish groups seem to be changing without any noticeable decrease in anti-Semitism.

Any careful observer of Jewish affairs is conscious of these transformations among the Jews since the end of the war. To a large extent they are attributable to the profound shock which followed the discovery that almost six million fellow Jews had been slaughtered by Hitler. That they died was one blow; how they died another; the way the rest of the world reacted to the news a third. It is safe to say that the Jews as a whole will never be the same again. As a historical event, the extermination of the greater part of European Jewry will take its place with the Exodus and the destruction of the Temple. Even if the brotherhood of man had followed hard upon the fall of Hitler, it would have taken a long time for the wounds to heal. As it is, these wounds are torn open afresh by every sign that the world does not feel it owes the pitiful survivors anything, and by the multiplying evidences that anti-Semitism has now reached an intensity in some Western countries almost equal to that observed in Germany a few years before the Nazis came to power.

Some liberals and friends of the Jews are puzzled. After all, they point out, this is not the first time in recent history that millions of innocent human beings have been destroyed by despots. Without making comparisons between degrees of infamy and differences in the techniques of murder, Stalin has probably killed more people from the time of the man-made Ukrainian famine in 1932 to the present than even Hitler. When these events happened, and similar ones in China and India, the Jews were no more and no less indignant than anyone else. Why do they seem so "hysterical" now?

The answer is simple. When six million Jews are slaughtered, the remaining Jews cannot but feel uneasy about their own position; when six million Gentiles are slaughtered, the remaining Gentiles do not feel uneasy. Whether the feeling in the case of the Jews is justified—and I believe it is not—is hardly the point. That it exists is a sufficient explanation of the great differences in attitude, speech, and behavior of many Jews throughout the world, and not least in the United States.

In certain respects these differences are not desirable even from the standpoint of Jewish survival and the quality of Jewish life. A people that has, by and large, been rational and pacific now seeks by an act of resolution to be belligerent and to cultivate the *mystique* of action. The desperate courage and will-to-death-through-resistance which would have been appropriate throughout Europe—and not only in the last days of the Warsaw ghetto—in combating the Nazi extermination squads, is now on tap to meet difficulties that are honorably negotiable. It was not Hitler who was assassinated by Bernadotte. And the Jews have now created their own non-Jewish D.P.'s [displaced persons], more numerous than the remaining Jewish D.P's in Europe. Because the Nazis fooled them again and again, they have become overly suspicious of those who kept the Nazis at bay. Goebbels used to assert that the Jews were not as intelligent as they or the world believed because they persisted in misreading Hitler's clearly expressed intentions with respect to them. To prove their intelligence now, many read Clement Atlee's words in such a way that only a Nazi could have uttered them. And as for Bevin!

It is as if the Jews were out to prove that they are like everyone else—inconsistent, fanatical, atavistic. Even those Jews who are distressed by these changes, who prefer to look at Jews as Sartre sees them, "mild," endowed with "a sense of justice and reason," "spontaneous and warm," full of "obstinate sweetness which they conserve in the midst of the most atrocious persecution"—even such Jews, despite themselves, feel a throb of satisfaction at the feat of Jewish arms in a world that has cast slurs over Jewish willingness or ability to fight. Some Jews—fortunately a minority—judge all issues of foreign policy not by their bearings on the preservation of democracy throughout the world but by the way in which the fortunes of the State of Israel are affected. And not unlike the fellow-traveling Christian clergyman, there has emerged the disingenuous Jewish rabbi who permits his name to be used by Communist Front organizations.

All this is reflected in cultural and theoretical matters. The same liberal Jewish periodical which denounces in unmeasured terms—"undemocratic," "unconstitutional," "utterly indecent"—the Mundt-Nixon Bill calling for the registration of subversive organizations plotting the overthrow of the U.S. government by force and violence grows lyrical over the Israeli Constitution that condemns as criminal any propaganda against democracy—a provision which in effect makes Plato's *Republic* seditious literature. Opposition to any official Zionist measure, condemnation even of the Irgun, is sure to bring a raft of scabrous anonymous letters. A people of dissenters have become impatient of their own dissenters and have almost succeeded in cowing them. There has been an upsurge in religious orthodoxy in many Jewish communities outside of Palestine—an orthodoxy not a whit less superstitious than that of other religions. And as if to add a comic touch, the "new failure of nerve" is observable among some young literary Jewish intellectuals, who, looking enviously at the Church, are prepared to join the Synagogue if only Kafka is added to the Apocryphal Books of the Old Testament. One is tempted to characterize them, modifying a phrase of Horace Kallen's, as "amateur Catholics."

If Sartre is right, all this is in vain. It is a matter of profound unconcern to the anti-Semite what the Jews believe and how they behave—whether they are communists or democrats, pious or agnostic, aggressive or shy. The anti-Semite hates them all. The existence of the state of Israel will not disminish anti-Semitism. It will merely furnish the anti-Semites with another charge. We can expect to hear references to Jews as "hyphenated Americans." Sartre here sees truly and sees what some Jews themselves do not see. It is pathetic to observe how many Jews seek to pin on other Jews, those who differ in some perceptible manner from themselves, the blame for a discrimination whose explanation lies not in them, save in the tautologous sense that if there were no Jews there would be no anti-Semitism, but in the beliefs and habits and culture of the non-Jews. A whole volume can be written about the illusions Jews harbor concerning the disabilities imposed upon them by public disapproval of *other* Jews—nonbelieving Jews or rich Jews or radical Jews or second-generation Jews or what not—and the resistance they set up to recognizing the truth that in the eyes of those who "don't like Jews" these differences are utterly irrelevant.

II

What, then, is anti-Semitism? This is Sartre's first question. What is a Jew? is his second. What is an authentic Jew? is his third. Sartre's metaphysics muddies all his answers but he has something psychologically illuminating to say about each question.

Anti-Semitism is not so much an opinion as a *passion.* This passion is not a result of a personal or direct experience with Jews but is a "predisposition" which lies in the psyche of the anti-Semite, his uneasiness about himself, his mediocrity. The idea that the anti-Semite has about the Jew is not explained by "any social fact." "It precedes the facts that are supposed to call it forth." Although Sartre contradicts this by his Marxist derivations of anti-Semitism, this is his deeper, underlying thought. He even goes so far as to say that, "If the Jew did not exist (today), the anti-Semite would invent him."

But why would he invent the *Jew* and not someone else? One would imagine that some historical answer to this question is necessary. Sartre boldly denies it. The *idea* of the Jew as a special and detestable creature must first be present in the anti-Semite before he lets historical facts influence him. Consequently "no external factor can induce anti-Semitism in the anti-Semite." It is an idea or passion that has no adequate cause in its object. *Whence,* then, does it spring?

Instead of answering this question Sartre gives us a phenomenology of the anti-Semitic consciousness. And here he is at his best. He pictures the anti-Semite as a man who is afraid of the human estate, as a sadist with a "pure heart" who justifies infamies in a good cause, a coward and malcontent, a would-be murderer, who glorifies his mediocrity, and legitimizes his right to belong to the world by assimilating himself "to the permanence and impenetrability of stone."

Brilliant as all this is, it is overdrawn. It is too narrow. It does not recognize distinctions and degrees in an appropriate way. This is the psychology of the active anti-Semite who has either harmed Jews by act or libelous word or is aware that under favorable circumstances he would be happy to do it. But what of the much more numerous group who are aware that they have no use for Jews, who desire neither to buy from, nor sell nor rent to Jews, to hire them or compete with them, who at most can only be taxed with participation in a cold pogrom, and yet are free of the vicious traits detailed above? Sartre lets them off lightly. They are really not anti-Semites but mindless nonentities who unconsciously serve as the medium through which the active anti-Semites exercise power. Sartre falters at the point. His eloquence, as well as his insight, stops short. For there are so many of them. To account for *their* moral culpability, comparatively minor as it may be, he would have to face the question he evades all the time (except in a few hasty lines): Why are the Jews, of all possible pretexts, of all possible scapegoats, selected as the sacrificial objects of Western culture?

Before considering this question, let us note that in its fullness Sartre's psychological analysis applies only to the professional anti-Semite, to those who in a sense make a political and social career of anti-Semitism. But there is a significant group of anti-Semites to whom it does not apply.

It is true that in any competitive situation, where inner security or assured social status is lacking, *mediocrity* generates fear of personal failure and hatred of the successful competitor. Where Jew and Gentile are involved, the greater the fear, the more likely it is that the nonmediocre Jew will become the object of embittered hatred by the mediocre Gentile. The latter solidarizes himself with all the Gentiles in a contrived defense of their common interests against the insidious "plot" of the Jew, all the more insidious for being invisible, in order that probing concern about his own failure of achievement be averted from him. Mediocrity, a hopeless, fuming, nervous mediocrity, particularly when it burns with ambition for power or fame, is almost invariably anti-Semitic.

But there is still another type of anti-Semite who is barely touched by Sartre's psychological analysis. This is the anti-Semite who, far from being mediocre, has a touch of genius. He is not a sadist or moral degenerate in the sense of Sartre's active anti-Semite. Nor does he belong among the mindless ones who constitute the latter's mass base. Yet he has provided a great deal of the ammunition for the vulgar advocates of extermination and made anti-Semitism a respectable sentiment in the salons, and among the literary hangers-on of the genteel tradition, who fancy themselves liberal because they make exceptions for one "white haired boy" among the Jews they know.

What Sartre says applies to creatures like Hitler, Goebbels, Rosenberg and their corresponding type in other countries, Drumont, Mosley, Gerald Smith but not to figures like Schopenhauer, Wagner, Dühring, Houston Chamberlain, Proudhon, Bourget, Maurras, Sorel, Dostoyevsky, Henry Adams, Dreiser, Chesterton and Belloc—who, for all their gifts, have helped poison the little minds of Europe and America, and prepared the way for the easy credulities which, while dismissing the Protocols of Zion and the charges of ritual blood-murder, murmur: "After all, there must be something in it." The sensibilities of the Ezra Pounds are finer than those of the Himmlers, the stomachs of the Célines are weaker than those of the Streichers but is the objective meaning of their statements about the Jews so fundamentally different? Yet their psychology is certainly not the same. Every anti-Semitic "genius" has a unique psychology. Even as social psychologies the anti-Semitisms of Central European clericalism, anti-Dreyfus French nationalism, German racialism, English snobbism, must be distinguished. Perhaps the psychology is not so important as that it has a common object.

A study of the literary history of the West reinforces the same point, to be sure, in a gentler and much more indirect way. The reasons are complex and vary somewhat from country to country but it is undeniable that the role assigned to Jewish characters in literature has been unedifying when not actually odious. What seems to me more telling is that despite their tremendously rich imaginative power, the depths of their compassion, and the range of their understanding, the great creative spirits in poetry, novel and drama have never treated the tragic theme of Jewish experience in the modern world in a manner befitting its universal human significance.

Time and again Sartre tries to bring his analysis into line with what he conceives the Marxist position to be by pressing into use a series of sociological banalities. Having read in Communist literature that the intellectual is more undisciplined (i.e., more inclined to question Party Dogma) than the worker because he has not been educated by the compulsions of the processes of production, Sartre believes he can show why anti-Semitism is present in some classes and absent in others. "Shaped by the daily influence of the materials he works with, the workman sees society as the product of real forces acting in accordance with rigorous laws." That is why workers and engineers are not anti-Semites. One wonders how many workers and engineers Sartre knows. In Germany and the United States the engineering profession was probably the most anti-Semitic of all. And it is a myth that the workers are more "disciplined" than the intellectuals. It is only when the Communists have established job control that they can keep the workers in line. If the behavior of the intellectuals in Western Europe and the United States, during the last fifteen years is studied, it will be found that an amazingly large number of them jump to the crack of the Communist whip on matters of belief with far greater enthusiasm than the workers.

There is ample evidence to show that anti-Semitism is present in every class in Western Society from top to bottom. There are, to be sure, variations in the intensity of its expression but they perhaps are more significantly correlated with *the number* of Jews which a given group encounters than with the degree to which it deals directly with the "material" world. Professor Philip Frank, a shrewd observer, tells us that the German students who put up the greatest resistance to Hitler were drawn from the faculties of pure science and philosophy which specialized in "abstractions," and were not disciplined by direct contact with the material world.

There is no one cause of anti-Semitism, or of any other mass movement, but it is possible to find certain constant factors which are present, in all its manifestations in diverse countries, conditions, and times. These indicate that anti-Semitism is not so much a bourgeois phenomenon as a Christian phenomenon, that it is endemic to every Christian culture, whose religions made the Jews the eternal villain in the Christian drama of salvation. Sartre mentions this only to dismiss it. It was once true but is no longer true. Again his psychology is better than his history. "Have we ever stopped to consider the intolerable situation of men condemned to live in a society that adores the God they have killed? Originally, the Jew was a murderer or a son of a murderer—which in the eyes of a community with a prelogical concept of responsibility amounts inevitably to the same thing—it was as such that he was taboo. It is evident that we cannot find the explanation of modern anti-Semitism here. . . ."

No, not *the* explanation but one which goes a long way to explain the *persistence* of anti-Semitism in a world that recognizes the differences between Jew and non-Jew, and in which the Christian dogma—Sartre rightly calls it a legend—that the Jews killed Christ is still taught at some time or other to almost every non-Jewish child. And it is the child who conspicuously lives by the pre-logical concept of responsibility. Even when the legend fades out of the focus of consciousness or belief, the natural horror and resentment, the curl of repulsion and hateful rejection, leave scar-tissue deep in the unconscious which bursts into angry infection later in adult life often to the surprise of the carrier. This does not have to be universally true to be generally true. There are exceptions. The community, too, has its cultural scar tissue—e.g., the use of the term "Jew" as an epithet of disparagement—which may act as host to any passing evil germ. And there obviously cannot be a germ-free life. This is not past history but present history, and its meaning is reinforced by the findings of modern psychiatry.

There is, of course, an anti-Semitism which precedes Christianity; and there is, and probably will continue to be, an anti-Semitism in Moslem countries. But these anti-Semitisms are of the same kind as oppositions between Moslem and Christian, Chrisitian and pagans, or between Christians of different sects. They are not so integral to one another as anti-Semitism is to the Christian epic.

That is why it is safe to predict that anti-Semitism will endure as long as orthodox Christian religious education which pictures the Jew as a deicide.

That is why, for genuine democrats, religion must be a private matter in fact as well as profession, why secular humanism and not Christian humanism is a safer, as well as truer, philosophy for democratic life. That is why every revival of religious orthodoxy, every manifestation of intense *public* concern with the *truth* of religious dogma—to which some foolish literary Jewish sophisticates seem eager to contribute—churns up the already troubled waters of secular liberalism with dangerous historical sediment. That is why it becomes necessary to distinguish between kinds and degrees of anti-Semitism, and avoid the generous illusions of Sartre that everyone's life is at stake when any Jew is threatened in any way anywhere. The Jews, I am sure, would be willing to settle for much less than this Utopian universal brotherhood—for security and justice under a common law for free men. They do not ask to be loved, nor even that people cease feeling prejudices which in a free society everyone is entitled to—including Jews. Legislation against certain discriminatory practices is legitimate but one can no more legislate against social and personal prejudice than one can make all lies actionable at law.

"Anti-Semitism leads straight to National Socialism," declares Sartre. This is preposterously and dangerously false, else all the Jews would by now have long since been dead.

III

The second question: What is a Jew? is one which Sartre answers correctly but for the wrong reasons—correctly, insofar as he says "a Jew is one whom other men consider a Jew"; wrong, because he suggests that there are distinctive Jewish traits, physical and psychical and cultural which are created by this pejorative consideration. The problem deserves some independent analysis. Nothing is to be gained from that pose of profundity which affects a deep metaphysical approach to the question of what is a Jew, illustrated in the procedure of one Jewish philosopher, not noted for his modesty, who, with unctuous cheek, writes: "No one is a Jew who is not ethical, reflective and modest."[3]

What definition of the Jew is most adequate to the various usages of the term "Jew" in current life? There are approximately five million Jews in America. Nothing is so absurd as the attempt to find some one trait, or combination of traits, which will explain the usage of the term "Jew" or which marks off Jews from non-Jews. Whether it be religion, history, culture, language or political aspiration, every criterion breaks down in the face of the multiplicity of facts concerning the beliefs and behavior of those who call themselves Jews or are called such by others.

Religion, for example, is not a differentiating factor. Those who subscribe to a particular form of Jewish religion still regard those in the Jewish community who reject this form—or any form of religion—as Jews. What is even more to the point, the non-Jewish community does not regard religion as a differentiating factor. It does not distinguish between religious and irreligious Jews or believe that "Jewishness" is washed in the waters of baptism. I recall being asked, during the thirties, to join an organization which called itself, "The Society for the Help of Non-Aryan (!) Christian Refugees."

What is true for religion is true for any other trait of differentiation—physical appearance, psychology, culture, language, political faith. This may be roughly established as follows. Take any trait "x" or combination of traits, "x^s" which is presented as *the* mark of Jewishness. Classify all those who are regarded or who regard themselves as Jews, East or West, North or South, in an order ranging from those who manifest the least amount of x, or x^s, to those who display the most. It will then be found that the difference between Jews who possess the least and the most amount of x, or x^s, is greater than the difference between most Jews and most non-Jews in respect to this trait. This is clearly so in the United States, and if on a world-scale we include Jews in the vastness of Yemen, the Caucasus, and Abyssinia, it is even clearer.

Some think that they can define the Jew in terms of origin as one whose ancestors were of the Hebraic religious faith. The difficulty with this is twofold. There are some who are not regarded as Jews, and who do not regard themselves as Jews, whose ancestors many years ago were of the Hebraic faith. Second, how many ancestors professing the Jewish faith does one need—one grandparent, two or three, one great-grandparent, two or three? Every decision is purely arbitrary. No wonder an anti-Semitic mayor of Vienna, when taxed with close friendship with Jews, retorted: *"Wer Jude ist, dass bestimme ich."*

Paradoxical as it may sound, the only formal definition of a Jew that can be given which will do justice to the various ways in which the term "Jew" is used is this: *"A Jew is anyone who for any reason calls himself such or is called such in any community whose practices take note of the distinction."* Let any Catholic Irishman or Boston Brahman or Southern aristocrat move into a community in which he is unknown and pretend he is Jewish only to the extent of *saying* he is Jewish, and he will be treated like all other Jews including those who do not *say* they are Jewish but whom the Gentile community regards as Jews.

One may quarrel with the adequacy of the definition but not with the facts which suggest it. There is no trait or dogma or practice common to all Jews who recognize themselves as such or who are recognized as such by others. What they have in common is a condition or situation of exclusion from one or another pattern of social life, an exclusion which ranges from minor annoying restrictions in good historical weather to major discriminations in bad. What unifies them is nothing positive but, by and large, a common historical condition which, whether they like it or not or whether they like each other or not, cancels out in the eyes of others their not inconsiderable differences.

But what nonsense to say with Sartre that the Jew has been "poisoned" by these restrictions and pressures to the point that he lacks "a metaphysical sense" (would it were so!) and a feeling for "the vital values." The leaders of positivism from Hume to Mach, from Russell and Poincaré to Carnap, have not been Jews, and not a single great pragmatist—Peirce, Dewey, James and Schiller—is Jewish. Sartre has to convert Bergson's anti-intellectualism into rationalism, and the intuitionism of Spinoza and Husserl into intellectualism to make them fit his scheme. Yet every Jewish thinker of note in Western Europe owes more to his non-Jewish contemporaries and predecessors for his ideas than to his status, willing or unwilling, as a Jew. And as for movements that are distinctively Jewish like Hassidism and Zionism, which *can* be explained by the social and cultural pressures of Western Christendom, they are as far removed from rationalism as anything can be. Sartre is almost ready to agree with the anti-Semite that the Jew as such has certain obnoxious traits but mitigates the charge with the counter-impeachment: "You made him so." No group of people so heterogeneously constituted, who have so many assorted reasons for affirmatively or negatively expressing their "Jewishness," can be pressed into one characterological type.

IV

There are many kinds of escape which individual Jews try to make from the common situation of loose negative togetherness which the Christian culture of the West imposes upon them. It is in his account of the psychology of these Jews that Sartre writes his most powerful and poignant pages. But his psychological insight is obscured by an untenable distinction he makes between the "authentic" and "inauthentic" Jew—which I wish to discard in order to use these terms in a different sense. For Sartre "authenticity consists in having a true and lucid consciousness of the situation, in assuming the responsibilities and risks that it involves, in accepting it in pride or humiliation, sometimes in horror and hate." Although he pretends that no normative connotation is attached to "authentic living," he quite clearly indicates that the person who lives inauthentically lacks courage and dignity. Whatever else a man should be, he should be authentic! But this is obviously wrong. "A true and lucid consciousness of the situation"—by all means and in all situations. But whether one should *accept* the situation—why, that depends upon the situation. If one is a thief, a sadist, an anti-Semite, or a Communist Party functionary—it would be far better if he lived inauthentically. And if in any situation, one carries out the responsibilities and risks it involves with "humiliation" or "with horror," this is *prima facie* evidence that he has not accepted it.

The "authentic Jew" for Sartre is one "who lives to the full his condition as Jew"; the "inauthentic Jew" is one who denies it or attempts to escape from it. But to live to the full his condition as a Jew, according to Sartre, is "quite simply to lay claim to and live in the situation of a martyr." Now one may praise an individual for living like a hero or martyr; but one cannot condemn a human being for not living like a hero or martyr. More important, there are many ways in which a Jew can affirm his Jewishness without being a martyr. Sartre says nothing about this because he does not recognize the plural ways in which those who are recognized as Jews by Gentiles *can* live as Jews. What he is really concerned with is the Jew who is recognized as such by the Gentile community but who refuses to admit to himself, and sometimes to others, that he is so recognized and that consequences flow from that recognition. As I use the term "inauthentic" it applies only to the Jew who imagines that he can identify himself with non-Jewish experiences so completely that he can avoid the pains and penalties and discriminatory regard suffered by other Jews whose affirmations and behavior seem to him to be the main source of disabilities imposed upon Jews. According to Sartre, the Jew who is a socialist or liberal or anything else that a Gentile can be is an inauthentic Jew—a fantastic assumption which can only make sense on the notion that there is a metaphysical Jewish essence irreducibly different from a non-Jewish essence, so that the Jew appears to be another *kind* of human being, perhaps not a human being but something above or below him.

In describing the psychology of what he calls the "inauthentic Jew" among Gentiles, Sartre does not distinguish between the psychology of what I call the "inauthentic" Jew—the Jew who desires, so to speak, to pass himself off as a Gentile, and the psychology of what I call "the authentic Jew" who accepts himself as a Jew for any reason whatsoever. *La mauvaise foi* or inverted self-consciousness, as Sartre describes it in the few illuminating pages of his turgid and boring *L'Être et le néant* [*Being and Nothingness*], is different in both cases.

The "inauthentic Jew," in my sense, is afflicted with an additional dimension of self-consciousness. No matter how impeccable his conduct, he is always on guard in predominantly non-Jewish company, exquisitely conscious of the possibility that at any moment something he says or does will be regarded as a telltale sign. He feels that there are some things that are appropriate for him to do, and others which are not appropriate, *merely* because he is regarded as a Jew. Whether he is active in public life or in the professions, wherever his words or deeds affect his fellowmen, he is pursued by a nagging consciousness of the specific effect activity as a Jew has on others. In his utterances he must think not only of whether what he says is true or false, but of how, as coming from *him,* it will be received. He finds that he is bothered by what Jews do or leave undone in a way his own attempted escape makes it difficult for him to understand. He develops a guilty sense of Jewish responsibility despite the absence of any consciousness of Jewish loyalty. When he is pretty far down in the scale of creation, he does not overhear anti-Semitic remarks, and touches bottom when he regales the company with anti-Semitic jokes, told with an air that suggests the difference between himself and other Jews, usually too subtle for others to see. Sometimes, without any religious faith, he embraces another religious faith. There are very few inauthentic Jews of this kind. They are really inauthentic people. The main problem of the authentic Jews is to find some rational basis or ideal fulfillment of their authenticity. Sartre is no guide here.

The genuine problem which confronts those who are regarded as Jews in the modern world is whether they should regard themselves as Jews, and what meaning they can give to their lives as Jews once they acknowledge, as elementary decency and dignity demand, that in some sense they accept themselves as Jews. This is a problem of tremendous complexity just because there is no one thing that constitutes Jewishness and because of the ideological imperialism of so many different Jewish groups which seek to impose their own particular conception of Jewish life upon all other Jews. Before discussing this question, I wish to indicate how the problem arises.

Perhaps the best way to do this is to relate one of my experiences with Jewish and Gentile youth in many institutions of learning. Plato's *Republic* is an ideal introductory text in philosophy and I have always read it with my classes. In the concluding book of the *Republic,* and as a profound commentary on his Utopia, Plato relates an interesting myth about a Greek, named Er, who was left for dead on the field of battle. Er is transported to the meadows of the other world where he observes how the souls of those about to be born anew pick out their future lots on earth before they drink of the waters of forgetfulness from the river Lethe. After a discussion of the significance of this myth in Plato's *Republic* and an analysis of the idea of immortality, I would invite (I no longer do so) the students to partake in a kind of extra-philosophical homework exercise to motivate the next assignment. They were asked to list on one side of a card their sex, place of birth, religious origins, vocational interests and other information they considered relevant to the kind of person they were. On the other side, they were asked to indicate under corresponding heads, what they would choose, if, like the souls in the Platonic myth, they could determine their lot in a future reincarnation on earth. The entries were anonymous, and all students entered into the spirit of it although the results were never disclosed. The results, however, were very instructive. For example, all students want to be born again with the same sex in their next reincarnation. The only exceptions were those girls whose vocational choices indicated that they hoped to become physicians or engineers. They wanted to be reborn men. But more significant for present purposes was the fact that the overwhelming majority of Jewish students did not want to be born again as Jews but as something else—"no religion," "agnostic," "pagan," "Protestant" (mostly Unitarians with a few scattered Episcopalians), "nothing that would be a burden or be discriminated against"—were some of the typical responses. Not a single Gentile student ever wanted to be born Jewish.

This is no more an expression of "inauthenticity" in Sartre's sense than the desire to be born in a better age. But it does indicate a profound *malaise* on the part of Jewish youth. Sometimes it takes an acute form. Over the years I have met numbers of young Jewish men and women who wanted to know why they shouldn't change their name, why, if a job or life career was at stake, they shouldn't deny their origins. "After all," they complain, "we don't conform to, or believe in, anything distinctively Jewish." They wanted to know from me as a professor of ethics why it was wrong for them to seek to escape punishment for a condition for which they have no responsibility. It was not hard to point out that for most of them escape was practically impossible, that where it was possible the psychological costs were usually too burdensome, and that morally it was intrinsically degrading to capitulate to irrational prejudice and deny kinship with their own fathers and mothers who, often against heroic odds, had courageously kept their integrity and faith whatever it was. Except for one or two cases it turned out that these young men and women were content to remain Jews because they were fundamentally decent, not because they had any clear conception of what made them Jews.

This feeling of ambiguity and negation toward Jewish existence is characteristic not only of certain sections of Jewish youth but even of greater numbers of their elders, particularly in the United States. Many American Jews have acknowledged themselves as Jews for the sake of their Jewish brethren in distress. Many more have become concerned with their Jewishness for the sake of their children in hopes of providing them with psychological security and a sense of historical belonging with which they can meet the shocks of discrimination and rejection without neurosis. The Jewish child as a rule experiences the impact of scorn, hostility, and opprobrious rejection during his tender years. Sartre has some remarkable passages on this theme. It is difficult for any one not acquainted with specific cases to appreciate how deep the bewildered hurt goes into the psyche of the child, and how often these frustrations express themselves in tensions toward his parents, the innocent cause of the child's plight, or in a tortured silence that gives rise to self-doubt, and sometimes self-hatred. Most parents find it much easier to carry their own burdens of suffering than to stand by helplessly in the presence of their children's agony.

That is why so many Jewish parents, especially in this neurotic-conscious age, seek eagerly to supply some consciousness of historic or contemporary Jewish association. But they avoid facing frankly the question of what their own Jewishness consists in, and how it is related to the Jewish and world scene.

It is at this point, usually, that a quest for definitions begins and Jews cast around desperately for some conception or clear formula which will express "the essence" of their Jewishness. The quest is not only fruitless but foolish. It is a capitulation to the muddy metaphysics of the anti-Semite.

Far wiser, it seems to me, is to recognize the historic fact of Jewish existence, the plural sources of Jewish life, and its plural possibilities. No philosophy of Jewish life is required except one—identical with the democratic way of life—which enables Jews who for any reason at all accept their existence as Jews to lead a dignified and significant life, a life in which together with their fellowmen they strive collectively to improve the quality of democratic, secular cultures and thus encourage a maximum of cultural diversity, both Jewish and non-Jewish. Such a philosophy recognizes that there is no dignity in denying one's origins or in living as if they were something to be apologetic about. It recognizes that morally, even more significant than acceptance of one's origins are the *fruits* of such acceptance, what one does with it, what one makes it mean, what comes out of it.

This is not the place to discuss the various "positive solutions" that have been offered as a basis for Jewish life. I shall return to them on another occasion. Meanwhile I permit myself a preliminary comment.

One solution, very unpopular among Jews today, is the universalist solution in which the individual thinks of himself as a Jew by unfortunate accident but as a human being by enlightened choice. He usually looks to some form of universal democratic socialism in the future where the difference between Jew and non-Jew will forever disappear. This dream has its noble features, but it overlooks the fact that human beings live as Jews and non-Jews here and now and will continue to do so for a long time to come; that the dream itself is based upon the acceptance of differences among men and not on the hope of an undifferentiated unity; and that the microbes of anti-Semitism infect even movements which do not officially allow for its existence. The dream still has its uses as a guide in some ways but not as a home.

If it is pruned of its Utopianism and its failure to understand that the ethics of democracy presupposes not an equality of sameness or identity but an equality of differences, much of the universalist view still has a large measure of validity which Sartre, for one, completely ignores in his caricature of the attitude of the liberal and democrat toward the Jews.

According to Sartre the man of democratic principle, although a better person than the anti-Semite, is just as hostile to the Jew as a Jew. He wants him to disappear into the abstract universal, *man,* and annihilate himself as a concrete, historical individual. Whereas the anti-Semite "wishes to destroy the Jew as a man and leave nothing in him but the Jew, the pariah, the untouchable," the democrat "wishes to destroy him as a Jew and leave nothing in him but the man, the abstract and universal subject of the rights of man and the rights of the citizen." To the Jew, therefore, Sartre concludes, "there may not be so much difference between the anti-Semite and democrat."

No, not much difference except between death and life, between *Mein Kampf* and the Statute of Virginia for Religious Liberty. Now we know what surrealism in logic is! Because *the man* does not exist, Sartre tells us with a gesture of rigorous thinking, therefore only particular kinds of men exist. But the sense in which *the man* does not exist is precisely the sense in which *the Frenchman, the Ger-man, the Jew,* and *the* anti-Semite do not exist either. A subclass is just as much of an abstraction as a class. Only individuals exist. But whether they should exist as Jews or Gentiles, as Cathoics or Protestants or humanists, as Italians or Americans, as existentialists or as philosophers (in the etymological sense), should be, according to the democratic philosophy, *a matter of voluntary choice.* If individuals exist, they must exist as something. This is an analytic statement. But that they must continue to exist in the same social and cultural status in which they are born is a piece of antidemocratic presumption. The democrat wants to give all individuals the right to freely determine themselves as Jews or Gentiles, as citizens of one country or another, as cultural heirs of Socrates or Aquinas or Dewey. He no more wants to destroy the individual Jew than the individual Gentile. He wants only to destroy those individuals and social institutions which seek to deprive human beings of their power of uncoerced choice. This is what is perennially valid in the liberating ideas of the French and Anglo-American Enlightenment which Sartre has renounced for a noisome mess of Heideggerian anguish and neo-Marxist historicism. He is a better man than his doctrine because he lacks the courage of his confusions.

NOTES

1. The two countries of the world Sartre is most ignorant of are the U.S. and the U.S.S.R. for the position of the Jews in the Soviet Union, cf. two noteworthy articles, "The Soviet Partisans and the Jews" by Solomon M. Schwarz, *Modern Review* (January 1949), and "Has Russia Solved the Jewish Problem?" by Harry Schwartz, *Commentary* (February 1948).

2. Marx did not understand that Jewish capitalism was what Max Weber called "pariah" capitalism and that the Jews played no important role as a group in capitalism *"as a process of production"* whose study became his life work. He never returned to the theme of his essay "On the Jewish Question" written when he was a young man of twenty-seven. In that essay he argues for the emancipation of society not only from Judaism but from Christianity and all other religions.

3. *Commentary* (October 1946).

6

Toward Greater Equality

The concept of equality has moved into the center of intellectual and cultural interest in recent years. In some quarters it has become a verbal fetish, used synonymously with terms like "democracy" and "social justice." Reflection will show, however, that when it stands by itself, "equality" or the demand for equality is an incomplete and ambiguous expression. If we want to move "toward greater equality" we don't know what it is we want unless we can specify *what* we want in greater equality. In a country in which members of group A have the vote while members of group B have not, we can move toward greater equality either by granting members of both groups the vote or by *denying* it to both groups. If we stress only equality we could not distinguish between saying that "justice consists in treating all persons alike" and "justice consists in mistreating all persons alike." At best, then, equality is a necessary but not sufficient condition of a just society—since human beings can be equal in poverty or affluence, equally enslaved as well as equally free. That is why a just rule or law must go beyond mere impartial application. The rule or law itself must be morally valid.

My starting point, which I am assuming is common for all of us, is that we are interested in furthering greater equality of participation in democracy as a way of life. The commitment to democracy as a way of life does not entail a belief that all men and women are physically and mentally equal, but the postulate that, whatever their differences, they are *morally* equal. The recognition of the moral equality presupposed by democracy as a way of life is expressed as *an equality of concern* for all members of the community to develop themselves to their full capacities as human beings. This makes

---

From *Philosophy, History, and Social Action,* edited by S. Hook, W. L. O'Neill, and R. O'Toole (Dordrecht, Holland: Kluwer Academic Publishers, 1988), pp. 235–243.

it obligatory for the democratic community to equalize opportunities for its citizens regardless of race, color, religion, sex and national origin. Toward greater equality, then, means toward greater equality of opportunity, for persons in all areas, especially education, housing, health and employment, required for individuals to develop their best potential as human beings.

It is obvious that as long as the family and different home environment exists, as well as extreme genetic variations in capacities, *absolute* equality of opportunity is unattainable. But this is no more a justification for abandoning the continued quest for equalizing the conditions of opportunity than our failure to achieve absolute health, wisdom, and honesty undercuts the validity of these ideals. Properly understood, equality of opportunity commits us to programs of continuous reforms. It is the revolution *en permanence*.

But is equality of *opportunity* enough? Are competence and merit, which determine awards and rewards when careers are truly open to talents, sufficient? It is sometimes argued that equality of opportunity necessarily converts social life into a race or battlefield in which the consequence of the victor's triumphs is invidious defeat of his competitors. This is a non sequitur. If we remember that our controlling moral postulate is equality of concern for all persons to reach their potential, not all forms of competition are desirable; neither are all forms of competition undesirable; not all forms of competition need result in disaster for those who are not winners, and especially for their children. After all, we do not tolerate or encourage opportunity, no less equal opportunity, for many kinds of anti-social actions. Our moral postulate commits us at the very least to see that the basic human needs for food, clothing and shelter are gratified for all, regardless of the outcome of social programs geared to merit. It commits us to provide a floor or level of life, whose extent and nature is a function of our technological capacities, beneath which human beings should not be permitted to sink through no fault of their own.

It is further objected: if careers are to be open to talents, what about the fate of the untalented? To which I reply: it is a tolerable fate provided that there are opportunities of employment for all; provided that no persons, regardless of their vocations, are regarded as second-class citizens of the political community; and provided that all citizens have the assurance that the community in diverse ways will seek to equalize the opportunities open to their offspring.

So I cheerfully acknowledge that equality of opportunity is not enough because it does not absolve us from the responsibility of responding to basic human needs; and because, as Jefferson realized, not all the possible consequences of equal opportunity, especially extreme disproportions of wealth and power, are acceptable, particularly if their operation undermines through monopolies of press and other strategic goods and services, equal opportunities of development for subsequent generations.

Nonetheless because equality of opportunity with all its institutional reinforcements is not by itself adequate for an enlightened social philosophy, it does not in the least follow that we must supplement it or substitute for it, or use as a test of its presence the principle of equality of *result.* It is strange logic that argues from the undesirability of *some* extreme inequalities of result to the desirability of equal results in every form of social distribution, or seeks to justify equality of results as essential to social justice or to genuine democracy. In a world in which men and women vary in all sorts of ways, how can equality of concern eventuate in equality of result except by chance or ruthless design? The expectation is as absurd as the presumption that equality of medical concern for those who are ailing necessitates the same medical prescription or regimen for them all—the unfailing sign of a medical quack. Equality as a moral postulate envisages the moral equality of the different and not merely of the same; the application of an equal desirable standard to those relevantly situated, regardless of their differences. It was none other than Karl Marx who reminded us that since a right by its nature consists in the application of an equal standard, applied to different individuals, "and they would not be different individuals if they were not unequal . . . every right in its content is one of inequality." It is a gross misconception of the socialist ethic to interpret its principle of distributive justice as aiming at equality of result or situation regardless of merit, variations in need, responsibility, and social utility. After basic needs have been met, with respect to goods and services that are scarce, i.e., relative luxuries, it is not unfair to distribute these on the basis of desert. This makes it more likely that the availability of such goods and services will increase.

How shall we apply these general considerations to the concrete situations we face in the United States today? I start with the assertion that among the very highest items on the agenda of unfinished business of American life is the final elimination of all practices of civil, social and economic discrimination against any citizen on grounds of race, color, sex, religion, or national origin. We can move toward this objective by vigorous enforcement of all federal, state, and local statutory prohibitions against discrimination, not only in the field of civil and political rights but in public and private employment with respect to remuneration, promotion, and tenure, and in access to education, housing, recreation, and other areas that affect the development and fulfillment of human capacities.

It goes without saying that vigorous enforcement of existing laws against discrimination will not by themselves achieve the objective of equal opportunities. Where there are no opportunities, there is little solace in the assurance of equal opportunity to fill them. If decent housing is not available, equal opportunity of access to it is literally equal opportunity of access to nothing. It is therefore incumbent upon the federal government to commit itself to a program of full employment at a decent wage level. For those able and willing to work there must be posts for all who are qualified, and also for the unqualified, granting that the posts will naturally by different. In all areas, if private enterprise is unable to meet public need, public agencies must move to meet them. In education, particularly, special supplementary programs should be established to permit all *individuals* who have been disadvantaged in the past to make up for opportunities lost or denied to them. The basic strategy for realizing equality or opportunity is a combination of rational public and private policies, whose detailed nature we cannot explore here, that will expand opportunities for all. If there are not enough places in law school for all *qualified* students, where that has been determined on objective grounds, then instead of preferential racial or religious selection, let us establish more law schools. The same goes for medical schools. What we must avoid is, first, policies that discriminate *in favor* of any group at the cost of discriminating *against* some other group on grounds irrelevant to the objectives of the policy and, second, policies that fail to consider the rights and needs of the individual person, considering him or her only as a representative of a group. We must avoid them precisely because it has been such policies that in the past have resulted in gross injustices to racial and religious minorities and women. We are inconsistent, as well as insincere, if in attempts to rectify the arbitrary and invidious discrimination of the past we practice arbitrary and invidious descrimination in the present. Morally illicit proposals for such types of rectification have been made by partisans of preferential hiring, of quota systems, of schemes which require that "numerical goals and timetables" be mandatory for all institutions that have contractual relations with the government.

Let us consider this issue which currently divides those who are opposed to the patterns of prejudice and discrimination of the past.

It is sometimes denied that it is arbitrary to give preferential treatment to someone who has been the victim of preferential treatment. And with this we can agree. Any particular person who has suffered in consequence of injustices toward him or her is certainly entitled to compensatory treatment as an individual. But morally it is altogether different to say that since *other* individuals of his or her group have suffered in the past because their qualifications were disregarded that therefore individuals who belong to that group in the present, who were not themselves discriminated against, should be judged not on the basis of their qualifications, but on the basis of their group membership, even if this means barring individuals who are better qualified.

I say that it is altogether different because it violates the very principles of equity that justify compensatory treatment for the individual victimized by past discrimination. What I am asserting is that granting the evils of past and present discrimination, the remedy in *not* bureaucratically prescribed "numerical goals" and "time-tables," a quota system, imposed on educational institutions and other organizations. Such remedies are advanced on the basis of a highly questionable assumption, to wit, that a society of equality is one in which all the various groups and subgroups within that society are represented in all disciplines and professions in precise numerical proportion to their distribution in the total pool of the population, or in the community pool, or in the pool of those potentially utilizable. The additional assumption behind such remedies is that any statistical evidence that reveals a marked variation from these proportions is proof of a policy of discrimination.

Not only are these assumptions highly questionable, we never make them in other situations where abuses have been checked or abolished. No one would reasonably argue that because many years ago blacks were deprived of their right to vote and women denied the right to vote that today's generation of blacks and women should be compensated for past discrimination against their forebears by being given the right to cast an extra vote or two at the expense of their fellow citizens or that male descendants of some prejudiced white men of the past be deprived of their vote. Take a more relevant case. For years, blacks were shamefully barred from professional sports, until Jackie Robinson broke the color bar. Would it not be absurd to argue that, therefore, today in compensation for the past there should be discrimination against whites in professional athletics? Would any sensible and fair person try to determine what proportion of whites and blacks should be on basketball or football teams in relation to racial availability or utilizability? Do we not want the best players for the open positions regardless of the percentage distributions in proportion to numbers either in the general population or in the pool of candidates trying out? Why should it be any different when we are looking for the best qualified mathematician to teach topology or the best scholar to teach medieval philosophy? If we oppose all discrimination, why not drop all color, sex, religious and social bars in an honest quest for the best qualified—no matter what the distribution turns out to be? Of course the quest must be public and not only fair, but must be seen to be fair.

One might even consider the situation with respect to athletics as a paradigm. Since there should be equal opportunities for health and recreation, the community has the responsibility for providing facilities for all citizens to engage in sport and other exercise and, in fact, many communities are moving in this direction. There are still areas of discrimination here with respect to women. There is a neglect of their legitimate athletic interests, especially in competitive sports with men, and they have not yet cracked the sex bar in professional athletics. The law can properly prevent some types of discrimination in budgeting appropriations to enlarge the field of opportunity for women. The rest ultimately depends on them. In time, as more and more women participate in sports, and the social stereotypes about women in this field disappear—as they have in tennis and swimming—I am confident that opportunities will open to women in professional sports as they have to blacks.

Were a woman to appear who bats almost as well as Hank Aaron or who steals basis as well as Lou Brock, it would not be long before she broke into the big leagues. Where there is a vested interest in victory, one standard for everyone will sooner or later prevail. In a free and open society one standard for everyone should prevail, regardless of any vested interest.

We may even draw an analogy with equality of educational opportunity. On the basis of the principles I have outlined, we can support programs of open enrollment, in the sense that the community should provide opportunities for all young men and women to enter some institutions of higher or tertiary education, and beyond that to *compete* for entry into *any* educational institution. However, the right to receive an education, and to the schooling required for that education, does not carry with it the right to enter any specific institution at any specific time. But it does carry with it the right to be judged and evaluated by the same standards as all others who have been admitted.

There are some institutions that seek to staff themselves with the most talented faculty available, with the aim of serving the ablest students, engaging themselves in an educational experience and in a process of learning and discovery of inestimable social value and human benefit to the entire community. Provided that one standard of excellence is applied to all applicants, when all the programs of remedial and special training and coaching to enhance the skills of those who need this support to compete have been concluded, the percentage distributions of students in various ethnic groups or among men and women are irrelevant.

But of course these are not the only kind of students that should be of educational concern to us. The ordinary students, even the dull students, have the same right to the best educational experience for their aptitudes as have the superior students. That is why there must be a provision for various types of educational institutions for students of various interests and capacities. That is why there must be provision for continuing education. After all, not all teachers can be the most talented nor all students the ablest. There is a uniqueness about every student that must be respected. That respect is perfectly compatible with the application of a single standard of achievement or award in any given institution. We may and should guarantee the basic needs of food, shelter, education and, whenever possible, vocation, too, but we cannot guarantee anyone against educational failure.

It should be obvious that my whole approach is based on the belief that it is the individual who is the carrier of human rights and not the ethnic or national or racial group. Once we disregard this universalist approach which is blind to color, deaf to religious dogma, indifferent to sex where only merit should count, we practically insure the presence of endemic conflicts in which invidious discriminations are rife and tensions mount until they burst with explosive force. The pluralist society then becomes a polarized society. A pluralistic society is one in which the *individual* is a member of many different associations, in which he does not stand stripped of all ties and parochial loyalties before the power of the all-encompassing State. A pluralistic society is *not* one in which individual rights are bestowed by different contending groups or possessed by virtue of membership in these groups. Such a society, whether it is called multi-ethnic or multi-racial, whether it be Malaysia, Northern Ireland, Cyprus, South Africa, Uganda and other areas where persons do not enjoy equal rights unless their mothering groups possess equal power, is in an incipient state of civil war.

There are many cultural and psychological side-effects that derive from employment practices based on membership in groups rather than from individual merit. First, there is a tendency to dilute and debase academic and professional standards in order to accommodate members of groups who, it is feared, would not make the grade. There is something offensively patronizing in assuming that members of some groups, even when given educational opportunities commensurate with others, cannot, without preferential treatment, compete on equal terms with their fellow citizens. Second, a double standard of status begins to emerge among the personnel of institutions recruited in this way. Invidious distinctions are drawn between those who have made it strictly on their own merits, selected by their professional peers in open competition, and those who have made it by virtue of membership in some group. Qualified members of disadvantaged groups who have succeeded without benefit of preferential selection have been quite eloquent on that score.

I want to conclude by presenting a program of nondiscriminatory hiring for institutions of higher learning—the institutions I know best—and by recommending the underlying principle, *mutatis mutandis,* to all other institutions of our society.

Let us assume for the moment that institutions of higher learning have been asked and have agreed to comply with the following rules:[1]

(1) that they publicize in the most open and evenhanded way all their academic and other job openings;
(2) that they recruit applicants from *all available* sources;
(3) that they maintain fully nondiscriminatory hiring procedures and keep full records of such items as interviews;
(4) that they comply fully with nondiscriminatory promotion and tenure policies;
(5) that they abolish all rules and regulations which are discriminatory with regard to pay, leave or fringe benefits.

Let us also assume that our colleges and universities:

(1) open up fully their respective institutions to all qualified student applicants;
(2) recruit their student body evenhandedly from *all* secondary schools and other possible preparatory channels;
(3) maintain vigorous remedial programs for entrants who wish to remove deficiencies;
(4) maintain comprehensive counseling and other auxiliary programs to facilitate the entry of disadvantaged students into the mainstream of academic life.

Let us further assume that there be maintained a *simple, speedy,* and *effective* complaint and grievance mechanism made inside and outside the academic institutions (lower and appellate levels) to handle promptly complaints involving alleged discrimination on grounds of race, sex, or creed.

Let there be academic and mixed academic/nonacademic study groups and standing commissions to investigate continuously the employment *possibilities* and *practices* and, when necessary, recommend censure and the withholding of government funding.

Here is a practical program of positive commitments, remedial measures, and monitoring bodies that constitutes a plan as comprehensive as any in existence to combat discrimination—without demanding "numerical goals," "timetables," or quotas of any kind.

I ask: wherein is it lacking? In what respects is it unfair? Why will it not work if it has the active support of all persons of conscience and good will?

NOTE

1. These are substantially the proposals made by University Centers for Rational Alternatives, through its Executive-Secretary, Prof. Miro Todorovitch, to HEW [the former Department of Health, Education, and Welfare].

Part Two

ON EDUCATION

7

Minimum Indispensables of a Liberal Education

The present scene in higher education is marked by renewed concern with fundamental questions of what should be taught and why. To some the picture is one of curricular chaos. But if the chaos leads faculty members, regardless of their specialty, to recognize their role and responsibility as educators, the situation is not to be deplored. In what follows, I present considerations that bear on the construction of a liberal arts or general education curriculum. By a liberal arts or general education I mean a prescribed course of study for all students with the exception of those who can provide evidence of adequate mastery in the subject matters and skills that constitute the curriculum requirement. If our discussion is to have any point or relevance for higher or tertiary education today, we must not lose sight of the fact—deplore it as one may (and I do not deplore it)—that it must be germane to the general education not just of an elite or selected body of students at Columbia, Harvard, or Swarthmore but of *all students beginning their college careers.*

The first question we must face is this: If the course of study is to be related to the student's individual needs, capacities, and background, by what right or justification do we impose any general requirements upon him, aside from the power we have to award or withhold degrees? In the affairs of the mind, coercive power should be irrelevant. Besides, we do not need reminding that in education today power is a very uncertain and shifting commodity. It has been in the wake of student power—as a corollary of student strength and potential for disruption, not as a corollary of reasoned analysis—that requirements on many campuses have been replaced by an unrestricted elective system at the outset of the student's career. The situation has been aggravated

---

From *The Philosophy of the Curriculum: The Need for General Education,* edited by S. Hook, P. Kurtz, and M. Todorovich (Buffalo, N.Y.: Prometheus Books, 1975).

by shrinking enrollments in many institutions; many are luring applicants to enroll with the promise that they can write their own educational ticket so long as they pay their tuition. In such institutions there is no field of inquiry, no skill, no body of knowledge that all students are expected to have some familiarity with, not to speak of competence in, before being awarded a baccalaureate degree. Each does his own thing—and not always on the campus.

The challenge to us to justify a required course of general education is often quite explicit. I recall one occasion not so many years ago when a highly vocal and not unintelligent student put it to us at a faculty meeting at Washington Square College.

"After all," she said, "the intrinsic value or interest of a subject isn't enough to justify prescribing it. Every subject has intrinsic value but not to everybody, and judging by some of our teachers, not even to those who make their living teaching it. If education is to be effective and relevant, it must be related to the personal needs of the students. Without us, you have no justification for your being as teachers." And, turning to me, the acting spokesman for the curriculum committee, she let fly: "Who are you, or anyone else, to tell *me* what my educational needs are? I, and I alone, am the best judge of what I want and what I need. What goes for me, goes for everybody. That's democracy in education."

This seems to me now, as it did then, a fair challenge. We must meet it not as specialist scholars but as educators. It is a challenge very often evaded because so many teachers in our colleges do not regard themselves as educators but as scholars, whose primary, if not exclusive, allegiance is to their subject matter. Teaching, for them, is the training of apprentices, who will someday be their successors.

We can grant two things in this challenge to us. The first is that an education that will bear permanent intellectual fruit must be related in larger measure to students' individual needs. The second is that students are aware of what they want although they may not know the consequences of what they want. But these two truths by no means entail that students know what they need, or know what is educationally good for them. Indeed, after more than forty-five years of teaching on the college level, the proposition that most students, upon immediate entry, know what their genuine educational needs are seems to me quite dubious. As a rule, they no more know what their educational needs are than they know their medical needs. Sometimes their needs, and almost always their wants, are altered as they become acquainted with different fields of study. The notion that the generality of students (I am not speaking of the precocious or exceptionally gifted) can make an informed and intelligent decision about their abiding educational needs before being exposed to the great subject matters and disciplines of the liberal tradition is highly questionable. The notion that they are capable of making sensible, lifelong vocational or professional commitments in late adolescence—which is expected of them in some institutions—seems to me gratuitously cruel, and overlooks students' natural capacities for growth and the difficulties of self-knowledge.

Granted that students will ultimately have to make their own curricular choices when the time comes for specialization or the choice of a career. Granted the important role of formal critical education in resisting the tyrannies of the peer group and other social pressures as maturing men and women make the free choice of the pattern of their lives. But so long as we believe that the wisdom of such choice depends upon its being informed, the less occasion there will be for regret. This justifies the exposure to a variety of disciplines, problems, and challenges that general education counterposes to a too early specialization.

There is another point about need. The educational needs of students cannot be considered in isolation from the needs of the society in which they live, which nurtures and subsidizes them and which justifiably expects that they will be active, mature, and responsible citizens. Indeed, the chief justification for the community's underwriting the immense costs of universal access to higher education is not that it will increase earning power or social status or even provide enjoyment but that it will enhance the prospects of developing an intelligent and responsible citizenry. But that depends on what students learn and how.

John Dewey said that there are three important reference points that must be considered in developing a curriculum on any level. The first is the nature and needs of the student; the second is the nature and needs of the society of which students are a part; the third is the subject matter by which the students develop themselves as persons and relate to other persons in their society.

Our problem, as I see it, is this: Given our society, our potential student body, the accumulated knowledge, traditions, and skills of a large number of disciplines, given the spectrum of conflicting values in the present juncture of history, can we as educators devise a program of studies (I do not mean specific courses) that we can and should require of all students on their way to adulthood and vocation? Or, to use one of the felicitous distinctions of Professor deBary: Has the university, in the exercise of its "magisterial role" rather than its "prophetic or pontifical role," not only the authority but the intellectual confidence and courage to say to all students, "Here in our considered judgment, based on experience and reflection, are the minimum indispensables of liberal or general education for the modern man and woman. We shall require a certain proficiency in these minimum indispensables before you are allowed to do your own curricular thing. We are prepared to sit down with you to discuss the educational validity of a curriculum, listen carefully to your criticisms and suggestions in the never-ending process of curricular modification, experiment, and revision, and make allowance for your special aptitudes and conditions. But in the end, the decision will be ours if you elect to stay and continue your studies."

If we were to stop at this point, we might as well have not begun. For the thrust of the argument may be accepted and yet the content of education consist of a miscellany of studies that will not reflect the common needs of students and of our society. I hope we can be sufficiently concrete to reach a consensus not only on the desirability of general education but also, allowing for some peripheral diversity and variation, on its basic content. I shall very briefly put forward some curricular proposals to that end.

Permit me first to address myself to some of the larger considerations that I fear may distract us from our task. By striving to do too much we may achieve too little. There is a danger in the overly ambitious attempt to envisage and plan for the general or liberal education of students over their entire educational career, including their technical or specialized education as well as their vocational or professional education. As I understand general education, it is an integral part of liberal education, defined as the knowledge and sensibility, the attitudes and intellectual skills that men and women, in Professor deBary's words, "can reasonably be expected to have in common as a basis for their individual development and participation in the human community." It introduces students in a coherent and systematic way to "those areas of human experience [and knowledge], concerns, values, and ends [and problems] that extend into virtually all forms of study and give them relevance both to the inner life of the individual and the common human enterprise."

Granted that this does not exhaust the range and depth of liberal education, that it is desirable for students to renew and strengthen their liberal orientation regardless of their subsequent experience, or subsequent specialized or professional education. But that is something we cannot plan for, for our primary concern is with the foundational years. To be sure, liberal learning is lifelong learning, but how it should be integrated into the professional education of lawyers, physicians, architects, and engineers must be worked out by educators in those disciplines, with reference to their own problems. Having served on committees that have sought to humanize the curricula of law and medical schools, I am convinced of both the relevance of liberal education and its concerns for professional education and also the wisdom of leaving the curricular broadening in these fields to the professional practitioners, in consultation with others. After all, most students do not go on to professional or graduate schools. The best we can do is to try to make liberal education so intense and meaningful an experience before the onset of specialization that the interest evoked will feed itself in all subsequent experience.

The second danger I wish to caution against is the attempt to derive the liberal-education curriculum from some metaphysical or philosophical or theological conception of the nature of man, or from some overall view of "first and last things," about which the possibility of establishing a consensus is impossible. Instead of trying to devise a curriculum that will fit some antecedent beliefs about what differentiates man from other creatures, we can probably make better progress by taking a prospective point of view, by asking what courses of study are likely to achieve more desirable outcomes than others for the men and women in our community, regardless of whether we believe that they are ultimately analyzable into complexes of electrons or sense data or spiritual emanations of the One. This makes wise decisions in curricular matters dependent upon the fruits or consequences of alternative proposals, not a matter of deduction or interference from the essential nature of man or other problematic conclusions from philosophical anthropology.

And now, I wish to sketch very briefly the areas of study that should, I think, constitute the curricular substance of general education, and dwell on some of the open problems. I classify them under six rubrics.

1. Every student has an objective need to be able to communicate clearly and effectively with his fellows, to grasp with comprehension and accuracy the meaning of different types of discourse, and to express himself in a literate way. (Judging by the student levels of reading and writing accepted at some colleges, we may expect in the future that students will sue their educational alma maters, not for failure to teach them wisdom, but for failure to make them literate or teach them the good language habits of their own tongue.)

2. Every student needs to have at least some rudimentary knowledge about his own body and mind, about the world of nature and its determining forces, about evolution and genetics, and allied matters that are central to a rational belief about the place of man in the universe. If he is to have any understanding of these things, he must possess more than the capacity to remember and parrot isolated facts. He must have some grasp of the principles that explain what he observes, some conception of the nature of scientific method. After all, the modern world is what it is in virtue of the impact of science and technology on nature and society. He cannot feel at home in the modern world ignorant of science.

3. Every student has a need to become intelligently aware of how his society functions, of the great historical, economic, and social forces shaping its future, of the alternatives of development still open to us, of the problems, predicaments, and programs he and his fellow citizens must face. Whether he wants to revolutionize the world or save it from revolution, he must acquire an historical *perspective,* without which old evils may reappear under new faces and labels. Those who act as if they were born yesterday are the great simplifiers, who mistake their own audacity for objective readiness and often wreck the lives of others in the wreckage of their hopes.

4. Every student needs to be informed, not only of significant facts and theories about nature, society, and the human psyche, but also of the conflict of values and ideals in our time, of the great maps of life, the paths to salvation or damnation, under which human beings are enrolled. He must learn how to uncover the inescapable presence of values in every policy, how to relate them to their causes and consequences and costs in other values, and the difference between arbitrary and reasonable value judgments.

5. Every student needs to acquire some methodological sophistication that should sharpen his sense for evidence, relevance, and canons of validity. He should, at least in popular discourse and debate, be able to distinguish between disguised definitions and genuine empirical statements, between resolutions and generalizations, to nail the obvious statistical lie, and acquire an immunity to rhetorical claptrap. This is what I mean when I speak of the centrality of method in the curriculum. Is it expecting too much of effective general education that it develop within students a permanent defense against gullibility? It is astonishing to discover how superstitious students are, how vulnerable to demogogic appeal, to empty show and eloquence. There are, for example, more students enrolled in courses in astrology than astrophysics.

I ask this question under the influence of the report of a bizarre experiment published in the July 1973 issue of *The Journal of Medical Education,* which has a bearing on the weight now being given to student evaluations in the assessment of teachers. A medical team hired a professional actor to teach "charismatically and nonsubstantively on a topic about which he knew nothing." Under the pseudonymous name of Dr. Fox, in an inspired and seductive fashion, his lectures spiced with humor, he delivered himself of an hour-long lecture that consisted of pure gobbledygook, "nothing more than a goulash of double talk, neologisms, non sequiturs, and contradictory statements." The audience was composed of fifty-five educators, psychiatrists, psychologists, social workers, and administrators of courses in educational philosophy. All respondents were very favorably impressed. One even believed he had read Dr. Fox's papers. There seemed to be only one criticism: "The presentation was too intellectual." The topic of the lecture was "Mathematical Game Theory Applied to the Education of Physicians" and was ostensibly designed to be understood by laymen. If general education cannot immunize professionals against such farragoes of absurdity, it seems to me a failure no matter what else it does.

6. Finally, every student has a need to be inducted into the cultural legacies of his civilization, its art, literature, and music. His sensibilities should be developed and disciplined because they provide not only an unfailing occasion of delight and enjoyment in the present but also a source of enrichment of experience in the future.

These needs, I submit, define required areas of study. The creative task we face is to devise specific courses from campus to campus that will give these studies body and depth, that will truly challenge and interest students before the point of specialization, and continue to do so beyond it. I hope that others in the humanities, natural sciences, and social sciences will come forward with vital and practicable proposals for curriculum construction, and will grapple with well-known difficulties. What history, for example, should be taught, and how? Is it feasible to include the systematic study of Oriental literature and culture without cutting too much away from the study of Western literature and culture? How should the sciences be taught? Should mathematics be additionally required? Should a reading or speaking knowledge of a foreign language be required of all students? I used to think so, on the ground that it introduces us to new ways of thought and feeling, spurs imaginative and empathic identification with others, besides constituting the best way of getting to know a foreign culture. Today I no longer think it should be required. The time necessary to acquire a useful and usable linguistic mastery may be too great; it should be left to specialized education.

It is not necessary that we agree on detailed answers, but our abstractions about liberal education should give some guide to curricular practices. (I repeat, we are concerned here primarily with the philosophy of the *curriculum,* not the philosophy of the subject matters.)

Before concluding, I must say a word about objections to my emphasis on the centrality of method in liberal education. These objections assert that such emphasis results in a hypertrophic critical stance to all positive laws and institutions, to a value rootlessness that takes the forms of apathy or nihilism or exaggerated skepticism, to a demand for a shallow clarity, comparable in André Gide's words, to "the shining clarity of empty glasses." It is on this point that I find Professor deBary's observations puzzling and rather questionable. There seems to be an intimation in his essay that a powerful cause of our academic time of troubles, its disorders and violence, is "an overdose of critical skepticism," of questioning for questioning's sake, of too much debunking of ideals.

Problems of causation are complex, of course, but two things seem to me to be true. First, the issues that sparked campus disruptions were most often extra-academic, related to off-campus events and not to defects of the curriculum; arguments about the latter were later brought in as sheer rationalization. Second, having confronted militant students of every sect and persuasion, I would say that, far from suffering from an overdose of skepticism, they seem to be in the grip of a double dose of absolutism—cocksure, intellectually arrogant, and intolerant. Some are obsessed by a Marxism so crude and vulgar that it would make the doctrinaire Yipsils (Young People's Socialist League) of my own revolutionary youth blush with shame. Others are credulous prophets of immediacy or apologists of violence, while professing belief in the natural goodness of man. All are full of messianic zeal without any tincture of skepticism.

Why indeed should the awareness of method and the cultivation of methodological sophistication necessarily result in skepticism and the absence of grounded belief? After all, it is a commonplace that we can only doubt intelligently on the basis of something we believe. Genuine skepticism is not the foundation of knowledge, but its crown. Ignorance, inexperience, naiveté are free of doubt. Methodological skepticism does not so much undermine beliefs as limit them by placing them in context. It moderates the coefficient of the intensity of belief with which they are held by relating them to the body of available evidence. What it undermines is *absolutism,* the arrogance of partial perspectives claiming a total and incandescent vision.

A proper understanding of method is aware of the differences that different subject matters make—differences reflected in the varying degrees of certitude appropriate to different disciplines. It is true that students have shown an alarming distrust of democracy and the democratic process. In part, this has been an impatience with the pace of reforms, in part an understandable reaction to the abuses and failures of the democratic process. This would not be so disquieting were it accompanied by as pervasive a distrust of the alternatives advanced to cure its evils. But surely when, as many students do, they go beyond legitimate criticism of democracy and espouse unabashed forms of elitism, and even outright dictatorship of the "righteous," they are not carried there by skepticism but rather by their ignorance and innocence of the nature of ideals. Lacking an historical perspective, they are acutely aware of the ever present disparity between our ideals and existing realities. Combined with a failure to understand the heuristic function of ideals, they ignore or dismiss the substantial gains that have been made, both in the areas of welfare and freedom, and the extent to which our ideal sights have been raised with our advance. With the loss of a sense of proportion, there is loss in their sense of reality.

Nor can I accept the view that the academic and cultural barbarism that grows out of the implicit notion that *Alles ist Gefühl* came into existence to fill the vacuum created by too much intellection in higher education. I agree that man is a believing animal and that the exigencies of life and its troubles require that he act on some beliefs. I would argue, however, that the very interest of successful action reinforces the view that the ways in which he holds his beliefs, and the study of such ways, are as important as and sometimes even more important than any particular belief. I have long argued that dissent is no more virtuous than conformity, that the significant question is always whether either one is reasoned or unreasoned. On this I agree with Professor deBary, but I cannot see why the process of critical inquiry must always terminate in dissent. One widely accepted definition of science is that it is the study of propositions concerning which universal agreement is possible. Karl Popper to the contrary notwithstanding, the scientist is not always a "nay-sayer." And when he does say "nay" it is a way station in a process that terminates in warranted assertions that provide reliable knowledge.

General or liberal education studies different ideologies. It does not itself express or presuppose any ideology unless the term "ideology" is used synonymously with "ideal." In the language of ideals, general education is neither capitalist nor socialist; neither nationalist nor internationalist; neither theist nor atheist. The ideal it exemplifies is the ideal of untrammeled free inquiry, inquiry into fact and value and their interrelations. The hope is that commitment to free inquiry about nature, society, and man will lead to well-being and human happiness. But no guarantees can be given. What we can be reasonably sure about is that it will increase the range and freedom of human choice. And that is justification enough.

Where general education has been tried and failed, its failures have resulted, not from an overdose of skepticism generated by its curricular practices, but from a lack of belief in its validity on the part of those who have been responsible for its operation and especially by abysmal failures to teach it properly—a task of greater magnitude than the teaching of specialties. Here the students cannot be faulted. Like so many other things for which students are blamed, it is the faculties who are primarily responsible for the deplorable state of undergraduate education.

8

John Dewey's Philosophy of Education

With the possible exception of some elements of the chapter on "Vocational Aspects of Education," John Dewey's *Democracy and Education* continues to be a classic in the philosophy of education and in the related fields of social, political, and moral philosophy. Though it was written some seventy-odd years ago, there is a refreshing sense of contemporaneity about the book. The ideas discussed and the position taken still have a remarkable impact on, and relevance to, the major problems faced by modern man when he reflectively examines what we should educate for and why. It illuminates directly or indirectly all the basic issues that are central today to the concerns of intelligent educators or laymen interested in education. At the same time it throws light on several obscure corners in Dewey's general philosophy in a vigorous, simple prose style often absent in his more technical writings.[1] And it is the only work in any field originally published as a textbook that has not merely acquired the status of a classic, but has become the one book that no student concerned with the philosophy of education today should leave unread.

DEFINITIONS

What each reader regards as the continuing significance of *Democracy and Education* to some extent reflects his own interests. In referring to Dewey's conception of democracy in education, however, we raise questions that take us into the thick of some of the most embattled sectors of contemporary education. Conflict rages among various groups who all flaunt their allegiance to democratic principles. This suggests that different conceptions of democracy

---

are operating despite the common rhetoric. Sometimes *democracy* is used in the narrow political sense; sometimes in the broad sense as "openness to experience"; and sometimes as synonymous with education itself.

Let us sort out the meaning of these terms in Dewey's discussion. For him experience is not everything or anything that happens to a person, although there is a sense in ordinary discourse in which any happening is an experience, like birth or death, an accidental fall, or an unexpected blow. As Dewey uses the term, it refers to a pattern of events in which the organism is deliberately or with some awareness attending or acting upon something and undergoing or suffering the consequences of the action. Education is the process by which on the basis of present experiences we make future experiences more accessible, meaningful, or controllable. That is why for Dewey experience and education are not synonymous. Those who talk of life as a school and any or every experience as its curriculum, so to speak, miss this crucial distinction and overlook the fact that some experiences may be uneducational, crippling the powers to meet, understand, and possibly control the inescapable flow of future experiences. They also overlook the fact that one learns not only from one's own experience but from the experiences of others too, something ignored or denied by some fashionable movements in education. Education goes on in all types of society, democratic or undemocratic. Consequently it cannot be identified with democratic processes.

The most striking and insightful contributions of *Democracy and Education* fall within the field of the psychology of education or learning. In inquiring into the conditions, factors, and activities that make for effective education, especially teaching and learning in schools and classrooms, what Dewey has to say about interest and discipline, motivation and effort, method and subject matter, and a number of allied themes has stood the test of further inquiry since his day. In exploring these topics Dewey uncovers the profound influence of certain philosophical and psychological assumptions of the past on some deplorable present-day educational practices. Most of these practices are derived from a dualistic theory of mind and body which, according to Dewey's analysis, converts functional distinctions in the "moving unities of experience" into separations of existence. Thus mind is considered separate from the body, whose activity is viewed as an alien influence on how the mind learns; the self is divided from its environing physical and social world; the objects of experience are regarded as completely external to the modes of experiencing them; and, therefore, the methods of learning are isolated from the subject matters learned. Among the evils of education, or rather schooling, that Dewey sees as consequences of isolating the way we learn from what we learn are the failure to make use of "the concrete situations of experience," reliance upon the twin inducements of fear and bribes to motivate learning, and mindless use of rote methods and mechanical routines.

So far, regardless of the social philosophy one holds, it would be possible to accept and implement what Dewey says about how to improve the quality of education for any particular person or group. Dewey's insights into the psychology of education could be used in educating an absolute monarch or the guardians and rulers of a Platonic republic. But when we ask ourselves what should education be for society as a whole, we cannot give an intelligible answer unless we have a definable notion of a desirable society. The criteria of a desirable society are derived by Dewey from the features that are found wherever any social group exists and prospers. These criteria are twofold—the degree of shared interests within the society and the freedom to develop new interests, both common and personal. "How numerous and varied are the interests which are commonly shared? How full and free is the interplay with other forms of association?" Using these as moral criteria, the superiority of the democratic community to all other forms of communal association is easy to establish.

Actually this derivation of the validity of democratic society is circular, and some may even claim it is question-begging because the very choice of criteria presupposes an ideal family. In a series of later writings, especially his *The Public and Its Problems, Liberalism and Social Action,* and *Freedom and Culture,* Dewey returns to the question of the justification of democracy. But the point that is central here is not the justification of democracy but its conception—how it is to be understood—and the educational corollaries of that conception. It is a warranted surmise that had *Democracy and Education* been written after the rise of totalitarianism and its challenge to the democratic faith, Dewey would have devoted more pages to the problem of justification. At the time he wrote it, he could assume at least verbal commitment to the ideals of democracy on the part of the national community. He therefore addressed himself primarily to an analysis of their implications and corollaries.

MORAL EQUALITY

Does the democratic conception of education mean that all students are equal in capacity, whether of intelligence or creative ability, and that schools should be organized like politically democratic communities in which the majority rules what is to be learned, when, and how? Or does it mean that individuals should be permitted to do their own thing without let or hindrance by others as Nature takes its free and benevolent course?

These and similar views are travesties of Dewey's meaning. The equality that Dewey speaks of is not one of fact or ideal goal but of *moral* equality among human beings whose value or worth is incommensurable and cannot be quantified. For him a democratic society is one whose institutions are so organized that they exhibit an equality of concern for all human beings to develop themselves to their full stature as persons, free to choose patterns of life that are compatible with those of their fellows within the environing social frame. A political democracy is a necessary condition for such a society but it is not sufficient, for the growth of the individual is affected by other dimensions and aspects of his life—by his economic, religious, cultural, racial, and national experience. Education in and for a democratic society must provide the *schooling* required for each student to develop his powers and interests to their full, to find himself, and to learn to live at least peacefully if not cooperatively with others.

Such an education takes as its point of departure the individual and his needs, and, to the extent that individuals differ, effective teaching must take note of the fact. That is why Dewey never opposed individual testing but only the abuses of it, which typed students into fixed categories or classes and then treated them primarily as members of a class or group, overlooking their plasticity and differences *as individuals.* Of course students have common educational needs just as they have common medical needs. Just as it is helpful to have all the relevant medical data and measurement about a person in order to treat his or her health problems properly, so it is helpful to know whether a child is tone-deaf, acute or defective in vision, what his or her present powers of memory or imagination are, whether an individual child's IQ is high or low. The point is not to make invidious comparisons between children but to determine whether they are working below or up to their own powers and to help them grow. Equality of medical treatment does not consist in imposing the same regimen on everyone but in equality of medical care. Medical measurements are not invidious. Similarly educational measurements need not be a sentence of doom but a guide to good teaching. In a criticism of some early applications of IQ tests written after the publication of *Democracy and Education,* Dewey wrote: "How one person's abilities compare in quantity with those of another is none of the teacher's business. It is irrelevant to his work. What is required is that every individual shall have opportunities to employ his own powers in activities that have meaning."

INDIVIDUAL DIFFERENCES

In a democratic society there is recognition that original capacities are "indefinitely numerous and variable," and that its institutions should seek to provide the opportunities in which the specific, variable, and differential capacities of individuals find fulfillment in some significant calling or vocation. For certain important social tasks it may be somebody's business to determine "how one person's abilities compare in quantity with those of another."

Otherwise our buildings may collapse on our heads and our planes collide in midair. But in no circumstances are individuals to be stratified into classes or groups or, in the selection of qualified persons, be discriminated against on the basis of their exclusion from or inclusion in any group whatsoever. Plato's vision of a world in which each person finds fulfillment in doing what all the resources of an enlightened, scientific and humanistic education discovers that he is best qualified to do, is acceptable to Dewey. Dewey denies, however, that this vision can be realized in Plato's class society or any other class society.

What would Dewey have said about the work of some modern-day biologists and psychologists who are concerned with the genetic capacities of racial groups or subgroups and their findings of some statistically significant differences? First of all, as the founder of the American Association of University Professors and of the American Committee for Cultural Freedom he would have been up in arms against recent attempts to curb their inquiries or deny them a hearing. Just as there are some inherently different natural capacities among individuals, there may be some inherently different capacities among the families that constitute an ethnic group. But whatever the findings, Dewey would maintain that they are *educationally irrelevant* to the kind of education a democracy should provide for its *individual* citizens. The reasons are obvious. What may be true for a group may be false for any particular member of that group. For example, men as a sexual group are naturally physically stronger than women. (Plato, who was a feminist but not a democrat, regarded this as the only inherent difference between the sexes.) But it would be absurd, therefore, to infer that any man is stronger than any woman. For some physical tasks the most qualified person available could very well be a woman. Women as a group have stronger natural predispositions to treat infants with tender, loving care than men do. But some men may make better nursery teachers than some women.

Perhaps a more graphic illustration is the not unusual family whose children's IQ varies from 90 to 140. This would have no bearing on the equal right of each child to the best medical, educational, and personal care to which its needs entitled it. There are ordinary and extraordinary talents, but no person is ordinary to himself. Each one morally counts for one in a democracy and no more than one. Individuals must no more earn the right to the best education from which they can profit than they must earn the right to speak or vote or have a fair trial.

The paradigm of an ideal family in which the parents are wise and benevolent cannot, of course, be used with respect to democratic society as a whole. For such a society is self-governing and must strictly abide by majority rule after respecting the rights of other individuals. Dewey, it should be noted, even in politics was never an absolute majoritarian or believer in unlimited government; the validity of majority rule presupposes respect for the equal political and civil rights of minorities. The family model is more appropriate to the school, especially on the elementary level, for it recognizes the indispensable and active role of the teacher and the legitimate restraints that may be put on students when their experimental activities may result in harm to themselves or others. Until students are mature enough to take over the direction of their own education, of necessity there must be an asymmetry in the role and intellectual authority of the teacher with respect to them. The excesses of progressive education, which made it a byword among those who took the curriculum of studies seriously, flowed from a failure to realize this.

CITIZEN PARTICIPATION

With this conception of democracy in education, we can see how Dewey uses it in masterly fashion to criticize the traditional methods of education and its curricular content, down to the specific details of the three Rs, history, geography, and other academic disciplines. In every case he traces the effect of inherited class interests and prejudices in narrowing and mechanizing what was considered "essential," in separating the purely intellectual studies from purely practical ones, in identifying the former with liberal education, and by separating such education from concern with the great social problems and responsibilities of the age infecting it with illiberality. At the same time he evaluates the institutions of existing society in the light of what would be required to make democratic education pervasive. While this might seem to involve an adjustment of the schools to the existing economic, political, and nationalist order, he argues convincingly that, rather, it entails a continuous and profound tranformation of social life which will bring all citizens into a greater participation in determining the ends and goals of their activity. In the processes of production, distribution, communication, and exchange, individuals should more and more enter actively in the planning of goals, the sharing of roles and responsibilities instead of being, like machines and raw material, at the beck of decisions that they cannot influence or even indirectly control. From the vantage point of his educational ideal,

> An undesirable society, in other words, is one which internally and externally sets up barriers to free intercourse and communication of experience. A society which makes provision for participation in its good of all its members on equal terms and which secures flexible readjustment of its institutions through interaction of the different forms of associated life is in so far democratic. Such a society must have a type of education which gives individuals a personal interest in social relationships and control, and the habits of mind which secure social changes without introducing disorder.[2]

Once these social changes are introduced, and they must be introduced democratically, not from above by a beloved leader or a vanguard political party, and without violence which usually serves the purpose of reaction, then the division or separation between the concepts of culture and utility, and their attendant curricular practices, can be banished from formal schooling.

The centrality of multiple forms of active participation in Dewey's conception of democracy distinguishes it from conventional views of formal political democracy in which citizens merely choose at stated intervals between alternatives set by others. It must not be confused with some New Left perversions which imply that all individuals are capable of doing everything, that all must be not only equally considered but equally rewarded, that responsible leadership is incompatible with accountability and control, and that the principle of majority rule be disdainfully rejected. At the same time we can see why Dewey rejects any view, whether Platonic or technocratic, which makes one small group by virtue of its theoretical concern with the ends of life the best qualified to rule over the masses who have been educated only in the use of means and instruments in behalf of goals beyond their ken or competence. For him, when education has not been narrowly circumscribed by the needs of a class society, there are no experts in wisdom. And as for the rule of experts in any field, without disputing their expertise, Dewey holds that one does not need to be an expert in order to evaluate the recommendations of experts. Otherwise democratic government would be impossible.

VOCATIONAL EDUCATION

At the outset reference was made to certain elements of Dewey's chapter on the "Vocational Aspects of Education" that might trouble the reader. This is because it is difficult to shed the connotations of the phrase "vocational education" that suggest the kind of narrow trade-school training into which students are shunted when they are considered uneducable for traditional liberal arts programs. Yet the chapter both summarizes and brings to a peak Dewey's distinctive views. It would have been better if Dewey had consistently used the term "calling" and had argued that schooling be so organized as to make possible the self-discovery of the capacities and powers which under proper educational guidance and stimulus would blossom into a career or series of careers for every normal person. "There is danger," he writes, "that vocational education will be interpreted in theory and practice as trade education: as a means of securing technical efficiency in specialized future pursuits" (p. 326). It is a danger because that is what most vocational education has been until now. He deplores it because such education "becomes an instrument of perpetuating unchanged the existing industrial order of society, instead of operating as a means of its transformation." It reinforces "the feudal dogma of social predestination." Dewey exaggerates here. Even under existing conditions a militant trade union can counteract the feudal aspects of modern industrial organization. But even under the best of circumstances in modern industrial or post-industrial society, there are malaise and discontent in work.

What Dewey has in mind is clear. He had observed that the happiest human beings are those who have satisfactory personal relations in love, friendship, and family, and in a calling that gives them a sense of creative fulfillment. He was aware that for many human beings "earning their living" and what they regarded as "living their life" were quite different modes of experience. The task is, if possible, to universalize the happy situation so that every person is living and enjoying his life as he earns his living. The function of schooling is to enable the individual to discover the calling or vocational center around which he can organize his life, both on and off the job.

At this point there arise many problems that remain to be solved if Dewey's views are not to appear in some respects Utopian. He grappled with some of them in subsequent writings. First, even if schooling were to reconstruct its methods and curricula along the lines Dewey and other scientific psychologists recommend, and enable each student to find himself or herself, who would provide—much less guarantee—the callings or vocational opportunities? And how would this be provided—and enforced? Society and industry would have to cooperate with, or in some degree be controlled by, the school. This would require some form of democratic socialism or genuine welfare society far different from what we now have.

Secondly, some forms of work are brutalizing, deadening to sensibilities, narcotizing in their monotony, and yet necessary to the production of goods and service that people demand. It is hard to imagine anyone finding creative fulfillment on an assembly line. Its rigors could be mitigated by high pay and shorter hours, but no matter how varied the organization of work it could not qualify as a calling by any of Dewey's own criteria.

Thirdly, mechanization of work of this charcacter, may be carried to a point of automation. But there are many kinds of work that are dull and boring that are not mechanized, e.g., in the service trades. It was once thought that automation would ultimately make most physical labor superfluous. This is not likely to happen soon. If and when it does, the problem will shift to the creative use of leisure. Schooling then will be challenged to provide educational experiences that will enable individuals in a mass society to find a significant life in the way they spend their leisure. The way masses of people spend their leisure in contemporary society can hardly be considered educationally rewarding .

Finally, one can seek to reorder society and its economy to meet human needs by sacrificing efficiency and the price and profit system. But in a world where human beings and human needs are multiplying, this may result only in socializing hunger unless certain controls are introduced.

Dewey would be the first to recognize the difficulties that face the implementation of his program of finding satisfactory callings even in an order more equitable and enlightened than our own. But such difficulties by no means justify acceptance of the status quo and compliance with educational and industrial practices that stunt the lives of so many. Dewey was no Utopian and insisted that ideals must be practicable. It is not a case of all or nothing. He was convinced that the resources of scientific intelligence would enable us to democratize our social institutions further, that in the light of the fruits of the gains and progress he had witnessed in his own lifetime, the United States, despite setbacks, would continue in the same direction by democratic political means, eschewing the evils of social chaos and the despotism it breeds. In that faith—by which he lived and died—*Democracy and Education* was penned.

The misunderstandings of Dewey's educational philosophy are legion and it may be that if Dewey had written with greater precision, some of them could have been obviated. Each generation reads him in the light of its own problems and predicaments. A year after *Democracy and Education* was published, the United States became embroiled in the First World War. The period since then has witnessed more profound transformations in the cultural and social life of the nation and, indeed, of the world, than in any comparable span of years in human history. That Dewey's educational writings still have contemporary relevance is a great tribute to them despite the limitations and corrections that current needs and interests impose upon them.

Many of the criticisms of Dewey's views are really more properly addressed to the pronouncements of self-styled disciples. But some are directed against Dewey himself and a few words may be in order about two central types of criticism. The first type can be characterized as based on distortion. The second, which has a measure of legitimacy, is a matter of relative emphasis.

A paradigm illustration of the first type of criticism is the charge that Dewey's general and educational philosophy is guilty of "anti-intellectualism." (This has been popularized by Richard Hofstadter's *Anti-Intellectualism in American Life*.)[3] The term "anti-intellectualism" is not clearly defined. But if "anti-intellectualism" is a vice, is intellectualism a virtue? It is true that Dewey like Peirce and William James was opposed to intellectual*ism*. But opposition to intellectual*ism* is by no means incompatible with emphasis on the role and value of *intelligence*. In fact the central emphasis Dewey places on "the methods of intelligence" in all areas of human experience, especially inquiry, suggests that "intelligence" functions as the only absolute value in Dewey's ethical and educational philosophy, since in contradistinction to all other human values considered ultimate, it alone is the judge of its own limitations.

"It is not wisdom to be only wise" was a line from one of Santayana's sonnets that Dewey would endorse.

Intellectual*ism,* condemned by Dewey, is the view that thinking is an autonomous activity unrelated to any interest, desire or passion, that ideas possess some magical, creative power independent of determining material conditions, physical, biological, and social. It is a view that Dewey rejects as not only incompatible with all post-Darwinian scientific findings but incompatible also with psychological truths established by Spinoza and Hume.

If by intellectual*ism* one means Cartesianism, Dewey accepted and developed Peirce's devastating critique of the notion that the foundations of knowledge rested upon clear and simple ideas that gave immediate and certain truth.

From any philosophically informed perspective, the charge of "anti-intellectualism" against Dewey, where it means opposition to the cultivation and use of all available methods of intelligence, both as means and ends in education, is simply bizarre.

There is more substance in the second type of criticism, illustrated by the contention that Dewey's philosophy is "social, all too social," that too much emphasis is placed upon the conjoint, cooperative activities with others in the learning process, and not enough recognition given to the private and inner sphere of experience and its delights in which the knowledge experience culminates. Allied to this is the criticism that Dewey's stress is more on the education of the citizen aware of his social responsibilities and duties and not enough on the development of the individual who in the last analysis lives and dies alone and whose greatest joys are found in cultivating his or her internal landscape.

It is true that for Dewey the opposition between the individual and social is untenable and the source of much confusion. His Hegelian antecedents had led him to the understanding that the individual outside of society was an abstraction, that individuality or personality is an outgrowth of social differentiation, and that historically and analytically, the community is the matrix out of which man as a human being develops in virtue of culture and language. From this point of view Hobbes's "war of all against all" is a myth. No community could ever originate from it.

There is nothing in this analysis which is incompatible with the recognition of the importance of the individual, even the supreme importance of the individual, as Emerson and Thoreau understood it. Why, then, did Dewey stress so strongly the social elements in education and democracy?

The explanation, it seems to me, is to be found in the dominant ideological climate of his own life. It was marked by the raw, rugged individualism of the expanding industrial society with still open frontiers. It was buttressed by a Social-Darwinism that transferred the biological categories of "struggle for existence" and "the survival of the fittest" to society. This generated an indifference and cruelty, no less harmful for being unconscious, to those who were unfortunate, unlucky or unsuccessful in the competitive struggles for place or position, and for living. It was Dewey's humane feelings that led him to stress the cooperative approach to the problems that beset man and the importance of extending the professed democratic credo from the political sphere to education and the economy.

Indeed, the motivation for Dewey's concern with the social coefficients of "equal opportunity" flows from his appreciation of the unique value of the individual. What he saw as the pursuit of individuality and personality with its cultivation of the refinements of inner experience seemed to him to be a monopoly of the leisured free from which the working masses were barred because of the absence of cooperative social action and social control.

This permanent and overriding concern for the character of individual experience comes to the fore in Dewey's later writings on the aesthetic experience. But it is implied if not apparent in his earlier works, and even in his criticism of some varieties of intellectualism. One kind of intellectualism he condemned, in which he was joined by James who appended the term "vicious" to it, was the view that all we need to know about things, events, and persons was their class membership, that because two individuals were properly classified as members of the same class, this made their specific differences unimportant or irrelevant to anything else. It meant that, for Dewey, although the individual could be properly understood by abstractions, he or she was not to be conceived merely as a bundle or complex of, so to speak, intersecting abstractions—an attitude manifested in practical affairs when we judge people *only* by whether they are men or women, black or white, Jew or Gentile, American or foreign and thereby overlook the specificity, the individuality, and the uniqueness of the person.

That is why it seeems to me that although Dewey repeatedly stressed the social components of human experience, the spirit of his philosophy recognizes the indefeasibility and irreducibility of the individual. The relations to others are internalized in each individual but in the beginning and in the end and in between the individual also remains in external relation. Just as in the scientific community the control of evidence by the weight of tradition and the repeatability of results leaves the individual scientist free to develop his own style and find his own way to new truths, so in the democratic community the participation in the political and social process leaves the indivdual free to contribute in his own distinctive way to the common life. This is not, of course, to equate the scientific and democratic communities, for only in the latter does each one count for one and no more than one.

In his eightieth year, not long after the Second World War had begun, Dewey declared that whatever else democracy was, it was also "a *personal* way of individual life." It was an acknowledgment that the pervasiveness of the social is compatible with different modes of personal life. For Dewey, democracy was a social way of life which permitted us at least to live together peacefully if not fruitfully with our privacies. That is why for him democracy was based on faith—faith that intelligence could discover or create shared interests sufficient to perserve civilized society. "To take as far as possible every conflict which arises—and they are bound to arise—out of the atmosphere and medium of force, of violence as a means of settlement, into that of discussion and of intelligence, is to treat those who disagree—even profoundly—with us as those from whom we may learn, and in so far, as friends."[4]

Education among other things should seek to cultivate that faith and encourage the willingness to take risks for it. It should also seek to prepare the individual for the contingency of failure.

NOTES

1. In one of his rare autobiographical references to his own work, Dewey wrote:

> Although a book called *Democracy and Education* was for many years that in which my philosophy, such as it is, was most fully expounded. I do not know that philosophic critics, as distinct from teachers, have ever had recourse to it. I have wondered whether such facts signified that philosophers in general, although they are themselves usually teachers, have not taken education with sufficient seriousness for it to occur to them that any rational person could actually think it possible that philosophizing should focus about education as the supreme human interest in which, moreover, other problems, cosmological, moral, logical, come to a head.

("From Absolutism to Experimentalism," in *Contemporary American Philosophy*, ed. George P. Adams and William P. Montague [New York: Macmillan Co., 1930], 2:22-23.)

2. *Democracy and Education* (New York: Macmillan Co., 1916 [Carbondale: Southern Illinois University Press, 1980, 9:105]). Subsequent page references are to the present edition.

3. *Anti-Intellectualism in American Life* (New York: Alfred A. Knopf, 1963).

4. John Dewey, "Creative Democracy—The Task Before Us," in *The Philosopher of the Common Man*, ed. Sidney Ratner (New York: G. P. Putnam's Sons, 1940), p. 226.

9

Education in Defense of a Free Society

As we approach the bicentenary of the American Constitution, it seems to me fitting and fruitful to explore two related themes in the intellectual legacy of Thomas Jefferson, the first philosopher-statesman of the fledgling American republic to call himself a democrat. These themes are, first, his conception of a free self-governing society; and second, his faith in the processes of education to guide, strengthen, and defend this free self-governing society from the dangers—internal and external—that might threaten its survival. Since Jefferson's own time, discussion of the relation between democracy and education has not been absent from political discourse, but as a rule, it has been subordinated to narrow curricular issues. Periodically, however, the question becomes focal whenever we seek, as we are doing today, to rethink, revise, and reform the educational establishment of the nation.

Jefferson was not a systematic thinker and his rhetoric sometimes carried him beyond the bounds of good sense. A revolution every twenty years or so, which he advocated to nourish the tree of liberty, would have destroyed the American republic long before the Civil War came near to doing so. Nor were all elements of his thought consistent. Jefferson once wrote that man was "the only animal which devours its own kind." Yet in the very passage in which man is so characterized, he declared that "were it left to me to decide whether we should have a government without newspapers or newspapers without government, I should not hesitate for a moment to prefer the latter." The case for a free press does not rest on such an absurd position, which overlooks the fact that in a state of anarchy, one without government, there would be no press at all. It would be destroyed by mob rule when it exercised its critical functions, as indeed happened during some stormy years of American history in various regions of the country. Of course, government is not a sufficient condition of a free press, but it is a necessary condition not only

---

From *Commentary* 78, No. 1 (July 1984), by permission;

of press freedom but of any freedom. For how can any freedom be exercised unless those who would violate it are not free to do so?

Rhetorical excesses and logical inconsistencies apart, the most profound feature of Jefferson's political philosophy, and what all major political groups in American life today regard as possessing a perennially valid significance, is its emphasis on self-government. Self-government in Jefferson's conception has three central figures. It is based on freely given or uncoerced consent. Secondly, freely given consent entails the guaranteed right to *dissent,* to wit, the freedoms of speech, press, association, and assembly, and all other freedoms legitimately derived from them. It is this feature that distinguishes the Jeffersonian, or modern, conception of self-government from the ancient and transient democratic orders of the past which recognized no limits on government power, and treated opponents within the democratic system as enemies. Finally, given the recognition of the right to dissent, a *sine qua non* of a self-governing community is the principle of majority rule. In the absence of a consensus, rarely to be expected in the inescapable conflicts of human interests and opinions, this rule is the only way to reach orderly decision and effect a peaceful succession of government. Jefferson stressed this, as did many years later the uncompromising individualist, William James. "The first principle of republicanism," writes Jefferson, "is that the *lex majoris partis* is the fundamental law of every society of individuals of equal rights. To consider the will of society enunciated by a single vote, as sacred as if unanimous, is the first of all lessons in importance. This law, once disregarded, no other remains but the use of force."

Jefferson was acutely aware, as are we all, that majorities may go astray, be injudicious, and even be morally tyrannical within the letter of the law. For this he had only one remedy: not the rule of presumably enlightened minorities, but the education of experience. His not unreasonable assumption is that, given access to knowledge, most adult human beings are better judges of their own interests than are others. However, to be able to learn effectively from their present experience, to make it available for their future experience, citizens should have access to education of the narrower kind—to schooling that develops the intellectual skills and imparts the relevant knowledge necessary to sustain a free society. The people themselves, Jefferson continually observes, are "the only safe depositories" of nonoppressive rightful government.

One may ask, of course, whether such government is not only safe, but whether it is sound, not only whether it is right, but whether it is good. Jefferson's reply indicates where he puts his faith: "To render them [the people] safe, their minds must be improved to a certain degree. This is indeed not all that is necessary though it be essentially necessary. An amendment of our Constitution must here come in aid of the public education. The influence on government must be shared by all the people."

How far we have come from the Jeffersonian faith that the people or their representatives are the only safe depositories of a free society is evidenced by current discussion of a constitutional convention. I am not a partisan of any particular measure advocated for the agenda of such a convention and I disapprove of most. But I am appalled at the reasons offered by some who oppose its convocation and who cry out in alarm that it will run amok and even abolish the Bill of Rights. No more flagrant contradiction of the Jeffersonian faith is imaginable than such a sentiment. It confidently predicts that measures threatening the foundations of a free society will not only be adopted by a majority of the delegates but also by three-quarters of our fifty states, and by both freely elected legislative assemblies in those states. If such a thing were to come to pass, it would certainly establish that a majority of citizens are either too obtuse or too vicious to be entrusted with self-government. And if this were indeed true, as some philosophers from Plato to Santayana have asserted, why should anyone be in favor of a politically free society? The current state of civic education and behavior is indeed deplorable. But the situation is not so far gone as to make the case for a free society a lost cause.

Far from fearing a constitutional convention, I believe its convocation, timed for our bicentenary, could become the occasion for a great historic debate. Reviewing and interpreting the experience of two centuries, it might strike a more adequate balance among the branches of our government and clarify some central ambiguities in present constitutional provisions that sometimes generate dangerous deadlocks.

Jefferson, as we know, was in advance of his time. He provided the rationale for the systems of public education that developed in the United States after his day, especially for instruction going beyond the fundamentals of literacy—reading, writing, and the arts of calculation. He even ventured on the outlines of a curriculum of studies, mainly based on science and history, to strengthen faith in a free society and safeguard it from the corruptions of human ambition and power.

Now suppose that, in the spirit of Jefferson, we wanted to devise an educational system that would indeed strengthen allegiance to our self-governing democratic society: how would we do this today? One possible way—consistent with Jefferson's own prescriptions—would be to modify our educational system so that its central emphasis became the detailed study of the sciences. But is there really any convincing reason to believe that this would result in an increase of support for a free, self-governing society? After all, the subject matters and techniques of the sciences can be mastered in any kind of society. Even though it is true that the greatest burgeoning and bursts of creative discovery in science have occurred during the last two centuries in modern democratic countries, it does not tax our imagination to conceive a world in which, once political freedom has been lost, the sciences become not only the organon of continuous inquiry into nature but also the instrument of enforcing a cruel and ruthless despotism over society. The domination man exercises over nature has often been used to fasten bonds of domination over other men.

To be sure, as John Dewey often pointed out, there is much in the process of scientific inquiry—its openness, sense of evidence, tentativeness, and co-operative intelligence—that when carried over into the discussion and practice of human affairs vitalizes the free society. But Dewey also never ceased to remind us that, desirable as it is to carry over scientific methods in the pursuit and testing of human ends, science and politics differ in several crucial respects. For one thing, not everyone is qualified to be a scientist or has a right to a scientific judgment, while all citizens of a free society are deemed qualified to participate in determining judgments of political policy. Deny this and one is committed to the view of government by experts, which is incompatible with the premises of a self-governing society. For those premises imply that on crucial questions of policy one does not have to be an expert to judge the work of experts or choose among their oft-conflicting proposals.

Further, scientists are united in one overriding interest—the interest in the pursuit of truth; human affairs, on the other hand, are a field of conflicting interests. The agreements scientists reach are ultimately determined by the compulsions of fact; in human affairs, even when there is agreement on facts, the resolution of differences may require tolerance and compromise of interests. In a free society, it may be necessary to forgo demands for the full measure of justified claims in order to preserve the *process* by which future claims may be peacefully negotiated. Science develops by the elimination of error. But the life of a free society consists not so much in the elimination of interests as in their reconciliation. In science, a wrong judgment loses all value as soon as it is shown to be wrong; in a democracy, even the interest which is outvoted has value. It must be respected in defeat if only because it has submitted itself to the arbitrament of argument and persuasion.

In short, a curriculum concentrating entirely on science could not be expected to achieve the aim Jefferson sought. Not that Jefferson himself was a simple-minded believer in the effect of science and science education on the moral estate of humanity. He called freedom "the first-born daughter of science"; yet he was aware that science could "produce the bitter fruits of tyranny and rapine." He never wavered in his belief that through the diffusion of scientific knowledge the human condition could be advanced. And if by the advance of the human condition we mean the material improvement of the human estate, the extension of longevity, and the increase of our power over nature, none can gainsay him. Yet even if we grant the dubious proposition that all knowledge is good, surely not all of it is relevant for our political purpose. Henry Adams to the contrary notwithstanding, no law of physics has any bearing on the justification for a free society. Einstein's theory overthrew Newton's, not the Declaration of Independence.

It is a commonplace but an important one that it is not science and technology that are fateful to man, but the uses to which they are put. When we speak of uses, we imply purposes and ends, goals and policies. We therewith find ourselves in the realm of values. The humanities, broadly speaking, are concerned with the exploration of this realm. Though Jefferson prescribed a mainly scientific course of study for the intellectual elite, a curriculum built on the humanities is roughly what he had in mind for the ordinary citizen, whose studies should, he thought, be chiefly historical. Might not such a curriculum today provide what the sciences cannot—a strengthened faith in a free self-governing society?

I wish to declare at once that regardless of how we answer this question, the humanities—primarily the disciplines of language and literature, history, art, and philosophy—should have a central place in the education of *any* society. For their subject matter is perennial and transcends, even when it touches on, the temporalities of politics.

The reasons for this are manifest and heralded in many ways from ancient days to the present. The study of the humanities nurtures an understanding and appreciation of the great and often unfamiliar visions and modes of life. Within any mode of life, they present "the problems of the human heart in conflict with itself" (William Faulkner). They therefore embrace but go beyond the dimensions of the political and ideological. They strike no consensus. They have no flag or creed, even when they celebrate ways of life and death fought under warring battle cries. They take us out of ourselves and enable us to see with the eyes and minds of others, just as we become aware of the reach and power of others in us. Define the humanities and limit their concerns for curricular purposes as one will, their cultivation leads to the permanent enrichment of the internal landscape of the mind in any clime or social station. For they provide an ever renewed source of delight, consolation, insight, sometimes hope.

Surely this is merit enough to justify the place of the humanities in any curriculum of liberal studies. Surely this justifies us in maintaining that their absence is the sign of a truncated, one-sided, and impoverished education—whatever other virtues such education may have.

Nonetheless, we cannot honestly maintain that the study of the humanities of itself generates allegiance to the free society. Two considerations prevent us from doing so. The first is the historical fact that the student population of Western Europe, who until recently were brought up in their *lycées* and *gymnasia* largely on classical studies, were certainly not noteworthy for their ardor and enthusiasm for free democratic societies. Indeed, not infrequently in countries like Spain, Italy, France, and Germany, it was students who provided the intellectual shock troops for anti-democratic movements.

There is a second troubling reason why we cannot maintain that an organic relationship exists between the humanist tradition in life and letters and commitment to the free or liberal society. This is the fact that many of the monumental writers of the past regarded the promise of democratic progress as a threat to the life of the mind and to the creative spirit, as the political gloss on the mechanisms that were leveling and standardizing culture and taste. No one can reasonably dispute the record. From the age of Plato to the present, the dominating figures in the humanistic disciplines have been critical of, sometimes even hostile to, the extension of political power to the masses, even when safeguards against the excesses of popular sovereignty have been adopted. In the nineteenth century, writers like Dickens, George Eliot, and Shelley were sympathetic to the advance of the democratic idea, but their influence was more than counterbalanced by Wordsworth, Balzac, Goethe, Dostoevsky, and many others. In our own time, such major literary figures as T. S. Eliot, Yeats, Pound, Faulkner, and D. H. Lawrence typify the distrust and suspicion of democratic society prevalent among the creative vanguard.

Why there should be this "adversary" relationship, as Lionel Trilling called it, between the sympathies and values of so many great humanists and the democratic tendencies of their culture, and why there should be a corresponding bias toward the artistocratic tradition, is hard to explain. A partial answer may lie in the greater receptivity among aristocratic classes to the novel and experimental than is generally found in the larger public. ("Nothing is so foreign to the plain man," observes Santayana, "as the corrupt desire for simplicity.") To this may be added the fact that where the people are sovereign they have sometimes been less tolerant of heresies that challenge accepted beliefs than have some benevolent despotisms, which under the mantle of a patronizing *Narrenfreiheit,* the freedom accorded to the court jester, sometimes sheltered purveyors of doctrines dangerous to the state.

Whatever the explanation, we cannot plausibly deny that the outstanding humanist figures have rarely been protagonists of the ordered freedoms we associate with democratic life and republican virtue in a self-governing society. The growth of such a society in the West owes more to the dissident, non-conformist religious sects, to the agitation and battles of the early trade unions and other manifestations of class struggle than to the classical humanist tradition. It was not a scholar inspired by Plato or Aristotle, Aquinas or Dante, or any figures of the Renaissance, but a spokesman of the Protestant Levellers who proclaimed that "the poorest he that is in England has a life to live as the greatest he," and therefore argued for the right "to choose those who are to make the laws for them to live under."

In pointing to the considerations that prevent us from making the easy inference that a liberal-arts education centered around the study of the humanities is integral to the existence and survival of a liberal society, I do not mean to suggest that there is a simple causal relation between curricular study and political behavior. A contemporary literary critic (George Steiner) has written in a tone of bitter discovery: "We know now that a man can read Goethe and Rilke in the evening, that he can play Bach and Schubert, and go to his day's work at Auschwitz in the morning." But he could have added that those who studied Euclid and Newton also built the crematoria at Auschwitz. And he undoubtedly is aware that those in previous times who led the massacres of innocents in their holy wars against heretics or infidels invoked the blessings of the God of love on their dedicated work. This is an old story. The face of evil can wear the mask of learning. The devil can play the role not only of a gentleman but of a scholar—but this does not make learning or manners evil or less desirable. The guilt of a criminal does not stain the means by which he commits or conceals his crime. As well maintain that the abuse of language is an argument for permanent silence.

Moreover, after one has said everything there is to be said to the contrary, there still remains at least some positive connection between the rationale of a free society and the great expressions of the human spirit in art and literature. Regardless of their specific political orientation, these works are usually animated by a passion or vision of opposition to the customary. They move by challenging complacency. They are essentially nonconformist. To reach their mark they must disturb, upset, and sometimes frighten.

To the extent, then, that a free society thrives on diversity, the play and struggle of varied perspectives, the dialectic of confrontation, it *is* served by the humanities, just as in turn the free society often serves the humanities better than the authoritarian societies some humanists tend to favor. For a free society offers an unlimited theater for works of the spirit to develop, in contrast with authoritarian societies that always in some crucial area of the mind invoke the Augustinian dictum that "error has no rights," as a bar to further inquiry and experiment.

To be sure, free societies sometimes sin against the light of cultural freedom. But when they do, they are violating their own ethos. Conversely, some unfree societies may tolerate, even encourage, experiment and variation in some restricted area, but never in all the realms of the human spirit. I am struck by a story told about General de Gaulle. In refusing to endorse the arrest of Sartre for an infraction of the law, he is reputed to have said: "In a free society one does not arrest Voltaire." Sartre was no Voltaire, and he was to boot an apologist for Stalinism; but we know what his fate would have been as a dissident under a Stalinist regime.

I do not want to go beyond the modest claim that there is no essential or necessary hostility between the humanities and a free society, and that there need be no conflict between a love of the humanities and a commitment to liberal democracy. But I believe I have also shown that a curriculum concentrating on the humanities can no more be expected to achieve the Jeffersonian objective of strengthening faith in the free society than a curriculum based on the sciences.

I have brought up Jefferson's ideas about the relation between education and freedom not out of an academic concern with those ideas, but rather in the hope that examining them might yield some guidance in dealing with our urgent contemporary crisis. It is a crisis that threatens the very survival of a free, self-governing society in the United States. For it consists precisely of an eroding allegiance to the ideals of a free, self-governing society itself. It would require volumes to document the failure to abide by the democratic ethos in American life today. Restricting ourselves only to phenomena observable without enlisting batteries of research teams to report on them, we find: (1) the vehement assertion of rights and entitlements without the acceptance of corresponding duties and obligations; (2) the invocation of group rights to justify overriding the rights of individuals; (3) the growth of violence, and the tolerance of violence, in schools and local assemblies; (4) the open defiance of laws authorized by democratic process, and the indulgence of courts toward repeated and unrepentant violators; (5) the continued invasion by the courts themselves into the legislative process; (6) the loss of faith in the electorate as the ultimate custodian of its own freedom.

Each reflective observer can make his own list of the multiple threats from *within* our own society to the health, security, and civility of the processes of self-government. However conceived, they raise the question of whether we possess the basic social cohesion and solidarity today to survive the challenge to our society from *without,* particularly that posed by the global expansion of communism. Although there are different views of the immediacy and magnitude of the Communist threat to the free world, it is plain political folly to deny its existence. The map of the world from 1945 to the present bears witness to the fact that the policy of containment, initiated by President Truman after the Baruch-Lilienthal and the Marshall Plan had been rejected by the Kremlin, does not contain.

The threat of Communist expansion is compounded by the fear that the defensive use of nuclear weapons will result in a nuclear holocaust. The artful, unremitting, and often unscrupulous propaganda by fanatical groups, exemplified by television programs like *The Day After* and by terrifying classroom scenarios on every level of our school system from a kindergarten to university, has generated a mood of fear not far removed from hysteria. The fallout from this sustained propaganda has often short-circuited reflection. It has led to the mistaken belief in some circles that we are confronted by the stark alternatives of unilateral disarmament or inevitable war, and to a disregard of the well-grounded position that an effective deterrent is the best way of preserving peace without sacrificing freedom. Clarity, however, requires recognition that to renounce in advance the retaliatory use of a deterrent is to proclaim in effect that we have no deterrent, thus inviting the very aggression the policy of deterrence was designed to discourage.

In our precarious world every policy has risks. What shall we risk for freedom? What shall we sacrifice for mere survival? If our nation were confronted by a nuclear ultimatum, would there be enough loyalty to a free society to generate the necessary resolution to cope with the threats without bluster or paralyzing panic? To many the answer seems doubtful, and this in itself is an alarming sign of the state of the national mind. Past generalizations about the American character are no guide, whether drawn from de Tocqueville, Whitman, or Lord Bryce.

What then must be done? Not long ago our President proposed and our Congress approved the organization of a National Endowment for Democracy to encourage the spread of democratic forces abroad. As welcome as such a program is, I submit that it is even more necessary to organize a National Endowment for Democracy at home. The first goal of such an endowment would be to develop programs to study the basic elements of a free society, and suggest them as required parts of instruction on every educational level.

Today it is widely agreed that fundamental educational reforms are needed to improve the levels of skill and literacy of American students so that they may cope with the present and future problems arising from multiple changes in our complex world. Agreeing with this proposition, I am suggesting that it is just as important to sharpen the students' understanding of a free society, its responsibilities and opportunities, the burdens and dangers it faces. Instead of relying primarily on the sciences and humanities to inspire loyalty to the processes of self-government, we should seek to develop that loyalty directly through honest inquiry into the functioning of a democratic community, by learning its history, celebrating its heroes, and noting its achievements. Integral to the inquiry would be the intensive study of the theory and practice of contemporary totalitarian societies, especially the fate of human rights in those areas where communism has triumphed.

The first retort to such a proposal is sure to be that it is just a variant of the propaganda and indoctrination we find so objectionable in Communist society. As to propaganda, Karl Jaspers somewhere says that the truth sometimes needs propaganda—a dark saying. I interpret it to mean that we require courage to defend the truth when challenged and the skills both to make it more persuasive and to combat its distortions. But as to indoctrination, the retort misses the basic difference between the open and closed society. This lies not in the presence or absence of indoctrination, but in the presence or absence of the critical, questioning spirit. Indoctrination is the process by which assent to belief is induced by non-rational means, and *all* education in *all* societies at home and in school *in the tender years* is based on it. The habits of character, hygiene, elementary sociality and morality are acquired by indoctrination and become the basis of all further learning. In a free society, however, such methods are, and always should be, accompanied by, and gradually become subordinate to, the methods of reflective, critical thought at every appropriate level. When students achieve greater maturity they are able to assess for themselves step by step the validity of the beliefs and the justifications of the habits in which they have been nurtured. A free society not only permits but encourages questioning, commensurate with the intellectual powers of students, as integral to learning.

In a closed society indoctrination induces assent by irrational as well as non-rational means, beyond the early years, and throughout the entire course of study in all except certain technical areas. It never permits a critical study of its first principles and the alternatives to them. The unfree society regards its subjects as in a permanent state of political childhood; it controls what they read and hear by a monopoly of all means of communication. The free society can live with honest doubt and with faith in itself short of certainty. Skeptical of perfect solutions, it eschews the quest for absolutes. In contrast with the closed society, it can live with the truth about itself.

I am not making the utopian claim that anything we do in the schools today will of itself redeem or rebuild our society. Continued institutional changes must be made to strengthen the stake of all groups in freedom. But of this I am convinced. In our pluralistic, multi-ethnic, uncoordinated society, no institutional changes of themselves will develop that bond of community we need to sustain our nation in times of crisis without a prolonged schooling in the history of our free society, its martyrology, and its national tradition. In the decades of mass immigration in the nineteenth and twentieth centuries that bond was largely forged by the American public school. What I propose is that our schools, reinforced by our colleges and universities, do the same job today in a more intelligent, critical, and sophisticated way.

There was a time when most Americans understood that the free, self-governing society bequeathed to them by Jefferson and the other founding fathers was the "last best hope on earth." If anything, the experience of the twentieth century, and especially of the past fifty years, should have made that truth even more evident than it was to Jefferson himself. During that period, our own society has been able to make gigantic strides in the direction of greater freedom, prosperity, and social justice, while its totalitarian enemies—first Nazi Germany and then the Soviet Union—have produced war and holocaust, economic misery, cultural starvation, and concentration camps. Yet in spite of that record, the paradox is that faith and belief in the principles of liberal democracy have declined in the United States. Unless that faith and that belief can be restored and revivified, liberal democracy will perish.

Jefferson thought that proper education was necessary to the birth and establishment of a free society. He would not have been surprised to discover that it is also necessary to its perpetuation, and indeed to its very survival.

10

The Principles and Problems of Academic Freedom

ACCOUNTABILITY

In this day and age very few persons will be found who openly declare that they are opposed to academic freedom. But as is the case with the term "democracy," it would be extremely hazardous to predict the specific beliefs of those who profess democracy, particularly when prefaced with adjectives like "higher" or "directed" or simply "new" or "people's." Nonetheless, if we are careful, and are prepared to make relevant distinctions, I believe it is possible to clarify what academic freedom has meant in the history of higher education in the Western world, and particularly in the history of American higher education. Before we declare that academic freedom is present or absent or discuss its problem, we must begin a working definition.

I offer as a working definition of academic freedom the following: "Academic freedom is the freedom of professionally qualified persons to inquire or investigate, to discuss, publish or teach the truth as they see it in the discipline of their competence subject to no religious or political control or authority, except the control of standards of professional ethics or the authority of the rational methods by which truths and conclusions are established in the disciplines involved."

This definition is substantially the one elaborated in greater detail by Arthur O. Lovejoy who together with John Dewey founded the American Association of University Professors, the latter as President and the former as Secretary. At the time, 1915, academic freedom, as they defined it, could hardly be said to be recognized by most governing boards of American colleges and

From *Contemporary Education* 58, No. 1 (Fall 1986): 6–12. Reprinted by permission of the publisher.

universities. Even in the '30s when I served as a member of the Council of AAUP its principles were far from being universally accepted. Today there is hardly a college and university in the country which does not proclaim its allegiance to those principles. Indeed the proclamation and acceptance of these principles have become commonplace. And like other commonplaces some of its implications are overlooked.

I want to begin by exploring some its implications. First, it is important to note that academic freedom is defined here not as the freedom to teach the truth but as the freedom *to seek* the truth. What is the difference? Isn't the truth important? Of course it is, but just as important is recognition of the fact that even if one believes in absolute truth, human recognition of the truth, however it be defined, varies, that many things once believed true are no longer accepted by competent inquirers as true, and some things considered false like the heliocentric hypothesis are now considered true. That is why we cannot accept without qualification the Augustinian dictum that error has no rights.

Secondly, academic freedom is a special right, it is *not,* much rhetoric to the contrary notwithstanding, a human right, or a civil right or a constitutional right. It is the right of the professionally qualified teacher or researcher. What, one may ask, is the difference between *a special right* like academic freedom and these other rights—human, civil, or constitutional? To make a short answer—academic freedom is a right that must be *earned.* All these other rights we enjoy as members of the democratic community. They are our birthright as citizens; they do not have to be earned, and the community has an obligation to prevent others from denying or abridging them. The community and its law enforcing agencies in a democracy cannot arrogate to itself, except under carefully defined conditions, the power to limit the exercise of our human and constitutional rights. Freedom of speech gives anyone freedom to talk nonsense anytime, anywhere, barring for the moment, laws about public nuisance. But it does not give anyone the right to talk or teach nonsense in a university. One must, so to speak, be professionally qualified to talk nonsense in a university.

Of course, what may appear nonsense to you or the inexpert may turn out to be the latest or higher wisdom or knowledge. To some individuals the truths of non-Euclidian geometry, or the view that the simultaneity of two distant events is not absolute but relative to different frames of reference or current notions in cosmology, quantum physics, or genetic engineering, all appeared nonsensical to some when they were first enunciated.

Similarly, one can under the first amendment teach on the street or in one's home anyone who wants to be instructed. But he must be qualified to teach or engage in research before he can be permitted to teach in a university classroom or experiment in a laboratory. There are many problems connected with qualification some of which I shall discuss later. But we can't dispense with the principle of qualification without making a shambles of our educational system. The whole structure of our social life depends on the recognition of the indispensability of qualification as a necessary condition of professional performance. Every time we enter a hospital or clinic or entrust ourselves to a public conveyance, we stake our life on the assumption that some adequate tests of qualification have been conducted. And although going to a university is not so risky, no one who values his time or money would enter its classrooms unless he or she assumed that the teachers were qualified to teach their subject.

In this connection a certain feature of qualification must be mentioned which although not unique to university life is often misunderstood and productive of needless controversy. No institution, and certainly not a university, can function well if appointment to its staff conveys instant and permanent tenure. In the nature of the case there must be a probation period of varying length before full qualification can be established. When academic freedom is recognized, it holds for the probation period, too. The criteria that must be met before tenure is granted varies with different types of teaching. In those institutions where the greatest stress is placed on excellence of teaching, the criteria will be different from those in which excellence in research and quality of publication are given precedence. I shall not pursue this complex question here. Normally I have found that anyone who receives an appointment assumes that he or she is entitled to lifelong or permanent tenure if they conscientiously perform their duties. They are apt to be extremely suspicious of the grounds offered for their nonrenewal after the probation period.

It is at this point that cases allegedly involving breaches of academic freedom arise. For the grant of permanent tenure not only completes the rites of passage to full academic citizenship, it confers a lien on the university's future resources of almost three quarters of a million dollars. No responsible faculty or administration can permit the grant of tenure to be taken as a matter of course. Every decision must be considered a major serious educational decision.

A third remarkable implication of academic freedom is that if one subscribes to it, one is committed to the belief that the professionally qualified person in pursuit of the truth, and abiding by the Canons of professional ethics, has a right to reach any conclusions that seem to him valid. This means he has what I have called the right to heresy in the field of his competence. This is a very momentous inference, for to those who disagree with him it means the right in good faith to be wrong. It means that an honest inquirer will be defended not only when he reaches a heresy that we agree with but a heresy with which we disagree. That is easily said but experience shows that often it depends on whose ox is being gored. In disciplines where controversy is rife, especially the social sciences and the humanities, this means that where academic freedom exists it will protect the right of a qualified teacher to reach conclusions that some will regard as Communist or Fascist or racist or irreligious or un-American.

There is another implication of academic freedom that is even more remarkable. I as a professor can stand on a public platform with my grocer, my butcher, my physician or lawyer. We all exercise our constitutional right of freedom of speech to advocate the same unpopular or heretical proposal. Select your own particular abomination as an illustration. Let us say voluntary euthanasia or the deportation of illegal aliens or curtailing social security. Every one of my fellow speakers may pay a very large price for the expression of their opinions. They may lose trade, or patients, or clients to a point where their very livelihood may be affected. I, however, to the extent that I have academic freedom claim and enjoy complete immunity from any institutional sanctions. Neither my salary nor my prospects of promotion can be affected. In a sense I am experiencing a privilege or freedom that comparatively few of my fellow citizens have. I am absolved of the normal costs of unpopularity and sometimes even of my defiance of convention. Coupled with the fact that once I acquire tenure, I cannot be deprived of it except by a long and arduous due process—rarely invoked in universities—this reinforces the exceptional nature of my vocational rights as contrasted with most other vocations and professions.

It is necessary to stand off and examine in perspective the remarkable character of the right to academic freedom. It is remarkable in that as distinct from what existed in any other period of human history, it involves not only the tolerance of intellectual heresy but its legal support. It is remarkable in that it offers safeguards in ways that are unprecedented, against the price or costs of intellectual heresies, and in that it has upheld the right of teachers to exercise their responsibilities of citizenship on the same terms as their neighbors without suffering academic sanctions. And it is remarkable above all because of its uniqueness in the long history of civilization, in its limited jurisdiction to certain areas of the Western and American world, and in the recency of its emergence in those areas.

There was no academic freedom in the ancient world, not even in democratic Athens as the death of Socrates attests. There was no academic freedom during the medieval synthesis, the Renaissance, the Reformation, or the Enlightenment. There was no academic freedom in colonial or revolutionary America or in England where instruction was largely in the hands of the clergy. Academic freedom was an un-American importation from Imperial Germany where it first took root in the University of Berlin in 1810 at a time, interestingly enough, when there was less political democracy in Prussia and the rest of Germany than in the United States or Great Britain. When

I began teaching in the American University in 1927 academic freedom and faculty governance were in a very rudimentary state. Contracts were for one year with no legal presumption of renewal. The status of the faculty was little better than that of hired men in industry except that one's private life and public activity could more readily affect one's academic future than in other pursuits. Boards of Trustees often intervened directly into educational affairs. Gradually things improved, especially as members of the AAUP made their way up the administrative ladder. The turning point was the adoption of the AAUP's Basic Statement of Principles not only by the Association of American Colleges and Universities but by 47 national professional organizations of scholars and teachers embracing almost the entire spectrum of the arts and sciences. By the end of the Second World War, the battle for academic freedom was essentially won although several problems on procedural matters remained to be clarified.

The very recency and rarity of academic freedom gives rise to the question: why should the community which either directly or indirectly through tax exemption underwrites the great costs of university education support the institution of academic freedom? There are many reasons but we can sum them all up in the statement: because it believes that it is to its own ultimate interest to do so. It believes that the discovery of new truths and the extension of the frontiers of knowledge are more effectively furthered by the presence of academic freedom than by its absence. It believes that fidelity to the mission of the university will result in the accumulation of bodies of reliable objective knowledge that may be used as guides or tests of policy by legislators and citizens. It gives relative autonomy to the university not for the pleasure and enjoyment of its teachers and researchers but for the good of society.

But it should be obvious that this precious right to academic freedom carries with it certain duties and responsibilities about which we unfortunately hear less and less. It is certainly true that academic freedom protects the expression of heresy but that does not mean that "anything goes" in the way of classroom or research behavior, that one is free to do or not do *anything* he or she pleases to do. The grant of academic freedom is based on the assumption that the mission of the university is to search for the truth, and therefore on the assumption that the professor or researcher is truly *seeking* to reach the truth or the best warranted conclusion on the available evidence. The assumption is that he or she is a free agent, not under orders from an outside group to indoctrinate or to cook his evidence, not bought, not a fanatic committed in advance of inquiry to a predetermined conclusion regardless of the evidence. In short, the assumption behind the grant of academic freedom is that the professor is a scholar not a propagandist, and this is the source of the duties and responsibilities correlative to the exercise of his freedom.

It is noteworthy but rarely acknowledged that the 1940 Basic Statement on Academic Freedom of the AAUP explicitly asserts that academic freedom "carries with it duties correlative with rights." It enumerates quite a few, e.g., "The teacher is entitled to freedom in the classroom in discussing his subject but he should be careful not to introduce into his teaching controversial matter which has no relation to his subject." (It seems to me that even if the matter is noncontroversial but has no relation to the subject, it does not belong in the classroom.) The duties enumerated in the AAUP statement are not confined to the teacher's behavior in the classroom. It reminds him that "As a man of learning and an education officer, he should remember that the public may judge his profession and his institution by his utterances. Hence he should at all times be accurate, should exercise appropriate restraint, should show respect for the opinions of others, and should make every effort to indicate that he is not an institutional spokesman." In a further statement in 1956, the AAUP adds:

> The academic community has a duty to defend society and itself from subversion of the educational process by dishonest tactics, including political conspiracies to deceive students and lead them into acceptance of dogmas or false causes. Any member of the academic profession who has given reasonable evidence that he uses such tactics should be proceeded against forthwith, and should be expelled from his position if his guilt is established by rational procedure.

Similar sentiments are expressed in the famous declaration of the Graduate School of the New School for Social Research established by exiles from totalitarian countries.

> The New School knows that no man can teach well, nor should he be permitted to teach at all, unless he is prepared "to follow the truth of scholarship wherever it may lead." No inquiry is ever made as to whether a lecturer's private views are conservative, liberal, or radical; orthodox or agnostic; views of the aristocrat or commoner. Jealously safeguarding this precious principle, the New School stoutly affirms that a member of any political party or group which asserts the right to dictate in matters of science or scientific opinion is not free to teach the truth and thereby is disqualified as a teacher.
>
> Equally the New School holds that discrimination on grounds of race, religion or country of origin either among teachers or students runs counter to every profession of freedom and has no place in American education.[1]

It follows from this foregoing that the faculty which extends its *protection* to its members who exercise their right to academic freedom must also be *prepared* to discipline those who violate the duties and responsibilities of academic freedom. I have always held that there is no necessity for state legislatures or Congress to investigate where questions of professional ethics are involved, and that academic bodies are the best qualified to determine the fitness of their colleagues to teach and to give the benefit of due process to those charged with unfitness or violation of professional trust. It stands to reason that the unwillingness of a faculty to administer its own standards of objective scholarship and intellectual integrity, its indifference to what is taught, and how it is taught or to whether anything at all is taught in its classes is both wrong and foolish. It will not only degrade the quality of the degrees it bestows and affect its scholarly standing, but sooner or later it will provoke community alarm and interference. In public institutions whose budget is underwritten by tax money, it is safe to predict that any academic scandal that seems to indicate laxity in the application of proper scholarly standards is sure to give rise to legislative investigation.

An illustration that has its amusing sides occurred in a western state college that shall here remain unidentified. In a course on human sexuality it was reported that a teacher was giving class credit to students for their accounts of their novel sex experiences and activity. You may have read of the hullabaloo that ensued when word of this reached the press. After considerable turmoil in which some state legislators were very vocal and emergency sessions of faculty and administrative committees were convoked, the trouble blew over because the instructor resigned. But it is significant that the faculty and administration had no notion of what was going on and made no provision for examining the quality and relevance of the instruction until the outside community clamor arose and the budgetary prospects of the college before the Legislative Committee became quite cloudy.

It seems to me that faculties should be very jealous of their scholarly reputations on teaching and research. Self-appraisal and self-criticism of their curricular offering should be an ongoing process. The enforcement of the statement about the responsibilities and duties of scholarship should not be treated as pious platitudes. They should be as vigorously enforced as the principles of academic freedom are defended. When that is done faculties can be prepared to stand up to any relevant legislative inquiry. They can with eloquent dignity point out that the legislature has the legal power to establish or not establish any educational institution, whether liberal or professional. But once that decision is made, then it is within the professional competence of the educators to operate and control that institution without let or hindrance from those not professionally qualified, including the legislators. For that is the meaning of academic freedom. And if the university faculties have lived up to their academic mission, they will ultimately win community support.

There are many other problems that remain to be explored that I cannot treat in short compass, particularly whether the exercise of a constitutional right by a teacher gives him automatic immunity from any academic sanctions, and what safeguards exist against the abuse of faculty power. But I want to conclude by pointing to what I regard as the central question bearing on the future of the university freedom, viz., whether the ideals of academic freedom I have sketched can be sustained. Today those ideals are not so much endangered by the traditional enemies of academic freedom, the church and state, but sometimes from within the university.

I have referred to the mission of the university as providing the context of academic freedom. I have defined that mission in terms of the pursuit of intellectual ends—discovery, clarification, criticism aimed at reaching the various modes of truth. But during the last decades a new conception of the university has emerged in some quarters which discards the traditional objective of scholarship and regards the university as primarily an agency of social change to effect political goals. This view is not satisfied to present programs to the democratic electorate for acceptance or rejection but insists on the right to use the classrooms for political purposes. Now to be sure, in the past the classroom and university have often been used for such political and religious purposes but according to the conception of academic freedom I have defended, this has been a lapse from the mission of the university and the ideal of objectivity. But the new view challenges the very conception of objective truth as a superstition. In effect it regards the university as an arena of struggle for conflicting political views, and refuses to recognize any distinction between the quest for objective truth and propaganda. It accepts whatever freedom it can acquire but refuses to recognize any responsibilities and duties. It proudly carries the bias and partisanship of the hustings and marketplace into the university which then becomes transformed into a battlefield of warring groups struggling for domination.

Let me offer a typical statement by a representative of this point of view:

> The social university is not primarily concerned with the abstract pursuit of scholarship, but with the utilization of knowledge obtained thru [*sic*] scholarship to obtain social change. Therefore it does not recognize the right of its members to do anything they wish under the name of academic freedom; instead it assumes that all its members are committed to social change. To give an example, a course in riot control would simply be declared out of place in such a university, while a course in methods of rioting might be perfectly appropriate.[2]

There are even more extreme statements of this position.

If such a view of the university prevailed or even achieved wide currency, I doubt whether any community would support its existence for long. Now in my view of academic freedom any qualified teacher has the freedom to say or write or advocate such a view of the university, but if he were to *act* on it and subordinate his teaching and research not to the controls of scholarship and evidence, he would be in violation of the duties and responsibilities of academic freedom. He or she should be held to account by their faculty peers. And if they lacked the courage to do so, both their institutions and the cause of academic freedom would suffer irreparable damage.

ACCURACY IN ACADEMIA: CRITICISM

Unfortunately the politicalization of many American universities since the '60s and the introduction of some new disciplines in which the expression of only one point of view is tolerated have created a climate of opinion on some campuses very hostile to the principles of academic freedom as I have defined them. The situation is exacerbated by the intolerance of radical extremists among student bodies who refuse to permit the expression of views with which they are unsympathetic. It would hardly be an exaggeration to say that since the so-called Free Speech Movement at Berkeley, there is no longer freedom of speech for anyone, even invited scholars, publicly to present and uphold the views of the American government. Contrast the treatment meted out to Jeane Kirkpatrick, the violent disruption of her meetings, and the friendly reception accorded to Communist Angela Davis, the notorious apologist of the Soviet Gulag and other oppressive Communist regimes. Not so long ago the President of Harvard had to plead with the Cambridge academic community to extend the traditional courtesies of a hearing to visiting officials of the American government. These violations of elementary, political, and civic freedoms continue primarily as a result of faculty unwillingness to discipline disrupters in accordance with principles of due process worked out in collaboration with student bodies of recent years.

Even more widespread, continuous, and educationally disastrous is the conversion of many classrooms, especially in the humanities and social sciences, into political pulpits sometimes on matters unrelated to the theme of the course, and outside the field of competence of the instructor. Almost always the bias of the teaching and preaching is directed in one way—*against* American policies and institutions, without a scholarly, fair, or balanced presentation of the issues. Horror stories about such excesses abound. One English instructor whose area of specialization has nothing to do with political or foreign affairs teaches his class that there is currently more injustice in America than in Nazi Germany. Another instructor in history converts his class into guerilla theater to attack American policy in Nicaragua. A professor holding a joint appointment in psychology and anthropology teaches there are three varieties of racism of which Zionism is one. Another professor alleges that the holocaust of the Jewish population in Europe is a Zionist myth.

How can such violations of the ethics of teaching and scientific inquiry be combatted without opening the door to other and possibly worse evils? I repeat: certainly not by legislative investigation or action on a state or national level. This threatens the relative autonomy of the university and the whole conception of academic freedom which has developed to serve us well in this country only in our century.

Nor by a proposal recently presented by a group called Accuracy in Academia. This calls for the organization of concerned students and others on campuses to monitor the classrooms of teachers. Using tapes and notes they plan to record the statements of teachers which they deem seriously in error and send them to a central source where they will be vetted. If the statements are regarded as ill-founded, the professors will be requested to correct them in class, failing which wide publicity will be given to the offending remarks.

Those who have advanced this proposal are unwittingly damaging the cause of academic freedom and are playing into the hands of the very individuals whose excesses have arroused their sense of outrage.

First of all, most teachers will justifiably resent the assumption that what they say will be monitored and judged by persons who have no professional standing. Secondly, in pursuing and analyzing an idea, new or old, it may be necessary to explore critically positions and statements that may be at great variance from accepted views, even if they are ultimately rejected. Thirdly, anyone with any academic experience knows how hazardous it is to rely on students' notes to determine what has been said, and in what context. Fourthly, teachers with heretical views will be discouraged from expressing their judgments lest a hue and cry be raised by some hysterical devotee of orthodoxy thus depriving both students and the community of insights that challenge accepted doctrine. Finally, the grant of academic freedom carries with it a trust in the *bona fides* or the qualified teacher which is challenged in advance by this proposal.

Already among the most vehement critics of Accuracy in Academia have been the very persons who are committed to a propagandistic, illiberal, and predominately anti-Western stance in their teaching, and who are shouting that academic freedom is threatened while they continue to violate its duties and responsibilities. Others have rushed into the fray with hackles flaring who just recently kept a discreet silence when free speech and academic freedom were being denied to Jeane Kirkpatrick, as Jefferson Lecturer, at Berkeley, and at Minnesota and other universities. At Stanford University, one of the leaders of the movement to deprive the Fellows of the Hoover Institution (whose scholarship and recognized achievements are beyond his range) of their academic freedom on the alleged ground of their conservative orientation, now paints himself as a target of victimization. In the hubbub that has been raised by this thoughtless proposal, public attention will be distracted from the actual sapping and undermining of the principles of academic freedom that have accompanied the growing politicalization of American universities.

Where does this leave us? If we reject any legislative oversight and forego the shortsighted and self-defeating proposals of Accuracy in Academia, how shall we combat the multiple abuses of the academic ethic?

By exercising our academic freedom *publicly* to criticize its violations on the campuses on which they occur, by insisting that administrations enforce the guarantees of free speech to visiting scholars and other invited academic guests, and initiating disciplinary action against those guilty of disruption. If administrations persist in their policies of self-defeating appeasement and refuse to enforce the provisions of the disciplinary codes established on most campuses by joint student-faculty committees, resort should be made by concerned faculty, to the Civil Rights Law.

In the last analysis the academic health of the university and the integrity of the academic ethic can only be upheld by the faculties themselves. So far it seems that those members of the faculties who seek to subvert the academic mission, who deny that there are objective standards of scholarship, who insist that all teaching is a form of propaganda, seem to show more courage in proclaiming these absurdities and peddling their nostrums than those who disagree with them. On some campuses it may court unpopularity publicly to criticize the mouthings of radical fanatics and the duplicities of ritualistic liberals who deny that there is any danger to intellectual and political freedom from the left. But unpopularity is a small price to pay to recall the university to its mission.

Ultimately we must rest our faith in the intelligence of our students to assess for themselves the truth of conflicting claims. But they must be aware of the *existence* of conflicting claims; they must hear the other side; they must hear the criticism of the nonsense about the Nazification of American culture by the apologists for Gorbachev, Castro, Ortega, and their similars. Our students must be reassured that as a group their teaching faculties do subscribe to a tested body of knowledge painstakingly wrested from ignorance by our forebears; that they do actively participate in the process by which we differentiate between what is probably true from what is demonstrably false; that they are willing to stand up and defend the intellectual and scholarly legacy entrusted to them against politically inspired attacks, regardless of the political spectrum from which such attacks originate. Scholars cannot entrust to others the chores of intellectual hygiene. Compared to what other scholars have endured resisting the march of totalitarianism, in foreign countries, whose first victim is academic freedom, unpopularity is a small price to pay.

NOTES

1. American Association of University Professors, *New School Bulletin* 10, no. 19 (January 5, 1953): 2.
2. Alan Wolfe, "The Myth of a Free Scholar," *The Center Magazine* (July 1979): 77.

11

Allan Bloom's Critique of American Education

A Noble Failure

The phenomenal intellectual and commercial success of Allan Bloom's *The Closing of the American Mind* cannot be explained by the philosophical sophistication or political maturity of the American public. What it signifies is the widespread recognition that something is profoundly wrong with the American educational system. There is little agreement on what is wrong and why. But the dissatisfaction is periodically fed by government and foundation reports that are headlined in the press and become the subject of television programs. Despite increases in expenditures, the elementary schools seem unable to raise the level of functional literacy of those who complete their studies. Secondary education, especially in large metropolitan centers, is afflicted by increasing violence, drug addiction, and sexual promiscuity that contribute to a high dropout rate. Not only is there universal access to some form of higher—more accurately, tertiary—education but there is almost universal acceptance (except at Ivy League and a handful of other colleges), grade inflation, and declining standards, so that remedial courses in English and mathematics often make up a considerable portion of the curriculum for large numbers. It is unsafe to assume that those on whom degrees are bestowed possess the elements of what constituted a liberal arts education a generation or two ago. Whatever the specific reasons for the confusions and problems of the school system of the country—and the picture, granted, is certainly varied—every large section of the population has a grievance with some aspect of its operation.

Originally published as "*The Closing of the American Mind:* An Intellectual Best-Seller Revisited," *The American Scholar,* 58, no. 1 (Winter 1988–89):123–35.

Allan Bloom is convinced that he knows the reason for the failure of American education, particularly higher education—the headwaters of the system—whose products make their influence felt on all subordinate levels of instruction. He attributes the deficiences and troubles of higher education to its failure to grasp the central philosophical truths about human nature, and a consequent failure to devise a proper, ordered curriculum of studies that would transmit the perennial truths, problems, and aspirations of (in a term he often uses) "the human soul."

Any realistic conception of social causation would find rather naive Bloom's assumption that the social evils impinging on the school systems can be profoundly modified by curricular change or reorganization. On the other hand, given that the schools by themselves can neither reconstruct nor revolutionize society, it still remains true that they can gradually have *some* influence in modifying the attitudes and behavior of their students. They can do this not so much by the information they impart as by the values of appropriate conduct they stress, and especially the habits of mind (or mindlessness) they teach their students. Although Bloom himself sometimes gives the impression that, as a seeker after the truth, he is indifferent to whether he influences or affects anyone or anything, like all educators from Plato to the present he really is trying to improve society or at least prevent it from going to the dogs. He certainly cannot be faulted on this score.

Before assessing the validity of Bloom's analysis of the current educational scene and his proposals for improving it, I must credit him with two indisputable achievements. The first is to have evoked the astonishing spectacle of the intellectual bankruptcy of the so-called political and cultural Left in its response to the positions he has developed in his book. With the exception of two reviews (one by Richard Rorty in the *New Republic,* the other by Richard Gambino in *Freedom at Issue,* both scholars of independent mind), nowhere is the thesis of Bloom's book adequately stated and criticized in the large array of attacks made against it. Most of the attacks on *The Closing of the American Mind* and its author do not even reach the level of argument. Bloom has simply become the target of abuse, accused of subverting democracy. One extreme radical young fogy, David Reiff, taxes Bloom with being, if not responsible for Lt. Colonel North and the Iran-Contra scandals, a philosophical apologist for actions of this sort. And of all places in the *Times Literary Supplement,* which, before its now-evident politicization, was thought to be one of the most disinterested intellectual journals in the English-speaking world.

The second and greater distinction of Bloom's book is his sober, brilliant, and really quite devastating account of the barbarous attack on American universities in the sixties—an attack from whose consequences they are still suffering. Bloom is not the first to draw the parallel between the riotous

American students in the sixties and the behavior of the Nazi-infected students in German universities after Hitler came to power. Those who are too young to remember or who have tried to forget will find Bloom's account of what occurred at Cornell—which mutatis mutandis is what occurred at Harvard, NYU, Buffalo, San Francisco State, Berkeley, and other institutions—so galvanizing that it will overcome their initial incredulity. They will also find it shocking that he does not hold the riotous students themselves solely or even primarily responsible for the collapse of academic freedom and integrity during this period, but the faculties—their teachers. Students, Bloom writes, "discovered that the pompous teachers who catechized them about academic freedom could, with a little shove, be made into dancing bears." Most of the time only the threat of a shove sufficed, as it did in Nazi Germany, where distinguished intellectuals surprised the world by their servility. In mitigation to some extent of the German professors' behavior is that resistance required heroic conduct, since it invoked immediate dismissal, imprisonment, and worse. The American professors risked only unpopularity.

Much can be forgiven Bloom because of the story he tells, as distinct from his proposed remedy, all the more so because the memory of those violent days and the lessons that can be drawn from them have been largely ignored. It is striking that of the hundreds of millions of dollars expended on research projects by the great liberal educational foundations, not a single study can be found of the stormy period that transformed so many American universities into political battlefields. Someone has suggested that in part this can be explained by the fact that a considerable number of the university administrators of that era subsequently moved into positions of influence in the foundations as officers and board members.

This denial of the truth about the rampaging students of the sixties is reflected even in the most respectable of the critical reviews Bloom has received. Among the most disappointing of the reviews from a philosophical source is Martha Nussbaum's in the *New York Review of Books* (November 5, 1987). Through a pedantic display of classical learning she seeks to discredit Bloom's scholarship—scholarship that is not relevant to his central position. Her account of Bloom's criticism of the riotous behavior of the students of the sixties is a travesty. She pictures Bloom as a resolute defender of the political and social status quo, opposed to the improvement of society presumably because he was critical of the student demands. She refers to his "bitter account of the student movement of the sixties, during which Bloom, lonely opponent of corruption, attempted to stop various changes he deemed pernicious, such as changing the curriculum requirements and even of faculty appointment procedures in response to student demands. To this time of timidity and lowering of standards he traces today's rootlessness and narcissism."

So this is what the arson, firebombs, and violence was about—curricular disagreement. Extraordinary. The most charitable interpretation of anyone capable of writing this way about the demands and behavior of the rioting students of the sixties is that Professor Nussbaum is too young to have any memories of what occurred; or that for some odd reason she has not read the literature of and about the sixties; or she is fearful of the hostile judgment of those alumni of the sixties who, having escaped punishment at the hands of the cowardly faculties they intimidated, are now teaching in the universities. I don't know what explains Professor Nussbaum's case. She must have read Bloom's book with ideological blinders on if she failed to understand that the chief corruption Bloom was opposing was that of academic freedom. Despite my fundamental differences with Allan Bloom—and we are separated by an abyss—and despite the easy and frequent charges of his critics that his views would lead to the curtailment of academic freedom, I have much more confidence that my academic freedom is safer in an institution governed by him and his Straussian colleagues than in one governed by his critics.

Bloom indicts American students of the current generation for many things: a lack of understanding of the perennial ideals of Western civilization, an absence of coherent intellectual outlook on the world, an addiction to novelties in cultural life, a hypersensitivity to mind-numbing modern music, the pursuit of sex as a kind of organized sport, a glorification of freedom and an openness of mind whose consequences in fact close the student's mind to moral, metaphysical, and religious truths which constitute the true legacy of liberal civilization. It would not be unfair to ask him for empirical evidence of actual changes over the years in the basic beliefs of the American student body. Certain student practices, of course, are new and different—the vogue of new music, drugs, the flaunting of sexual promiscuity. But what seems to outrage Bloom most is what he calls the students' moral and historical relativism. Sometimes he calls it "cultural relativism," sometimes "relativity," sometimes the belief that "truth is relative." His opening sentence reads: "There is one thing a professor can be absolutely certain of: almost every student entering the university believes, or says he believes, that truth is relative." Students, he writes, "are unified only in their relativism and in their allegiance to equality." Here we focus on his views about relativity and disregard the fact that he is talking about students in our elite universities and not the vast numbers still enrolled in religious and church-related institutions.

It may be hard to believe, but Bloom's whole discussion of the theme from the first page to the last is vitiated by a fundamental blunder. He confuses subjectivism with moral relativity. He seems to be unaware of the difference between saying (1) all truth is relative, meaning nothing is true or false, good or bad, but that our saying so or feeling so makes it so, and saying (2) all truth is relational, depending upon a complex of things that determine its validity or objectivity. To Bloom the opposite of relational is absolute, not subjective. The subjectivist judgment is arbitrary: it does not call for reasons or evidence to buttress its claims. It does not make a cognitive claim at all. It merely declares a state of feeling. A relational or relativistic judgment, on the other hand, can be challenged to justify itself. Bloom seems not to have heard of the notion of objective relativism. Sometimes what a proposition is relational to is simple: "Milk is a nourishing food," in relation to the digestive systems of organisms of type *x*. This is perfectly compatible with the truth "Milk is not a nourishing food" in relation to the digestive systems of organisms of type *y*. No subjectivism here, only more specification. Bloom would recognize the point at once if someone were to ask him: "How far is Chicago?"

Often what makes a statement true or false, good or bad is much more complex, especially moral statements, since for the problem in hand they are related not only to facts but to shared values in that situation. The complexity of our moral statements depends on certain historical conditions and on the plurality of values always involved in a genuine moral problem. "What shall we do?" may be a technical problem merely concerning the best or most effective means to achieve a given end. But when it is a *moral* question, it always presupposes a conflict of ends that must be resolved here and now. No important policy issue is merely a technical problem of means. Bloom assumes that there exists one underlying good that can be grasped if we understand "the nature of man," and from which all moral judgments of good or bad can be ultimately derived in all situations. He also holds that there are a number of self-evident natural rights sufficient to answer all our questions of right and wrong.

Not only is this position false, but demonstrably false. He does not realize that our moral economy is one in which good often conflicts with good, and right with right. No matter what the particular good or right may be which we seek to absolutize, it may be overridden in the light of the possible consequences of our actions on other goods or rights to which we are committed in the particular historical situation we find ourselves.

Let us examine one of Bloom's own illustrations:

> The students, of course, cannot defend their opinion. It is something with which they have been indoctrinated. The best they can do is point out all the opinion and cultures there are and have been. What right, they ask, do I or anyone else have to say one is better than the others? If I pose the routine questions designed to confute them and make them think, such as, "If you had been a British administrator in India, would you have let the natives under your governance burn the widow at the funeral of a man who had died," they either remain silent or reply that the British should never have been there in the first place. It is not that they know very much about other nations, or about their own. The purpose of their education is not to make them scholars but to provide them with a moral virtue-openness.

Well, the students Bloom taught at Chicago were very different apparently from those I taught at New York University. My students would have replied, "Of course the administrator should hve tried to stamp out the barbarous practice . . . but not if the attempt was to result in communal riots and violence by fanatics resulting in widespread loss of life. The timing is important and it might be better to work through the Hindu religious authorities, not all of whom approved of the practice, even when it was really voluntary. As it is, it took the British almost fifty years before declaring the practice illegal." The students, in justifying their reply, probably would have brought up other historical instances in which an evil was tolerated for a time in order to avoid a greater evil. In passing, I doubt very much whether Bloom's students at Cornell, Toronto, or Chicago would have responded with the "openness" he reports if he had asked them about Hitler's racial laws, or the Holocaust.

The difference between Bloom and the objective relativists whose position he distorts is that, for him, good is good and right is right—and that's the end of it. To the objective relativist, however, morals are related to human weal and woe, to human and social needs, and to the feasible alternatives of action open to mankind at any historic time. But aren't there some practices that are intrinsically bad? Of course there are, as slavery is even when it has divine and religious institutional sanctions. But *intrinsic* does not mean *unrelated*—something utterly in itself. When the only alternative to enslaving prisoners of war was to slaughter them with their families, wouldn't Bloom have preferred the lesser evil of slavery, with its prospect of ultimate liberation? Would we not take it as a sign of some moral progress if a savage tribe were to enslave another defeated tribe, rather than to slaughter them, as was the custom?

Bloom, like his former colleague Harry Jaffa, glorifies Abraham Lincoln as a truly moral statesman inspired by the ideals of the Declaration of Independence. Hence it is surprising that Bloom does not recognize and appreciate Lincoln's pragmatic genius. Lincoln regarded slavery as a moral evil, yet he went to war not to abolish slavery but to save the Union. If the Union had not been preserved, there would have been no amendments to abolish slavery as an institution. It was the Thirteenth Amendment that outlawed slavery as an institution, not the Emancipation Proclamation, which emancipated slaves as a war measure. In the eyes of John Brown and other abolitionist fanatics, Lincoln would have been regarded as "a damned moral relativist," if the phrase had been in vogue in Bloom's sense. But Lincoln knew that prudence and a sense of timing were not only political virtues but moral ones. He feared the fanaticism of virtue, the idealisms focused only on one value or program pursued at *any* cost to other values violated by the means employed to achieve the ideal goal.

The facts of history, Bloom insists, have really nothing to do with the moral quality of an action. True, they have not *everything* to do with the moral judgment, because many of the qualities of human experience are transcultural, but sometimes the historic context is highly relevant. Both Bloom and his students, for example, would certainly be appalled if today horse thieves were subject to capital punishment. But had they lived centuries ago in regions where stealing a man's horse threatened his very survival, such punishment would not have been deemed cruel and unusual.

The conception of cultural and ethical relativism in American thought, as Bloom interprets it, leads to the view that "anything goes." The true conception, however, leads instead to a better understanding of the causes and conditions of the values and practices different groups hold, and the likely consequences of alternative policies in dealing with the conflicts that arise from such differences in order to discover the more reasonable and better way of preserving our democratic society. Bloom rejects this approach as "liberalism without natural rights"—rights, that is, enshrined in the Declaration of Independence and the Constitution, ultimately derivable from God and Nature. He makes no attempt to show how they can be derived from these theological and metaphysical notions. And he seems unaccountably indifferent to the obvious fact that the rights to life, liberty, and happiness in the Declaration are not always compatible with each other, and that the rights enumerated in the Constitution are often in direct conflict with each other. The right to due process and a fair trial may be threatened by the exercise of free speech. This makes it incoherent to regard all of them as inalienable, indefeasible, or absolute. The compulsions of an ordered society may make it necessary to override for a limited time any of the enumerated rights; hence none can be regarded as absolute. Only the use of intelligence or reason in making the decision can be deemed absolute.

To hold his view, Bloom is compelled to flagrantly distort history and to interpret the right to freedom of religion as belonging to the realm of knowledge rather than to practice. He must ignore also the fact that the practice is far from absolute, since a religion that practiced human sacrifice, or sacred prostitution, polygamy, or any other currently illegal action would not be tolerated under the constitutional right of freedom of religion. To cover up the glaring gaps in his argument—or rather the absence of argument—he charges that ethical relativism entails the lunatic doctrine that freedom, conceived as the right to do anything one pleases in the name of democracy, is absolute.

He taxes Oliver Wendell Holmes, as he does John Stuart Mill and John Dewey, with preparing the way to the present-day spurious openness he deplores. Holmes, he says, "renounced seeking for a principle to determine which speech is not tolerable in a democratic society and invoked instead an imprecise and practically meaningless standard, clear and present danger, which to all intents and purposes makes the preservation of public order the only common good."

The clear and present danger standard is imprecise because no one can foresee all the circumstances in which the consequences of speech, and even its modes, become problematic in a democracy. What is modifiably wrong with it is that some of Holmes's successors have made the declaration of what constitutes a clear and present danger—which is a *matter of fact* to be determined by a jury or Congress under certain safeguards—into a matter of law, as Judge Medina did. But Bloom's inference that to all intents and purposes the doctrine makes the preservation of public order under all circumstances an absolute desideratum is an arrant non sequitur. When it is properly invoked, it is best construed as an effort to preserve some of the other rights enumerated in the Constitution. The trouble with Holmes is that he was too optimistic and progressive, according to Bloom, and held that truth unaided by government "always triumphs in the market place of ideas. This optimism had not been shared by the Founders, who insisted that the principles of democratic government must be returned to and consulted, even though the consequences might be harsh for certain points of view—some merely tolerated and not respected, others forbidden outright. To their way of thinking, there should be no tolerance for the intolerant."

This is a strange reading both of Holmes and the Founding Fathers. What Bloom overlooks is that the Founders were intolerant only of the *actively* intolerant, otherwise they would not have tolerated Platonists, Catholics, fundamentalists of Protestant sects, Orthodox Jews, or philosophers like Bloom, whose theology (or constitutional theory in the case of Bloom) tolerated no heresy. Bloom is simply adapting to his own basic political theory the Augustinian dictum that error about first principles in theology has no rights. This is incompatible with the Jeffersonian legacy of the Founding Fathers developed by Holmes, Frankfurter, and Learned Hand. With respect to the most important issue that gave rise to the formulation of "the clear and present danger" doctrine, namely, the constitutional rights of members of the Communist party who are intolerant in both theory and practice, they held in effect that in a democratic polity communism may be tolerated as a heresy, but not as an active conspiracy. Communists (Leninists) are the true founders of twentieth-century totalitarian intolerance. In a democratic polity they can be tolerated as a heresy, but not as an *active* conspiracy.

Among the difficulties of Bloom's book is a certain lack of clarity in the use of his basic terms, chief among them "soul," "nature," and "reason." Is "soul," as Bloom uses it, a metaphor for the activity of an acculturated organism, or is he using it, in the Platonic and theological sense, as a substantial entity? When he speaks of "nature," is he speaking of the natural world, and of the human history or culture it supports, or of nature in some metaphysical sense, something over and above the quality and behavior patterns of things in their spatial and temporal dimensions? And when he speaks of "reason," is he speaking of a faculty or the capacity of intelligence? (In ordinary discourse when we say a person is intelligent, we mean, as a rule, that he or she is capable of giving adequate reasons or *grounds* for his or her judgments.)

The difficulty with Bloom's position is that, like Leo Strauss, he has not emancipated himself from the Greek notion that the cosmos is also an ethos, and that what is good and bad, right and wrong for man is essentially related to the cosmic order rather than to the reflective choices of men and women confronted by problems of what to do. Bloom speaks of "the rational quest for the good life according to nature." He tells us that "nature should be the standard by which we judge our own lives and the lives of people," but he does not tell us where we must go to find it. He certainly does not mean nature "red in tooth and claw" as a standard. Nor can the metaphysical or theological order be of any more help. We may hold that all men are biological brothers or brothers under the fatherhood of God. But this conviction does not clarify in the slightest why we believe it is wrong to act like Cain toward his brother Abel but right to act like Jonathan to David, who was not his brother. Nor does it follow from the theological doctrine that all men are equal in the sight of the Lord, that they are or should be equal in the sight of the Law, something well known both to the biblical Jews who petitioned the prophet Samuel to "appoint Thou a King over us," and to Charles I and the defenders of the divine right of kings.

Implicit in Bloom's analysis, and more explicit in the writings of his mentors, is his denial of the autonomy of the moral experiences. Without reference to the existence of God or to some metaphysical "order of the whole of things," we cannot, according to him, intelligibly determine what is right or wrong or rationally defend a belief in human rights conceived in Jeffersonian fashion as reasonable rights, not literally as natural rights. Bloom offers not a single plausible argument to defend his position but, to reassert it, falls back on pages upon pages about Nietzsche and relativity. He is strikingly and strangely sympathetic to Nietzsche under the twofold delusion that Nietzsche's declaration that "God is dead" left man not only bereft or in anguish but in terror without any compass to direct his life; and that the development of reason itself must lead to the rejection of reason.

All this is absurd. Hume long ago showed that there is no such thing as pure reason, that it always acts in the context of interest and passion. Thereafter a whole brigade of thinkers, including both Dewey and Freud (one of the few things they have in common) showed that the cultivation of reason or intelligence, by establishing new behavior or habit patterns, can modify and reorder the interests and passions to avoid self- and socially destructive consequences. Utopian fools believe that this can be done easily. It is just as foolish to believe that it is altogether impossible, that nothing can be done by intelligent nurture and education. Those who talk of "the bankruptcy of reason" or of science in virtue of the consequences of its development—which generates, of course, new problems and challenges—exhibit failure not only of nerve but of intelligence.

Let us finally return to the issue dividing Bloom from the pack of frenzied detractors of his book (among the latter, I note, are some of his ideological kinsmen, doubtless envious of his success)—that is, the issue of what the curriculum of a liberal arts college should be today. Bloom's approach rests upon the grasp and application of certain metaphysical truths about the nature of man and society. More comprehensive in its claim, and yet more detailed in its application, was the similar approach to higher education taken before him by Mortimer Adler and Robert Hutchins with an occasional assist from Alexander Meikeljohn as a justification of the curriculum of St. John's College. No protagonist of this approach has ever replied to my critical detailed evaluation of its program, an evaluation endorsed with respect to its scientific aspects by Richard Courant, Albert Einstein, and Bertrand Russell, and in whole by John Dewey. The book containing this critique, entitled *Education for Modern Man* (1946), presented an alternative required a program for the first two years of a liberal arts and science college education for *all* students before vocational specialization. It should also be noted that in the best critical review of Bloom's book so far published, that by Richard Rorty (which is really more critical of Strauss than of Bloom), Rorty, too, on empirical not metaphysical grounds, advocates a prescribed curriculum for "the first two years" of college life. Such a curriculum allows some adaptation to local conditions, but it includes the best features of the St. John's College curriculum. In range and depth, it covers much more ground than the recently emasculated course in Western Culture at Stanford University. The proposals deriving from this empirical approach, following Dewey's lead, are oriented to three reference points: first, the nature and needs of the students; second, the nature and needs of the society of which students are a part; and third, the subject matters, studies of which most effectively enable students to develop themselves as persons and live with mutual benefit among other persons in their society. I predict that Bloom will not be unhappy with what he finds in college curricula devised along these lines without benefit of any controlling metaphysics or theology.

Although written from an explicitly Deweyan standpoint, some of Rorty's formulations, however, may be misconstrued. He is quite right in saying that *with respect to the arena of public life,* "for Deweyans, the theoretical questions, 'Did Socrates answer Thrasymachus?' and 'Can we answer Hitler?' get replaced by practical questions like 'How can we arrange things so that people like Thrasymachus and Hitler will not come to power?' " But this should not be extended to Dewey's conception of the range of curricular questions open to consideration in the universities. "Did Socrates answer Thrasymachus?" is a perfectly legitimate, indeed, inescapable, question to any intelligent reader of Plato's *Republic,* and the answer seems to me obviously no. There are better answers to Thrasymachus. To the question "Can we answer Hitler?" the answer is "Easily, even if he is not likely to accept the answer." As for the practical questions on how to prevent people like Thrasymachus and Hitler from coming to power, universities may *discuss* all the proposals but *officially advocate* none. It is not likely in their present politicalized state that their faculties are likely to have better ideas than the trade unions, churches, political parties, or any randomly selected group of literate citizens.

The specific details of any college curriculum are, of course, never fixed. They are affected by contingencies of national crises as well as by slow changes in the encompassing society of which the educational system is always a part. But it is possible to develop on empirical grounds, regardless of differences on first or last things, broad outlines for certain required areas of study appropriate for the liberal education of men and women in our time.

I attempted to do this in the mid-sixties when the tide of student activism swept away in most colleges the structure of required courses. It was in answer to the challenges of a fiery young rebel who concluded her tirade against the "class-angled and biased" required curriculum of the college with the following:

> Who are you, or anyone else, to tell *me* what my educational needs are? I, and I alone, am the best judge of what I want and what I need. What goes for me, goes for everybody. That's democracy in education.

This was a perfectly fair question, although some of my colleagues resented the tone and manner in which it was asked. I still regard my reply to her as valid and sufficient to make it possible to justify a course of study which Allan Bloom can approve and which, if he doesn't, can, I believe, withstand any criticism he can make of it.

Here is an abbreviated account of my answer to what students, men and women, need to know, whether they know they need it or not.*

1. Every student has an objective need to be able to communicate clearly and effectively with his fellows, to grasp with comprehension and accuracy the meaning of different types of discourse, and to express himself in a literate way.
2. Every student needs to have at least some rudimentary knowledge about his or her own body and mind, about the world of nature and its determining

*The fully developed answer appears on pages 77-78 of this volume.

forces, about evolution and genetics, and allied matters that are central to a rational belief about the place of man in the universe. If they are to have any understanding of these things, they must possess more than the capacity to remember and parrot isolated facts. They must have some grasp of the principles that explain what they observe, some conception of the nature of scientific method. After all, the modern world is what it is in virtue of the influence of science and technology on nature and society. They cannot feel at home in the modern world ignorant of science.

3. Every student has a need to become intelligently aware of how his or her society functions, of the great historical, economic, and social forces shaping its future, of the alternatives of development still open to us, of the problems, predicaments, and programs they and their fellow citizens must face. Whether they want to revolutionize the world or save it from revolution, they must acquire a historical perspective, without which old evils may reappear under new faces and labels. Those who act as if they were born yesterday are the great simplifiers, who mistake their own audacity for objective readiness and often destroy the lives of others in the wreckage of their hopes.

4. Every student needs to be informed, not only of significant facts and theories about nature, society, and the human psyche, but also of the conflict of values and ideals in our time, of the great maps of life, the paths to salvation or damnation, under which human beings are enrolled. He or she must learn how to uncover the inescapable presence of values in every policy, how to relate them to their causes and consequences and costs in other values, and the difference between arbitrary and reasonable value judgments.

5. Every student needs to acquire some methodological sophistication that should sharpen his or her sense for evidence, relevance, and canons of validity. He or she should, at least in popular discourse and debate, be able to distinguish between disguised definitions and genuine empirical statements, between resolutions and generalizations, to nail the obvious statistical lie, and acquire an immunity to the rhetorical claptrap. . . .

6. Finally, every student has a need to be inducted into the cultural legacies of his civilization, its art, literature, and music. His sensibilities should be developed and disciplined, because they provide not only an unfailing occasion of delight and enjoyment in the present but also a source of enrichment of experience in the future.

A few months ago I had an interesting conversation with a bright young man who was on the dean's list at a prestigious eastern university. He had read my autobiography and complained with some justification that it didn't tell him enough about my personal life. "Aside from your political interests," he asked, "as students what were you and your friends really concerned with?" I thought back to the mid-twenties and the students of my day; almost all of us came from lower-middle-class or working-class homes. "What made life exciting for us," I said, "were books, music—Haydn, Mozart, Beethoven—and love. What about your classmates?"

He hesitated for a moment and replied, "Well, I'm not speaking for myself, but I can safely say that the general run of my classmates are interested in sex, drugs, and rock 'n' roll. They say, after all, we live only once."

I heard myself reply, "You don't know what you're missing! Yes, you live only once, but these days you are likely to live an awfully long time, and you can't sustain yourself for long with sex, drugs, and rock 'n' roll. It will first degrade you, and then kill you. 'Today you live and tomorrow you die,' the wilder kids of my own generation used to say. If that were true, something could be said for it. But it is more often true that today you live and tomorrow you suffer, and for many long days after, too."

I relate this exchange not to show my readiness to deliver a homily, but to indicate that I felt the students he was describing were missing something, that they were radically mistaken—and not unregenerate or degenerate—that somehow or other an obvious truth had eluded them. I believe I felt at that moment something of what Allan Bloom must have felt as he wrote *The Closing of the American Mind:* a profound sadness at the prospect of thousands of young men and women missing out on a good thing and accepting in its place something altogether inferior.

Although I reject Allan Bloom's analysis of what is wrong with higher education in our day, and therefore I reject as well his remedies, I nonetheless wish to pay tribute to his good will and intellectual effort, which has succeeded in arousing the country to the necessity, at long last, of a serious debate on what a serious education for modern men and women should be. His noble failure will do more to enrich and uphold the quality of higher education in the United States than the recent vaunted reforms of curricular offerings that in the name of an unlimited, and therefore educationally meaningless, diversity seek to politicalize our universities.

Part Three

IN DEFENSE OF WESTERN CULTURE

12

An Open Letter to the Stanford Faculty

An observer of the educational scene at Stanford during the last fourteen years, I am taking the liberty of offering some comments on the proposed reforms in the course on Western culture. Among my professional concerns has been a prolonged concern with the philosophy of education and with the philosophy of the curriculum. I noted with interest the reintroduction of the course in Western culture in 1980 and have followed closely the discussions of the various reform proposals for it. Such discussions about the courses on Western culture—their content, their organization, and the most effective methods of teaching them—have been held on many other campuses. Two things, however, are distinctive about the discussion at Stanford.

The first is the almost complete absence of reference to a considerable literature by highly qualified scholars on the genuine problems that are involved in exploring perfectly legitimate differences about methods of approach, content, Western or universal (world) orientation. For example, a few years ago a national conference was convened at Michigan State University on the subject: "What Americans Should Know: Western Civilization or World History?" The published proceedings were edited with an introduction by Professor Josef W. Konvitz.

There is hardly a single topic of educational interest broached in the discussion at Stanford during the last two years which is not considered in depth in those proceedings—including questions of periodization, chronological coverage, and the extent to which the cultures and histories of other areas of the world should be integrated into the required course. For all the differences among participants, the discussions were conducted on a distinguished intellectual level. The bibliographical references call attention to other scholarly writings on questions concerning world history and world culture courses.

The discussion at Stanford seems to have ignored a considerable amount of relevant literature on the central themes in dispute.

The second distinctive thing about the discussion at Stanford is the deplorable level of discourse and the denunciatory tones of abuse which have marked the exchange of different points of view. The course in Western culture at Stanford has been attacked as racist, sexist, and imperialistic. One critic of the course declared that Western culture as it stands is "not just racist education, it is the education of racists." More distressing even than this violation of the courtesies of civilized discourse is that it brought no appropriate response from the humanistic scholars who have taught in and designed the program, protesting the degradation of the intellectual level of the discussion.

Proposals were made to reform the alleged bias in the course on Western culture by the injection of material from non-Western culture, Third World countries, and from spokesmen for feminist and the various oppressed minorities. They elicited some relevant technical objections to their feasibility and desirability—limited time, inadequate personnel, and their relative significance for the perennial problems of reflective life central to the course. These objections were fiercely denounced as a mask for the expression of racism, and as a more subtle manifestation of the spirit of intolerance and violence evident in the outrages of Howard Beach and elsewhere. The pages of the *Stanford Daily* contain the most intemperate and irresponsible charges of racism against those who defended retaining the course on Western culture with some modification on various educational grounds. Among the grounds was that the overwhelming number of students who had completed the course over the years regarded it as very satisfactory. Some declared it to be the high point of their educational experience.

The extent to which the discussion of the course on Western culture became politicalized is evidenced in the shouting protest march of last January on the Stanford Senate led by the Reverend Jesse Jackson demanding the abolition of the course. Whatever his contributions to American life and culture, the Reverend Jackson is not known for his contributions to curricular reform on the collegiate level. That the members of the Senate and Academic Council of Stanford should be in need of instruction from the Reverend Jackson on the essentials of liberal education is preposterous. One can very well imagine what the reaction of the Stanford faculty would have been to a march on the Senate by the Reverend Jerry Falwell demanding that the course in Western culture be Christianized.

It goes without saying that there is no justification for any expression of racism, especially in an educational institution, and above all in an institution like Stanford. An assertion that Stanford's course in Western culture is an expression of racism is no more credible to any informed person than the assertion that the Hoover Institution is a hotbed of communism.

As morally offensive as is the expression of racism wherever it is found, a false charge of racism is equally offensive, perhaps even more so, because the consequences of a false charge of racism enables an authentic racist to conceal his racism by exploiting the loose way the term is used to cover up his actions. The same is true of a false charge of sexism or anti-Semitism. This is the lesson we should all have learned from the days of Senator Joseph McCarthy. Because of his false and irresponsible charges of communism against liberals, socialists, and others among his critics, many communists and agents of communist influence sought to pass themselves off as Jeffersonian democrats or merely idealistic reformers. They would all complain they were victims of red baiting to prevent criticism and exposure.

The First Amendment, of course, gives everyone the right to express his or her sentiments whatever they are—communist, fascist, racist, sexist, anti-Semitic, or whatnot—provided his or her words are not an incitement to violence. Students have a right to profess and hear all views. But there is such a thing as the ethics of words, as the great American philosopher Charles Peirce once observed, and their violation is an intellectual crime, especially in an academic community.

There is no need to go over the thoroughly plowed ground to justify the course in Western culture. Aside from the intrinsic value of the study of the outstanding books, ideas, movements, and personalities that constitute their subject matter, it seeks to familiarize students with their common legacy, including the conflicting cultural traditions of the past that have shaped the present and contributed to some of our current difficulties and dilemmas. The materials studied have in part provided us with the basic categories of thought, the conceptual tools, sentiments, and dispositions with which we approach the central problems of a reflective life.

Far from leading to a glorification of the status quo, as ignorant detractors charge, the knowledge imparted by such courses, properly taught, is essential to understanding the world of our own experience, regardless of whether one seeks to alter or preserve it. Indeed, the ideals of tolerance, the limitations of ethno-centrism, the Utopian visions invoked by critics of Western society and its institutions are all expressed in the literature studied in the course in Western culture. It would hardly be an exaggeration to say that of all cultures of which we have knowledge, Western culture has been the most critical of itself.

I have discussed elsewhere, and at length, the manifold ways in which a course in Western culture on the model of the existing courses at Stanford contributes to enriching the internal landscape of the student's mind, regardless of the individual's specialized vocational choice. Essential to such a course is a common core of readings, modifiable from time to time, in the absence of which a coherent, unified program of studies in Western culture, yet allowing for diversified approaches, cannot be achieved.[1]

Before examining more closely the proposed reform of the course on Western culture, some observations are in order. The fact that the overwhelming number of students who have completed the course in Western culture profess to be highly satisfied with the content and manner of instruction, although relevant, is not a decisive consideration. Students should be consulted on any matter that affects them, but the faculty, which confers their degrees, bears the ultimate responsibility for deciding what to teach them, how, and when. A faculty cannot surrender its authority to pressure groups inside or outside the university without stultification.

Second, I have already referred to the myth that the tradition of Western culture is something unitary or monolithic rather than a complex of conflicting traditions including those of dissent. I would go further. There is no definitive meaning or moral in any required text that is necessarily imposed on students by its study.

A competent teacher can, with any required text, play the role of devil's or angelic advocate. In my teaching days, confronted by a class of skeptics, I would make them see the force of the logic of beliefs in transcendence in its strongest and most sophisticated form. Faced with those frozen in dogmatic religious belief, I would make them aware of the formidable power of Humean skepticism.

The greatness of Plato's *Republic* as a perennial philosophical text is that it lends itself to the exciting counterposition of arguments and sentiments with respect to themes that have contemporary vibrancy such as feminism, censorship, the defects of democracy, the snares of totalitarianism, and many others. And this without reliance on the feeble dialectic of Socrates' interrogation; the teacher can further this open approach with occasional reference to supplementary reading.

Third, some of the criticisms of the course are clearly bizarre and others manifestly unwarranted. One of these criticisms asserts that the content and standards of Western culture were restricted to "elite members of Western society." But under the social conditions of the past who else but the elite could be the creators of culture? History has winnowed out the elite contributions of the elite. Does this criticism imply that the elite contributions of the past are beyond the capacity of Stanford students? What has happened to the pursuit of excellence? Not so long ago Dean Norman Wessells declared that Stanford "continues to assemble on the faculty a group of persons who are among this country's—and indeed the world's leading scholar/teachers." He goes on to say "the University's undergraduate body is elite by anyone's standards." With a teaching body and student body of this character, what objection can there be to a study of the elite culture of the elite? What else has come down to us?

We are also told "that the elite ideas are not the totality of meaningful ideas in a society." Of course, the elite ideas are not the totality of meaningful ideas. If they were, they wouldn't be elite. Yet his tautology is offered as a critique of Western culture. There is a wide variety of other courses in sociology, anthropology, economic history, politics, etc., in which other aspects of society can be studied. In my Jefferson Lecture, sponsored by the National Endowment for the Humanities, "The Humanities and the Defense of Freedom," I have argued that Western democracy owes more to the trade unions and the dissident churches than to the elite humanist tradition. But the justification for the study of the great works of Western culture is not political. The oft-repeated charge that the Western culture program "propounds white male values and slights the contributions of women and minority groups to the development of the Western tradition" is simply unwarranted.

Finally, the epistemology of the criticism of Western culture is primitive and mistaken especially in the demand that faculty be recruited from "women and people of color" to study ideas and aspects of culture that involve them. Where ideas are concerned, the primary consideration is mastery of subject matter and not identification with the subject studied. One does not have to be German to study Luther or the German Reformation or be sympathetic to the Nazis to study Hitler. As well argue that men cannot be gynecologists, that only women are best qualified to study family law, or that only fat physicians can study obesity or hungry people the phenomenon of starvation as that only people of color and women are uniquely qualified to do justice to the place, achievement, and oppression of minorities and their culture, wherever relevant, in Western culture. One of the greatest contributions to the exposure and struggle against racism in the United States was made by Gunnar Myrdal—a Swedish white man. Race, color, religion, national origin, and sexual orientation are neither necessary nor sufficient conditions for the fruitful study of the humanities or any subject matter. In scholarship as in sport today—alas! it was not always so!—the quest should always be for the best qualified.

Scholars in the natural and medical sciences may feel that aberrant notions such as those I have described above can prevail only in the soft disciplines of the humanities and social studies. Let them not delude themselves. If such views are not laid to rest, wherever they manifest themselves, they will make their presence felt in recruiting in the natural and medical sciences as well. In some of these fields in the past there have been disgraceful and invidious practices of discrimination on the basis of race, religion, and sex. The abolition of discrimination must not be a preface to any kind of reverse discrimination. In some areas we are already hearing criticism of the concept of objectivity and culture-free criteria of scientific validity and claims about the "efficiency of non-Western medical systems" which presumably should be integrated into the curriculum of our medical schools.

Many features of the proposed reform of the current course in Western culture are of dubious educational value when contrasted with their educational alternatives. Two of them are fatal to any worthwhile course. The first is the absence of a core of required texts in all tracks. The second is the restriction of the time period to be covered in the studies to 500 years, which in effect gives the impression that Western culture today is the residue of the cultural achievements of the fifteenth century to the present. Would it were so! Western culture would be less complex and in some respects better. But the legacy of the ancient and medieval world is still with us.

There is no need to despair that the contrasts, influence, and interactions of non-Western cultures on Western culture will be lost or neglected. Knowledgeable and skillful teaching can introduce references to parallel or analogous ideas and institutions in cultures other than our own when the material requires them. This can be done without the pretense or pretentious claims that the course in Western culture has or can be transformed into a course in world culture.

The Stanford Senate should take the organization or reorganization of the course in Western culture in its own hands, and appoint a committee consisting of outstanding scholars primarily in the humanities from the Stanford faculty to recommend the appropriate course of study in this area for its elite student body.

NOTE

1. *The Philosophy of the Curriculum,* Prometheus Books, 1975. A much earlier discussion will be found in my *Education for Modern Man,* which sought to apply the educational principles of John Dewey to the construction of a required curriculum of studies for the first two years of a liberal arts college.

13

The Attack on Western Civilization
An Interim Report

"Western civilization is under attack on many fronts" we were told by Professor Burns of Mt. Holyoke College in an Op Ed piece in *The New York Times.*[1] He is referring not only to Western civilization but specifically to courses in Western civilization and/or Western culture. And they are under attack for many reasons. For him one of the most valid reasons is the way these courses are organized. They tend to downplay and distort the historical and chronological dimension of Western civilization. In consequence students do not properly grasp the succession and order of the events, ideas, and movements they study. To the extent that his criticism is valid, it is easily remedied by providing for a more detailed examination of the historical context in which the great ideas and events of the past are embedded.

But there is another kind of attack on courses in Western civilization or Western culture and similar interdisciplinary courses in the humanities. This is that these courses are racist, sexist, and imperialistic. The prime example of this kind of attack on the courses on Western culture in an institution not noted for its political conservatism is the recent crusade, not yet complete, at Stanford University. A standard required course in Western culture was introduced about five years ago when the university was recovering from the prolonged consequences of the educational chaos of the sixties. One critic of that course in Western culture recently declared that "Western culture as it stands is not just racist education, it is the education of racists." Not only was this characterization untrue, unfair, ignorant, and an outrageous violation of the courtesies of civilized discourse, what was just as disheartening, it brought no appropriate response from most of the humanistic scholars who had designed and taught in the program.

From *Measure* 70 (February 1988): 1–6.

The situation at Stanford (or at any other institution) reflects local history and conditions. But it must be considered against the general background. One of the casualties of the anarchic sixties on many campuses was the very conception of a required curriculum for the first two years of the course of study in liberal arts, particularly in the humanities and social studies. The requirements were replaced by a cafeteria of miscellaneous courses limited by certain area distributions and course sequences. For years it was possible at some institutions for students to be awarded a liberal arts degree without having taken a course in history or the hard sciences and mathematics, or a foreign language. As the debilitating consequences of the relatively untrammeled elective process made itself felt, accompanied by grade inflation and deteriorating educational standards, a reaction set in. Required courses in Western civilization or Western culture were introduced to provide some elements of a common curriculum in the early years of college enrollment.

There is no need to go over thoroughly plowed ground to justify such courses. Aside from the intrinsic value of the study of the outstanding books, ideas, movements, and personalities that constitute their subject matter, such courses seek to familiarize students with their common legacy including the conflicting cultural traditions of the past that have shaped the present and contributed to some of our current difficulties and dilemmas. The materials studied have in part provided us with the basic categories of thought, the conceptual tools, and sentiments and dispositions with which we approach the central problems of a reflective life. Far from leading to a glorification of the status-quo, as their ignorant detractors charge, the knowledge imparted by such courses, properly taught, is essential to understanding the world of our own experience regardless of whether one seeks to revolutionize or reform or preserve it.

Properly taught, such courses should affect the spiritual and intellectual development of the individual student. It would hardly be an exaggeration to say that anyone ignorant of the parables and stories of the Bible taught as literature or of Greek tragedy and mythology would find many of the references and much of the language of modern literature and poetry incomprehensible. To a considerable extent the cultivation of the internal landscape of the students' minds, regardless of the individuals' specialized vocational choice, is enriched by the development of their sensibilities to the art, literature, and music in the courses in Western culture required in any liberal education worthy of the name.

There are a great many problems involved in the organization of an educationally adequate curriculum in Western culture. It is a theme which is relevant to the educational experience of the faculties and students. It invites reflective discussion and revision on the basis of actual classroom performance and tested results. There is no one model that serves all desirable purposes for all campuses. But a good case can be made for at least a one-year prescribed course in the humanities broadly understood. Presumably, distribution requirements will insure that students will come to analytic grips with the problems of contemporary civilization. One can distinguish for pedagogical purposes between the study of a great work that contributes to the student's understanding of it as an expression of the culture of its time, its influence on subsequent generations including the present, and an analysis of the problems and questions it generates in contemporary society. Plato's *Republic* is a good instance. A skillful teacher can show how the central issues of our times, problems of war, peace, social justice, feminism, education, and government are adumbrated in Plato's argument, but what is *distinctive* about Plato and Greek culture would be lost if *The Republic* were studied merely as a text in social problems which could be more fruitfully explored in other ways. Failure to recognize this distinction, as well as the expectation that a course in Western culture can embrace all areas of social and political life, is sure to generate misunderstanding. It will also overlook the perennial problems of philosophy, among them the definition and quest of a meaningful and satisfying life.

A significant thing about the course in Western culture at Stanford was that the overwhelming majority of the students, when polled, declared that they had found it interesting and educationally profitable. For some it was the high point of their experience at Stanford. This consideration by itself is not decisive in determining the educational desirability of a course but is certainly relevant. The agitation for its reform or rather its transformation and the allegations that the course was imperialistic, racially and sexually *biased* came from a relative handful of students and a scattering of faculty members. Now it is one thing to say that a given course in Western culture excludes what is relevant to its legitimate subject matter; it is another thing to say that what is relevant does not get sufficient attention; and a completely third thing to say that its relevant subject matter is taught in such a way as to downgrade, disparage, or contemn other cultures, women, and nonwhite minorities. The most vocal critics of the course did not distinguish among the three grounds. On the whole, they gave chief emphasis to the charge that it was racist, sexist, and imperialistic. No one ever gave a specific illustration of a theme whose treatment in any basic reading or text, or in any lecture or section discussion devoted to it, even remotely justified this charge. The general criticism assumed that because the course in Western culture naturally *focused* on the great works of the West, this necessarily implied "the superiority of Western culture" to all other cultures of the world. Of course it implied nothing of the sort. It implied that the ideas expressed in these works, the traditions and controversies they generated including the social, political, national and class struggles they inspired, played a greater role in the development and nature of present-day society, than the works and oral traditions of other cultures. Nor does it follow, nor does any rational person assert, that a course in Western culture is sufficient to understand the problems and predicaments that face the present world, either nationally or globally. It goes without saying that any teacher worth his or her salt in explicating the great works of the past, many of which have been sources of divergent interpretations, would make references to other cultures that have developed comparable or critical notions. For example, whether with reference to Leviticus or the New Testament, the injunction "Thou shalt love thy neighbor as yourself" could be compared with parallel texts from Buddhism or from Lao-Tse or from African sources if they can be found. It could also inspire an appreciation of the differences between the positive and negative formulations of the maxim: "Do unto others (or do not do) what you would (or would not) have done to yourself," as well as the virtues and evils of absolute pacifism.

The dean of undergraduate studies, at the close of the spring semester in 1986, declared that "the Western culture program has borne out its promise as the most important innovation in Stanford undergraduate education in the past two decades." This is high praise, indeed! Nonetheless the small handful of students and faculty members intensified their criticism of the course on the ground that it neglected the non-European contributions to Western culture as well as those of "women and people of color." Donald Kennedy, President of Stanford, who won his academic spurs as a biologist not as an educator, added his voice to the criticism of the course in Western culture. "I think it should be changed, and changed in significant ways." Several forums on the Stanford course in Western culture were conducted, most of whose participants were highly critical of its existing program. In view of the student evaluation of the course and the tribute paid to its educational value by the dean of undergraduate studies, the disproportion among the critics and defenders of the course was surprising. The editors of the student newspaper endorsed some of the criticisms of the program.

By the fall semester of 1986 a specific program of reform had been drawn up by some faculty members who had agitated for the revision of the existing course, and proposed to the Committee on Undergraduate Instruction for adoption. It provided for the development and teaching of a third spring quarter course option in Western culture which would drop the standard basic texts and focus on the place and contributions of women and minority groups within Western culture. In short order the committee approved the reform. The final decision was to be made by the Faculty Senate. On the day scheduled for the Senate vote a noisy demonstration led by the Reverend Jesse Jackson, not previously known for his educational contributions, who happened to be on the Stanford campus, marched to the site of the Senate meeting, protesting the racism of the existing course and demanding the adoption of the reform proposal. They chanted again and again, "Hey, hey, ho, ho Western culture has got to go!" No one, certainly not the administration or faculty committees, seemed to take umbrage at the intervention of Reverend Jackson in the curricular affairs of Stanford, although it is safe to predict that the intervention of Reverend Jerry Falwell or Pat Robertson and others of their kind would have been strongly and volubly resented. The Faculty Senate, without any expressed opposition, approved the recommendation of the Committee on Undergraduate Instruction. This occurred early in the winter semester of 1987, which began in January. The option approved *on a one time basis only* was duly introduced in the spring semester that began in April. It permitted students in any of the eight tracks in which Western culture was studied to substitute this option for the third quarter of their track.

It would be appropriate here to examine the details of this third quarter curricular option devoted to the contributions of women and minorities. And we shall return to it later as an indication of what some of those who charge the course in Western culture with bias against women and people of color propose to put in its stead. But other issues soon developed. Emboldened by their success in revising the curriculum of the course in Western culture, the architects of revision went further. The Western Culture Task Force now proposed the abolition of the course in Western culture and a substitution for it of a course in global and world culture in which the contributions of all cultures of the world would be considered, with special concern for the trials, tribulations, and achievements of women and minorities and the exploited masses. (Later on the title of the proposed course was revised to read "Culture, Ideas, and Values.")

At this point some of the distinguished senior members of the Humanities came alive to the enormity of what was being proposed and offered some obvious objections to it. They indicated several difficulties to the transformation of the course in Western culture into a course that was tantamount to one in world culture. There was some ambiguity about exactly what was intended but obviously a proposal that calls for "courses that examine other cultures on a fully equal basis as that of Europe" is certainly not a course in Western culture. A few students and other members of the Stanford community voiced their concern. One of the editors of the student paper reasonably countered the assertion of a faculty spokesman for the new proposal that "people can learn about Marx as he is seen and absorbed by Third World countries," with the observation: "of course they can, and they should. But first Marx's work should be read in itself, as a product of the time in which it is written." He could have added, had he known more about Marx, that otherwise students would not know that Marx gave the English imperialists credit for introducing the first social revolution in India in 1500 years! Nor would they know, something far more questionable than the Marxist justification for the progressive imperialism of early capitalism that Marx and especially Engels were guilty of denigrating expressions of racism. This is something that apparently is not known or taught by those who regard themselves as Marxist or who teach about Marx on campus.

Whereupon the whole level of discourse degenerated to an unbelievable level. Those who raised questions about the wisdom of abandoning the course were denounced as elitists and racists. The chairperson of the Black Student Union, in response to the perfectly reasonable doubts about the desirability and feasibility of the new course, replied with an hysterical outburst: "The vociferous and vicious response of members of the Stanford faculty have sent me reeling with surprise and pain."

But the response had actually questioned whether the existing faculty was sufficiently competent to teach the different cultures. It was neither vociferous nor vicious. It was mild and reasonable. Concerning a column and editorial in the student paper, the chairperson wrote further that she wonders whether "these are the same people that wrote the editorial about the persistence of racism." About another column and letter in the newspaper, she wrote: "These individuals are sending me, women and all women of color a message that says loud and clear 'niggers go home.' That is the battle cry of Howard Beach, New York, and that is what the Klan puts out everyday. 'We don't want you or your kind challenging our predominance and superiority.' "

There is nothing in what anyone wrote or said that implied anything of the sort, or that justified this torrent of abuse. There is no place for the expression of racism in civilized discourse nor for the false charge of racism. The false charge of racism is simply a tactic to choke off rational discussion, a strategy of intimidation to silence the expression of criticism of educationally dubious programs. It is based on a shrewd calculation of the moral cowardice of many members of the faculty who, fearful of becoming the target of such abuse, will swallow any and all doubts about this radical proposal to drop the course in Western culture for one in world culture or one in which Western culture is supplemented by a study of other cultures.

The magnitude of the problem of a course in the plural cultures of the world is apparent on its face. The standard criticism of the conventional courses in Western culture or civilization, from one end of the country to another, is that the essential ideas, books, traditions, and movements can hardly be covered in minimal depth in the course of one year. How, then, can minimal justice be done to the study of Western culture and other major cultures in the course of a year or less? *Properly taught,* a course in Third World cultures similar to the one offered on an experimental basis that was substituted unfortunately for the last third of the course in Western culture in the spring of 1987, could be offered as a legitimate elective independently of the basic requirement.

A whole cluster of problems cry out for discussion, and they deserve careful statement and consideration. Every reasoned expression of opinion should be invited, except the expression of racism and/or sexism and the false charge of racism or sexism which is often a manifestation of it.

One naturally looks to the educational leadership of the university for some guidance and insight in a matter of such critical curricular importance. The whole concept of liberal education is involved. But the first statement issued by President Donald Kennedy on the draft proposal to transform the course in Western culture into a course in World culture was an astonishing criticism of the few professors who had the courage to express some critical questions. He chided them for several reasons. First, the draft deserved more careful consideration before they criticized it. But if so, why did he not criticize the more numerous reactions that greeted the proposal with *Hosanna's*? Second, their criticism "is discouraging to minority students who may find in the rhetorical vigor and haste of these reactions a message that their concerns are to be dismissed with a prompt and heavy hand." This is a curious objection. Would the questions the few critics of the proposal asked be less cogent if they were expressed weakly? Is not the course in World cultures designed to benefit all students? And is not the faculty to have the ultimate authority, after discussion with all members of the Stanford community, to prescribe the educational requirement for the degree it bestows? Third, "the conduct of a discussion like this one in a newspaper instead of in dialogue with the proposers constitutes an irresistible temptation to hyperbole." But the proposal was published in the school newspaper! And there was an implied and shortly an explicit invitation welcoming comments on the proposal. The very issue of the faculty *Campus Report*[2] containing President Kennedy's rebuke to the few critics of the proposal for publishing their comments contained a well-organized, spirited defense of the proposal by several members of the faculty and student body. More significant than anything else was the failure of President Kennedy to condemn the false and contemptible charge of racism that had been hurled at the few critics of the proposal.

In my judgment, having spend a lifetime in the academy, constructing and deconstructing curricular programs for undergraduate education in liberal arts colleges, I regard as far more significant than the ultimate constitution and fate of the course in Western culture, the manner in which the discussion at Stanford has so far been conducted, and what it reveals about the faculty of Stanford University in the area of the humanities and social studies, as well as the character of its educational leadership.

* * *

The above was written some months ago and was unfortunately delayed in publication. At the present writing (mid-February), the fate of the course in Western culture is still undecided. It is under debate in the Stanford Faculty

Senate. The upshot of the debate has attracted national attention which began with Reverend Jesse Jackson's famous march and was intensified in consequence of a first page *New York Times* story. It may turn out that the debate in the Senate will have a healthy and healing educational effect since the discussion, although spirited and sometimes emotional, is being conducted in a rational fashion without demagogic rhetoric.

One beneficial fallout of the discussion is that representatives of the Student Rainbow Coalition on the Stanford Campus, who had been most vehement in denunciation of the course in Western culture as racist, sexist, and imperialist, no longer publicly utter these charges. They have been cautioned by some of the critics of the present course that their rhetoric is self-defeating. They have accepted as a lesser evil the proposal to abandon the present course in Western culture for a revised one entitled "Cultures, Ideas, and Values." There are some like President Kennedy who seek to play down the differences between these two courses as cosmetic, as merely over means to achieve the same ends. The differences are far from cosmetic.

After all, what would a course in world or global culture be, over and above a study in Cultures, Ideas, and Values? The present course centers on a core list of readings in order to insure a common coherent educational experience to build on, and to avoid the disintegration of that experience by a proliferation of different courses that have no relation to each other. That was the fate of a Western culture requirement many years ago. There is nothing to prevent changes in the core list through periodic reevaluation. The present course embraces a study of the various civilizations of the ancient world and the Medieval Age that are still at the root of much of the modern world. The proposed new course mandates no such study. This is not a cosmetic difference.

Sad to say, however, even those who wish to defend the existing course in Western culture have been forced to make a concession that compromised its intellectual integrity. The choice of the core list of works, its detractors to the contrary notwithstanding, is *not* a judgment that the works studied are "timelessly better" than any others that have been or will be written. The list can be changed. One can make an excellent case for substituting Locke's *Second Treatise on Government* or J. S. Mill on *Liberty* for More's *Utopia*. And the fact that there are no woman writers on the current list is no more evidence that the course is sexist than that the absence of American authors—not even of the *Federalist Papers*—is evidence that the course is anti-American. What troubles me is the proposal to add books "by women and people of color" to the list. This implies that the criteria of selection should be something other than the criteria of intellectual distinction and cultural importance regardless of the sex, race, or sexual orientation of the author.

Meanwhile, a faculty wag has been overheard to say about the furious debate over whether to retain or to abolish the core list of required readings:

"The agenda has been changed. It is not now a question of beheading the course in Western culture but what its hairstyle should be." There is some truth in this. There has been a shift in emphasis. But do some hairstyles make ultimate beheading easier than other hairstyles?

NOTES

1. (November 22, 1986.)
2. (April 29, 1987.)

14

Educational Disaster at Stanford University?

Before evaluating the educational significance of the curricular changes at Stanford University, approved by the Faculty Senate at its meeting of March 31, 1988, it is desirable to ascertain the nature of the changes. Since there seems to be some disagreement about some of the provisions of the new required course and the attendant circumstances of their adoption, it may be helpful to reproduce two news stories of the event—one from the local newspaper, *The Peninsula Times Tribune,* whose editors have taken no stand on the change, and the other from the student paper, *The Stanford Daily,* whose editors have approved it.

* * *

THE PENINSULA TIMES TRIBUNE
April 1, 1988
By Carol Watson
Times Tribune Staff

Ending a two-year struggle that pitted students against the faculty and faculty members against each other, Stanford University Thursday threw out its Western culture requirement in favor of a program promoting the study of women, minorities, and class issues.

The Faculty Senate voted 39–4 in favor of the new "Cultures, Ideas, and Values" [CIV] requirement. Five professors abstained.

"The change is a substantial improvement," said Stanford University President Donald Kennedy.

From *Measure* 21 (April 1988): 1–8. Reprinted by permission of the University Centers for Rational Alternatives.

Beginning next fall, freshmen will take classes from the CIV track to fulfill the first of eight breadth requirements.

It will replace the current Western culture program, which was branded as racist two years ago by the Black Student Union. The resulting debate captured national attention.

After the Faculty Senate voted for the new CIV, a student ran to the door to tell about 200 others waiting outside of the decision.

They cheered.

"We feel philosophically that the vote in favor of this was a vote in favor of moving forward and progression," said Black Student Union chairman Bill King. "They voted for moving toward ethnic studies, not teaching freshmen lies."

Students in the Western culture track, adopted by the Senate in 1980, currently choose from eight year-long sequences. Most, if not all, of these sequences will be adapted to meet the new guidelines.

The first CIV objective is to "provide students with the common intellectual experience of broadening their understanding of ideas and values drawn from different strands of our own culture, and to increase their understanding of cultural diversity and the process of cultural interaction," the CIV draft said.

To that end, students will study works from at least one non-European culture each quarter.

The program will give attention to race, gender, and class, and it will recruit Stanford minority faculty and faculty with knowledge of non-European cultures to teach.

Students will also study ancient and medieval cultures.

CIV faculty will decide each year on the program's most common elements —texts, authors, themes, or issues.

Members of the Black Student Union were concerned that the Western culture track was racist when it began, King said.

"We've invested two student generations in debates," King told the Senate before discussion began Thursday. "It's not one person's idea of what we'd like to see changed. It's a vision that keeps being reincarnated."

In April 1986, BSU members charged that the Western culture offerings focused on white, upper-class, European males.

They took the matter to the committee on Undergraduate Education, which voted unanimously to change the requirement.

A faculty-student task force was created to study the program and suggest changes.

Professors haggled over the definition of "democracy" and "Western," how many tracks should be offered and whether a core reading list was necessary.

In January, the debate drew comment from U.S. Secretary of Education William Bennett.

He said in a *New York Times* article that if the proposal were passed, it would be an act of "academic intimidation."

The 2½-hour session Thursday threatened to bog down several times as professors argued different points.

Students Wednesday staged a sit-in at the provost's office to express their anger over what they called the "betrayal" of the steering committee.

They claimed the committee had bypassed the legislative process in creating the second version and releasing it to Senate members and a campus publication.

On Thursday, the students were prepared to protest if the Senate voted on the second draft or significantly amended the first one.

"We would have walked in. We would have interrupted," King said. "Students would have resigned" from the committees.

Officers from the Stanford Department of Public Safety were on hand to monitor the response of 15 students attending the session and the crowd of 200 that waited outside.

But the Senate overwhelmingly favored the first draft.

* * *

THE STANFORD DAILY
Friday, April 1, 1988

Cheering "vote now, we want change" over 200 students rallied outside the law school before yesterday's Faculty Senate meeting (3/3/88) and maintained an attentive vigil throughout the proceedings, with plans to disrupt the meeting in case the Area One requirement vote was blocked or the proposal changed. . . .

Before the meeting convened, however, the mood was tense. Four speakers urgently called for continued student activism and emphasized the importance of the imminent decision concerning Western culture.

"We need to empower ourselves. This university is too rigid and too set in its ways, and we students need to change it," said the Chair of the Black Student Union, Bill King.

In case the Senate stalled or threatened not to pass the proposal, King introduced a "contingency plan" in which the few students inside the meeting would alert students to the changes. At five or six points during the meeting, when amendments were proposed, students inside the hall signalled to those outside to prepare to interrupt the proceedings, King said.

"If a vote had not occurred today, it would have been all over," according to King, explaining that such an event would have caused relations between the University and minority groups to degenerate into a "nasty, hard, bitter struggle" . . .

* * *

The course in Western culture will no longer exists at Stanford University as of the fall of 1989. It will be replaced by a course in Cultures, Ideas and Values in which only six of the required great classics of the original fifteen will be retained and which will be oriented to the study of race, sex, and class.

Certain issues of transcendent importance for American higher education have emerged from the current controversy at Stanford University over the required course in Western Culture. These are not essentially related to whether the title of the course should be changed to Cultures, Ideas, and Values; or to whether a core curriculum of great books should be mandatory for all students; or whether there should be one required course or a required distribution of courses from various disciplines. These are, to be sure, important educational questions but in accordance with American traditional practices, they can be left to the faculties of different universities to resolve them. Each institution in addition to its commitment to imparting a liberal education to its students has its own history, traditions, and specific goals that will be reflected in the outcome of faculty discussion.

What is noteworthy about what happened at Stanford is that, despite allegations to the contrary, the course in Western culture or civilization has not been merely repackaged or revised. It has been radically converted into a politically diluted course in sociology. The concepts of race, sex, class are perfectly legitimate notions and like a cluster of other concepts like state, nation, and kinship, have a place in the college education for modern men and women. The relevant question here is: Why has the new curriculum focused on them, and why was it necessary to repudiate the course in Western culture and civilization to do so?

The answer to that question is suggested by the nature of the criticisms that originally spurred the revision of the course in Western culture—a course which year after year had been judged by an overwhelming number of students who had completed it to be highly satisfactory. These criticisms centered on the charge that the course was "racist, sexist and imperialistic." They were made by small militant minority of students and echoed by a few junior members of the faculty. No specific illustration of the way the course was taught in any of its sections was ever cited by anyone in substantiation of the charge. The use of the epithets implied that race, sex, and class were being taught in an invidious and intellectually unacceptable manner. The only evidence offered was the list of books studied and inferentially, of books not studied.

Much was made of the fact that none of the authors of the core list of works was a woman or a person of color, and that there were no great works from foreign cultures. The Bible was not considered a work of non-Western culture, nor was Augustine, the Bishop of Hippo, regarded as a man of color.

When the proposal to revise the course to correct these deficiencies reached the Senate floor, however, there was hardly any mention of the original charges that had inspired the movement for revision. The impact of the Reverend Jesse Jackson's famous march at the head of several hundred chanting students demanding the abolition of the Western culture course threatened to be more damaging than helpful to the cause. The rhetorical abuse in the student newspaper by members and officers of the Black Student Union directed against a handful of faculty who had raised some critical questions about the proposal to substitute the revised course, had embarrassed some of its architects. They indignantly denied that the repeated charges of racism, sexism, and imperialism against the existing course in Western culture that had been heard at mass meetings and had filled columns of the press, had anything to do with the grounds for urging reform. Occasionally, however, these charges surfaced, as in the remarks of a professor, not in the humanities, who said: "I have no doubt but that the Western Culture requirement embodied chauvinistic, racist, and sexist values. The recommendation for change is, and is perceived to be, for a recognition of a need to teach a cultural history, to represent cultural values, the contributions of ethnic and racial groups which were given less than their due."[1] Again, no evidence was cited of specific contributions of women, ethnic, and racial groups to the dominant traditions of Western culture that in context had not been correctly acknowledged. The speaker seemed blissfully unaware that there was a plethora of courses in the social sciences and history in which these and related subjects were studied, and that the aim of the course in Western culture had never been to evaluate the contributions of the different ethnic and social groups to Western culture but to study their nature.

Despite denials to the contrary, the truth is that the initiating force and major continued pressure for abolition or revision came from those militant elements in the Stanford community who openly criticized the course as "racist, sexist, and imperialistic." Some members of the faculty, aware both of the falsity and irrelevance of the charge but eager to placate the militant students by gratifying some of their curricular demands, pleaded in extenuation of the students' discontent the avowals of these students that the existing course in Western culture had failed to cure them of their sense of alienation from Western culture.

Now for one thing, the aim of the course was never to cure students of their sense of alienation—whatever that may be—from Western culture but to enable them to understand the conflicting ideals and traditions of Western culture. These ideals and traditions had contributed to creating the world in which students were presently living. They had been formulated and expressed to some extent by authors who had themselves been alienated by the times and culture in which they had lived and whose works were being studied in the course.

There is something disingenuous about the notion that the dissatisfaction with the course in Western culture resulted from the special sense of alienation of a comparative handful of students. What about the overwhelming number who apparently were not alienated by the course but were quite happy with it? Further, one of the requirements of graduation at Stanford for all students is that they take a course in a non-Western culture. Why then was it necessary to introduce it into the course in Western culture? Also, there are additional elective courses in Black Studies, Chicano Studies, and Women's Studies, open to all students. If alienation can be cured by taking a course or a set of courses, the remedy is easily available. If it cannot be cured by taking courses, what is the point of the proposed revisions that would abolish or add to the core list of great works?

The assertion that the study of the great works that have influenced our present-day traditions generate a sense of alienation among students is really extraordinary. Normally, exposure to and active participation in such study overcomes preexisting feelings of alienation. The confession of a former Columbia College student, now the editor of a distinguished journal of opinion, on this point is highly relevant:

> Nor, speaking as a Jew, do I find it easy to believe these students when they claim that because of race or sex they feel left out or ignored by the great classic texts of the West. These texts, after all, are largely Christian and by no means friendly for the most part to Jews or Judaism. Yet when I encountered them as an undergraduate, I felt that an inheritance of indescribable richness which in the past had often been inaccessible to my own people was now mine for the taking. Far from being excluded, I was being invited in—and so are the Stanford students today.

Perhaps something else is intended. Perhaps it is believed that the alleged alienation results from the way the great books are being taught, from a feeling that their study does not sufficiently develop the proper political consciousness required to purify existing society from the evils of class, racial, and sexual oppression? If this is so, then it becomes apparent that for those who believe this, the reform of the Western culture program is a move to politicalize the curriculum.

The attitudes and assumptions implicit in some of the bizarre criticisms of the existing course, if widely shared, would constitute a profound threat to American higher education. One criticism protested that the content of the works studied and the standards of their evaluation were the products of individuals restricted to "elite members of Western society." But under the social conditions of the past—conditions that were criticized by some of the works studied in the course—and at a time when literacy was often a monopoly of the elite, who else but the elite could be the creators of culture? Western culture has winnowed out the elite contributions of the elite in the light of the continuing power of the great works of the past to illumine, stimulate and challenge the minds of those, elite or nonelite, willing to be engaged by them.

We are also reminded by some critics that elite ideas are not "the totality of meaningful ideas in a society." Of course, the elite ideas are not the totality of meaningful ideas. If they were, they wouldn't be elite. Yet this tautology is put forward as an objection to the course in Western culture. There is a wide variety of courses in sociology, politics, anthropology, economic history, etc., in which other aspects of a culture can and should be studied. It is doubtful that any course can do justice to "the totality of meaningful ideas," if that phrase is itself meaningful. Nor is it true that the course on Western culture is in any way an apologetic for Western imperialism or American chauvinism (there is not a single American book on the Stanford list—does that make the course un-American?) or even for political democracy. Personally I believe it can be established that political democracy in the modern world owes more to the dissenting churches and trade unions than to most of the classical tradition. The justification for the study of great works of Western culture is not political although it may contribute to our political sophistication. It gives no warrant to the oft repeated charge that the program devoted to a critical study of these works "propounds white male values and slights the contributions of women and minority groups to the development of the Western tradition."

The menace to the integrity of the educational process becomes more manifest in the primitive and mistaken view about how human beings learn. This is reflected in the demand by some critics of the existing program that faculty be recruited from "women and people of color" to study ideas and aspects of culture that involve them. Sad to say, even the group which originally opposed the emasculation of the program in Western culture, in an effort to save it, compromised its principles and urged that books by "women and people of color" be added to the core list of readings.

Where ideas are concerned, the primary consideration should be mastery of subject matter and not identification with the subject studied. One does not have to be a German to study Luther or the German Reformation, or be sympathetic to the Nazis to study Hitler. As well argue that men cannot be gynecologists, that only women are best qualified to study family law or that only fat physicians can study obesity or hungry people the phenomenon of starvation as that only people of color and women are uniquely qualified to do justice to the place, achievement, and oppression of minorities and their culture, wherever relevant, in Western culture. One of the greatest contributions to the exposure and struggle against racism in the United States was made by Gunnar Myrdal, a Swedish white man, in his famous book *The American Dilemma.* Race, color, religion, national origin, and sexual orientation are neither necessary nor sufficient conditions for the fruitful study of the humanities or any subject matter. In scholarship as in sports today—alas! It was not always so!—the quest should always be for the best qualified, assuming they know how to teach, as much for the sake of the students as for the international integrity of the subject taught.

Some of the criticisms are so transparently without merit that one wonders what is really behind them. For example, it is implied that once a core list is established, it is set in stone, unmodifiable in the light of educational experience, or by the emergence of new interests, and the continuing program of scholarship. Actually there has been some variation in the Stanford core list. But if one looks at the Columbia program in the Humanities established in 1937, which is the mother of most required courses in Western culture, one finds that 130 different works have appeared on its core list. It has even been suggested that a core list inhibits academic freedom despite the fact that no one is coerced into teaching the course! As well argue that insistence on the rules of grammar is a threatening imposition of conformity in academic life. Tied to these absurd criticisms is the charge that the existence of a core list is the basis "for a structure of exclusion that makes second-class citizens of faculty" whose primary interest is found in non-European literature and culture. Precisely the opposite is true! Those capable of teaching the core list could easily relate their expertise in non-European culture, wherever relevant, to the issues, problems and values that arise in the analysis of the great works.

One blushes to have to remind those who have endorsed the new course that the criteria of selection of the works studied should be their intrinsic aesthetic, literary or philosophical merit, and not whether the books are written by a person of color or a woman. If it is decided to study W. E. B. Du Bois' *The Souls of Black Folk* rather than Booker T. Washington's *Up from Slavery,* it is because the first is an intellectually and culturally more significant work than the second, and not because Du Bois is more of a black man than Washington. Similarly, if it is decided to include a work by Jane Austen rather than one by George Eliot, Edith Wharton, or Rebecca West, it is purely because of its literary quality, not because Jane Austen was more of a woman than the others.

There is even a more sinister implication in the decision of the Stanford Senate. One of the measures setting up the new course provides that the program be supervised by a special committee of nine faculty members, a lecturer or instructor (normally without tenure), three student members nominated by the official student body, the Dean of Undergraduate Studies, and the Deans of Humanities and Sciences, and Engineering *ex officio*. It then goes on to say: "To achieve the goals and objectives of the program, the membership of the committee shall be constituted taking into account such factors as gender, ethnicity, academic discipline, and field of expertise."[2]

This is truly unprecedented, and on its face horrendous. In my long life in the academy, I know of no university body that has established criteria of race and sex in the selection of personnel in setting up a committee to administer a purely academic intellectual function, where only academic discipline and field of expertise are relevant. Where have we heard of this before aside from South Africa and Nazi Germany? Possibly in the segregated areas of the South before *Brown* v. *Topeka Board of Education.*

Let us hope that this provision will not be implemented. That it was included in the motion adopted testifies to the hurried character of the proceedings of the Senate. It cannot possibly reflect the considered judgment of the fifty-five Senators or the thousands of faculty members at Stanford whom they presumably represent.

NOTES

1. *Campus Report* (March 9, 1988):28.
2. *Campus Report* (April 6, 1988):6.

15

The Academic-Brawley Cases

Historians of the academic scene in the United States will be struck by a curious phenomenon that has developed on the campuses of some prestigious universities in recent years. Some institutions which to an objective observer have been exemplary illustrations of freedom from racial bias, comparatively speaking, have suddenly through their administrations or other official spokesmen publicly denounced themselves as guilty of "institutional racism." They have issued calls for general self-examination and repentance, organized conferences and demonstrations to confront the evil of racism, prescribed days of reorientation to purge entering students of alleged stereotypical responses to racial, religious, and national differences, and have engaged in an orgy of self-flagellation about lapses from proper behavior whose intensity seem inversely related to the absence of overt expressions of racism.

In the early colonial period when liberal arts colleges were primarily church-related institutions for the education of clergymen, on some campuses the academic year began with intense soul-searching and concern for purification from sin and sinful thought. And probably in those days when belief in the natural depravity of man was quite widespread, before the enlightenment of coeducational practices became common, there was probably some justification for initiating the academic year with spiritual exercises to strengthen the defenses against the temptations of sin. But it would be a sign of paranoia to assume that today, despite the tremendous gains the United States has made in human rights, American students are as inevitably steeped in racist prejudice as their forebears were in sinful depravity.

The bewildered observer who is impressed by the evidence of the institution's *special* concern for the social, educational, and sometimes financial needs of minority students, asks: "How, where, and when is this racist sentiment

---

From *Measure* 74 (September 1988): 1–4. Reprinted by permission of University Centers for Rational Alternatives.

or behavior expressed?" Not seldom he is told that the racism is unconscious, and is conveyed by tone, look, voice, and gesture that only the sensitively affected can properly interpret. Sometimes I have heard it said that the very denial that racism exists in the university of a society that is racist, is itself an expression of racism. It would seem that no matter how liberal a white person is or is reputed to be, only a confession of his or her racism makes them eligible to engage in a discussion of racism.

Rational discourse under such circumstances becomes difficult.

In these discussions, the very term "racism" is used with mischievous ambiguity. It involves more than the recognition of the existence of races or national differences. In the sense in which racism is unacceptable in a liberal society or university community, it is the belief and practices based on the belief that some races or national groups are intrinsically morally inferior to others and therefore not entitled to the enjoyment of the rights of other citizens in the community.

In every case where administrators have confessed that their institutions have been guilty of institutional racism, they have done so *after* the charge has been made by a group of militant minority students. Sometimes these students have taken unlawful possession of administrative offices and made a series of "demands," never "requests," with respect to their living conditions, or to recruitment of more minority students and faculty members, and adoption of programs to combat racism. Sometimes it seems that administrators have come forward to acknowledge institutional sin to forestall the seizure of buildings or the disruption of the academic process. In no case that I am aware of have students been disciplined for violating the university's own guidelines of legitimate dissent. They have always been granted amnesty.

I shall briefly discuss only two institutions—Stanford University and the University of Vermont—with which I have some special relationship. About Stanford one would have to write a book to do justice to the situation. I restrict myself to one incident. On May 10, 1986 under big bold headlines, there appeared a story in the local Palo Alto newspaper in which a visiting law professor alleged that he had become a victim of racism at the Stanford Law School. The allegations were made by a black visiting assistant professor of law who was giving a course in constitutional law. A committee of his students who represented themselves as expressing the class sentiment had complained to the dean that all they were being treated to was a discussion of a small set of cases involving racial discrimination, to which they had no objection, but that other important aspects of constitutional law together with the relevant cases were being ignored. They felt they were not getting an adequate education in one of the basic courses of the curriculum. The dean should have taken the matter up with the visiting professor himself but, probably fearful of offending his sensibilities approved instead a proposal to organize a series of supplementary lectures on various aspects of constitutional law. These were to be given by several distinguished professors of constitutional law from Stanford's own faculty and neighboring institutions. In order to stress the supplemental educational nature of the courses, the visiting assistant professor was invited to deliver one of the lectures, and he gladly accepted. Here was a praiseworthy example of educational initiative on the part of the students that certainly deserved encouragement.

On the eve of the first lecture in the series a flyer was circulated by some militant members of the Black Student Caucus charging that the whole enterprise was racist. Whereupon with the courage of rabbits all the lecturers panicked and fled the scene. The visiting professor went into high dudgeon and now proclaimed himself a victim of racism. "We find it difficult to imagine" he complained, "that this could happen to a white professor." It is obvious, however, it could happen to any professor. I can think of a half dozen incidents in which students usually in the sciences have complained about the pedagogic inadequacies of their teachers. Unfortunately they do not complain enough. All we have here is the reaction of a hypersensitive teacher to students who, rightly or wrongly, believe his instruction, as good as it may appear to him, inadequate to their educational needs.

One simple way of determining what the motivation of the students really was would have been to question the students themselves. Why were they not quoted? Would not any professionally fair reporter seek them out and give them a chance to state their case against this ugly charge of racism? As written, the story condemns them and the Stanford Law School unheard, and was angled to reinforce the unproven charge of racism. It was clearly the story of an advocate journalist.

I waited in expectation for a spirited response by members of the Stanford Law School against the defamatory charges of racism. Those whom I spoke to, indignantly denied its truth. In response to my puzzled query about their silence, I gathered that they felt that a reply would needlessly prolong a controversy that would disappear of itself with the visiting assistant professor's departure at the end of the semester.

They could not have been more mistaken. Assistant Professor Derek Bell made a "federal case" of it, so to speak. He lectured whenever he could about this act of racism against him, and even wrote about it. Last spring, a new dean of the Stanford Law School took it upon himself without authorization of his faculty to offer Professor Bell a public apology for the racist behavior presumably of the Stanford Law students, faculty, and previous dean. This was done with pomp, ceremony, and maximum publicity. It was accompanied by a pledge to enroll more minority students and to move more energetically and expeditiously to recruit minority faculty. Professor Bell was gracious enough to accept the apology.

News travels fast. Emboldened by victories at Stanford and other institutions, Black Student Unions on other campuses moved into action. The University of Vermont was one of them. In the spring of 1988 students seized control of the executive offices and made the traditional demands for measures to counteract the alleged rampant racism at the university. Anyone familiar with the history and practices at the University of Vermont cannot help being surprised. Its most distinguished graduate is John Dewey whose philosophy, among others, has always had some influence on the institution. Its faculty contains scholars of the highest intellectual calibre and international standing. The president of the university capitulated to most minority student demands, protesting at the same time that he would have been willing to grant them without any sit-in. It was commonly admitted that there was no evidence of overt discrimination, but in the eyes of the protesting students and compliant administration the institutional and unconscious racism was clearly manifest in the relative scarcity of black students, faculty, and studies. To counteract this a Center for Cultural Pluralism was established, but despite this the complaint was that the university really "is not a center of cultural pluralism," a concept that like diversity has escaped clear definition or description.

The gravemen of the charge of racism against the University of Vermont is really the relative scarcity of black students and faculty for which the university is being blamed and is blaming itself. Black admissions tripled between 1983 and 1987, but in 1988 there were only half the number of blacks on campus that were enrolled in 1981. Black students dropped out and the university didn't do enough to retain them—it is claimed. But there is no evidence that different standards of scholarship were applied in their cases, or that even if more financial aid were offered black students, more would come and more would remain. There is intense competition for minority students among all universities and even fiercer competition for black faculty. The extent to which this competition goes may be gauged from the fact that Dean McCrory is quoted as saying "we may have to pay extra for black professors because they, too, bring something special to the campus." This unprecedented acknowledgment that the specialty that qualifies black professors for extra compensation is their blackness is really an insult to the qualified blacks who have made it on their own. When black students complain that sometimes white students and some members of other minorities like Asian-Americans automatically assume that their presence indicates that they are not there by their own merit, what really is to blame is the affirmative action programs based on fixed goals and timetables (in effect quotas), which is a perversion of the original principles of affirmative action. President Coor is pledged to hire four new black professors to the faculty this academic year. Why only four? And what if he cannot find four qualified professors? Will he resign?

Surely the University of Vermont cannot be faulted for the failure of the elementary and secondary schools to prepare more black students for college and university careers. Nonetheless this seems in part to be the motivation behind a veritable orgy of denunciations of actual and incipient racism at the University of Vermont in the orientation sessions of entering freshmen. The story of the mobilization of the Vermont campus against racism in *The New York Times* of August 31, 1988, reflects the bewilderment of some of the students and their indignation, too, at being treated as suspects already infected with the disease of racism. It probably is true that in the eyes of the administrators who organized the program, the white students, despite themselves, suffer from racial prejudices imbibed from their previous experience in the same way as students of the colonial period suffered from their burden of sin. The only difference is that the first was acquired, and the second was an expression of natural depravity.

Actually, the University of Vermont is among the universities known for episodes which resisted racism when it was widely current. During the twenties, one of its sororities enrolled a black co-ed. The national organization threatened to expel the Vermont chapter for violating its unwritten rule. The Vermont chapter held its ground to the plaudits of the entire university, and was expelled. There are other illustrations of its enlightened spirit.

Of course universities and their students cannot completely at one step and by mere resolution emancipate themselves from patterns of prejudice against blacks, Jews, foreigners, and dissenters that prevade all societies. Given the presence of young males bubbling over with energy, often under the influence of alcohol, there are occasions of conflict that sometimes take ill-mannered and ugly form. Where there are racial differences, these are sometimes seized upon to exacerbate differences. Such disagreements can be found among student bodies that are all black or all white. Only a cretin can deny that if one searches carefully one will unearth examples of sexist, racial, and religious prejudice. But this is no warrant for the charge of institutional racism that we hear from one end of the country to another, or what is more incomprehensible, confessions of institutional racism from administrators of institutions like Stanford which are demonstrably free of it.

If there is one thing that can be established, it is this. Although here and there an isolated incident of racism in the behavior of students, and even of teachers, may be found, it is precisely the institutions of higher education that are free of it, judging by their procedures of admission, financial support, and special provisions of housing for minority students. Administrators who eagerly confess to institutional racism do so in the hope that they will be spared sit-ins by militant members of minorities. They are suffering from illusion and have yet to learn the unhappy lesson of President Perkins at Cornell.

* * *

Editor's Note—A year ago a young black woman, Tawana Brawley, claimed to have been assaulted and brutalized by a group of white men including a police officer. When the authorities sought to investigate at the advice of her mother and advisors she refused to testify before a grand jury or present any evidence. Her advisor, the Reverend Al Sharpton, denounced New York State officials and helped her to relocate to another state beyond the jurisdiction of the State of New York. It has been reported in *The New York Times* that the Grand Jury has concluded that the whole incident has been concocted by Tawana Brawley and her advisors. To date no public evidence has been submitted in the case.

16

"Diversity"
A New Code Word?

From one end of the country to another, the quest or cult for "diversity" has become the new watchword for criticisms of courses in Western culture. Sometimes the term is used loosely as a synonym for "cultural pluralism." When affirmative action programs fail to produce expected numbers of minority students, college communities are taken to task for failure to appreciate the virtues of "diversity" and "cultural pluralism." These terms and phrases are used without adequate definition, and to club recalcitrant members of the faculty who ask questions about the educational relevance of "diversity" or who contend that the limits of diversity must be set by certain standards. None too subtly it is suggested that such queries smack of racism which is not so much an epithet of description but of abuse. Saul Bellow, Nobel Prize novelist, was charged by William Chace, Vice Provost for Academic Planning and Development at Stanford, with racism for criticizing the reverse discrimination practices of affirmative action. Chace is now President of Wesleyan University. He himself had been branded as a racist by some minority students at Stanford for originally opposing the proposal to emasculate the course in Western culture.

Those who espouse "diversity" as a goal assume that, and sometimes say, "the more diversity the better." But this makes no sense at all in most contexts. Taken literally it would mean no limits on who studies, what they study, and how they study. Students are individuals and should be treated as individuals, especially with respect to their capacity to study and their educational achievements and not as representatives of groups or classes. Some who cry up the educational desirability of more diversity insist that it is not

---

From *Measure* 74 (September 1988): 5–6. Reprinted by permission of University Centers for Rational Alternatives.

enough to enroll black minority students in our institutions, we must also make sure to enroll poor black minority students as well as middle-class blacks, inner-city blacks, rural and out-of-state blacks. Presumably, we must also make sure to diversify Chicano and Asian students, and see to it that our Jewish students are Orthodox, Conservative, Reformist, and free thinking in their religious belief rather than an undifferentiated group. Think of the kinds of diversity one can find if one seeks it among white students—elite and dull; those addicted to alcohol and other drugs, and those who are teetotalers; those who are athletic and those who are not; the bearded, the bald, the red-haired, etc. Unless one makes out a case or an educational need for a specific kind of diversity, the call for diversity in the blue is self-defeating and incoherent. Shall we enroll students who do not believe in diversity, too? One gets the impression that those who invoke the virtues of "diversity" feel that the positive emotive connotation of the word can be exploited to justify any program whose outline is not clear in their own minds. Mephistopheles' wry comment comes to mind:

> "Denn eben wo Begriffe fehlen,
> da stellt ein wort zur rechten Zeit sich ein."
>
> ("Precisely when a meaning does forsake you,
> a neat, pat word comes in quite readily.")

Robert Gordon, an anthropologist at the University of Vermont, protests that "Diversity is also a matter of class and age." So it is—does this mean that every age cohort, every class, and subclass must be represented in the student body and faculty? Apparently it does. He goes on to say "We can't simply educate a global elite. For true diversity we also should be enrolling, for example, peasants from the Third World and poor minority students." What makes this diversity "true"? Wouldn't it be a truer diversity to also invite the artisans from these Third World countries, the lower middle classes, and the government officials as well as the peasants?

Of course, one cannot simply educate a global elite but does it follow from this that institutions for elite students anywhere are impermissible? Why must all students from everywhere be represented at the same institution? And how are standards of educational acceptability for students from the strata of various countries and various cultures to be determined and applied?

The criterion of diversity or pluralism is being advanced not only to spur the quest for a more heterogeneous student body and faculty but to build a curriculum. But it is altogether worthless as a guide to a desirable curriculum for intelligent men and women anywhere. Even the most utopian of educators must realize that in the limited time period of a college or university or a life's education not everything can be studied. Some knowledge and skills may reasonably be required of all students; and some knowledge and skills of a specialized kind may be left to the individual students assessing their career prospects in the time and place they find themselves. But here is Professor Peter Saybolt, a champion of diversity and pluralism, berating the University of Vermont because only recently it reinstated courses in Chinese, "a language spoken by more people than any other language except English. That we don't teach Japanese is a disgrace." But what is relevant to the educational justification for offering language instruction is not the number of people speaking it, but the need of the individual student or its bearing on some problems of present-day culture or politics. More people speak Hindi than Japanese. Should the university therefore offer courses in Hindi? Comparatively few poeple speak Hebrew or Pharsi but what bearing does that have on the wisdom of a student's request to study the language or the investment by the university of its limited funds to lure scholars capable of teaching the language and culture of these nations properly? Should all languages be offered so that every campus functions like a Berlitz school? And what if the languages are offered but students don't enroll in them?

The absurdity of these questions reflects the absurdity of the whole drive for diversity *per se.* Yet administrators can be found who solemnly repeat these vacuous statements accompanied by sly insinuations that those who take umbrage at this nonsense are covering up their racism. What is worse, additional and costly personnel are being hired to fill administrative posts created to carry out programs of diversity.

The pursuit of diversity without the control of certain standards of maturity, prior achievement, and readiness can only bedevil the problems of teaching on the undergraduate level. These already constitute a scandal on many campuses where it is assumed that anyone who knows a subject is competent to teach it effectively. This is notoriously not the case especially in some disciplines. Teaching is an art that can even improve natural talent when present, which is not always true. Unfortunately, too many academics have a patronizing, if not contemptuous attitude toward the art of pedagogy. They assume they are under no obligation to communicate effectively, and that the responsibility for getting the point and mastering difficulties lies primarily with the students. This is or should be true on the graduate level where teachers and students are in effect colleagues in research, but not where undergraduates are involved.

In the nature of the case, no college can legitimately segregate individuals from any particular culture, class, or group into separate sections. This would defeat one of the presumed purposes of the pursuit of diversity. In consequence, teaching sections are likely to reflect a greater heterogeneity of capacity, knowledge, and interest than is usual today. It would require master teachers to cope with the problem and to avoid presenting material and challenges at the least common denominator of student comprehension. The bright students will be bored and the other students will sleep with glazed open eyes. Everyone's experience will resemble that of teachers in adult education classes, which are open to enrollment by anyone who can pay for the course. I once found myself in an adult education course in contemporary philosophy trying to expound Whitehead's criticism of the cosmology of Einstein to students who were ignorant of Newton. Only deconstructionists could do that! The example may be extreme but I imagine certain standards of literacy must be assumed to teach Shakespeare in a way that makes it a significant educational experience.

There is another element in the picture that I find mystifying and somewhat disquieting. On the campus of every university in which this cult of diversity is gathering force there are scholars of international standing whose analytical power could easily make mincemeat of the rhetorical piffle of the faculty and administrative spokesmen of the new dispensation. But their voices have not been heard.

17

The Mischief Makers

From all quarters of the academic campus we have been witnessing a display of synthetic indignation about manifestation of racism, sexism, and discrimination in all its varieties. I use the term "synthetic" because examination will show that it is fueled by pronouncements of "crisis" in student relations by administrators who seize upon some crude or rude remarks by some foolish students to declare a state of university emergency. It is hoped that in the days of general breast beating that follow, all students will be infected with a sense of guilt about the prejudices they have acquired from their parents, previous experiences, and associates. The more vehemently students protest that they are free of racism and sexism—ill-defined words that are used as epithets of abuse—the likelier it is that this will be taken as testimony of their prejudice—all the stronger for being unconscious.

What makes this phenomenon all the more puzzling is the remarkable progress that has been made in removing the institutional obstacles to academic careers for qualified minorities and women. Whether it is measured by the number of confirmed incidents of racial or sexual discrimination, the quality and nature of public discourse on campuses about race and sex, the access to new opportunities of academic advancement, it is no exaggeration to say that at no time in the past have American universities as a whole been freer of racial and sexual discrimination.

The very fact that when racial and sexual slurs, graffiti, and flyers are found, they are almost always anonymous, is an indication that they have no root in the academic community. Almost always outside groups seem to be involved and, ever since the Brawley case, doubts have emerged whether all the incidences are genuine.

Here we wish to call attention to the possibility of mischief making cre-

From *Measure* 76 (November/December 1988): 5–6. Reprinted by permission of University Centers for Rational Alternatives.

dited by an official document issued by the University of Michigan. What we report will hardly seem credible particularly since the document explicitly states that "The University recognizes and respects the fundamental right of free speech."

The document is entitled "What Students Should Know About Discrimination and Discriminatory Harassment by Students in the University Environment." It bravely declares that the university prohibits discrimination and discriminatory harassment and sternly warns that anyone guilty of such action will be subject to disciplinary action of sanctions ranging from formal reprimand to expulsion. Unfortunately, with all the profound intellectual resources of the university at its disposal, the document offers no analysis of the meaning of the term so that one can distinguish when it is not insidious—after all, how could a university function without intellectual discrimination—and when it is unacceptable on moral even if not legal grounds. Instead, it describes certain situations in which the discrimination is beyond the pale: for example, if a person is "victimized" on the basis of race or experiences "an unequal effect based on gender." We are not told whether this means when a person *feels* victimized or is objectively victimized; whether a person *feels* he or she has been unequally affected or is actually differently treated in an observable way.

With language as loose as this one could make a case to haul up half the student body and faculty before the discipline committee. Aware of this and of the necessity of being concrete, the document gives specific examples of what is discriminatory harassment and when a student is a harasser. Among the examples are the following:

1. A male student makes remarks in class like, "Women just aren't as good in this field as men. . . ."
2. Two men demand that their roommate in the residence hall move out and be tested for AIDS.
3. You tell jokes about gay men and lesbians.
4. A Black student is confronted and racially insulted by two white students in a cafeteria.

1. What if a student says: "Women just aren't as good in this field as men," and it is true! Will he have to face a discipline committee? Notice how the document completes the sentence. " 'Women just aren't as good in this field as men,' *thus* creating a hostile learning atmosphere for female classmates." But why should it? There may be a good reason why they aren't as good as men in many fields because of social prejudice, opportunity, etc.

But the truth is the truth. Should students be penalized for stating it? Suppose in a music class in composition a student says: "Women as musical performers equal men but as composers they are not as good. Look at the record." Or in a drama class he says: "Women are equal or better than men in acting but not in playwriting. Look at the record."

2. Why is it wrong, if they fear being infected, for the two men to demand that the third be tested for AIDS? Perhaps they are all homosexuals? Why should they be disciplined for making a reasonable demand? It doesn't have to be granted.

3. Why is it wrong to tell jokes about gay men and lesbians and not wrong to joke about straight men and ordinary women. What about equality under the law?

4. A student who insults anybody of any race on *racial* grounds should be reprimanded. Why only Black students? Haven't Chinese and Jews feelings too? And why must the insult be by *two* white students and only in the cafeteria? Isn't it an act of discriminatory harassment if a student is insulted by another student on racial grounds anywhere on campus?

It is safe to venture the guess that this document was concocted by administrators hired to deal with problems of racism and allied disorders on campus. On almost every campus a bevy of administrators have been recently hired. They must keep busy to justify their presence and their cost to the budget.

The irony of the situation is that the University of Michigan insists it "recognizes and respects" freedom of speech. Anyone there whose sensibilities have been affected by any remark can plead harassment and psychological injury and add yet another prohibition. What we need now is a list of permitted and forbidden expressions posted on all classrooms and an Orwellian word police to enforce it. Lewis Carroll should come back to life to compose a new *Alice in Blunderland!*

Readers are advised to write to the University of Michigan to acquire a copy of this document. It will make a choice item in the museum of the intellectual absurdities of our time.

18

The Politics of Curriculum Building

We are in a new phase of educational change inspired by developments in minority and feminist militancy in the last few years. As American higher education has progressively abandoned institutional obstacles to universal access to higher education flowing from racial, sexual, and national differences, demands have increased that the nature of the educational experience itself reflect the very differences that liberal education has sought to transcend. The new movement has announced its opposition to the very concept of Western culture as inherently infected with racial, sexual, and imperialistic prejudices. At Stanford University under the leadership of the Black Student Union and a few sympathetic faculty members, its famous course in Western culture—the one required of all students—and heralded for a decade by the students themselves as a high point in their educational experience, has been abolished and a new course in Cultures, Ideas, and Values (CIV) has been substituted. In many other universities curricular changes have been proposed, some under the same slogans against racism, sexism, and imperialism, and others under the quest for vague, ill-defined pluralism or diversity.

The reaction in the larger community to the changes at Stanford and elsewhere was not long in coming. There was surprise, outrage, ridicule, and incomprehension in some scholarly quarters, and a spirited defense among the organized ethnic campus groups, especially the university administrators who have the burden of explaining the changes to bewildered alumni, parents, and the public.

Since the proposed new courses are not yet completely in place, it is still too early to determine what is being proposed in lieu of the courses in Western culture. Are the new courses, for example, providing the unified (not uniform) common educational experience that liberal arts colleges in the past

---

From *Measure* 77 (January 1989): 1–11. Reprinted by permission of University Centers for Rational Alternatives.

prided themselves on? Or, under the guise of increasing elements of cultural diversity and purifying Western culture courses of their alleged racism, sexism, and imperialism—charges never proved—are they actually fracturing the common liberal arts experience, which should be the legacy of all students? It is to be hoped that one positive outcome of the controversy will be to make all members of the faculty aware of their role and responsibility as educators rather than as specialists of a narrow discipline unrelated to the goals and meaning of a liberal education.

The first observation that comes to mind on the basis of the materials so far made available is the uncertainty in the minds of the architects of the new program at Stanford as to the actual nature of the contemplated curricular change. On the one hand, the claim has repeatedly been made that the change is fundamental or, as the headlined story of *The Chronicle of Higher Education*[1] put it, "sweeping" and "monumental." And indeed, the leaders of the Black and Chicano students, and a scattering of faculty, originally demanded a radical transformation of the course in Western culture and the abolition of the entire core list of readings that constituted the skeletal structure of the course. They didn't get their way on this point. Not all the fifteen basic texts were abolished: They were reduced to six. The spokesmen of the radical reformers regarded this as a partial victory, a compromise.

On the other hand, we hear voices in defense of the new course asserting that there is no need for alarm and disquiet. The fact that six core readings of the old Western culture course have been retained for study in all eight tracks or divisions of the basic course is cited as evidence of continuity by those who wish to downplay the magnitude of the change. They hope this will counter the impression that Western culture has been "trashed" at Stanford. They assert that the changes have been moderate and evolutionary, and reassure startled parents and alumni that all the critical comments by Bennett, Bloom, and others, are demagogic exaggerations. The administration has poured great quantities of this soothing oil on the troubled waters of public opinion.

But there has obviously been a lack of candor in both responses. For the truly sweeping and monumental change is the fact that the entire *orientation* of the old course in Western culture has been altered. The new course specifies, in accordance with the mandate which established it, that the curriculum of all the tracks beginning in the fall quarter of 1989 be oriented towards "race," "sex," and "class." *If* the new course carries out the sense of the motion as it was understood by its most enthusiastic adherents among the minority students and faculty, it will be among other things, a comprehensive, diluted course in social studies dedicated to the appreciation of the contributions and systematic oppressions of racial minorities, women, and working masses in history, past and present, in all cultures studied, especially Western culture.

If it were not for this reorientation towards race, sex, and class, the claim that the changes in the basic curriculum were "sweeping" or "monumental" would be transparently disingenuous. For in the natural course of events changes in the core curriculum of Western culture were made from time to time. Without changing the structure of the course in Western culture, great works by women and people of color could easily have been incorporated, not because of the sex and color of the authors but because of the inherent qualities of their works. Indeed, in many courses in Western culture on other campuses this is actually the case or about to be done.

I cite as an example of this the curriculum of Boston University's proposed Humanities Core Curriculum, "The Making of the Modern World," in which at key points the *Analects* of Confucius, the *Tao Te Ching* of Lao Tzu, the *Bhagavad Gita,* the Qour'an, and the place of women in Greek and Roman society are examined. Many other illustrations from the recent past in the curriculum of American colleges can be cited. It required no revolution in the curriculum of Stanford's Western culture course to incorporate any educationally reasonable proposal for readings from a different culture at points of intersection or diffusion between them.

For the current year (1988–1989) at Stanford, only one track out of eight, "Europe and the Americas," presages the changes that may be introduced in the fall of 1989. Although all the tracks will gradually be modified along the lines mandated by the change from the old Western culture program to the new CIV program only the "Europe and the Americas" track has been described as departing "fairly significantly from the prevailing pattern" of the past. It may or may not be a reliable indication of how the other tracks will evolve. Since it is the only one available, it may be instructive to look more closely at this particular track as a possible guide to what to adopt or to avoid in constructing curricula.

We list the required readings of the fall quarter of 1988 for the "Europe and the Americas" track in the order in which they were scheduled to be studied:

Augustine, *Confessions*
Son of Old Man Hat: A Navaho Autobiography (Recorded by Dyk)
Freud, *The Psychopathology of Everyday Life*
Marx, *The Communist Manifesto*
Weber, *The Protestant Ethic*
Melville, *Bartleby*
Selections from the Old Testament (Genesis) and New Testament (Revelations)
Hurston, *Their Eyes Were Watching God*
Paredes, *With His Parasol in His Hand*
Fanon, *The Wretched of the Earth*

Rulfe, *The Burning Plain and Other Stories*
Popul-Vuh, *Mayan Book of the Dawn of Life*
Burgos-Debray, *I . . . Rigoberto Manchu*
Cisneros, *The House on Mango Street*

Two odd things are striking about this list, both its unhistorical order and its content. Freud and Marx are read before the Bible. Fanon's tract and paean of praise for revolutionary violence may be intelligible in understanding some of the reactions to African colonialism in the twentieth century, but it certainly has no important historical bearing on the diffusion of cultures or the impact of Europe on early American civilizations. One of the great weaknesses of courses in general education is the neglect of chronology. Ideas have histories. And although they can and should be considered analytically their cultural impact cannot be grasped without attention to the historical context.

Even more dubious is to regard minor works that may rate a place on a collateral reading list as having the status of works by Augustine and Marx. The rationalization for this mishmash is that a thematic approach is being taken and that the course is a study of the development of selves—starting with Conventions of Selfhood, the Labor and the Social Self, followed by Making Other Cultural Selves, Forging Revolutionary Selves, and ending with a one-day study of Urban Selves Today. Suddenly the course has been transformed into one of social psychology! But the architects of the course are out of their depths. They begin with a study of Conventions of Selfhood. But there is no such thing. Every conventional self presupposes a definite culture and history. Aside from biological and psychophysical phenomena like the study of afterimages, there is no such things as *the* self invariant at all times and all cultures. Even our dreams reflect our cultures. Instead of using Freud's *Psychopathology of Everyday Life* in the first rubric of the course, his *Civilization and Its Discontents* would be far more relevant, as would selected pages from Augustine's *City of God* rather than his *Confessions.* This thematic approach cannot be taken seriously, if it is intended as such, for even a thematic approach in order to do justice to our own time is best approached historically. It is a most dubious anthropological excursion to assume that the symbolic meanings of subconscious life are culturally invariant.

The most conspicuous of the readings elevated to a classic worthy of detailed study in this track is obviously Fanon's *The Wretched of the Earth.* It has truly become a classic among Third World terrorist guerilla groups. It preaches revolutionary terror and force without limit against colonialists and all native elements supporting them, and against any independent native party that proposes peaceful solutions. It is not enough that colonial peoples achieve their independence, according to Fanon. That liberation, to be genuine, must and can only be achieved by violence. One must not shrink from the hecatombs of victims that result from violence because they indicate that "between oppressors and oppressed everything [sic] can be solved by force." Fanon believed this literally—even the economic problems at the basis of colonialism can be solved by the creative potential of force. The basket-case economies of countries never occupied by colonialists are of course a legacy of colonial terror on this hysterical view.

Some persons have been shocked by the appearance of Fanon's book on the required reading list because of its rhetorical incitement to blood lust. This reaction is misguided. True, it is a very bad book. But one of the limitations of Great Books courses is the absence of the study of some very bad books that have had momentous historical significance like Hitler's *Mein Kampf*. Pedagogically one of the best preparations for membership in a liberal society is some familiarity with the mixture of sophism, fable, distorted fact, and self-sacrificial mindless fanaticism that constitutes so much of the literature of the political, religious, and racial totalitarian doctrines. If time permits, error should be confronted and countered even in its most persuasive form.

What is scandalous is not the appearance of Fanon's jeremiad on this list but the absence of any replies to the cult of violence. Let the students read Fanon but also Gandhi, if not Gandhi then Martin Luther King or the most powerful of all voices in behalf of nonviolence, Leo Tolstoy. Not that these works are beyond legitimate criticism but they make an effective intellectual reply to Fanon. Even when the opposite of an error if absolutized is itself an error, both errors are not *equally* in error or equally mischievous in their end effects. I am assuming, of course, that as educators we are primarily interested in stimulating or clarifying the minds of our students and not stirring them to some sort of political action.

These general considerations apply to the study of imperialism, too, of whose many evils students should be well aware. But is, or was, imperialism an absolute evil at all times and in every respect? Did the culture and economy of an imperial power in addition to its cruelties ever make a positive contribution to the health, standard of living, and public order of the region it ruthlessly exploited? There are several schools of thought on this complex of questions. But one school of thought whose most notable representative is Lord Peter Bauer, is never discussed. The works of Bauer and his school are never listed in the bibliography of courses in Black Studies, Chicano Studies or in any of the tracks of the old course in Western culture or the new course in CIV in which reference to colonialism is made. Nor are the writings of other foremost scholars of imperialism like Hoover's Lewis Gann or Peter Duignan ever listed, although occasionally orally denounced. Members of this school are not apologists of imperialism: Some of them even believe that colonialism was sometimes a bad economic investment. But they argue that not all the present-day economic evils of decolonized states are due to colonialism, that some of the worst economic problems today are found in states that were never colonized.

Right or wrong, it is a view that merits discussion. For the view that colonialism had some progressive features was held among others by none other than Karl Marx who wrote some years after he published the *Communist Manifesto* that India owed its only social revolution in 1,500 years to British imperialism. I suspect that many at Stanford and elsewhere who regard themselves as Marxists will suspect the authenticity of my quotation (as did Jarawahal Nehru) although it follows strictly from Marx's own theory of history and economics. The passage I refer to reflects the stigmata of racism with which Marx himself unfortunately was personally afflicted, and Engels even more. But it does not affect the point he was making.

To be sure, Marx is unsparing in his criticism of the needless cruelties of the British subjection of India. But he is just as unsparing in his eloquent account of the still greater infamies to which the British put an end. He mentions the "small semi-barbarian, semi-civilized communities" that were destroyed by "the greatest, and to speak the truth, the only social revolution ever heard of in Asia," and then goes on:

> . . . [W]e must not forget that these idyllic village-communities, inoffensive though they may appear, had always been the solid foundation of Oriental despotism, that they restrained the human mind within the smallest possible compass, making it the unresisting tool of superstition, enslaving it beneath traditional rules, depriving it of all grandeur and historical energies. We must not forget the barbarian egotism which, concentrating on some miserable patch of land, had quietly witnessed the ruin of empires, the perpetration of unspeakable cruelties, the massacre of the population of large towns, with no other consideration bestowed upon them than on natural events, itself the helpless prey of any aggressor who deigned to notice it at all.
>
> We must not forget that this undignified, stagnatory, and vegetative life, that this passive sort of existence evoked on the other part, in contradistinction, wild, aimless, unbounded forces of destruction and rendered murder itself a religious rite in Hindustan. We must not forget that these little communities were contaminated by distinctions of caste and by slavery, that they subjugated man to external circumstances instead of elevating man to the sovereign of circumstances, that they transformed a self-developing social state into never changing natural destiny, and thus brought about a brutalizing worship of nature, exhibiting its degradation in the fact that man, the sovereign of nature, fell down on his knees in adoration of Kanuman the monkey, and Sabbala, the cow.
>
> England, it is true, in causing a social revolution in Hindustan, was actuated only by the vilest interests, and was stupid in its manner of enforcing them. But that is not the question. The question is, can mankind fulfill its destiny without

> a fundamental revolution in the social state of Asia? If not, whatever may have been the crimes of England, it was the unconscious tool of history in bringing about that revolution.[1]

As usual Marx overstates his case. There were other, more benign aspects of the cultures he described. Although right about the pervasive effects of the mode of economic production on a culture, he ignored the reciprocal influence of a number of other irreducible factors on the alleged economic base, although giving lip acknowledgment to their presence. The man who said that the workers had no fatherland disbelieved the evidence of his own country, and died before the intensifying nationalism (as well as the economic conflicts) of the early twentieth century led to what can be more fittingly called the Second Fall of Man, World War I, than any other historical event. Marx ignored all the psychological forces of pride, tradition, cultural autonomy that may lead people to resist modernization and Westernization. One may wonder if the fetish of national independence was worth the nine million lives lost in consequence of the departure of the British Raj, and cite the complaints of the Sikhs, Moslems, Singhalese, Tamil minority ethnic groups today, that they are less safe in their lives and prosperity since the British left. It would still not serve as a justification for imperial rule imposed on a people that does not want it. Pehaps the best answer to Marx's tribute to the progressive character of British rule was made by an Indian patriot and jurist addressing his British colleagues.

> Yes, you gave us law and justice, roads, public hygiene and hospitals, museums, parks and much else. But you took away what we now value much more, our sense of self-respect.

It is not necessary to pursue the question any further here to determine whether this value was always indigenous to Indian culture or whether it, too, had been imbibed from the Western tradition. If its roots were truly native to the local culture, why had it taken so long to come to flower under British rule? It is sufficient to develop a sense of historical sophistication among students so that they realize that the moral imperatives of our own times cannot be automatically applied outside the specific historical context that limits the viable political and cultural possibilities of the past. One may recite the much misunderstood phrase of Marx about changing the present world instead of interpreting it. But Marx would have scorned the idea that the past could ever be changed by present-day moral edicts or interpretation. Not even God can change the past!

Almost all of the old courses in Western culture or civilization or the new courses proposed to replace them list Marx and Engel's *The Communist*

Manifesto as a core text. And this is as it should be. Without an understanding of the theory and practice of Marxism and the history of movements allegedly based on it, the modern age and culture would be no more intelligible than the middle ages without a knowledge of Christianity. Presumably when the student sections are oriented to the study of "class" in the analysis of ideas, values, and traditions, *The Communist Manifesto* and other writings will throw some light on it. But as valuable as his insights are, Marx's theory of class is the weakest aspect of his sociological analysis. Only his theory of economic value is weaker. To evaluate Marx and his claims properly—and scientifically as he hoped they would be—would require at least some familiarity with the writings of his critics (classical, Keynesian, Hayekian). Students are and should be required to read Marx. But should not a supplementary reading list contain suggestions of some works critical of Marx? I do not know what is the case with other tracks of the new Stanford CIV course but there is not a single work critical of Marx listed in the "Europe and the Americas" track.

After all, history itself has been guilty of *lèse-Marxism!* Capitalism for all its recurrent crises has not collapsed. Its working class has not been pauperized. Marx never anticipated the rise of totalitarianism either in its Fascist or Stalinist form. The first attempt at a Socialist revolution came not where he expected it but where his own theory of historical materialism asserted it was impossible. He himself had declared in *Die Deutsche Ideologie* (*The German Ideology*), in the very year he became a Marxist, that a high degree of "development of productive forces . . . is an absolutely necessary practical premise [of communism] because without it, privation, *want,* is merely made general, and with *want* the struggle for necessities would begin again, and all the old shitty business would be restored."[3] And as if to prove him right on this point, the very countries, the Soviet Union and mainland China, which, in defiance of his predictions, socialized their economies, are now jettisoning collectivist principles, while retaining the Leninist state, a perversion of the Marxist ideal which never envisaged the absolute dictatorship of a minority party based on brutal force as an expression of a democratic, socialist commonwealth.

Indoctrination is a process of teaching through which acceptance of belief is induced by nonrational or irrational means, or both. It may be unavoidable when teaching very young children who must acquire certain social habits before they are mature enough to understand their justification. But it has no place whatsoever in the curriculum of a liberal arts college. Any course of study that does not consider, where relevant, dissenting views where matters of opinion are involved, especially in the fields of the humanities and social studies, is an exercise in indoctrination, and often undisguised. That is the source of so much pedagogical concern and, except among partisan and fanatical elements, intelligent student rejection on many campuses of Black Studies, Feminist Studies, Chicano Studies, etc., in which only one position is heard on controversial issues about which reasonable men and women may differ. Whoever heard of a teacher in Black Studies who does not believe in *total* divestment of American corporation holdings in South Africa, regardless of its effects on the local Black population, or who agrees with the Zulu chief Buthelezi, spokesman for a considerable portion, if not a majority, of the Black population? Whoever has heard of an anti-feminist or of someone who agrees with Eleanor Roosevelt's opinion on the Equal Rights Amendment, teaching in Women Studies? Or a teacher of Chicano Studies who dares to agree with American policy in El Salvador, Nicaragua, or even Grenada? So long as these studies are elective or voluntary their fall out affects those who have surrendered their minds to them. But if the content and method of these studies are smuggled into the required courses, this constitutes an outrageous betrayal of the liberal tradition. We are already hearing complaints that there are not enough teachers available to discuss these questions in a scholarly way, coupled with the preposterous notion that those qualified to teach the great works of Western culture are incapable of mastering the relevant materials on these themes, and that therefore the teaching staff must be expanded to bring in persons specially qualified by race, sex, or class to present themes in these areas sympathetically.

Such views are sometimes heard even among those who imagine that they are Marxists of sorts in the fields of comparative literature or literary criticism, in which deconstructionist dogmas about "the myth of objectivity" give them license to take any liberties with texts or verifiable events. One almost feels sorry for poor Marx because of those who invoke his name. Marx naively believed that his position rested on historical evidence. His was intended to be an empirical view. To be scientifically credible it had to be refutable, i.e., stand the test of experience. Marx had left the irresponsible voluntarism, revived by twentieth-century existentialism, behind him with the swaddling clothes of his idealistic Hegelianism, which now reappears in the patched-up garments of the Frankfurt school.

We hear a great deal of the *Marxian* allegiance of university faculties in the humanities and social studies, especially among the not insubstantial number who were activist students in the sixties. Because of the collapse of rigorous standards of scholarship, some of these activists have survived as tenured teachers in the institutions they once sought to destroy. Once scholars have won their professional spurs, they have as much right to be Marxists as Straussians or Thomists or what not. There are good and bad among all schools of thought. But the astonishing thing is the degree to which those who pretend to or profess, as Marxist orientation, interpret Marxism, not as a scholarly scientific approach but as a *commitment* to a variety of political causes. The chief component of this commitment is opposition to American foreign policy whenever it involves a conflict in Third World countries or with the Soviet Union and its satellites. What they expound as Marxism is a blatant variety of vulgar Marxism, which is more Benthamite than Marxist, or a form of pseudo-Marxism in which there is no distinction between the causal efficacy of "the foundations" and "superstructure" of culture, and Marx's materialism disappears in an eclectic melange.

All this may appear peripheral to the problems of curriculur construction and evaluation. But it is not. The future of Stanford's only required course depends on whether the obvious political bias and indoctrination in the track on "Europe and the Americas" is to be reflected in the other tracks.* The

---

*For reasons that are quite understandable in the absence of details (certainly not the fault of critics), some of the doubts about the shortcomings of the complete set of CIV tracks may appear unfounded. Dante will not be read in the "Europe and the Americas" track but it may or may not be read in one or another of the seven other tracks.

On the other hand, some of the replies to critics fall back on the truism that times change and that even if the perennial questions of life remain the same, different books may suggest different answers. Replying to a critical *Wall Street Journal* editorial, the assistant dean of undergraduate studies at Stanford, an ardent advocate of the new program writes: "For example, 50 years ago John Locke seemed indispensable in answering a question like 'What is Social Justice?' In 1989, with a more interdependent world order, a more heterogeneous domestic population, and mass media and communications systems that complicate our definitions of 'society' and 'individual,' it may be that someone like Franz Fanon, a black Algerian psychoanalyst, will get us closer to the answer we need" (*Wall Street Journal,* 1/6/89).

What a curious and irrelevant defense of the new program! The two most notable works of John Locke are his *Essay Concerning Human Understanding* and *Two Treatises on Government.* Neither is concerned centrally with social justice. The first is about the theory of knowledge, the second about the philosophical foundation of human rights, which should be more relevant to the human rights revolution of our times than any of the new works in the course. On the other hand, Fanon's *The Wretched of the Earth* has nothing to say about "social justice" or even about psychoanalysis. It is an eloquent tract inciting victims of colonialism to revolutionary violence. It does not treat seriously any of the complex social phenomena listed as bearing on the modern quest for social justice. If one were concerned with theories of social justice in 1989, one would normally require the study of excerpts from John Rawls's *A Theory of Justice* and Robert Nozick's *Anarchy, State and Utopia* and from writings of critics of the natural rights tradition Rawls and Nozick have brilliantly revived rather than the study of Fanon's *The Wretched of the Earth.* And if, as the assistant dean writes, we are looking for works that "will get us closer to the answer we need," how does he know that the answer we need is a true or adequate answer? A purported answer to a question may meet our needs or hopes but it may not

current year is supposed to be transitional and, as in the past, changes normally would be made in the course of events. The disquietude generated by the course on "Europe and the Americas" was natural because of the publicity it received in the *Chronicle of Higher Education* and the *Wall Street Journal*.[4] The changes in no other track have been so widely heralded. Taken together with the Senatorial mandate that the concepts of race, sex, and class are to be stressed, and the explicit provision that books written by women and persons of color are to be added to the required reading list while nine of the fifteen core readings are to be dropped, it was inevitable that the academic community be alarmed. That alarm may contribute to the sobriety and reflectiveness of further curriculum developments at Stanford.

There is one great danger not properly faced in any institution where, as in Stanford, a course of study, devised to provide a common unitary educational experience for all students, is presented in different sections or tracks that reflect the specialized interests students bring *to* the course rather than letting their intellectual interests develop *out* of the course. The great danger is that despite the fact that the core curriculum of readings may be the same for all sections or tracks, in actuality the students are really taking

---

be a true or adequate answer to the question. A university is an institution that should study with critical care and understanding *all* proposed answers to the central questions and concerns of our time. It cannot as an institution become a partisan advocate or agency of any proposed solution. That is the function of legislative bodies in our democracy.

The basic educational or philosophical issue raised by reflections on curriculum building involves a larger question than the particular required course of study at Stanford or Boston Universities or anywhere else. It is whether we are to develop informed men and women capable of continuing their own education, with open minds, free of zealotry, aware of the challenges to their first principles and yet confident in the validity of their own reflective choices, prepared to defend the principles of a free and liberal civilization against enemies from any quarter, and with the imaginative capacity to see the human being even in the enemy. Those so educated, in a world of tension and conflict, are more likely to adopt the policy of live-and-help-live with others, and failing that, the policy of live-and-let-live.

The schools and universities are not the only educational agencies in society. In addition to the home, our economic, political, and cultural organizations have a pervasive educational influence, too. Unless they also reflect the basic values of democracy as a way of life, schools and universities cannot have much influence beyond their own precincts. Our hope should be that a proper educational experience will develop citizens with the knowledge, skills, and values required for intelligent action. This is in no way a defense of the status quo. Because, as John Dewey used to say, literally in a world of change, there is no *status quo*. The influence of the past for good or bad is always present. It is the task of creative intelligence to use what is valid in the past and present to face and hopefully determine the future.

different courses. The danger is intensified when the core curriculum readings are not the same or when each section or track can require different supplementary readings. (In a sense it is even true that in almost every discipline the identical material taught by a brilliant, imaginative teacher will result in a different course from one taught by a dull teacher who comes alive only in the laboratory, but there is no remedy for such situations.) A good case can be made for the view that the syllabus of one of the tracks in the old course in Western culture could have served adequately for all the students enrolled in the course. For example, of all the syllabi I have seen, I would say that the Syllabus for Structured Liberal Education, modified to include an analysis of central concepts of science and scientific method as well as references to other cultures, could very well serve as a paradigm course for all students. But there is no possibility of making that choice now. What is necessary is to curb the great divergence among the eight (some envisage ten) different tracks that will try to implement the mandated changes. The upshot may well be a series of unrelated courses so different from each other that the whole notion of a common unitary educational experience will be defeated. This has happened before and unless the engaged faculty keeps before it the ideals of a liberal arts education, it may happen again.

NOTES

1. (December 14, 1988.)
2. *Collected Works of Marx and Engels,* Volume 12 (Lawrence and Wishart, London and Moscow), p. 132.
3. *Collected Works,* Volume 5, p. 49.
4. (December 22, 1988.)

19

In Defense of the Humanities

The humanities have been part and sometimes the whole of the curriculum of institutions of higher education since antiquity. They embraced the scientific disciplines of the classical and medieval world. The impact of modern experimental science and technology, resulting in the multiplication and greater specialization of scientific studies, dwarfed the place of the humanities both by their novelty and revolutionary consequences of science on the life of society. But they did not eliminate the humanities, even when higher education became central for professional and vocational preparation. When higher education was the monopoly of a small leisure class, the very question of its bearing on how one earned one's living seemed irrelevant and vulgar. When higher education became universally accessible, however, such questions became inescapable. Even so, although scanted, the humanities remained a part of the curriculum distinguished from the rest by its subject matter, and justified by its significance.

During the sixties, the last great crisis in American education, the university as an institution came under political attack, but not its curriculum. The irony is that by the sixties the movement towards the *depoliticization* of the university, in consequence of the labors of the American Association of University Professors (AAUP), founded by John Dewey and Arthur O. Lovejoy, had largely succeeded. It had become, so to speak, the common law of the academy that the university was not to penalize faculty members or students for exercising their rights as citizens and that the university was not to make allegiance to capitalism or any other social or political ideology a condition for membership in the academic community. Individual members of the university as *citizens* could be partisan, but the university as a corporate body could not. During the sixties, highly militant bodies of students demanded that the university as a corporate body take stands on issues that had arisen

From *Measure* 81 (August/September 1989): 1–8. Reprinted by permission of University Centers for Rational Alternatives.

in the general community which fell within the province of representative legislative bodies. In some institutions, the abolition of required courses was part of the fallout of the crisis of the sixties, but within the last decade most of those required courses have been restored.

The current crisis of education in the United States may legitimately be characterized as an attempt to politicize the curriculum itself. Those who have provoked it contend that the existing curriculum in the humanities is already politicized in virtue of the fact that its basic texts have been composed by Western white males and that, in consequence, the required courses are intrinsically infected with racism, sexism, and imperialism. The remedy proposed for this deplorable situation is that the traditional texts be partly replaced and supplemented by books composed by women and people of color and by representatives of the oppressed masses and classes of the past and present, and further, that the study of foreign cultures in depth be introduced into required study. To insure that these texts be properly taught, it is urged that additional personnel of instruction, wherever possible, be recruited from minorities and women, if there is any doubt about the willingness or capacity of existing faculties to do so.

This transformation or revision (call it what you will) has been carried out fully at Stanford University, and criticized in some educational circles as a politicizing of a curriculum designed for other purposes. Such criticism has provoked the rejoinder from the architects of the new curriculum that the criticism is itself politically oriented, indeed, an expression of the same repressive politics embodied in the canonic texts of the course in Western culture. Even before these developments, in a report to Congress on *The Humanities in American,* Lynn Cheney, the present chair of the National Endowment for the Humanities, had deplored the fact that, in the teaching of the Humanities on every level and not only in required courses,

> viewing humanities texts as though they were primarily political documents is the most noticeable trend in academic study of the humanities today. Truth and beauty and excellence are regarded as irrelevant; questions of aesthetic and intellectual quality dismissed.

Her report has been itself subjected to a strong criticism by a committee of six scholars sponsored by the ACLS *Speaking for the Humanities,* as itself a political document.

I am going to devote my main analysis to the concept of the "political" in this discussion, and to the hard and fast way its different connotations are being employed to obfuscate the issues. Before doing this, I wish to state a few assumptions, which I am prepared to defend if challenged, that relate to the humanities curriculum in the educational enterprise.

We acknowledge or assume that what differentiates the disciplines in the humanities, as they are understood today, from other disciplines is their central concern with human values, their interconnection and imaginative representation in human experience. We acknowledge the desirability of including a broadly based course in the humanities as a curricular *requirement* to provide all students with the legacy of their culture through the study of the outstanding books, ideas, movements, and creative personalities that have contributed to it, and with an understanding of the conflicting cultural traditions of the past that have shaped the present and affected our current difficulties and tensions. The materials in such study have provided us in part with the basic categories of our thought and language, the conceptual tools, sentiments and dispositions with which we approach the central problems of reflective life, whatever our geography or region. We acknowledge that such study for many reasons cannot constitute the whole of the school's curriculum, that at most it will be confined to one year, preferably at the outset of the students' careers, before specialization begins. We acknowledge that there cannot be, in a decentralized educational system such as ours, only one program, however ideal, or a set of syllabi for a course of this character, whatever it is called, that the diversification will reflect local resources, capacities, and opportunities. Finally, we acknowledge that whatever texts are selected for a course of this character, they are not eternally fixed, they can be varied from time to time, reflecting available talents and shifting interests without affecting the overall goal of providing students from all backgrounds a unitary, but not uniform, education experience whose existence can be built on whatever educational and vocational differentiation follows.

The first point I want to make on the basis of a survey of courses in Western culture or civilization more or less like those previously offered at Stanford is that, despite what detractors have claimed, they are *not* a glorification of the *status quo.* On the contrary. The required reading gives an understanding of how the *status quo* has come into being, presents some of the revolutionary ideas that helped it come into being, and explores the struggle and debate among the great maps of personal and social salvation whose promises and dangers still engage our interest. As a matter of fact, it is from a curriculum of similar studies in Paris or London that some leaders of Third World countries absorbed the ideas and ideals they used to rally their peoples against colonialization. And in truth, since the standard texts express conflicting ideals, they could hardly lend themselves coherently to any one point of view. But their grasp and analysis is required by anyone who seeks intelligently to transform or conserve our society. Whether it is the ideals of tolerance, the limitations of ethnocentrism, the visions of utopia without which Wilde said no map of the world is complete—all are contained in every well-tailored course in the humanities. Any intelligent student completing such a course, if and when he acquaints himself with other cultures, can hardly help concluding that of all cultures of which we have any record, Western culture has been the most critical of itself, that its history has largely been a succession of heresies, and that it has been freer of the blind spots of ethnocentrism than any other.

More directly, addressing myself to the charge that courses in Western culture have been racist, sexist, and imperialistic, in the negative sense of these terms, despite every renewed request for evidence, no one has ever cited *specific* evidence that any of the basic texts has been systematically taught in the spirit and attitude of invidious discrimination that these terms currently have. There was certainly no evidence of this in any of the tracks of the course at Stanford, although, like all courses, they invited improvement. Of course, in discussing Greek drama, we cannot but become aware of how different the status of women was in the classical world from what it is in our own. But we would be guilty of the grossest distortion of scholarship if we denied the fact. Effective teaching can take one of its points of exploration from it whether we are reading the *Medea* or discussing the startling feminist views in Plato's *Republic.* Indeed, Plato's *Republic* in the hands of a good teacher lends itself to the exciting counterposition of arguments and themes on a whole variety of subjects that possess contemporary vibrancy like the recurrent temptations of censorship, the defects of democracy and the snares of totalitarianism. Nor should we forget for a moment that no text imposes one reading on all interpreters of its meaning.

At this point we are likely to hear that the absence of women and people of color among the authors of the basic texts is evidence of the inherent bias with which such courses are infected. Where, it is asked, is the imaginative presentation of the life of the common people, the spear carriers, the hewers of wood and drawers of water, of the victimization of women from biblical days, of the mute and inglorious lives of slaves, especially the black slaves? The texts of courses in Western culture, it is asserted, were written by elite members of Western society for the elite, and it therefore slights the contributions of women and minority groups, without whom there would be no culture at all.

The naivete of the complaint reflects the intensity of the political commitment of those who level this complaint, not their historical judgment. Of course the culture of the past was created by the elite members of the past! Who else could have created it at a time when literacy itself was the monopoly of the elite classes? It was that creation, winnowed by the criticism of successive elites, that produced our culture. And the quality of that creation is not affected by its origins. It was none other than Karl Marx himself, steeped to his very pores in the elite classical culture of the West, who declared that although Greek art and epics are products of a class society, "they still constitute a source of aesthetic enjoyment and in certain respects prevail as the standard and model beyond attainment." He was not exalting or looking for a proletarian or slave art that did not exist, but wanted to make the best of art and culture developed in every society part of the cultural birthright of the working class. To be sure, we may be curious to know how and why the masses and women were excluded from the creative cultural institutions of the past, why they were confined to the kitchens and workplaces and denied the light of learning, and what was the role of the sciences and technologies in their liberation. These are legitimate questions explored in a wide variety of other courses in sociology, politics, the sciences, economic history, and anthropology open to inquiring student minds. But to introduce all of these studies into a course in the *humanities* is to dilute it into a very thin soup of social matter.

The notion that the course in Western culture can be enriched by adding to its core list of readings books by women and persons of color, not because they are the best or most appropriate for the subject in hand but because of the race or sex or class of the author, a kind of affirmative action program in scholarship, is both patronizing and ludicrous form the standpoint of honest scholarship. And it compounds the folly when tacked onto this is a mandate to recruit from "women and people of color" the teachers of the ideas and aspects of culture that involve them. This is nothing more than a sophisticated revival of the old folk fantasy, and just as absurd, that only like can understand like. Does one have to be French to understand Napoleon, Russian to understand Lenin, Greek to read Homer or enjoy the figures of Praxteles? As well argue that men cannot be good gynecologists, that only women with children can best understand and administer family law, that only fat physicians can study obesity, and hungry ones the physiology of starvation as to assert or imply that only people of color or women are uniquely qualified to do justice, wherever relevant, to the place, achievements, and oppressions of minorities and their culture. Was it not the work of a white male and, to boot, a foreigner, a Swede, who in *The American Dilemma,* first moved the conscience of this country in recent times on the race question more than any other person before the appearance of Martin Luther King?

There is only one genuine educational question broached by the situation in Stanford that, unfortunately, had little to do with the actual decision made there but which has occasionally been asked and discussed elsewhere, notably at a national conference at Michigan State University a few years ago. Granted that Western culture is now operating in a world of global issues enveloping the entire world, should the required basic course we have been proposing be taught as a course in world culture or world civilization rather than as one in Western culture or civilization? If so, its core list would have to contain the great works of different peoples and cultures, the kind of literature, art, and history that denizens of these foreign cultures have been nurtured in. But could that be done in an educationally fruitful way? There are many reasons to doubt this. A great work that has exercised its influence in a culture is approached with a mindset that in part has been determined by the influence of that work in the culture. The Japanese student reading *The Tale of the Genji,* the Chinese student reading Confucious' *Analects,* the Pakistani student reading the Quaran, or the Hindi the *Bahghavad Gita,* has a knowledge of its symbols and world view that is certainly not beyond the grasp or comprehension of the American student but which manifestly would take him years to acquire. He hasn't the same background with which he approaches the Gospels or even Shakespeare. He cannot unmake himself and grow into these other cultures as he did in his own. The sphere of future activity will primarily be his own culture. So although he can contrast and compare the way the Golden Rule is formulated positively and negatively in Rabbi Hillel, the New Testament, Buddha, and Lao Tze, it cannot serve in any formulation as a key to the whole culture without the student knowing much more than even his teachers are likely to know. The point of building bridges of understanding to other cultures is to prepare students, using familiar examples, for the encounter of visiting them and imaginatively empathizing with them, not to live in them. Whatever the global future will be, it is not likely to result in a homogeneous global culture. There will not be one global village but a plurality of global villages.

The study and history of humanities in the West certainly touches the borders of other cultures. But it is the humanists themselves in pursuit of the pedagogical and research tasks, who know what is to be studied and when. The motivation of those who legislated that concerns for race, sex, and class be made central in the study of humanities at Stanford and elsewhere was not pedagogical but political. It was stated, often explicitly, that justice or fairness required that the needs of the exploited, oppressed, and hitherto unheard be recognized; that their voices be amplified; and their separateness be overcome. All worthy objectives of an enlightened political agenda. But however desirable this agenda is, its sphere of activity is the public and legislative forum, not the institutions for the dissemination of wisdom, let alone the curriculum of the humanities. In the study of the humanities, we can legitimately inquire into the influence of political decisions in the past on the ideals and models conceived to represent the best and most enduring in art and literature. But that is quite different from selecting readings in a course or teaching them in order to reshape the politics of the present or future.

This immediately brings the retort that the refusal to orient a course in the humanities politically is itself to take a political position. The refusal to take a stand, it is averred, is itself a political stand. And so, if we are not careful to make and abide by the proper distinctions, the question of whether and to what extent a work of art or literature exhibits a political aspect, the answer to which, if we know it, is yes or no, is transformed into whether or not our decision to study a subject and to stress this or that aspect of its work, becomes a *political* question, the answer to which depends on whether you are liberal or conservative, a reformer or a revolutionary.

Let us meet this position head on. Is it true that the refusal to take a stand is itself a political stand? No, unless we are dealing with an explicit political problem, where the consequences of not taking a stand, say proclaiming neutrality between aggressor and victim, has political consequences affecting everyone. But outside the sphere of partisan political issues, the refusal to take a stand on a disputed issue may mean nothing more than a decision to suspend judgment until more evidence is in. If I refuse to come down on one side or the other of the question of whether Lord Bacon or the Earl of Essex wrote the plays attributed to Shakespeare, or whether whoever wrote the play *Hamlet* portrayed Hamlet, the character, as genuinely mad or feigning madness or Polonius as a figure of fun or as genuinely a sage, my answer is decidedly *not* political in any ordinary sense of the term. It may be that in light of overwhelming or preponderant evidence, my continued suspension of judgment could be warrantably called unscholarly, but not political. It is often said that the choice of any set of books or writings in a course in the humanities is a political choice. What makes it political? That it is a choice? But how arbitrary that would be! Would the choice of textbooks in a course in mathematics be political too? Certainly not. Even in the case where a teacher is prescribing his own book instead of one clearly better, because of the anticipated royalties, his choice is not political but unethical and unprofessional. It certainly would be odd if anyone characterized the choice of musical works to be studied in a course on musical appreciation as "political." There could be all sorts of differences among the architects of such a course—or of any course—in the humanities about the justification for including each or any item, but unless one can show, and not merely assert, that there was a political reason for the selection, it is a plain abuse of what Charles Peirce called the ethics of words, to call the choice political.

Why, then, comes the renewed complaint, are there no books by women, workers, and people of color in the canon of the standard humanities courses? Does not that express a value judgment? To which the manifest answer is that, yes, it does express a value judgment, but *not* a political value judgment about women, workers, and minorities and their place in our culture. It is a judgment about which books have had the greatest influence on the culture of our time and of past times; which books have been the sources of renewed delight, intellectual stimulation, and challenge to their readers; which works of literature and art help us best understand our own contemporary culture, which is related in thousands of ways to the cultural achievements of the past.

Political passion still sustains the argument. It asks whether the standards of excellence themselves, the criticisms of judgment, even the "eternal values," do not "reflect" the social and class structure of the time. The word "reflects" is one of the most ambiguous terms in the vocabulary of criticism. If a writer or artist accepts the society of his time, his values "reflect" it; if he rejects the society, his action and values necessarily reflect it by his very negation. The question for scholarship is *how* do his values specifically reflect it? And the question whether his or her work is to be included in the canon of the humanities is not whether he reflects *his* society, as in some way it necessarily does, but whether it has something to say of abiding significance to other times and other societies as well. We don't have to use the rhetoric of eternal values to make the point that whatever makes a claim to eternal value must establish its validity as an enduring value *here* and *now;* that, of course, since all things have a history, values have a history; and that all we can ever mean by intrinsic, perennial, or eternal value is that the book, painting, or musical composition that embodies it, *still works its attractive power on us today,* regardless of our political partisanship.

What is basically objectionable in the contemporary movement to politicize the humanities is that it conflates different meanings of the term "political." It goes from a sense of "political," synonymous with a basic choice in any field, so broad that it lacks an intelligible opposite, so that to be is to be political, to a sense of the term "political" in its transparent, conventional sense. In order to conceal a predilection, and its relation to its overt political antecedents in the sixties as well as its political stance on the current scene, those who hold this view fall back on the comprehensive, confusing usage of the term "political" as meaning any choice. Sometimes the exemplars of the movement frankly proclaim they want to reform the humanities program *in order* to shape the political future of the nation. But, *logically,* these goals have nothing to do with each other. One can be for or against the Equal Rights Amendment or the Welfare State, regardless of the sex or color of the authors of the books studied. At this point the question they seem to imply is one of power, not logic. The situation is accurately characterized by Richard Rorty, who although critical is not himself unsympathetic to some of the social goals of this movement. He writes in a recent essay:

> A new American cultural left has come into being made of deconstructionists, new historicists, people in gender studies, ethnic studies, media studies, a few left over Marxists, and so on. This left would like to use the English, French, and Comparative Literature departments of the universities as staging areas for political action.[1]

A more representative, and in a sense official, view is expressed by Professor Linda K. Kerber, recent past president of the American Studies Association:

> We have celebrated the speed with which we have discovered diversity—of race, class, gender, and ethnicity. But for all the skepticism, irony, and critical perspectives upon which we pride ourselves, we have remained too much part of the *status quo* we deplore.
>
> Freed from the defensive contraints of cold war ideology, empowered by our new sensitivity to the distinctions of race, class, and gender, we are ready to begin to understand difference as a series of power relationships involving domination and subordination, and to use our understanding or power relations to reconceptualize both our interpretation and our teaching of American culture.[2]

Associated with this view and outlook is an attitude which gives me profound concern because it challenges the very notion of objective truth on the ground that the quest for truth is itself affected by interests that are ultimately tied up with the class structure of society. Accused of reading its own political bias into the interpretation and evaluation of events to further the indoctrination of their students, members of the New Left respond that their critics are themselves biased, that "objectivity" exists in the eye of the beholder, since no one is free from bias. It is not difficult to show that such a position is incoherent, flawed by its own assertions. It is true that no one can claim to have or to know the whole truth about anything, but it by no means follows from this that all assertions are equally true or false, that we cannot ground some statements on the basis of evidence, as better or truer than others. Indeed, to hold that objectivity is a myth is tantamount to denying the distinction between fiction and history, guilt and innocence *in relation to the admitted evidence.*

It is safe to predict that if such modes of thinking take over in the humanities, before long we will be hearing their echoes in medicine and the natural science, too. It was a mere fifty years ago when we were hearing about Aryan and Jewish physics and proletarian biology. Today once more there is talk of race, gender, and class not as a subject of scientific study but as characterizing the scientific approach itself. Nonsense, the literature reader will say. To be sure, but if unchecked, we have learned that nonsense will kill.

NOTES

1. From a public address on "General Education and Socialization" delivered at George Mason University (March 1, 1989).
2. *Chronicle of Higher Education* (March 29, 1989).

Part Four

POLITICAL AND POLEMICAL

20

The Faiths of Whittaker Chambers

The name of the author, the theme of his work, the nature of our times all conspire to make this volume one of the most significant autobiographies of the twentieth century. It is not among the hundred great books. Yet it throws more light on the conspiratorial and religious character of modern communism, on the tangled complex of motives which led men and women of goodwill to immolate themselves on the altars of a fancied historical necessity, than all of the hundred great books of the past combined. The phenomenon of which it treats is historically unique not only in scale but in meaning. It demands understanding, not mere denunciation. The keys to that understanding can be provided only by reflection on our present historical experience.

A certain perspective, especially freedom from partisanship, is essential if the reader of this book is to do justice to its different facets. Many will already have judged it before they have actually read it. This will be a pity because the book covers much more than the unhappy story of Alger Hiss. It contains interesting vignettes of the Communist movement, a record of religious conversion, the saga of a farm, an account of desperate courage alternating with moods of spiritual despair—all knit together by the essentially mystical and romantic personality of the author. The literary quality of the writing is impressive. In this respect serialization did the book a disservice.

The main theme, however, is the Communist movement, above and under ground, the men and women who served it, and the logic of the commitment which led them into an eager faithlessness not only to their country but to the moral values in which they were nurtured. Here we must sharply distinguish, as unfortunately Mr. Chambers does not, between the facts to which he bears witness and the interpretations he places upon them. Were these interpretations valid, they would have as fateful a bearing upon the prospects of democratic

---

A review of *Witness,* by Whittaker Chambers. (New York: Random House, n.d.), 808 pp.

survival as the revelations of the facts concerning Communist conspiracy. It will be necessary therefore to look hard at them.

First, about the facts. The internal evidence of this book is so overwhelmingly detailed and cumulative, it rings with such authenticity, that it is extremely unlikely any reasonable person will remain unconvinced by it. It is not that new facts about Hiss and his fellow conspirators are revealed but that the facts already known are placed in the historic context of Chambers's own development and almost day-to-day activities. To doubt them is tantamount to doubting Chambers's political existence as well as those of his collaborators. The absence of personal rancor against Hiss, the evidence that the author testified "reluctantly and in agony," the explanation of why he did not tell his entire story at once—a quixotic piece of foolishness—add credibility to his account.

As far as the charges that rocked the nation are concerned, the book, even more than the verdict of the trials, may well be called the vindication of Whittaker Chambers. Its pages show that he has long since atoned for his own complicity in conspiratorial work by his suffering at the hands of Hiss's friends whose outrageous smears against his personal life and that of his wife surpassed in virulence anything known in recent American history. It is indeed odd to observe that ritualistic liberals were much less indignant with those who betrayed the faith of their country than they were with the "informers" who revealed the betrayal—an attitude not displayed toward informers or renegades from fascism like Rauschning and Otto Strasser. The mood of anti-anti-communism, as the Hiss case shows, blinds one to political realities and creates an emotional vested interest in concealing the truth.

The facts in this book have a public side vastly more important than the private fortunes of Hiss and Chambers. What they show is that the highest instances of the government were informed on four separate occasions of Chambers's charges that an important group of American officials in the State Department, Treasury Department, Patent Office and Aberdeen Proving Grounds were functioning as members of a Communist party underground apparatus. One need only read the names and successive positions occupied by this group, among several in operation, to understand that, in the event of hostilities with the Soviet Union, they could easily have functioned with a deadliness comparable to the Foote ring in Switzerland and the Sorge ring in Japan, both of which made enormous contributions to Stalin's victory.

The truly puzzling and still inexplicable thing about these facts is not that the American government was deceived—American innocence of politics based on a *Weltanschauung* is almost invincible—but that no accredited government agency was asked to investigate the truth of Chambers's charges when he first made them. Had this been done and those whose guilt was subsequently revealed quietly dropped from government service, and elementary precautions taken against further penetration, the recent history of American political and even cultural life would have been profoundly different. As it is, one of the men in the Chambers ring, identified in 1939 as a Communist conspirator supplying top-secret information from the Aberdeen Proving Grounds, kept his post until 1948.

Given these facts and the organized campaign of calumny against him, one can understand the subjective compulsions which have led Chambers to interpret his experiences as he does. This interpretation takes two forms, political and philosophical, both none the less questionable for being widely shared.

Chambers is convinced that it was not by chance that the New Deal served as a host body for Communist infiltration. He argues that despite their differences, the New Dealers and the Communists were revolutionary brothers under the skin. The New Dealers sincerely abhorred the Communists but were unable, and then unwilling, to ferret them out because the latter were harder, brighter, vastly more knowing and unscrupulous protagonists of the same general line. Every move to oust Communists was regarded as a move against the administration, and all a Communist under threat of exposure need do was to cry "Witch hunt!" to rally the innocent New Dealers to deny the facts of Communist penetration. Chambers quotes a close friend, himself a New Dealer, saying to him: "I see why it might not pay the Communists to kill you at this point. But I don't see how the Administration dares to leave you alive."

To say that the New Deal—an eclectic, unorganized, popular reaction to the intolerable evils of an unstabilized capitalism—was a social revolutionary movement is to play with words. The principles of social welfare are indigenously Amercan, and Roosevelt, during the early months of 1933, could have led the country very much farther along these lines than he actually did.

Until the Seventh Congress of the Communist International in 1935, Roosevelt in the eyes of the Communists was a Fascist. It was only when the Popular Front strategy and the tactics of the Trojan horse was adopted that the Communists organized their mass infiltrations and began to speak the language of the New Deal. Chambers should know that when it suits their purposes Communists can speak anybody's language, the language of the Church Fathers as of America's Founding Fathers—and the ignorant or foolish will fall for it all the time.

The only thing that could have kept Communists out of any administration, New Deal or Old, was the knowledge that communism since Lenin's time was not an open and honestly avowed heresy but an international conspiracy, centered in the Kremlin, in a state of undeclared war against democratic institutions. The corollary would have been the realization that the Communists were and are prepared to use any and every means to achieve power, nationally and internationally.

That this knowledge was absent in almost all government agencies is not surprising in view of the fact that both American Presidents during World War II were convinced that England and France would be greater threats to post-war world peace and freedom than the Soviet Union. Nor was this knowledge more conspicuously evident in influential circles outside the government, in universities, for example, in churches, the press and even business.

Most of Chambers's facts are rendered intelligible by a less sinister hypothesis than the one he offers. It is that stupidity is sometimes the greatest of all historical forces. Stupidity explains why Communists were permitted to infiltrate into the government. But why were they retained so long after the data about them were in official hands? Here Chambers forgets that some of the most vocal opponents of Communists in government services seemed more interested in discrediting the administration and New Deal than in defending freedom. The passions of American parochial politics blinded both sides to the fact that an international civil war was raging in relation to which prestige, votes, patronage and many issues of domestic policy were irrelevant. Nor does the author's account do justice to the climate of cloudy opinion which saw in Hitler the sole incarnation of historical evil in our generation.

Chambers himself places the greatest stress upon the philosophical interpretation of his experiences. The international civil war so correctly described is regarded not as a struggle between the free society and the society of total terror but as the struggle between the Party of God and the Party of Man. The political differences among men are ultimately reducible to differences in theology, between the vision of a world with God and the vision of a world without Him. This in a sense is the thesis of Chambers's autobiography. He offers his life as testimony to its truth. And he writes as a moving and eloquent witness.

Chambers's story of his life is a minor classic in the history of religious conversions. No one can doubt the sincerity of his hard-won faith, that he has found in it, after much agony, a healing peace and humility. As a quest for personal salvation, it will command the respect of those who cannot share his cosmic hope and whose natural piety takes other forms.

But to make this faith a basis for social salvation is a hazardous enterprise, all the more so because of the desperate lengths to which Chambers carries it. He fervently and repeatedly asserts that the most revolutionary question in history is: God or Man? and that whoever answers "Man" shares the Communist vision whether he is aware of it or not. He recklessly lumps Socialists, progressives, liberals, and men of good will together with the Communists. All are bound according to him by the same faith; but only the Communists have the gumption and guts to live by it and pay the price. The others are the unwitting accomplices of communism precisely because they have put their trust in intelligence, not God. Only theists, not humanists, can resist communism, and in the end save man.

The view that man must worship either God or Stalin faces many formidable theoretical difficulties and has the most mischievous practical consequences. For one thing the disjunction is neither exhaustive nor exclusive. There exists a not inconsiderable body of men who worship both, even without counting those like the Dean of Canterbury and the Patriarch of the Russian Synod, and a still larger body who worship neither. After all, religious faiths have been compatible with the most diverse social principles. Not a single policy about empirical arrangements in human life can be logically derived from transcendental religious premises or from propositions of rational theology.

Deeply religious men speak with the same divided counsels as nonreligious men about the specific problems of war, peace, poverty, and foreign policy which must find empirical solutions if communism's false answers are to be rejected. Precisely because, as Chambers admits in an unguarded moment, "religion is not ethics or social reform," it is neither necessary nor sufficient for the discovery of the social programs and political strategy essential to the survival of freedom. Here there is no substitute for creative intelligence.

At one point Chambers invokes against liberalism and humanism, the theology of Barth, Dostoevsky and Kierkegaard without awareness of the irony in these references. The first is a "neutralist" in the current secular struggle; the second, perhaps the greatest dramatist of the human spirit but no friend of a free society; the third taught that between God's purposes in eternity and human purposes in history there is an "infinite qualitative difference." The fact that some of Chambers's fellow-Quakers are appeasers of Stalin while others are valiant fighters in the cause of freedom is enough to establish the irrelevance of his theology to his politics.

Indeed, Chambers has reflected poorly about the facts of his own disillusionment with communism. He writes dramatically of the "screams" of the victims of communism, of the shattering effect of these messages from souls in torment on even hardened Communists. He is silent about the fact that the truth about the Moscow trials, to whose victims' screams he was originally deaf was first proclaimed by liberals and humanists like John Dewey. While Chambers still worked for Stalin's underground, it was *they* who sought to arouse the world to the painful knowledge he is now frantically urging on it. He glosses over the fact that he himself closed his ears to the screams of the victims until his own life was threatened by Stalin's agents, and that in his hour of flight, need, and political repentance, it was to the Party of Man that he turned for aid first of all.

Chambers does not consider the possibility that the opposition of genuine American liberals to the cultural and physical terror of the Kremlin was deeper and more sustained than that of any other group because it was fed by a passion for freedom, and an opposition to all forms of authoritarianism. One would have thought it obvious that Franco, Hitler, and Mussolini, and other dictators with religious faith or support, have more in common with Stalin and the Politburo than either group has with the liberals and humanists Chambers condemns.

It is unfortunate that Chambers could not have given a wiser and more generous expression to his faith. The logic by which he now classifies liberals and humanists with the Communists is not unlike the logic by which, when a Communist, he classified them with Fascists. Stalinism permits no loyal opposition, for opposition, the lifeblood of democracy, is *the* enemy in the politics of every totalitarianism. I should hope that Chambers himself would recoil from the implications of his present view that there is no loyal political opposition outside the Faith. When heresy is identified with the enemy, we shall have seen the end of democracy.

Since Chambers is a self-declared mystic and irrationalist, it is pointless to take issue with him on matters he regards as transcending human intelligence. But in the very interest of religious freedom itself, as well as of the effective struggle for democracy, it is necessary to repudiate his contrast between faith in God on the one hand, and intelligence and scientific method on the other, and his further equation of intelligence and scientific method with communism. This is a monstrous piece of dogmatism and a gratuitous gift to communism. It no more follows that faith in intelligence and scientific method must lead to torture and death in the cellars of the Lubianka than that faith in God must lead to the Inquisition or the rack and the stake.

It remains to ask what kind of man is portrayed in this massive book and in the multiplicity of lives he has led. The first and lasting impression is of a man who has suffered much, whose humility is born of a genuine surprise at his own tenacity and survival. These seem to him to be the result of a divine grace, unearned yet partly paid for by a willingness to be a witness to things secular and divine, irrespective of personal consequences. There is also a great honesty in the book, even if it is incomplete about the natural history of his break and conversion. Above all, one is moved by the magnificent courage of this stubborn and sensitive man, who refused to die to please Stalin, who built a new life, threw it away to atone for his past, and found it again. May it inspire others who until now have feared the wolf-pack of the anti-anti-Communists to come forward to testify to the truth not only for the sake of their own country but for the sake of their fellow men everywhere.

On another level, one senses that Chambers has always been a man of feeling, always more interested in salvation of one kind or another than in disciplined thought. The result is an intellectual impatience, a hunger for absolutes, a failure of intelligence concealed in a surge of rapture or in a total commitment to action which requires a basis in irrational belief to sustain and renew itself. From the mysteries of dialectical materialism to the mysteries of dialectical theology is no great leap.

The American experience itself is after all the best answer to Chambers. For its secular humanism has developed gradually through grudging tolerance of religious differences to positive respect for all religious beliefs or disbeliefs. No longer is any man's spiritual freedom threatened with the doctrinal either-ors of fanatical sectarianism. It is not unlikely that the same humanistic spirit may be the best defense on a world scale against the Communist crusade because it can unite all human beings who, despite their religious differences about first and last things, value truth, justice, kindness, and freedom among men. For these values are justified both intrinsically and by their consequences, not by their alleged presuppositions.

Chambers's book will be widely read and deservedly so. That is why it seems to me all the more necessary to conclude by saying that in the war for human freedom the twice-born life of Whittaker Chambers is a tragic casualty. Instructive to the last about the mortal threat of the Communist movement, for which we should be deeply grateful to him, it does not offer us an intelligent guide to victory or even survival.

21

The Rationale of a Non-Partisan Welfare State

I am sure that many of you are surprised to find me on this program. I must confess to some surprise myself. I accepted this engagement with considerable reluctance, but finally viewed it as a challenge to my vocation as a philosopher and to my interest in social philosophy. I am profoundly ignorant of the intricacies of your subject: "The Health and Medical Care Issues of Our Time." In a sense, I am the only genuine layman at this conference. Those panelists who referred to themselves as laymen have revealed by their remarks that they are as competent in the affairs discussed as the professional physicians. They have given a large part of a lifetime of study to the details of medical care. It is true that I have devoted a few weeks to an intensive study of the papers that were submitted, and I have listened attentively to every word which has been uttered at this Symposium. I think I have learned something but not enough to lose my amateur standing. I remain a philosopher, an ignorant man in quest of truth. Ah, but you have already been warned against philosophy. Although in his flattering introductory remarks, Mr. Larson referred to what I am going to say as climaxing your proceedings, I fear very much that you will regard it as anticlimactic, and that when I get through, you will echo one of the panelists in saying, "That's just a lot of—philosophy!"

In extenuation of my role as a philosopher, however, I should like to plead that the kind of philosophy I am going to profess at this conference is no esoteric doctrine, but expresses a concern and activity to which every man is committed when he is a reflective human being. In a sense, all of you are philosophers when you grapple with basic issues of policy. The differences between you and me is that I know when I am philosophizing and am, therefore, careful about the philosophy I uphold, while most of you are committed to a philosophy without being aware of it. Even when you

---

Group Health Insurance Inc.: "The Health Cure Issues of the 1960s. A National Symposium Oct. 2, 3, 4, 1961," New York, 1963.

dismiss philosophy as a form of consolation, and claim that the locus of important problems is to be found only in economics, that's expressing a philosophy, too, indeed, a definite philosophy. Every time one takes a position on any large issue which has consequences that affect other human beings, one is taking a philosophical position. When one adopts a commitment to a large point of view which affects others besides oneself, one is a philosopher. This is sometimes true even of the man who claims to be neutral about important issues. In many situations, a person will say, "Well, I'm not taking any sides, I'm neutral on this issue, count me out." But if the problem or issue is momentous, and the consequences of being neutral have a bearing on how it is going to be decided, then he is taking a position, just as much as the person who, upbraided for the state of municipal affairs in his community, says, "Why blame me; I take no sides on the matter. I don't even vote!" There is a difference between suspending judgment in order to get more evidence and refusing to make a judgment on an important ethical or professional issue no matter what the evidence shows. What is true in foreign policy is sometimes true in professional policy—the garb of neutrality is a transparent commitment to the established and customary, or a cloak of naked self-interest.

I am not only a philosopher but a pragmatic philosopher and although you have been warned about pragmatism—one of the panelists spoke of "a pragmatic way of running away from problems"—you will find that of all philosophic approaches, the pragmatic approach is the one which grapples with problems and which tests all grandiose abstractions by their relevance to the problems which are the starting point of fruitful inquiry.

And this brings me to some of my composite impressions of the Symposium. Thinking, as you know, is impossible without words, but words often get in the way of our thinking. Again and again in the course of the discussions during the last two days on and off the podium, I felt that at crucial points where serious problems and purported solutions were about to be considered, problems of the first importance not merely to physicians but to the general public, when words like "free enterprise," "planning," "socialism," "individualism," "government control," were introduced they seemed to stop further inquiry at that point. They functioned as terrifying abstractions and sometimes set in train mechanical responses. The word, "control," for example, I found very interesting. Mr. Larson referred to Aneurin Bevins's famous contention that once you begin to charge even a nominal fee for certain medical services under an insurance plan, then you will not stop until you bring down in ruin the whole structure of socialized medicine. These Cassandra warnings turned out to be absurd. But something of the same kind of thinking seemed to me to be in evidence in what I have read, in what I have heard in conversation with many of the participants, and in the dark intimations of some of the panelists.

When a word like "control" is introduced and especially when it is conjoined with the term "government" the standard objection rises almost automatically. Once you introduce any government control, in the end the government will move in to determine or dictate the very content of medicine. I call this the argument of "the slippery slope"—once you begin, where will you stop? The answer to a question of that sort is: "You stop where your intelligence tells you to stop, and an intelligent decision proceeds from case to case, from problem to problem." I actually read a letter in *The New York Times* a few months ago protesting against the fluoridation of water on the ground that once we begin to introduce poisonous chemicals into drinking water, who knows where we'll stop? Presumably the writer feared we might end up adding potassium cyanide. Of course there may be legitimate objections to fluoridation because of the retention of fluorides in the body, but that is quite a different kind of argument. The other kind of an argument seems to me to characterize what one might call the "unpragmatic mind."

Or, take another thought-stopping phrase, "free enterprise," which, I gather from my reading, is a recurrent slogan in medical literature—especially official medical literature. For many years I have been genuinely puzzled by the meaning of the phrase "free enterprise" to those who use it. Certainly, the General Electric Company professes fervent belief in "free enterprise" and yet it has gotten into the news because it administered prices. Apparently it sensed no incompatibility between the practice and the profession of faith. The government, however, charged it with violating the canons of free enterprise. That seemed clear enough until the government turned around, after winning its action and said, "We will prosecute other suits against you unless you sign an agreement not to sell your products at an unreasonably low price in the open market." Now what kind of free enterprise is that? Where does it apply or where not? One begins to wonder whether those who talk about "free enterprise," whether in industry or government, really understand what they mean by it. I am not, of course, committing myself to the justice or injustice, the legality or illegality, of any particular action or decision by industry or government. I am only calling attention to the fact that a great many of our discussions are bedeviled by abstractions that have no specifiable content or concrete cash value in the way of specific consequences. I sometimes think that if we could forget terms like "socialism" and "capitalism"—keep them out of our discussions—that there would be a far greater likelihood of reaching agreement about the most desirable means of gratifying the objective needs of the situation.

Abstractions must also always be tied down to concrete proposals and policies in specific historical situations. Even a word like "freedom," despite its aura of warm emotive associations, perhaps because of them, is deceptive. We believe in freedom, of course, but when we understand what we believe we always take for granted a historical context, a particular context, and refer to a specific sort of freedom. No one can intelligently believe in freedom as such. For the very nature of any particular freedom, if it is to be fulfilled, requires that the freedom of individuals who wish to frustrate that freedom must itself be denied. The paradox of freedom is that you cannot universalize it as a rule of action. Every law which is passed by virtue of its legitimacy restricts someone's freedom. In the nature of the case, it must be so. Therefore, when we speak sensibly about "freedom" it is always a freedom to do something specific, or the freedom to adopt a certain kind of policy. The problem of what policies to adopt, of what medical policies to adopt, cannot be deduced from general considerations about freedom or expressions of allegiance to it.

Before turning to the question of policy decisions, I wish to say something about the character and level of the discussion. I was profoundly impressed by the plane on which it was conducted, its urbanity, its knowledgeability, and by the sense of high commitment to professional ideals by the participants. What puzzled me was the failure to grapple directly with fundamental problems and proposals which have agitated the public mind and produced something like a crisis of confidence in medicine. This was touched upon in this afternoon's panel but not adequately explored. Forgive me for saying so but I would be lacking in candor if I were silent about it. There seemed to me to be a kind of genteel timidity in facing alternatives, a failure, for example, to meet the challenge of the proponents of the different varieties of "socialized medicine," or even to state the challenge, a reluctance to consider the patterns of medical practice in other countries and to make objective comparative evaluations. I sensed that there were certain "sacred cows" to which even this group of emancipated physicians felt that they had to pay deference. I may be mistaken in this impression, but often when I hoped that the discussion would go deeper and further into these moot themes, it was diverted to something else.

How are we to judge the wisdom and adequacy of policies? It seems to me obvious that no intelligent consideration of policy is possible without reference to the facts in the case. Any acceptable policy must be relevant to or reponsible to the facts. And certainly, in these two days we have had a rich feast of facts and figures, trends and forecasts set before us without eliciting any major challenge to their pertinence and validity. Although there was some disagreement about the relative effectiveness of certain types of group medical practice and the relative value of different emphasis in the curricula of medical schools, the enormously impressive facts about unmet medical needs, the acute shortages in plant and personnel of hospitals and schools and nursing homes as well as of practicing physicians were not contested. Despite the record of remarkable medical triumphs, a very bleak picture of the future was presented and, by and large, accepted for the prospects of adequate medical care in light of our increasing medical knowledge and skills.

Now, why is it that despite this impressive agreement concerning the facts, no comparable consensus was established concerning policies to cope with them? The answer is obvious—knowledge of relevant fact is a necessary but not a sufficient condition for agreement on policy. By *themselves* the facts are not decisive. For no aggregate of facts can determine a policy without reference to some guiding social values—to some basic social philosophy, if you will pardon the expression—which determines the significance of these facts for action. Implicit in your discussion were certain values which must be brought to the surface so that we can see them more clearly, and see what they imply in the light of the agreed facts. The task is complicated because we will find, not one value, but a cluster of values to which you are committed, some of which conflict. This is an old story. We are not looking for the good but the *better* and the better is found not when we have a choice between the good and the bad—this defines no choice—but when we are choosing between the good and the good.

What I propose to do is to focus on these values, on some of the difficulties which your commitment to them creates, and on the choices which face you. I shall raise certain questions which may require redefining your commitment.

Your concern with human need in its most universal and imperious form, and the way you spoke of it, indicates that you believe that values, and especially moral values, are essentially related to basic felt needs, and to their relief or gratification. More concretely, you seem to be prepared to accept, partly on the basis of your professional commitment, partly on the basis of your implicit social philosophy, the far-reaching proposition that all human beings have a right, rooted in need, not only to certain minimum standards of food, clothing, shelter, and education but to the best available standards of health and medical treatment which insures it. This is not a self-evident proposition. It can and has been disputed. But it is a tremendously important proposition because of the sweep of its implications.

The minimum standards of need, with respect to food, shelter, and allied goods and services are not fixed. They are historically variable. But they are at a relatively low rate and may be revised in periods of scarcity. But the standard of accepted medical need is a continuous function of our medical knowledge. It is always progressing and in recent times spectacularly. Many of the things said in the last two days have made this dramatically clear. The great paradox of medicine is that its triumphs create additional needs. I do not mean merely that by increasing the life span, you increase the numbers of those who will need additional and progressively more costly treatment. I mean that at any stage, no one resigns himself to the evils to which the flesh is heir, if he becomes aware that they are remediable. Humans who want a long life, want a healthy life, but not one on a mattress grave. The very desire for immortality—as the classical fable about the goddess Juno and her earth-born lover so profoundly suggests—is not a desire for unending life but for eternal health. Medicine, of course, cannot ever give it, but if it could, every human being denied or deprived of it would be convinced that he was not receiving adequate medical care.

As I understand what you have been saying, whether or not a patient is receiving adequate medical care is not a matter of his subjective judgment. The standard of what constitutes adequate medical care is variable, dependent upon the discovery of new knowledge and emergence of new skills, but it is objective. It doesn't depend *merely* on how or what the patient feels or thinks. A man may feel perfectly content with a kind of treatment which you may professionally judge as outrageous; and he may be dissatisfied despite the fact that the best treatment has been lavished upon him with the appropriate tender and loving care. To the extent that medicine as a theoretical discipline and practical art is scientific, the question whether a community is receiving adequate medical care cannot be decided by popular feeling of consciousness—something which is not without considerable significance—but by the disinterested judgment of the medical profession itself. And to a layman like myself, who has not kept abreast with modern medicine, one of the most striking things which has been apparent from the data presented and accepted at this conference is that the medical profession itself is convinced that in the light of the technological possibilities of modern medicine on the whole, the people of the United States are not getting adequate comprehensive medical care.

I am particularly concerned with the objective validity of that judgment which is reinforced by the evidence that millions of people have no form of medical insurance, of the limited nature of most types of medical insurance and of what surveys show concerning the presence of unsuspected conditions requiring medical treatment among groups that have not had the benefit of diagnostic and preventive services. I do not believe that this conclusion is a consequence of the semantic manipulation of the concept of disease. In passing, may I mention that I was somewhat troubled by the suggestion of one of the panelists that health should be defined "not in terms of the absence of disease but the presence of physical, mental, and social well-being." The notion of "well-being," especially "social well-being," seems to me too subjective. I had thought that there are even some physical ailments which a person might have, at least in their early stages, without it affecting his "well-being." And not only ordinary but medical language refers to individuals as "healthy" who may not enjoy "social well-being." No matter how one defines disease, one must have some operational objective criteria for determining its presence or absence. Without them it is impossible to make responsible judgments about the inadequacy or adequacy of medical care.

I return now to the key assumption that all members of the community have a right to adequate medical care, broadly understood as including remedial and preventive treatment of disease. Suppose one were to deny the claim to such a right. How would we justify it? After all the claim that all human beings have a right to adequate medical care is relatively modern. Some religious traditions of the past have assumed it on the ground that we are all members of one another's body or all children of God. But it is only within the last generation, so to speak, that the human right to health and medical care has been introduced into the Bill of Rights which have taken the United Nations Declaration of Human Rights as a paradigm. Not everyone who is silent about this right or who does not contest it really accepts it. And one of the ways of making individuals articulate who really oppose this right is to phrase it in such a way that a vested interest is affected. We can restate this right to bring out the logic of the commitment. For what this right means is that all human beings have a right to adequate medical care *independently of their ability to pay for it.* Put this way, it is challenged—sometimes directly, sometimes indirectly. In discussion and conversation, as well as in the literature of this question, I have often heard individuals, physicians among others, ask: "Why should we use tax money to provide everyone with medical or health insurance?" The whole notion seems to fall in the general area of "the vaguely un-American ideas" to which Mr. Larson earlier referred. It is ruled out of court with pious and intense indignation by those who make a fetish of the abstraction "free enterprise."

Let us leave the large and vague abstractions aside. How does one resolve such fundamental differences in value judgment? If it is not done by fiat or authority, by physical force or psychological conditioning, which is another kind of force—if it is not done by these irrational methods, then the only way we can negotiate our differences is to find or create a shared interest, a shared point of view, a shared commitment or agreement which offers a principle that can be extended into the area of difference. Now I believe we can discover a commitment or assumption on the part of those who are prepared to question the right of all human beings to adequate medical care from which we can derive this right and make it more acceptable to them. Even those who conceive the function of the government to be merely that of an umpire establishing and enforcing rules of the road for free social intercourse—and I know few who still hold to this view consistently!—will grant that all members of the community have a right to protection of life against physical violence independently of their capacity to pay for it. The very recognition of the necessity of police power, without which no government can function, seems to imply that we recognize every citizen's right to life against physical violence whether he is rich or poor, irrespective of his social status and his tax status. The man who pays the most taxes doesn't necessarily get the most or best police protection. Nor would he be exempt from taxation if he were willing to forego police protection. It is no more possible to strike an equation between the social right to protection and ability to pay than between the right to a basic education, or the right to use the public roads and the ability to pay. We see no injustice in taxing a bachelor for the public education of his neighbor's children or levying taxes for the upkeep of motor highways on those who own no cars.

It seems to me a short step from the recognition that all citizens have a right to protection against the human agents who threaten their existence or survival to the acceptance of their right to protection against the natural, nonhuman agents which threaten their health and ultimately their life. No more in the first case than in the second does it seem just or fair to expect a human being to pauperize himself before he can legitimately expect adequate protection. There are certain differences in the two cases but they are not ethically central. When we speak of the right to adequate medical care we must qualify it with reference to the *availability* of social resources, since the first right—the right to security of person against violence—has an obvious priority. But *if* a society could afford adequate medical care for all its citizens, without sacrificing things that are more precious or immediately pressing than health, I can see no important difference.

I am confident that when we examine our attitudes in related situations we will discover that our commitments are compatible with the sense of general obligation to do what we can for everyone's health. Even our penal institutions assume that if a human being has not forfeited his life by some capital crime, he has a certain right to the preservation of his health and society a corresponding obligation to provide medical care. The costs of the maintenance of the health of prisoners is a charge upon the community. And when we reflect upon the right to health or medical care, we also discover that it enjoys a special status which marks it off from some other classes of rights. Rights to many things depend upon certain achievements or talents. Rewards, preferments and promotions, even opportunities for special study, are distributed according to merit. But I have never found anyone prepared to argue that the right to health is or should be a function of worth—any kind of worth, moral, financial, or creative. It seems to be acknowledged as a right which belongs to all human beings touched with mortality.

From these considerations alone nothing follows of a specific nature concerning how medical services are to be organized and distributed to the public. It is perfectly possible to acknowledge that everybody has a right to adequate medical care independently of means, and still agree as to how this can be done most effectively. The wisdom of the pragmatic approach is its recognition of the possibility of pluralistic solutions and its willingness to explore them. It may even grant, in virtue of our traditions, that *if* the medical needs of the population can be adequately met by voluntary forms of group insurance and group practice or even by a sufficient number of sufficiently well-trained and equipped solo medical practitioners, then despite the costs of duplication and the chaos of overlapping plans, it would be preferable to introducing the government into the picture. But—and this is the point of marrying the moral principle to the pragmatic approach—if the private and voluntary agencies are unable to cope with existing need, then we should not, because of some semantic fetish or negative tropism to words, rule out the alternative of government intervention. Indeed, if the right to adequate medical treatment is sincerely accepted as part of the modern Bill of Rights, it is hard to see how, in the face of the lacks and failures of existing medical practices, how on moral grounds one can oppose such intervention. I am woefully ignorant of the history of American medicine, and I warned the program committees which invited me of that fact. I was startled to learn that leading medical organizations in their official capacities have automatically resisted the attempts made by governments, national and local, to supply or subsidize objectively needed medical care which private practice in all its varieties has failed to provide. If this be so, then the most urgent issue before the medical profession is not a technical one of medicine but an issue in social philosophy in its broadest sense.

There was another consideration which appeared on the periphery of this discussion as something presupposed which I found a little disturbing in relation to the universal right to adequate medical care. It flashed into focus for a moment in the course of the paper Dr. Fox delivered at the luncheon meeting yesterday. He quoted, with obvious disapproval I was happy to note, some leading medical practitioner who said that the profession of medicine was moving into an epoch or era in which it had to come to terms with business and reorient itself with an eye to medicine as a modern business enterprise—or words to that effect. This, I confess, puzzles me. I trust I am not betraying my naïveté about both business and medicine when I say that the juxtaposition of the devices and incentives of business with the traditions and high responsibilities of the profession of medicine is almost as extraneous as coupling business with the ministry or the foreign and civil service. The notion of the business enterprise is such that it must be dominated by considerations of the ledger. How can it be otherwise? A banker can be philanthropic: but his bank cannot without betraying *its* business trust or the business interests of its stockholders. If a person sets up a proprietary hospital or home for the aged as a business enterprise in expectation of making a profit, *he* can legitimately say, using the colloquialism, that he is not in business for *his* health. We can legitimately suspect and sometimes say that neither is he in business for the health of his patients, if a high return on capital investment was his primary goal.

Now I do not mean to suggest for a moment that physicians are not entitled to appropriate economic returns or that they need be uneasy over the fact that they thrive on others' misfortunes. The misfortunes of others would not be abated by a jot or tittle if physicians were deprived of their economic security. Renan once referred to the life of a scholar as a life pledged to genteel poverty. But those were days in which the ideal of the scholar was of a celibate or at any rate of one unwed. No more than the scholar today has the physician the desire or the right to doom his wife and children to poverty. The same charter of social and personal rights by which we extend adequate medical care to all justify him in his expectations of an adequate social and economic return. But because physicians must be properly paid for their services, it does not follow that medicine must be considered as a business. Whatever they are paid, the relevant question here is whether this should depend upon the way the market operates and its vicissitudes or upon some assessment of the place, value, and aspirations of his profession in the community. Any man who has ventured into medicine to make a fortune is in the wrong profession. What I should have liked to have heard is more detailed consideration of viable alternative plans which would make it possible for the physician to pursue his professional work liberated from the burden of economic problems. When Mr. Larson spoke of the possibility of comprehensive insurance for all members of the population, I expected someone to consider and discuss the possibility that some such plan could guarantee physicians a more than "a living wage" and make it unlikely that any medical decision concerning treatment would be taken except on strictly medical grounds.

Particularly appalling to a layman is the obvious disparity between anticipated medical needs and the available resources, not only with respect to the number of practitioners of medicine to the general population but with respect to the brick and mortar provision for hospitals and medical schools, and with respect to their staffing all along the line. Few laymen are aware of the alarming figures and trends until you, the professionals, point them out. *Their* natural reaction is to invite the government in to meet these needs by underwriting costs and by the necessary controls. As a layman, I ask: "If the government doesn't do this, who will?" And I expect *you,* the professional physicians, who fear the menacing shadow of the government to tell me, now that private philanthropy is drying up, about *alternative* ways of establishing new hospitals, new medical schools, new homes for the aged, larger and better groups of students and teachers. You sounded the alarm and cried havoc about the future but I heard few new, positive proposals as to how to raise the colossal costs of even a partial program without appealing to the government in a sort of shamefaced way. Voluntary group insurance plans which also provide preventive medicine and extended care to the aging population cannot operate on a purely actuarial basis. They need subsidy and support. Where is it to come from—if not from the government? Why does this reference to governmental or state action, even by indirection, generate discomfort and embarrassment?

It seems to me that those who are doctrinaire about the state and see in its controls the beginning of a totalitarian state system are as deluded about the nature of the state today as the orthodox Marxists whom they rightfully see as their arch foes. According to orthodox Marxism, the state more or less acts as an executive committee of the dominant economic class which is always the ruling class. There was some truth to the doctrine in the nineteenth century when suffrage was restricted by property qualifications and large sections of the working population were either disenfranchised or had little influence in the political process. Since the emergence of the welfare state, however, most workers, especially in England and the United States, have refused to buy this view. Their own experience has convinced them that the state or government is not inherently hostile, that public policy can reflect public opinion as determined by "the give and take and learn" of the democratic process. The state is no longer "them" but "us" as much as anyone. This distrust of the state now seems to have become the legacy of groups who believe that its function is to blindly erode all vested economic interest, including vested medical interest. Just as much as the Marxists, they deny in an *a priori* way that public welfare is a meaningful concept which emerges from the inescapable conflict of economic interests. Without some conception of public welfare, social and political life is no more than an exemplification of the Hobbesian war of all against all. In a genuine democracy the state must serve as the organ which administers the public welfare of the common good. In most situations in which we legitimately deplore state action, the cure is not no state action but better and more intelligently planned state action.

There is another source of fear or distrust of government. The government is associated with the inertia, the inefficiency, the mechanical administration of rules which we associate with bureaucracy. The term bureaucracy is another word that all too often functions as a substitute for thought. A bureaucrat is an administrator. We call him a bureaucrat when he is a bad administrator. Why, then, does it follow that bureaucracy is necessarily involved in government? Do we not often speak, and justly, of bureaucracy in universities, in large corporations and trade unions, even in professional organizations as well as other associations? The evils of bureaucracy are usually a consequence of size and not of administration *per se*. Problems of bureaucracy result from the failure to perform specific functions properly at the point of consumer impact or experience. These failures are challenges not to the existence of organization but to the lack of intelligence in programming, in defining goals, and checking performance. To be sure, we must pay a price for organization just as much as we pay a price for a good traffic system that curbs our freedom of individual action. But think of the price we should have to pay if there was no traffic system. Let us have done, then, with fear of government plans as such. If we have better plans let us present them. But some plans we must have—because of the mounting needs and the potential human agony which will result if these needs are unmet.

On some of the peripheral problems you have discussed, I can speak with a little more authority. But here, too, although I have no solutions, I may be able to illumine their problems in the light of some general considerations. We have heard laments that in medical schools improper relative emphasis has been placed upon research and clinical teaching. This is an old problem and not restricted to medical schools. For many years teaching has been at a discount in liberal arts colleges and universities. The operating maxim has been, "Publish or perish." To this day, the worst teaching in the country in the general educational system occurs on the college level because of the assumption that anyone who knows a subject expertly can teach it well. It is not only in medical schools that the man who is primarily an effective teacher often feels that he lacks status and recognition in the republic of arts and science. Now I should have thought that teaching in medical schools is much more important than teaching in ordinary schools, for the same generic reason that a mistaken medical diagnosis is so much graver than a mistaken or confused historical or literary analysis. At the same time I do not think that there will ever be time when the researchers and discoverers do not regard themselves as more important than teachers. They are on the frontiers of knowledge. There is the excitement of the quest, the honors that beckon, the reflection that what the researcher discovers others will teach. In all professions there are hierarchies—perhaps in the medical profession, too. Where imagination is absent, an orthopedic surgeon may take a patronizing attitude toward an internist. Recoveries among his patients are dramatic, he knows what's wrong and what to do about it whereas the internist, who may be keeping a chronically ill patient alive and functioning by remarkable care and much greater intellection than the surgeon, can't point to anything comparably impressive. He can't always be sure that the patient will not do as well without his minstrations.

Problems of this kind are not soluble by general rules but only *per ambulandum.* And not always then. We must recognize the possibility that we have to live with problems that may not be soluble and that we have to make them bearable. In specific situations the actual pedagogical needs of students in medical schools should have institutional priority, which means that research should not be prosecuted to a point where medical instruction falls below par. So much I think even most researchers will grant and accept some teaching assignments on the basis of their professional responsibility.

Whether more than this can be done depends upon the development of a kind of mutuality of esteem for all members of a profession who are doing their particular work well. Every human being has a desire to count. He wants to feel that his work makes a difference, that someone is aware or cares about what he is doing and how he is doing it. A great many professional, psychological, and social evils result when the person asks himself the question: "Who cares?" and has to answer, "No one." Of course the ideal person works because of the intrinsic rewards of his work, but most of us are not ideal and most people's work—here physicians are fortunate—is not intrinsically justifying and interesting. It is difficult for this mutuality of esteem to operate not only in relation to those who are higher than we are in the hierarchy of status—that we can see—but to those who are lower. It is unlikely to flourish in the academy, or in any particular profession, unless it is nurtured in the general community, too, which means ultimately in the values we educate for. But this opens a door I have no time to go through.

A related question: "Why don't enough students—why don't enough good students—apply for admission to medical schools?" Well, why not ask them, as I have? The answer or answers should not be particularly difficult to discover. For whatever it is worth, let me tell you of my experience. I have been teaching for nigh on thirty-five years, and have observed and helped influence generations of students make their vocational choices. When I have questioned the recent generations about their professional interests and choices, and pointedly inquired of those I thought qualified for medicine why they passed it up, I have received several different answers. The one I heard most often is that the preliminary grind is too prolonged. Interestingly enough I do not hear this complaint from those who do go on into medicine. What somone observed earlier today seems true. Once students are in medical school, they become so involved and absorbed in their work that they do not complain about its prolonged and onerous character. But it is the response given by so many who do not elect medicine which should be your special concern. All the more so because the temptations and rewards from other fields competing for their interest is so strong. It goes without saying that under current conditions medical students, interns, and residents should be provided with a decent wage. Since the budgets of the universities can't afford it, and the government seems willing to underwrite it, I am at a loss to understand medical opposition to such measures except in terms of an anachronistic response to what the government does. If there is a fear that the modest sums involved will attract those who are looking merely for safe berths, certain intellectual and psychological tests can weed them out. At any rate it will weaken the rationalizations of physicians who justify their rapacity in private practice by the memory of the lean years of deprivation.

My own feeling is that the failure to recruit the best types of students for medicine reflects the failure of our teaching to cultivate the powers of imagination. These are not the same as the powers of thinking. It is what brings thinking into play, and provides the springs of thoughtful action. I have forgotten who it was that observed that if we were all seated at the same table, no one would go hungry. In so many of our predicaments in life, we actually are seated at the same table but are unaware of it. The cultivation of the imagination is necessary to bring the faces that we can't see into the focus of our vision. It is necessary to make us alive to possibilities that once grasped stir the emotions and give motor force to resolution. I have the feeling that students today have no strong imaginative vision of medicine as a vocation and that representatives of the medical profession are not sufficiently in touch with vocational advisors in the colleges in an effort to restore the image that medicine once had in the minds of youth. Not every gifted student can be, should be, or even try to be, a physician but the pity of it is that so many who seem specially gifted for medicine are unaware of it.

I heard someone murmur when the absence of students was being deplored: "What would the medical schools do with them if they had more students?" One needs medical schools to accommodate medical students and there is an acute shortage of medical schools. But I was thinking of quality rather than quantity. I recognize that all these problems are interrelated. One must begin somewhere. Perhaps if more medical schools were built, the problems of qualitative recruiting would be faced more directly.

Among the things I learned at this symposium was the importance of the ancillary services in medicine, and how much effective medical care is dependent upon the daily ministrations of nurses, hospital aides, and hosts of others who are not in the foreground of the stereotyped picture. I have only one suggestion to make which grows out of a very important experience in my life. When I was in Asia a few years ago, I made the acquaintance of a number of medical missionaries. As you know, I am a humanist and secularist, but these medical missionaries who were more interested in helping human beings and relieving their distress than in converting them to doctrinal creed or theology were the most impressive men and women I had ever encountered. They were performing services for human beings whose communities had rejected them, because of the nature of their disease, or ignored them because of the depths of poverty in which so many lived. They cured and comforted the sick, consoled the dying, and washed the dead. Their devotion to others was gradually having an effect upon the attitudes of the communities which had been traditionally indifferent. The total and selfless nature of their dedication was, I confess, a challenge to my own view to find a common faith in humanity a basis for similar service in such circumstances. This is a private matter. But it certainly brought home to me how powerful among the sources and motivations which lead people to medicine and nursing is the religious impulse. Whether the religious experience is nurtured by the belief that all human beings are children of God or by the humanist view that they have a common origin, lot, end, and ethical ideal, it should not be difficult to draw upon religious groups for ancillary medical services in greater measure than ever before in these days of emergency. No matter how God is defined, who serves men in their pain and helplessness serves God, too.

I should like to close on two points that have bearing of great importance on the theme of the symposium. Both are in a sense educational. Both are largely the responsibility of the profession. The first concerns the cost of medical care to the public. Since it is true, as one of the participants said, that health in its broadest reach is the only indispensable asset human beings have, the relevant economic question is not how much money will a good health program cost but whether the money available is being spent wisely, effectively, and with minimum waste. Whether we appeal to the community or to the specific individuals, we can teach them that the tremendous social resources running into millions upon millions of dollars which goes into gadgetry, into advertising the nonexistent advantages of one cigarette, or tooth paste, or airline over another, and similar excrescences of an affluent society, can be diverted to better uses. If the medical profession makes an organized effort to teach the people of the United States what they might have in the way of medical care and educates them to appreciate its significance, support for the necessary expansion of services will become available from both public and private sources.

My second point concerns the changing image of the physician in our time. The popular literature concerning medicine in our periodicals is largely a literature of protest. In the light of that literature, this assembled group of physicians is unrecognizable. The public, despite its discontents, must be brought to a greater awareness of the significance of the vocation, or better still, "the calling," of a physician. Until the profession recaptures that ideal for itself and keeps it always before it, the public will tend to regard it as just another kind of business or job, and measure it with the same skeptical criteria as it does any other business or job in which individuals profess their allegiance to the public service in order to enhance their private profit. What is the difference between a calling or a vocation and a mere job? A calling, it seems to me, is a mode of activity in which the individual is able to fulfill himself, in which making a living and living one's life are not opposed to each other, but are one and the same. Unfortunately, for most human beings in our communities today, earning one's living and living one's life are two separate things. Teachers, physicians, and a small number of other professional and skilled craftsmen groups are enjoying a privilege which is all too rare in our machine economy—one which is a far more reliable assurance of happiness than the money they earn and bank. There are two great components of happiness which you can discover for yourself when you make a survey of the happiest people you know. They are satisfactory personal relations—fulfillment in love and marriage and children—and fulfillment in some task or profession which makes a call upon their creative capacities, their insight, their ability to solve recurrent problems. As things are organized today, most individuals find happiness only in their personal life and in the lives of their children. That is why when their children no longer need them and when they are unprepared for a life of creative leisure, their existence seems empty and boring. They have no calling or vocation to serve as a significiant center around which to organize their experiences, no road to self-fulfillment.

The unending tasks of the physician provide him with a series of constant challenges in which defeats may be as significant as triumphs. And his calling, more than most, and like very few others, enables him to fulfill himself as he bestows a boon upon his fellow men. This may not be an avenue to blessedness but it is a path of life on which one can find that rarest of things, serenity in action. It is this conception of medicine as a calling, and not so much the emphasis upon the elite status, entrepreneurial independence, financial returns and security—although it does not exclude them—which should attract the intellectually gifted and the emotionally qualified students. To do this the profession itself must be convinced of it. It must also be jealously concerned about the distorted public image which emerges when any large segment of the population feels that the interests of the medical profession stand in the way of their finding fulfillment.

I do not know whether I can successfully accept Mr. Larson's challenge to show how our deliberations and commitments are relevant to our democratic faith. Only if we conceive of democracy as more than a political system can their relevance be established. We do so conceive of it whenever we condemn on democratic grounds a system of political democracy, whenever we condemn its exclusions, its abuses, its failure to act in the proper spirit. We sometimes say that a democracy is not functioning in a proper democratic way even when it adopts a measure by a majority vote, when it crushes a minority by legalistic methods. When we speak that way what do we mean by it? I think we mean that democracy is a way of life as well as a political system. But is that not another large and empty phrase—"the democratic way of life?" No, it expresses a basic social philosophy—an ethical commitment to a society in which there is an equality of concern for all human beings—not only men, not only white, not only Christian—all human beings to fulfill themselves as persons, and to enjoy a rich and significant experience. No one who rejects this principle will staunchly defend for long a political democracy. An equality of concern for all individuals to achieve their full cultural and spiritual growth requires the continual revision and improvement of the social institutions and practices which transform members of an animal species into self-governing citizens. To be denied or deprived of adequate medical care for any reason at all is to be denied the possibility of entering into, experiencing, and enjoying our democratic heritage. Democracy as a political system and as a way of life involves much more, very much more, than the organization of adequate health services for the community. But without it, democracy is incomplete.

22

How Democratic Is America?

Howard Zinn

To give a sensible answer to the question "How democratic is America?" I find it necessary to make three clarifying preliminary statements. First, I want to define "democracy," not conclusively, but operationally, so we can know what we are arguing about, or at least what I am talking about. Second, I want to state what my criteria are for measuring the "how" in the question. And third, I think it necessary to issue a warning about how a certain source of bias (although not the only source) is likely to distort our judgments.

Our definition is crucial. This becomes clear if we note how relatively easy is the answer to our question when we define democracy as a set of formal institutions and let it go at that. If we describe as "democratic" a country that has a representative system of government, with universal suffrage, a bill of rights, and party competition for office, it becomes easy to answer the question "how" with the enthusiastic reply, "Very!" . . .

I propose a set of criteria for the description "democratic" which goes beyond formal political institutions, to the quality of life in the society (economic, social, psychological), beyond majority rule to a concern for minorities, and beyond national boundaries to a global view of what is meant by "the people," in that rough, but essentially correct view of democracy as "government of, by, and for the people."

Let me list these criteria quickly, because I will go on to discuss them in some detail later:

1. To what extent can various people in the society participate in those decisions which affect their lives: decisions in the political process and decisions in the economic structure?

From *Points of View,* edited by R. E. DiClerico and A. S. Hammond (Reading, Mass.: Addison-Wesley Publishing). Reprinted by permission of the author.

2. As a corollary of the above: do people have equal access to the information which they need to make important decisions?
3. Are the members of the society equally protected on matters of life and death—in the most literal sense of that phrase?
4. Is there equality before the law: police, courts, the judicial process—as well as equality *with* the law-enforcing institutions, so as to safeguard equally everyone's person, and his freedom from interference by others, and by the government?
5. Is there equality in the distribution of available resources: those economic goods necessary for health, life, recreation, leisure, growth?
6. Is there equal access to education, to knowledge and training, so as to enable persons in the society to live their lives as fully as possible, to enlarge their range of possibilities?
7. Is there freedom of expression on all matters, and equally for all, to communicate with other members of the society?
8. Is there freedom for individuality in private life, in sexual relations, family relations, the right of privacy?
9. To minimize regulation: do education and the culture in general foster a spirit of cooperation and amity to sustain the above conditions?
10. As a final safety feature: is there opportunity to protest, to disobey the laws, when the foregoing objectives are being lost—as a way of restoring them? . . .

Two historical facts support my enlarged definition of democracy. One is that the industrialized Western societies have outgrown the original notions which accompanied their early development: that constitutional and procedural tests sufficed for the "democracy" that overthrew the old order; that democracy was quite adequately fulfilled by the Bill of Rights in England at the time of the Glorious Revolution, the Constitution of the United States, and the Declaration of the Rights of Man in France. It came to be acknowledged that the rhetoric of these revolutions was not matched by their real achievements. In other words, the limitations of that "democracy" led to the reformist and radical movements that grew up in the West in the middle and late nineteenth century. The other historical note is that the new revolutions in our century, in Africa, Asia, Latin America, while rejecting either in whole or in part the earlier revolutions, profess a similar democratic aim, but with an even broader rhetoric. . . .

My second preliminary point is on standards. By this I mean that we can judge in several ways the fulfillment of these ten criteria I have listed. We can measure the present against the past, so that if we find that in 1988 we are doing better in these matters than we were doing in 1860 or 1910, the society will get a good grade for its "democracy." I would adjure such an approach because it supports complacency. With such a standard, Russians in 1910 could point with pride to how much progress they had made toward parliamentary democracy; as Russians in 1988 can point to their post-Stalin progress away from the gulag; as Americans could point in 1939 to how far they had come toward solving the problem of economic equality; as Americans in the South could point in 1950 to the progress of the southern Negro. Indeed, the American government gives military aid to brutal regimes in Latin America on the ground that a decrease in the murders by semiofficial death squads is a sign of progress.

Or, we could measure our democracy against other places in the world. Given the high incidence of tyranny in the world, polarization of wealth, and lack of freedom of expression, the United States, even with very serious defects, could declare itself successful. Again, the result is to let us all off easily; some of our most enthusiastic self-congratulation is based on such a standard.

On the other hand, we could measure our democracy against an ideal (even if admittedly unachievable) standard. I would argue for such an approach, because, in what may seem to some a paradox, the ideal standard is the pragmatic one; it affects what we *do*. To grade a student on the basis of an improvement over past performance is justifiable if the intention is to encourage someone discouraged about his ability. But if he is rather pompous about his superiority in relation to other students (and I suggest this is frequently true of Americans evaluating American "democracy"), and if in addition he is a medical student about to graduate into a world ridden with disease, it would be best to judge him by an ideal standard. That might spur him to an improvement fast enough to save lives. . . .

My third preliminary point is a caution based on the obvious fact that we make our appraisals through the prism of our own status in society. This is particularly important in assessing democracy, because if "democracy" refers to the condition of masses of people, and if we as the assessors belong to a number of elites, we will tend (and I am not declaring an inevitability, just warning of a tendency) to see the present situation in America more benignly than it deserves. To be more specific, if democracy requires a keen awareness of the condition of black people, of poor people, of young people, of that majority of the world who are not American—and we are white, prosperous, beyond draft age, and American—then we have a number of pressures tending to dull our sense of inequity. We are, if not doomed to err, likely to err on the side of complacency—and we should try to take this into account in making our judgments.

1. PARTICIPATION IN DECISIONS

We need to recognize, first, that whatever decisions are made politically are made by representatives of one sort or another: state legislators, congressmen, senators, and other elected officials, governors and presidents; also by those appointed by elected officials, like Supreme Court justices. These are important decisions, affecting our lives, liberties, and ability to pursue happiness. Congress and the president decide on the tax structure, which affects the distribution of resources. They decide how to spend the monies received; whether or not we go to war; who serves in the armed forces; what behavior is considered a crime; which crimes are prosecuted and which are not. They decide what limitations there should be on our travel, or on our right to speak freely. They decide on the availability of education and health services.

If representation by its very nature is undemocratic, as I would argue, this is an important fact for our evaluation. Representative government is *closer* to democracy than monarchy, and for this reason it has been hailed as one of the great political advances of modern times; yet, it is only a step in the direction of democracy, at its best. It has certain inherent flaws—pointed out by Rousseau in the eighteenth century, Victor Considerant in the nineteenth century, Robert Michels in the beginning of the twentieth century, Hannah Arendt in our own time. No representative can adequately represent another's needs; the representative tends to become a member of a special elite; he has privileges which weaken his sense of concern at others' grievances; the passions of the troubled lose force (as Madison noted in *The Federalist* 10) as they are filtered through the representative system; the elected official develops an expertise which tends toward its own perpetuation. Leaders develop what Michels called "a mutual insurance contract" against the rest of society. . . .

If only radicals pointed to the inadequacy of the political processes in the United States, we might be suspicious. But established political scientists of a moderate bent talk quite bluntly of the limitations of the voting system in the United States. Robert Dahl, in *A Preface to Democratic Theory,* drawing on the voting studies of American political scientists, concludes that "political activity, at least in the United States, is positively associated to a significant extent with such variables as income, socio-economic status, and education." He says:

> By their propensity for political passivity the poor and uneducated disfranchise themselves. . . . Since they also have less access than the wealthy to the organizational, financial, and propaganda resources that weigh so heavily in campaign, elections, legislative, and executive decisions, anything like equal control over government policy is triply barred to the members of Madison's unpropertied masses. They are barred by their relative greater inactivity, by their relatively

limited access to resources, and by Madison's nicely contrived system of constitutional checks.[1]

Dahl thinks that our society is essentially democratic, but this is because he expects very little. (His book was written in the 1950s, when lack of commotion in the society might well have persuaded him that no one else expected much more than he did.) Even if democracy were to be superficially defined as "majority rule," the United States would not fulfill that, according to Dahl, who says that "on matters of specific policy, the majority rarely rules."[2] After noting that "the election is the critical technique for insuring that governmental leaders will be relatively responsive to nonleaders," he goes on to say that "it is important to notice how little a national election tells us about the preferences of majorities. Strictly speaking, all an election reveals is the first preferences of some citizens among the candidates standing for office."[3] About 45 percent of the potential voters in national elections, and about 60 percent of the voters in local elections do not vote, and this cannot be attributed, Dahl says, simply to indifference. And if, as Dahl points out, "in no large nation state can elections tell us much about the preferences of majorities and minorities," this is "even more true of the interelection period." . . .

Dahl goes on to assert that the election process and interelection activity "are crucial processes for insuring that political leaders will be *somewhat* responsive to the preferences of *some* ordinary citizens."[4] I submit (the emphasized words are mine) that if an admirer of democracy in America can say no more than this, democracy is not doing very well.

Dahl tells us the election process is one of "two fundamental methods of social control which, operating together, make governmental leaders so responsive to nonleaders that the distinction between democracy and dictatorship still makes sense." Since his description of the election process leaves that dubious, let's look at his second requirement for distinguishing democracy: "The other method of social control is continuous political competition among individuals, parties, or both." What it comes down to is "not minority rule but minorities rule."[5]

If it turns out that this—like the election process—also has little democratic content, we will not be left with very much difference—by Dahl's own admission—between "dictatorship" and the "democracy" practiced in the United States. Indeed, there is much evidence on this: the lack of democracy within the major political parties, the vastly disproportionate influence of wealthy groups over poorer ones (what consumers' group in 1983 could match the $1 million spent by the Natural Gas Supply Association to lobby, in fifteen key congressional districts, for full control of natural gas prices?);[6] the unrepresentative nature of the major lobbies (the wealthy doctors speaking for all through the AMA, the wealthy farmers speaking for the poorer ones through the American Farm Bureau Federation, the most affluent trade unions speaking for all workers). All of this, and more, supports the idea of a "decline of American pluralism" that Henry Kariel has written about. What Dahl's democracy comes down to is "the steady appeasement of relatively small groups."[7] If these relatively small groups turn out to be the aircraft industry far more than the aged, the space industry far more than the poor, the Pentagon far more than the college youth—what is left of democracy?

Sometimes the elitism of decision-making is defended (by Dahl and by others) on the ground that the elite is enacting decisions passively supported by the mass, whose tolerance is proof of an underlying consensus in society. But Murray Levin's studies in *The Alienated Voter* indicate how much nonparticipation in elections is a result of hopelessness rather than approval. And Robert Wiebe, a historian at Northwestern University, talks of "consensus" becoming a "new stereotype." He approaches the question historically.

> Industrialization arrived so peacefully not because all Americans secretly shared the same values or implicitly willed its success but because its millions of bitter enemies lacked the mentality and the means to organize an effective counterattack.[8]

Wiebe's point is that the passivity of most Americans in the face of elitist decision-making has not been due to acquiescence but to the lack of resources for effective combat, as well as a gulf so wide between the haves and have-nots that there was no ground on which to dispute. Americans neither revolted violently nor reacted at the polls; instead they were subservient, or else worked out their hostilities in personal ways. . . .

Presidental nominations and elections are more democratic than monarchical rule or the procedures of totalitarian states, but they are far from some reasonable expectation of democracy. The two major parties have a monopoly of presidential power, taking turns in the White House. The candidates of minority parties don't have a chance. They do not have access to the financial backing of the major parties, and there is not the semblance of equal attention in the mass media; it is only the two major candidates who have free access to prime time on national television.

More important, both parties almost always agree on the fundamentals of domestic and foreign policy, despite the election-year rhetoric which attempts to find important differences. Both parties arranged for United States intervention in Vietnam in the 1950s and 1960s, and both, when public opinion changed, promised to get out (note the Humphrey-Nixon contest of 1968). In 1984, Democratic candidate Walter Mondale agreed with Republican candidate Ronald Reagan that the United States (which had ten thousand thermonuclear warheads) needed to continue increasing its arms budgets, although he asked for a smaller increase than the Republicans. Such a position left Mondale unable to promise representatives of the black community (where unemployment was over 20 percent) that he would spend even a few billion dollars for a jobs program. Meanwhile, Democrats and Republicans in Congress were agreeing on a $297 billion arms bill for the 1985 fiscal year.[9]

With all the inadequacies of the representative system, it does not even operate in the field of foreign policy. In exactly those decisions which are the most vital—matters of war and peace, life and death—power rests in the hands of the president and a small group of advisers. We don't notice this when wars seem to have a large degree of justification (as World war II); we begin to notice it when we find ourselves in the midst of a particularly pointless war.

I have been talking so far about democracy in the political process. But there is another serious weakness that I will only mention here, although it is of enormous importance: the powerlessness of the American to participate in economic decision-making, which affects his life at every moment. As a consumer, that is, as the person whom the economy is presumably intended to serve, he has virtually nothing to say about what is produced for him. The corporations make what is profitable; the advertising industry persuades him to buy what the corporations produce. He becomes the passive victim of the misallocation of resources, the production of dangerous commodities, the spoiling of his air, water, forests, beaches, cities.

2. ACCESS TO INFORMATION

Adequate information for the electorate is a precondition for any kind of action (whether electoral or demonstrative) to affect national policy. As for the voting process, Berelson, Lazarsfeld, and McPhee tell us (in their book, *Voting*) after extensive empirical research: "One persistent conclusion is that the public is not particularly well informed about the specific issues of the day." . . .

Furthermore, . . . there are certain issues which never even reach the public because they are decided behind the scenes. . . .

Consider the information available to voters on two major kinds of issues. One of them is the tax structure, so bewilderingly complex that the corporation, with its corps of accountants and financial experts, can prime itself for lobbying activities, while the average voter, hardly able to comprehend his own income tax, stands by helplessly as the president, the Office of Management and Budget, and the Congress decide the tax laws. The dominant influences are those of big business, which has the resources both to understand and to act.

Then there is foreign policy. The government leads the citizenry to believe it has special expertise which, if it could only be revealed, would support its position against critics. At the same time, it hides the very information which would reveal its position to be indefensible. The mendacity of the government on the Bay of Pigs operation, the secret operations of the CIA in Iran, Indonesia, Guatemala, and other places, the withholding of vital information about the Tonkin Gulf events are only a few examples of the way the average person becomes a victim of government deception.

When the United States invaded the tiny island of Grenada in the fall of 1983, no reporters were allowed to observe the invasion, and the American public had little opportunity to get independent verification of the reasons given by the government for the invasion. As a result, President Reagan could glibly tell the nation what even one of his own supporters, journalist George Will, admitted was a lie: that he was invading Grenada to protect the lives of American medical students on the island. He could also claim that documents found on the island indicated plans for a Cuban–Soviet takeover of Grenada; the documents showed no such thing.[10]

Furthermore, the distribution of information to the public is a function of power and wealth. The government itself can color the citizens' understanding of events by its control of news at the source: the presidential press conference, the "leak to the press," the White Papers, the teams of "truth experts" going around the country at the taxpayers' expense. As for private media, the large networks and mass-circulation magazines have the greatest access to the public mind. There is no "equal time" for critics of public policy. . . .

3. EQUAL PROTECTION

Let us go now from the procedural to the substantive, indeed to the *most* substantive of questions: the right of all the people to life itself. Here we find democracy in America tragically inadequate. The draft, which has been a part of American law since 1940 (when it passed by one vote) decides, in wartime, who lives and who dies. Not only Locke, one of the leading theorists of the democratic tradition, declared the ultimate right of any person to safeguard his own life when threatened by the government; Hobbes, often looked on as the foe of democratic thought, agreed. The draft violates this principle, because it compels young people to sacrifice their lives for any cause which the leaders of government deem just; further, it discriminates against the poor, the uneducated, the young.

It is in connection with this most basic of rights—life itself, the first and most important of those substantive ends which democratic participation is designed to safeguard—that I would assert the need for a global view of democracy. One can at least conceive of a democratic decision for martial sacrifice by those ready to make the sacrifice; a "democratic" war is thus a theoretical possibility. But that presumption of democracy becomes obviously false at the first shot because then *others* are affected who did not decide. . . . Nations making decisions to slaughter their own sons are at least theoretically subject to internal check. The victims on the other side fall without any such chance. For the United States today, this failure of democracy is total; we have the capacity to destroy the world without giving it a chance to murmur a dissent; we did, in fact, destroy a part of southest Asia on the basis of a unilateral decision made in Washington. There is no more pernicious manifestation of the lack of democracy in America than this single fact.

4. EQUALITY BEFORE THE LAW

Is there equality before the law? At every stage of the judicial process—facing the policeman, appearing in court, being freed on bond, being sentenced by the judge—the poor person is treated worse than the rich, the black treated worse than the white, the politically or personally odd character is treated worse than the orthodox. The details are given in the 1963 report of the Attorney General's Committee on Poverty and the Administration of Federal Criminal Justice. There a defendant's poverty is shown to affect his preliminary hearing, his right to bail, the quality of his counsel. The evidence is plentiful in the daily newspapers, which inform us that a Negro boy fleeing the scene of a two-dollar theft may be shot and killed by a pursuing policeman, while a wealthy man who goes to South America after a million-dollar swindle, even if apprehended, need never fear a scratch. The wealthy price-fixer for General Motors, who costs consumers millions, will get ninety days in jail; the burglar of a liquor store will get five years. A Negro youth, or a bearded white youth poorly dressed, has much more chance of being clubbed by a policeman on the street than a well-dressed white man, given the fact that both respond with equal tartness to a question. . . .

Aside from inequality among citizens, there is inequality between the citizen and his government, when they face one another in a court of law. Take the matter of counsel: the well-trained government prosecutor faces the indigent's court-appointed counsel. Four of my students did a study of the City Court of Boston several years ago. They sat in the court for weeks, taking notes, and found that the average time spent by court-appointed counsel with his client, before arguing the case at the bench, was seven minutes.

5. DISTRIBUTION OF RESOURCES

Democracy is devoid of meaning if it does not include equal access to the available resources of the society. In India, democracy might still mean poverty; in the United States, with a Gross National Product of $3 trillion a year, democracy should mean that every American, working a short work-week, has adequate food, clothing, shelter, health care, education for himself and his family—in short, the material resources necessary to enjoy life and freedom. Even if only 20 percent of the American population is desperately poor . . . in a country so rich, that is an inexcusable breach of the democratic principle. Even if there is a large, prosperous middle class, there is something grossly unfair in the wealthiest fifth of the population getting 40 percent of the nation's income, and the poorest fifth getting 5 percent (a ratio virtually unchanged from 1947 to 1980). . . .[11]

Whether you are rich or poor determines the most fundamental facts about your life: whether you are cold in the winter while trying to sleep, whether you suffocate in the summer; whether you live among vermin or rats; whether the smells around you all day are sweet or foul; whether you have adequate medical care; whether you have good teeth; whether you can send your children to college; whether you can go on vacation or have to take an extra job at night; whether you can afford a divorce, or an abortion, or a wife, or another child. . . .

6. ACCESS TO EDUCATION

In a highly industrialized society, education is a crucial determinant of wealth, political power, social status, leisure, and the ability to work in one's chosen field. Educational resources in our society are not equitably distributed. Among high-school graduates of the some IQ levels, a far higher percentage of the well-to-do go on to college than the poor.[12] A mediocre student with money can always go to college. A mediocre student without money may not be able to go, even to a state college, because he may have to work to support his family. Furthermore, the educational resources in the schools—equipment, teachers, etc.—are far superior in the wealthy suburbs than in the poor sections of the city, whether white or black.

7. FREEDOM OF EXPRESSION

Like money, freedom of expression is available to all in America, but in widely varying quantities. The First Amendment formally guarantees freedom of speech, press, assembly, and petition to all—but certain realities of wealth, power, and status stand in the way of the equal distribution of these rights. Anyone can stand on a street corner and talk to ten or a hundred people. But someone with the resources to buy loudspeaker equipment, go through the necessary red tape, and post a bond with the city may hold a meeting downtown and reach a thousand or five thousand people. A person or a corporation with $100,000 can buy time on television and reach 10 million people. A rich person simply has much more freedom of speech than a poor person. The government has much more freedom of expression than a private individual, because the president can command the airwaves when he wishes, and reach 60 million people in one night.

Freedom of the press also is guaranteed to all. But the student selling an underground newspaper on the street with a nude woman on the cover may be arrested by a policeman, while the airport newsstand selling *Playboy* and ten magazines like it will remain safe. Anyone with $10,000 can put out a newspaper to reach a few thousand people. Anyone with $10 million can buy a few newspapers that will reach a few million people. Anyone who is penniless had better have a loud voice; and then he might be arrested for disturbing the peace.

8. FREEDOM FOR INDIVIDUALITY

The right to live one's life, in privacy and freedom, in whatever way one wants, so long as others are not harmed, should be a sacred principle in a democracy. But there are hundreds of laws, varying from state to state, and sometimes joined by federal laws, which regulate the personal lives of people in this country: their marriages, their divorces, their sexual relations. Furthermore, both laws and court decisions protect policemen and the FBI in their use of secret devices which listen in on private conversations, or peer in on private conduct.

9. THE SPIRIT OF COOPERATION

The maintenance of those substantive elements of democracy which I have just sketched, if dependent on a pervasive network of coercion, would cancel out much of the benefit of that democracy. Democracy needs rather to be sustained by a spirit in society, the tone and the values of the culture. I am speaking of something as elusive as a mood, alongside something as hard as law, both of which would have to substitute cooperation tinged with friendly competition for the fierce combat of our business culture. I am speaking of the underlying drive that keeps people going in the society. So long as that drive is for money and power, with no ceiling on either, so long as ruthlessness is built into the rules of the game, democracy does not have a chance. If there is one crucial cause in the failure of American democracy—not the only one, of course, but a fundamental one—it is the drive for corporate profit, and the overwhelming influence of money in every aspect of our daily lives. That is the uncontrolled libido of our society from which the rape of democratic values necessarily follows.

The manifestations are diverse and endless: the Kefauver hearings on the drug industry in 1961 disclosed that the drive for profit in that industry has led to incredible overpricing of drugs for consumers (700 percent markup, for instance, for tablets to arthritic patients) as well as bodily harm resulting from "the fact that they market so many of their failures."

It was disclosed in 1979 that Johns-Manville, the nation's largest asbestos manufacturer, had deliberately withheld from its workers X-ray results which showed they were developing cancer.[13] The careless disposition of toxic wastes throughout the country and the repeated accidents at nuclear plants were testimony to the concern for corporate profit over human life.

If these were isolated cases, reported and then eliminated, they could be dismissed as unfortunate blemishes on an otherwise healthy social body. But the major allocations of resources in our society are made on the basis of money profit rather than social use. . . .

Recent news items buttress what I have said. The oil that polluted California's beautiful beaches in the 1960s . . . was produced by a system in which the oil companies' hunger for profit has far more weight than the ordinary person's need to swim in clean water. This is not to be attributed to Republicanism overriding the concern for the little fellow of the Democratic Party. Profit is master whichever party is in power; it was the liberal Secretary of the Interior Stewart Udall who allowed the dangerous drilling to go on. . . .

In 1984, the suit of several thousand veterans against the Dow Chemical Company, claiming that they and their families had suffered terrible illnesses as a result of exposure in Vietnam to the poisonous chemical Agent Orange, was settled. The Dow corporation avoided the disclosures of thousands of documents in open court by agreeing to pay $180 million to the veterans. One thing seemed clear: the company had known that the defoliant used in Vietnam might be dangerous, but it held back the news, and blamed the government for ordering use of the chemical. The government itself, apparently wanting to shift blame to the corporation, declared publicly that Dow Chemical had been motivated in its actions by greed for profit.

10. OPPORTUNITY TO PROTEST

The first two elements in my list for democracy—decision-making and information to help make them—are procedural. The next six are substantive, dealing with the consequences of such procedures on life, liberty, and the pursuit of happiness. My ninth point, the one I have just discussed, shows how the money motive of our society corrupts both procedures and their consequences by its existence and suggests we need a different motive as a fundamental requisite of a democratic society. The point I am about to discuss is an ultimate requisite for democracy, a safety feature if nothing else—neither procedures nor consequences nor motivation—works. It is the right of citizens to break through the impasse of a legal and cultural structure, which sustains inequality, greed, and murder, to initiate processes for change. I am speaking of civil disobedience, which is an essential safeguard even in a successful society, and which is an absolute necessity in a society which is not going well.

If the institutional structure itself bars any change but the most picayune and grievances are serious, it is silly to insist that change must be mediated through the processes of that legal structure. In such a situation, dramatic expressions of protest and challenge are necessary to help change ways of thinking, to build up political power for drastic change. A society that calls itself democratic (whether accurately or not) must, as its ultimate safeguard, allow such acts of disobedience. If the government prohibits them (as we must expect from a government committed to the existent) then the members of a society concerned with democracy must not only defend such acts, but encourage them. Somewhere near the root of democratic thought is the theory of popular sovereignty, declaring that government and laws are instruments for certain ends, and are not to be deified with absolute obedience; they must constantly be checked by the citizenry, and challenged, opposed, even overthrown, if they become threats to fundamental rights.

Any abstract assessment of *when* disobedience is justified is pointless. Proper conclusions depend on empirical evidence about how bad things are at the moment, and how adequate are the institutional mechanisms for correcting them. . . .

One of these is the matter of race. The intolerable position of the black person, in both North and South, has traditionally been handled with a low muttered apologies and tokens of reform. Then the civil disobedience of militants in the South forced our attention on the most dramatic (southern) manifestations of racism in America. The massive black urban uprisings of 1967 and 1968 showed that nothing less than civil disobedience (for riots and uprisings go beyond that) could make the nation see that the race problem is an American—not a southern—problem and that it needs bold, revolutionary action.

As for poverty: it seems clear that the normal mechanisms of congressional pretense and presidential rhetoric are not going to change things very much. Acts of civil disobedience by the poor will be required, at the least, to make middle-class America take notice, to bring national decisions that begin to reallocate wealth.

The war in Vietnam showed that we could not depend on the normal processes of "law and order," of the election process, of letters to *The Times,* to stop a series of especially brutal acts against the Vietnamese and against our own sons. It took a nationwide storm of protest, including thousands of acts of civil disobedience (14,000 people were arrested in one day in 1971 in Washington, D.C.) to help bring the war to an end. The role of draft resistance in affecting Lyndon Johnson's 1968 decision not to escalate the war further is told in the Defense Department secret documents of that period. In the 1980s civil disobedience continues, with religious pacifists and others risking prison in order to protest the arms race and the plans for nuclear war.

The great danger for American democracy is not from the protesters. That democracy is too poorly realized for us to consider critics—even rebels—as the chief problem. Its fulfillment requires us all, living in an ossified system which sustains too much killing and too much selfishness, to join the protest.

NOTES

1. Robert A. Dahl, *A Preface to Democratic Theory* (Chicago: University of Chicago Press, 1963), p.81.
2. Ibid., p. 124.
3. Ibid., p. 125.
4. Ibid., p. 131.
5. Ibid., pp. 131–32.
6. Thomas B. Edsall, *The New Politics of Inequality* (New York: Norton, 1984), p. 112.
7. Dahl, *A Preface to Democratic Theory,* p. 146.
8. Robert Wiebe, "The Confinements of Consensus," *TriQuarterly* (1966). Copyright by TriQuarterly 1966. All rights reserved.
9. *New York Times,* September 25, 1984.
10. The *New York Times,* reported November 5, 1983: "There is nothing in the documents, however, that specifically indicates that Cuba and the Soviet Union were on the verge of taking over Grenada, as Administration officials have suggested."
11. Edsall, *The New Politics of Inequality,* p. 221.
12. See the Carnegie Council on Children study, *Small Futures,* by Richard deLore (1979).
13. *Los Angeles Times,* May 3, 1979.

23

How Democratic Is America?
A Response to Howard Zinn

Charles Peirce, the great American philosopher, once observed that there was such a thing as the "ethics of words." The "ethics of words" are violated whenever ordinary terms are used in an unusual context or arbitrarily identified with another concept for which other terms are in common use. Mr. Zinn is guilty of a systematic violation of the "ethics of words." In consequence, his discussion of "democracy" results in a great many methodological errors as well as inconsistencies. To conserve space, I shall focus on three.

I

First of all, he confuses democracy as a political *process* with democracy as a political *product* or state of welfare; democracy as a "*free* society" with democracy as a "*good* society," where good is defined in terms of equality or justice (or both) or some other constellation of values. One of the reasons for choosing to live under a democratic political system rather than a nondemocratic system is our belief that it makes possible a better society. That is something that must be empirically established, something denied by critics of democracy from Plato to Santayana. The equality which is relevant to democracy as a *political process* is, in the first instance, political equality with respect to the rights of citizenship. Theoretically, a politically democratic community could vote, wisely or unwisely, to abolish, retain, or establish certain economic inequalities. Theoretically, a benevolent despotism could institute certain kinds of social and even juridical equalities. Historically, the Bismarckian

---

From *Points of View*, edited by R. E. DiClerico and A. S. Hammond (Reading, Mass.: Addison-Wesley Publishing).

political dictatorship introduced social welfare legislation for the masses at a time when such legislation would have been repudiated by the existing British and American political democracies. Some of Mr. Zinn's proposed reforms could be introduced under a dictatorship or benevolent despotism. Therefore, they are not logically or organically related to democracy.

The second error in Mr. Zinn's approach to democracy is "to measure our democracy against an ideal (even if inadvertently unachievable) standard . . . even if utopian . . ." without *defining* the standard. His criteria admittedly are neither necessary nor sufficient for determining the presence of democracy since he himself admits that they are applicable to societies that are not democratic. Further, even if we were to take his criteria as severally defining the presence of democracy—as we might take certain physical and mental traits as constituting a definition of health—he gives no operational test for determining whether or not they have been fulfilled. For example, among the criteria he lists for determining whether a society is democratic is this: "Are the members of the society equally protected on matters of life and death—in the most literal sense of that phrase?" A moment's reflection will show that here—as well as in other cases where Zinn speaks of equality—it is impossible for all members to be equally protected on matters of life and death—certainly not in a world in which men do the fighting and women give birth to children, where children need *more* protection than adults, and where some risk-seeking adults require and deserve less protection (since resources are not infinite) than others. As Karl Marx realized, "in the most literal sense of that phrase," there cannot be absolute equality even in a classless society. . . .

The only sensible procedure in determining the absence or presence of equality from a democratic perspective is comparative. We must ask whether a culture is more or less democratic in comparison to the past with respect to some *desirable* feature of equality (Zinn ignores the fact that not all equalities are desirable). It is better for some people to be more intelligent and more knowledgeable than others than for all to be unintelligent and ignorant. There never is literally equal access to education, to knowledge and training in any society. The question is: Is there more access today for more people than yesterday, and how can we increase the access tomorrow?

Mr. Zinn refuses to take this approach because, he asserts, "it supports complacency." It does nothing of the sort! On the contrary, it shows that progress is possible, and encourages us to exert our efforts in the same direction if we regard the direction as desirable.

It will be instructive to look at the passage in which Mr. Zinn objects to this sensible comparative approach because it reveals the bias in his approach:

"With such a standard," he writes, "Russia in 1910 could point with pride to how much progress they had made toward parliamentary democracy; as

Russians in 1985 could point to their post-Stalin progress away from the gulag; as Americans could point in 1939 to how far they had come in solving the problem of economic equality; as Americans in the South could point in 1950 to the progress of the southern Negro."

* * *

a. In 1910 the Russians were indeed moving toward greater progress in local parliamentary institutions. Far from making them complacent, they moved towards more inclusive representative institutions which culminated in elections to the constituent assembly in 1918, which was bayoneted out of existence by Lenin and the Communist Party,with a minority party dictatorship established.

b. Only Mr. Zinn would regard the slight diminution in terror from the days of Stalin to the regime of Chernenko as progress toward democracy. Those who observe the ethics of words would normally say that the screws of repression had been slightly relaxed. Mr. Zinn seems unaware that as bad as the terror was under Lenin, it was not as pervasive as it is today. But no one with any respect for the ethics of words would speak of "the progress of democracy" in the Soviet Union from Lenin to Stalin to Khrushchev to Chernenko. Their regimes were varying degrees of dictatorship and terror.

c. Americans could justifiably say that in 1939 progress had been made in giving workers a greater role, not as Mr. Zinn says in "solving the problem of economic equality" (a meaningless phrase), but in determining the conditions and rewards of work that prevailed in 1929 or previously because the existence of the Wagner Labor Relations Act made collective bargaining the law of the land. They could say this *not* to rest in complacency, but to use the organized force of their trade unions to influence further the political life of the country. And indeed, it was the organized labor movement in 1984 which in effect chose the candidate of the Democratic Party.

d. Americans in the South in 1950 could rightfully speak of the progress of the southern Negro over the days of unrestricted Jim Crow and lynching bees of the past, *not* to rest in complacency, but to agitate for further progress through the Supreme Court decision of *Brown* v. *Board of Education in Topeka* and through the Civil Rights Act of Congress. This has not made them complacent, but more resolved to press further to eliminate remaining practices of invidious discrimination.

Even Mr. Zinn should admit that with respect to some of his other criteria this is the only sensible approach. Otherwise we get unhistorical answers, the hallmark of the doctrinaire. He asks—criterion 1—"To what extent can various people in the society participate in those decisions which affect their lives?" and—criterion 7—"Is there freedom of expression on all matters, and equally for all, to communicate with other members of the society?" Why doesn't Mr. Zinn adopt this sensible comparative approach? Because it would lead him to inquire into the extent to which people are free to participate in decisions that affect their lives *today,* free to express themselves, free to organize, free to protest and dissent today, *in comparison with the past.* It would lead him to the judgment *which he wishes to avoid at all costs,* to wit, that despite the grave problems, gaps, and tasks before us, the United States is *more* democratic today than it was a hundred years ago, fifty years ago, twenty years ago, five years ago with respect to every one of the criteria he has listed. To recognize this is *not* an invitation to complacency. On the contrary, it indicates the possibility of broadening, deepening, and using the democratic political process to improve the quality of human life, to modify and redirect social institutions in order to realize on a wider scale the moral commitment of democracy to an equality of concern for all its citizens to achieve their fullest growth as persons. This commitment is to a process, not a transcendent goal or a fixed, ideal standard.

In a halting, imperfect manner, set back by periods of violence, vigilantism, and xenophobia, the political democratic process in the United States has been used to modify the operation of the economic system. The improvements and reforms won from time to time make the still-existing problems and evils more acute in that people become more aware of them. The more the democratic process extends human freedoms, and the more it introduces justice in social relations and the distribution of wealth, the greater grows the desire for *more* freedom and justice. Historically and psychologically, it is false to assume that reforms breed a spirit of complacency. . . .

The third and perhaps most serious weakness in Mr. Zinn's view is his conception of the nature of the formal political democratic process. It suffers from several related defects. First, it overlooks the central importance of majority rule in the democratic process. Second, it denies in effect that majority rule is possible by defining democracy in such a way that it becomes impossible. . . .

"Representation by its very nature," claims Mr. Zinn, "is undemocratic." This is Rousseauistic nonsense. For it would mean that no democracy—including all societies that Mr. Zinn ever claimed at any time to be democratic—could possibly exist, not even the direct democracies or assemblies of Athens or the New England town meetings. For all such assemblies must elect officials to carry out their will. If no representative (and an official is a representative, too) can adequately represent another's needs, there is no assurance that in the actual details of governance, the selectmen, road commissioners, or other town or assembly officials will, in fact, carry out their directives. No assembly or meeting can sit in continuous session or collectively carry out the common decision. In the nature of the case, officials, like representatives, constitute an elite and their actions *may* reflect their interests more than the interests of the governed. This makes crucial the questions whether and how an elite can be removed, whether the consent on which the rule of the officials or representatives rests is free or coerced, whether a minority can peacefully use these mechanisms, by which freely given consent is registered, to win over or become a majority. The existence of representative assemblies makes democracy difficult, not impossible.

Since Mr. Zinn believes that a majority never has any authority to bind a minority as well as itself by decisions taken after free discussion and debate, he is logically committed to anarchy. Failing to see this, he confuses two fundamentally different things—the meaning or definition of democracy, and its justification.

1. A democratic government is one in which the general direction of policy rests directly or indirectly upon the freely given consent of a majority of the adults governed. Ambiguities and niceties aside, that is what democracy means. It is not anarchy. The absence of a unanimous consensus does not entail the absence of democracy.

2. One may reject on moral or religious or personal grounds a democratic society. Plato, as well as modern totalitarians, contends that a majority of mankind is either too stupid or vicious to be entrusted with self-government, or to be given the power to accept or reject their ruling elites, and that the only viable alternative to democracy is the self-selecting and self-perpetuating elite of "the wise," or "the efficient," or "the holy," or "the strong," depending upon the particular ideology of the totalitarian apologist. The only thing they have in common with democrats is their rejection of anarchy.

3. No intelligent and moral person can make an *absolute* of democracy in the sense that he believes it is always, everywhere, under any conditions, and no matter what its consequences, ethically legitimate. Democracy is obviously not desirable in a head-hunting or cannibalistic society or in an institution of the feeble-minded. But wherever and whenever a principled democrat accepts the political system of democracy, he must accept the binding authority of legislative decisions, reached after the free give-and-take of debate and discussion, as binding upon him whether he is a member of the majority or minority. Otherwise the consequence is incipient or overt anarchy or civil war, the usual preface to despotism or tyranny. Accepting the decision of the majority as binding does not mean that it is final or irreversible. The processes of freely given consent must make it possible for a minority to urge amendment or repeal of any decision of the majority. Under carefully guarded provisions, a democrat may resort to civil disobedience of a properly enacted law in order to bear witness to the depths of his commitment in an effort *to reeducate* his fellow citizens. But in that case he must voluntarily accept punishment for his civil disobedience, and so long as he remains a democrat, voluntarily abandon his violation or noncompliance with law at the point where its consequences threaten to destroy the democratic process and open the floodgates either to the violent disorders of anarchy or to the dictatorship of a despot or a minority political party.

4. That Mr. Zinn is not a democrat but an anarchist in his views is apparent in his contention that not only must a democracy allow or tolerate civil disobedience within limits, but that "members of a society concerned with democracy must not only defend such acts, but encourage them." On this view, if southern segregationists resort to civil disobedience to negate the long-delayed but eminently just measures adopted by the government to implement the amendments that outlaw slavery, they should be encouraged to do so. On this view, any group that defies any law that violates its conscience—with respect to marriage, taxation, vaccination, abortion, education—should be encouraged to do so. Mr. Zinn, like most anarchists, refuses to generalize the principles behind his action. He fails to see that if all fanatics of causes deemed by them to be morally just were encouraged to resort to civil disobedience, even our imperfect existing political democracy would dissolve in chaos, and that civil disobedience would soon become quite uncivil. He fails to see that *in a democracy the processes of intelligence, not individual conscience, must be supreme.*

II

I turn now to some of the issues that Mr. Zinn declares are substantive. Before doing so I wish to make clear my belief that the most substantive issue of all is the procedural one by which the inescapable differences of interests among men, once a certain moral level of civilization has been reached, are to be negotiated. The belief in the validity of democratic procedures rests upon the conviction that where adult human beings have freedom of access to relevant information, they are, by and large, better judges of their own interests than are those who set themselves up as their betters and rulers, that, to use the homely maxim, those who wear the shoes know best where they pinch and therefore have the right to change their political shoes in the light of their experience. . . .

Looking at the question "How democratic is America?" with respect to the problems of poverty, race, education, etc., we must say "Not democratic enough!" but not for the reasons Mr. Zinn gives. For he seems to believe that the failure to adopt *his* solutions and proposals with respect to foreign policy, slum clearance, pollution, etc., is evidence of the failure of the democratic process itself. He overlooks the crucial difference between the procedural process and the substantive issues. When he writes that democracy is devoid of meaning if it does not include "equal access to the available resources of the society," he is simply abusing language. Assuming such equal access is desirable (which some might question who believe that access to *some* of society's resources—for example, to specialized training or to scarce supplies—should go not equally to all but to the most needful or sometimes to the most qualified), a democracy may or may not legislate such equal access. The crucial question is whether the electorate has the power to make the choice, or to elect those who would carry out the mandate chosen. . . .

When Mr. Zinn goes on to say that "in the United States . . . democracy should mean that every American, working a short work-week, has adequate food, clothing, shelter, health care, . . ." he is not only abusing language, he is revealing the fact that the procedural processes that are essential to the meaning of democracy, in ordinary usage, are not essential to his conception. He is violating the basic ethics of discourse. If democracy "should mean" what Zinn says it should, then were Huey Long or any other dictator to seize power and introduce a "short work-week" and distribute "adequate food, clothing, shelter, health care" to the masses, Mr. Zinn would have to regard his regime as democratic.

After all, when Hitler came to power and abolished free elections in Germany, he at the same time reduced unemployment, increased the real wages of the German worker, and provided more adequate food, clothing, shelter, and health care than was available under the Weimar Republic. On Zinn's view of what democracy "should mean," this made Hitler's rule more democratic than that of Weimar. . . .

Not surprisingly, Mr. Zinn is a very unreliable guide even in his account of the procedural features of the American political system. In one breath he maintains that not enough information is available to voters to make intelligent choices on major political issues like tax laws. (The voter, of course, does not vote on such laws but for representatives who have taken stands on a number of complex issues.) "The dominant influences are those of big business, which has the resources both to understand and to act." In another breath, he complains that the electorate is at the mercy of the propagandist. "The propagandist does not need to lie; he overwhelms the public with so much imformation as to lead it to believe that it is all too complicated for anyone but the experts."

Mr. Zinn is certainly hard to please! The American political process is not democratic because the electorate hasn't got enough information. It is also undemocratic because it receives too much information. What would Zinn have us do so that the public gets just the right amount of information and propaganda? Have the government control the press? Restrict freedom of propaganda? But these are precisely the devices of totalitarian societies. The evils of the press, even when it is free of government control, are many indeed. The great problem is to keep the press free and responsible. And as defective as the press and other public media are today, surely it is an exaggeration to say that with respect to tax laws "the dominant influences are those of big business." If they were, how can we account for the existence of the income tax laws? If the influence of big business on the press is so dominant and the press is so biased, how can we account for the fact that although 92 percent of the press opposed Truman's candidacy in 1948, he was reelected? How can we account for the profound dissatisfaction of Vice President Agnew with the press and other mass media? And since Mr. Zinn believes that big business dominates our educational system, especially our universities, how can we account for the fact that the universities are the centers of the strongest dissent in the nation to public and national policy, that the National Association of Manufacturers bitterly complained a few years ago that the economics of the free enterprise system was derided, and often not even taught, in most Departments of Economics in the colleges and universities of the nation?

Mr. Zinn's exaggerations are really caricatures of complex realities. Far from being controlled by the monolithic American corporate economy, American public opinion is today marked by a greater scope and depth of dissent than at any time in its history, except for the days preceding the Civil War. The voice and the votes of Main Street still count for more in a democratic polity than those of Wall Street. Congress has limited, and can still further limit, the influence of money on the electoral process by federal subsidy and regulations. There are always abuses needing reforms. By failing to take a comparative approach and instead focusing on some absolute utopian standard of perfection, Mr. Zinn gives an exaggerated, tendentious, and fundamentally false picture of the United States. There is hardly a sentence in his essay that is free of some serious flaw in perspective, accuracy, or emphasis. Sometimes they have a comic effect, as when Mr. Zinn talks about the lack of "equal distribution of the right of freedom of expression." What kind of "equal distribution" is he talking about? Of course, a person with more money can talk to more people than one with less, although this does not mean that more persons will listen to him, agree with him, or be influenced by him. But a person with a more eloquent voice or a better brain can reach more people than you or I. What shall we therefore do to insure equal distribution of the right of freedom of expression? Insist on equality of voice volume or pattern, and equality of brain power? More money gives not only greater opportunity to talk to people than less money but the ability to do thousands of things barred to those who have less money. Shall we then decree that all people have the same amount of money all the time and forbid anyone from depriving anyone else of any of his money even by fair means? "The government," writes Mr. Zinn, "has much more freedom of expression than a private individual because the president can command the airwaves when he wishes, and reach 60 million people in one night."

Alas! Mr. Zinn is not joking. Either he wants to bar the president or any public official from using the airwaves or he wants all of us to take turns. One wonders what country Mr. Zinn is living in. Nixon spoke to 60 million people several times, and so did Jimmy Carter. What was the result? More significant than the fact that 60 million people hear the president is that 60 million or more can hear his critics, sometimes right after he speaks, and that no one is compelled to listen.

Mr. Zinn does not understand the basic meaning of equality in a free, open democratic society. Its philosophy does not presuppose that all citizens are physically or intellectually equal or that all are equally gifted in every or any respect. It holds that all enjoy a *moral* equality, and that therefore, as far as is practicable, given finite resources, the institutions of a democratic society should seek to provide an equal opportunity to all its citizens to develop themselves to their full desirable potential.

Of course, we cannot ever provide complete equal opportunity. More and more is enough. For one thing, so long as children have different parents and home environments, they cannot enjoy the same or equal opportunities. Nonetheless, the family has compensating advantages for all that. Let us hope that Mr. Zinn does not wish to wipe out the family to avoid differences in opportunity. Plato believed that the family, as we know it, should be abolished because it did not provide equality of opportunity, and that all children should be brought up by the state.

Belief in the moral equality of men and women does not require that all individuals be treated identically or that equal treatment must be measured or determined by equality of outcome or result. Every citizen should have an equal right to an education, but that does not mean that, regardless of capacity and interest, he or she should have the same amount of schooling beyond the adolescent years, and at the same schools, and take the same course of study. With the increase in national wealth, a good case can be made for an equal right of all citizens to health care or medical treatment. But only a quack or ideological fanatic would insist that therefore all individuals should have the same medical regimen no matter what ails them. This would truly be putting all human beings in the bed of Procrustes.

This conception of moral equality as distinct from Mr. Zinn's notions of equality is perfectly compatible with intelligent recognition of human inequalities and relevant ways of treating their inequalities to further both the individual and common good. Intelligent and loving parents are equally concerned with the welfare of all their children. But precisely because they are, they may provide different specific strategies in health care, education, psychological motivation, and intellectual stimulation to develop the best in all of them. The logic of Mr. Zinn's position—although he seems blissfully unaware of it—leads to the most degrading kind of egalitarian socialism, the kind which Marx and Engels in their early years denounced as "barracks socialism."

It is demonstrable that democracy is healthier and more effective where human beings do not suffer from poverty, unemployment, and disease. It is also demonstrable that to the extent that property gives power, private property in the means of social production gives power over the lives of those who must live by its use, and, therefore, that such property, whether public or private, should be responsible to those who are affected by its operation. Consequently one can argue that political democracy depends not only on the extension of the franchise to all adults, not only on its active exercise, but on programs of social welfare that provide for collective bargaining by free trade unions of workers and employees, unemployment insurance, minimum wages, guaranteed health care, and other social services that are integral to the welfare state. It is demonstrable that although the existing American welfare state provides far more welfare than was ever provided in the past—my own lifetime furnishes graphic evidence of the vast changes—it is still very far from being a genuine welfare state. Political democracy can exist without a welfare state, but it is stronger and better with it.

The basic issue that divides Mr. Zinn from others no less concerned about human welfare, but less fanatical than he, is how a genuine welfare state is to be brought about. My contention is that this can be achieved by the vigorous exercise of the existing democratic process, and that by the same coalition politics through which great gains have been achieved in the past, even greater gains can be won in the future.

For purposes of economy, I focus on the problem of poverty, or, since this is a relative term, hunger. If the presence of hunger entails the absence of the democratic political process, then democracy has never existed in the past—which would be an arbitrary use of words. Nonetheless, the existence of hunger is always a *threat* to the continued existence of the democratic process because of the standing temptation of those who hunger to exchange freedom for the promise of bread. This, of course, is an additional ground to the even weightier moral reasons for gratifying basic human needs.

That fewer people go hungry today in the United States than ever before may show that our democracy is better than it used to be but not that it is as good as it can be. Even the existence of one hungry person is one too many. How then can hunger or the extremes of poverty be abolished? Certainly not by the method Mr. Zinn advises: "Acts of civil disobedience by the poor will be required, at the least, to make middle-class America take notice, to bring national decisions that begin to reallocate wealth."

This is not only a piece of foolish advice, it is dangerously foolish advice. Many national decisions to reallocate wealth have been made through the political process—what else is the system of taxation if not a method of reallocating wealth?—without resort to civil disobedience. Indeed, resort to civil disobedience on this issue is very likely to produce a backlash among those active and influential political groups in the community who are aware that normal political means are available for social and economic reform. The refusal to engage in such normal political processes could easily be exploited by demagogues to portray the movement towards the abolition of hunger and extreme poverty as a movement towards the confiscation and equalization of all wealth.

The simplest and most effective way of abolishing hunger is to act on the truly revolutionary principle, enunciated by the federal government, that it is responsible for maintaining a standard of relief as a minmum beneath which a family will not be permitted to sink. . . .

For reasons that need no elaboration here, the greatest of the problems faced by American democracy today is the race problem. Although tied to the problems of poverty and urban reconstruction, it has independent aspects exacerbated by the legacy of the Civil War and the Reconstruction period.

Next to the American Indians, the American Negroes have suffered most from the failure of the democratic political process to extend the rights and privileges of citizenship to those whose labor and suffering have contributed so much to the conquest of the continent. The remarkable gains that have been made by the Negroes in the last twenty years have been made primarily through the political process. If the same rate of improvement continues, the year 2000 may see a rough equality established. The growth of Negro suffrage, especially in the South, the increasing sense of responsibility by the white community, despite periodic setbacks resulting from outbursts of violence, opens up a perspective of continuous and cumulative reform. The man and the organization he headed, chiefly responsible for the great gains made by the Negroes, Roy Wilkins and the NAACP, were convinced that the democratic political process can be more effectively used to further the integration of Negroes into our national life than by reliance on any other method. . . .

The only statement in Mr. Zinn's essay that I can wholeheartedly endorse is his assertion that the great danger to American democracy does not come from the phenomena of protest as such. Dissent and protest are integral to the democratic process. The danger comes from certain modes of dissent, from the substitution of violence and threats of violence for the mechanisms of the political process, from the escalation of that violence as the best hope of those who still have grievances against our imperfect American democracy, and from views such as those expressed by Mr. Zinn which downgrade the possibility of peaceful social reform and encourage rebellion. It is safe to predict that large-scale violence by impatient minorities will fail. It is almost as certain that attempts at violence will backfire, that they will create a climate of repression that may reverse the course of social progress and expanded civil liberties of the last generation. . . .

It is when Mr. Zinn is discussing racial problems that his writing ceases to be comic and silly and becomes irresponsible and mischievous. He writes:

> The massive black urban uprisings of 1967 and 1968 showed that nothing less than civil disobedience (for riots and uprisings go beyond that) could make the nation see that the race problem is an American—not a southern—problem and that it needs bold, revolutionary action.

First of all, every literate person knows that the race problem is an American problem, not exclusively a southern one. It needs no civil disobedience or "black uprisings" to remind us of that. Second, the massive uprisings of 1967 and 1968 were violent and uncivil, and resulted in needless loss of life and suffering. The Civil Rights Acts, according to Roy Wilkins, then head of the NAACP, were imperiled by them. They were adopted despite, not because, of them. Third, what kind of "revolutionary" action is Mr. Zinn calling for? And by whom? He seems to lack the courage of his confusions. Massive civil disobedience when sustained becomes a form of civil war.

Despite Mr. Zinn and others, violence is more likely to produce reaction than reform. In 1827 a resolution to manumit slaves by purchase (later, Lincoln's preferred solution) was defeated by three votes in the House of Burgesses of the State of Virginia. It was slated to be reintroduced in a subsequent session with excellent prospects of being adopted. Had Virginia adopted it, North Carolina would shortly have followed suit. But before it could be reintroduced, Nat Turner's rebellion broke out. Its violent excesses frightened the South into a complete rejection of a possibility that might have prevented the American Civil War—the fiercest and bloodiest war in human history up to that time, from whose consequences American society is still suffering. Mr. Zinn's intentions are as innocent as those of a child playing with matches.

III

One final word about "the global" dimension of democracy of which Mr. Zinn speaks. Here, too, he speaks sympathetically of actions that would undermine the willingness and capacity of a free society to resist totalitarian aggression.

The principles that should guide a free democratic society in a world where dictatorial regimes seek to impose their rule on other nations were formulated by John Stuart Mill, the great defender of liberty and representative government, more than a century ago:

> To go to war for an idea, if the war is aggressive not defensive, is as criminal as to go to war for territory or revenue, for it is as little justifiable to force our ideas on other people, as to compel them to submit to our will in any other aspect. . . . *The doctrine of non-intervention, to be a legitimate principle of morality, must be accepted by all governments.* The despots must consent to be bound by it as well as the free states. Unless they do, the profession of it by free countries comes but to this miserable issue, that the wrong side may help the wrong side but the right may not help the right side. Intervention to enforce non-intervention is always right, always moral *if not always prudent.* Though it may be a mistake to give freedom (or independence—S. H.) to a people who do not value the boon, it cannot but be right to insist that if they do value it, they shall not be hindered from the pursuit of it by foreign coercion (*Fraser's Magazine,* 1859, emphasis mine).

Unfortunately, these principles were disregarded by the United States in 1936 when Hitler and Mussolini sent troops into Spain to help Franco overthrow the legally elected democratic Loyalist regime. The U.S. Congress, at the behest of the administration, adopted a Neutrality Resolution which prevented the democratic government of Spain from purchasing arms here. This compelled the Spanish government to make a deal with Stalin, who not only demanded its entire gold supply but the acceptance of the dread Soviet secret police, the NKVD, to supervise the operations. The main operation of the NKVD in Spain was to engage in a murderous purge of the democratic ranks of anti-Communists which led to the victory of Franco. The story is told in George Orwell's *Homage to Catalonia.* He was on the scene.

The prudence of American intervention in Vietnam may be debatable but there is little doubt that Adlai Stevenson, sometimes referred to as the liberal conscience of the nation, correctly stated the American motivation when he said at the UN on the very day of his death: "My hope in Vietnam is that resistance there may establish the fact that changes in Asia are not to be precipitated by outside force. This was the point of the Korean War. This is the point of the conflict in Vietnam."

Today the Soviet Union and Communist Cuba are engaged in extensive operations to help indigenous elements overthrow regimes in Central America. Mr. Zinn's remarks about Grenada show he is opposed to the liberal principles expressed by J. S. Mill in the passage cited above. His report of the facts about Grenada is as distorted as his account of present-day American democracy. On tiny Grenada, whose government was seized by Communist terrorists, were representatives of every Communist regime in the Kremlin's orbit, Cuban troops, and a Soviet general. I have read the documents captured by the American troops. They conclusively establish that the Communists were preparing the island as part of the Communist strategy of expansion.[1]

It is sad but significant that Mr. Zinn, whose heart bleeds for the poor Asians who suffered in the struggle to prevent the Communist takeover in Southeast Asia, has not a word of protest, not a tear of compassion for the hundreds of thousands of tortured, imprisoned, and drowned in flight after the victory of the North Vietnamese "liberators," not to mention the even greater number of victims of the Cambodian and Cuban Communists.

One summary question may be asked whose answer bears on the issue of how democratic America is. Suppose all the iron and bamboo and passport curtains of the world were lifted today, in what direction would freedom-loving and democratic people move? Anyone is free to leave the United States today, except someone fleeing from the law, but in the countries arrayed against the United States people are penned in like animals and cannot cross a boundary without risking death. Has this no significance for the "global" aspect of our question?

NOTE

1. *THE GRENADA PAPERS: The Inside Story of the Grenadian Revolution—and the Making of a Totalitarian State as Told in Captured Documents* (San Francisco: Institute of Contemporary Studies, 1984).

24

Rebuttal to Sidney Hook

Howard Zinn

Mr. Hook *does* have the courage of his confusions. I have space to point out only a few.

1. He chooses to define democracy as a "process," thus omitting its substance. Lincoln's definition was quite good—"government of, by, and for the people." Mr. Hook pooh-poohs the last part as something that could be done by a despot. My definition, like Lincoln's, requires "of" and "by" as well as "for," process as well as content. Mr. Hook is wild about voting, which can also be allowed by despots. Voting is an improvement over autocracy, but insufficient to make any society democratic. Voting, as Emma Goldman said (true, she was an anarchist), and as Helen Keller agreed (true, she was a socialist), is "our modern fetish." It is Mr. Hook's fetish.

Mr. Hook's "democracy" is easily satisfied by hypocrisy, by forms and procedures which look good on paper, and behind which the same old injustices go on. Concealed behind the haughty pedant's charge of "methodological errors" is a definition of democracy which is empty of human meaning, a lifeless set of structures and procedures, which our elementary school teachers tried to pawn off on us as democracy—elections, checks and balances, how a bill becomes a law. Of course, we can't have perfect democracy, and can't avoid representation, but we get closer to democracy when representation is supplemented by the direct action of citizens.

The missing heart, the flowing blood, the life-giving element in democracy is the constant struggle of people inside, around, outside, and despite the ordinary political processes. That means protest, strikes, boycotts, demon-

---

From *Points of View,* edited by R. E. DiClerico and A. S. Hammond (Reading, Mass.: Addison-Wesley Publishing). Reprinted by permission of the author.

strations, petitions, agitation, education, sometimes the slow buildup of public opinion, sometimes civil disobedience.

2. Mr. Hook seems oblivious of historical experience in the United States. His infatuation with "political process" comes out of ancient textbooks in which presidents and congresses act in the nick of time to save us when we're in trouble. In fact, that political process has never been sufficient to solve any crucial problem of human rights in our country: slavery, corporate despotism, war—all required popular movements to oppose them, movements outside those channels into which Mr. Hook and other apologists for the status quo constantly invite us, so we can get lost. Only when popular movements go into action do the channels themselves suddenly come to life.

The test is in history. When Mr. Hook says blacks got their gains "primarily through the political process" he simply does not know what he is talking about. The new consciousness of the rights of blacks, the gains made in the past twenty years—were they initiated by the "political process"? That process was dead for one hundred years while five thousand blacks were lynched, segregation flourished, and presidents, Congress, and the Supreme Court turned the other cheek. Only when blacks took to the streets by the tens of thousands, sat-in, demonstrated, even broke the law, did the "political process" awaken from its long lethargy. Only then did Congress rush to pass civil rights laws, just in time for Mr. Hook to say, cheerily, "You see, the process works."

Another test. Mr. Hook talks about the progress made "because the existence of the Wagner Labor Relations Act made collective bargaining the law of the land." He seems unaware of the wave of strikes in 1933–34 throughout the nation that brought a dead labor relations act to life. Peter Irons, in his prize-winning study, *The New Deal Lawyers,* carefully examines the chronology of 1934, and concludes: "It is likely that the existing National Labor Relations Board would have limped along, unable to enforce its orders, had not the industrial workforce erupted in late April, engulfing the country in virtual class war. . . . Roosevelt and the Congress were suddenly jolted into action." Even after the act was passed in 1935, employers resisted it, and it took the sit-down strikes of 1936–37—yes, civil disobedience—to get contracts with General Motors and U.S. Steel.

A third test. The political process was pitifully inept as a handful of decision-makers, telling lies, propelled this country into the ugly war in Vietnam. (Mr. Hook joins them, when he quotes Adlai Stevenson that we were in Vietnam to act against "outside force"; the overwhelming "outside force" in Vietnam was the United States, with 525,000 troops, dropping 7 million tons of bombs on Southeast Asia.) A president elected in 1964 on his promises to keep the peace took us into war; Congress, like sheep, voted the money; the Supreme Court enveloped itself in its black robes and refused to discuss the constitutionality of the war. It took an unprecedented movement of protest to arouse the nation, to send a surge of energy moving through those clogged processes, and finally bring the war to an end.

3. Mr. Hook doesn't understand civil disobedience. He makes the common error of thinking that a supporter of Martin Luther King's civil disobedience must also support that of the Ku Klux Klan. He seems to think that if you believe civil disobedience is sometimes justified, for some causes, you must support civil disobedience done any time, by any group, for any reason. He does not grasp that the principle is not one of absolute civil disobedience; it simply denies absolute obedience. It says we should not be fanatics about "law and order" because sometimes the law supports the disorder of poverty, or racism, or war.

We can certainly distinguish between civil disobedience for good causes and for bad causes. That's what our intelligence is for. Will this lead to "chaos," as Mr. Hook warns? Again, historical experience is instructive: Did the civil disobedience of blacks in the sixties lead to chaos? Or the civil disobedience of antiwar protesters in the Vietnam years? Yes, they involved some disorder, as all social change does; they upset the false tranquility of segregation, they demanded an end to the chaos of war.

4. Mr. Hook thinks he is telling us something new when he says we can't, and sometimes should not, have perfect equality. Of course. But the point of having ideals is not that they can be perfectly achieved, but that they do not let us rest content, as Mr. Hook is, with being somewhat better off today than yesterday. By his standard, we can give just enough more to the poor to appease anger, while keeping the basic injustice of a wealthy society. In a country where some people live in mansions and others in slums, should we congratulate ourselves because the slums now have TV antennas sticking out of the leaky roofs? His prescription for equality would have us clean out the Augean stables with a spoon, and boast of our progress, while comparing us to all the terrible places in the world where they don't even have spoons. Mr. Hook tries to avoid this issue of inequality by confusing inequality in intellect and physique, which obviously can't be helped much, with that of wealth, which is intolerably crass in a country as wealthy as ours.

Mr. Hook becomes ludicrous when he tries to deny the crucial importance of wealth in elections and in control of the media. When he says, "The voice and votes of Main Street still count for more in a democratic polity than those of Wall Street," I wonder where he has been. If Main Street counts more than Wall Street, how come congressional cutbacks in social programs in 1981-82 brought the number of people officially defined as poor to its highest level since 1965—25.3 million—while at the same time eight thousand millionaires saved a billion dollars in lowered taxes? And how can we account for this news item of October 16, 1984, in the *New York Times:* "Five of the nation's top dozen military contractors earned profits in the years 1981, 1982, and 1983, but paid no Federal income taxes." Can you name five schoolteachers or five social workers who paid no federal income taxes?

What of the system of justice—has it not always favored Wall Street over Main Street? Compare the punishment given to corporation executives found guilty of robbing billions from consumers by price-fixing with the punishment given to auto thieves and house burglars.

Money talks loudly in this "democratic polity." But, Mr. Hook says, in an absurd defense of the control of the media, you don't have to listen! No, the mother needing medical aid doesn't have to listen, but whether her children live or die may result from the fact that the rich dominate the media, control the elections, and get legislation passed which hurts the poor. A *Boston Globe* dispatch, May 24, 1984:

> Infant mortality, which had been declining steadily in Boston and other cities in the 1970s, shot up suddenly after the Reagan Administration reduced grants for health care for mothers and children and cut back sharply on Medicaid eligibility among poor women and children in 1981, according to new research.

5. As for "the global dimension of democracy," Mr. Hook's simple view of the world as divided between "free society" and "totalitarian agression" suggests he is still living back in the heroic battles of World War II. We are now in the nuclear age, and that neat division into "free" and "totalitarian" is both factually wrong and dangerous. Yes, the United States is relatively free society, and the Soviet Union is a shameful corruption of Marx's dreams of freedom. But the United States has established or supported some of the most brutal totalitarian states in the world: Chile, South Africa, El Salvador, Guatemala, South Korea, the Philippines. Yes, the Soviet Union has committed cruel acts of aggression in Hungary, Czechoslovakia, and especially Afghanistan. But the United States has also, whether by the military of the CIA, committed aggression in Iran, Guatemala, Cuba, and the Dominican Republic, and especially in Vietnam, Laos, and Cambodia.

You cannot draw a line across the globe, as Mr. Hook does, to find good on one side and evil on the other. We get a sense of Mr. Hook's refusal to face the complexities of evil when he passes off the horror of the American invasion of Southeast Asia, which left a million dead, with: "The prudence of American intervention in Vietnam may be debatable." One can hear Mr. Hook's intellectual counterparts in the Soviet Union saying about the invasion of Afghanistan: "Our prudence . . . may be debatable." Such moral blindness will have to be overcome if there is to be movement toward real democracy in the United States, and toward real socialism in the Soviet Union. It is the fanaticism on both sides, justifying war "to defend freedom," or "to defend socialism," or simply, vaguely, "national security," that may yet kill us all. That will leave the issue of "how democratic we are" for archeologists of a future era.

25

Rejoinder to Howard Zinn

I may have been mistaken about Mr. Zinn's courage. I am not mistaken about his confusion—his persistent confusion of a free or democratic society with a good society as he defines a good society. Zinn has not understood my criticism and therefore not replied to it. Perhaps on rereading he will grasp the point.

1. Of course, there is no guarantee that the democratic process will yield a good society regardless of how Zinn or anyone else defines it. Democratic-like majorities, may sometimes be wrong or unwise. But if the decisions are the result of a free and fair discussion and vote, it is still democratic. If those who lose in the electoral process resort to civil disobedience, democratic government ultimately breaks down. Even though the processes of democracy are slow and cumbersome and sometimes result in unwise action, its functioning Bill of Rights makes it possible to set them right. That is why Churchill observed, "Democracy is the worst of all forms of government except all the others that have been tried," including, we should add, anarchism.

Zinn dismisses our democratic processes as "a lifeless set of structures and procedures." But it is these very structures and procedures which have enabled us to transform our society from one in which only white men who had property voted to one in which all white men voted, then all men, then all men and women. It is these structures and procedures which have extended and protected the right to dissent, even for all sorts of foolishness like Zinn's. They currently protect Mr. Zinn in his academic freedom post, in his right to utter any criticism of the democratic system under which he lives—a right he would never enjoy in any so called socialist society in the world today.

Mr. Zinn gives his case away when he refers to the democratic process,

---

From *Points of View,* edited R. E. DiClerico and A. S. Hammond (Reading, Mass.: Addison-Wesley Publishing).

which requires voting in *free* elections, as a "fetish." A fetish is the object of irrational and superstitious devotion which enlightened persons reject. Like Marx, Zinn rejects "the fetishism of commodities." Is he prepared to reject the democratic process, too, if its results do not jibe with his conception of the good society?

How, one wonders, does Zinn know that his conception is inherently more desirable than that of his fellow citizens? The democrat says: *Let us leave this choice to the arbitrament of the democratic process.* Zinn has a shorter way. He labels any conception other than his own as undemocratic; and if it prevails, he urges the masses to take to the streets.

2. The space allotted to me does not permit adequate discussion of the international aspects of the struggle for a free society. (I refer readers to my *Philosophy and Public Policy* and *Marxism and Beyond.*) Suffice it to say here that sometimes when the feasible alternatives are limited, the wisest choice between evils is the lesser one. This is the same principle, supported by Zinn, that justified military aid to the Soviet Union when Nazi Germany invaded, although Stalin's regime at the time oppressed many more millions than Hitler's. From the standpoint of the free society, Stalin was the lesser evil then. Today Nazism is destroyed and globally expanding communism has taken its place. If, and only if, we are anywhere confronted by a choice of support between an authoritarian regime and a totalitarian one, the first is the lesser evil. This is not only because the second is far more oppressive of human rights (compare Batista to Castro, Thieu to Hanoi, Syngman Rhee to North Korea, Lon Nol to Pol Pot) but because authoritarian regimes sometimes develop peacefully into democracies (Spain, Portugal, Greece, Argentina), whereas no Communist regime allied to the Kremlin so far has.*

3. Within narrowly prescribed limits, a democracy may tolerate civil disobedience of those who on grounds of conscience violate its laws and willingly accept their punishment. (Cf. the chapter in my *Revolution, Reform and Social Justice.*) But Zinn does not advocate civil disobedience in this sense. He urges what is clearly *uncivil* disobedience like the riotous actions that proceded the Civil Rights Acts from which the blacks, not white racists, suffered most, and the extensive destruction of property from factory sit-ins. Roy Wilkins, who should know, is my authority for asserting that the Civil Rights Acts were adopted by Congress not because of, but despite, these disorders. The most significant racial progress since 1865 was achieved by *Brown* v. *Topeka Board of Education* without "the disorders" Zinn recommends—a sly term that covers broken heads, loss of property, and sometimes loss of life, which are no part of civil disobedience.

---

*1988

Until now, the most charitable thing one could say of Zinn's position is what Cicero once said of another loose thinker: there is no absurdity to which a person will not resort to defend another absurdity. But when Zinn with calculated ambiguity includes "disorders" in the connotation of civil disobedience, *without denouncing violence as no part of it as Gandhi and Martin Luther King did,* he is verging on moral irresponsibility.

Law and order are possible without justice; but Mr. Zinn does not seem to understand that justice is impossible without law and order.

26

Can American Universities Be Depoliticized?

Henry David Aiken

In his inaugural address a year ago last autumn, Morris Abram, the second president of my own university, Brandeis, called for a general "depoliticizing" of our universities and colleges. Many others, both inside the universities and out, are making similar appeals. The hope, it seems, is for a return to a golden age of higher education when professors professed, and administrators, delighted to leave well enough alone, spent their time passing the hat, balancing budgets, acting as substitute parents, and performing such ceremonial acts as presiding at faculty meetings and commencement exercises. Of course such a golden age is long gone. It hasn't existed at private colleges for generations; at public colleges and universities, many of which evolved out of the old land-grant colleges, it never existed. In fact, another university president (or rather ex-president), James Perkins of Cornell, has argued approvingly that American institutions of higher learning generally have combined in a unique way the three "missions" of teaching, research, and service. By "service," however, Perkins seems originally to have had in mind primarily service to the state and to the national society over which the state presides. In times past, such services have often grudgingly been performed; indeed, faculties and students alike have frequently debated whether they do not compromise the integrity of the American scholar. And even when members of the university have accepted the principle that the college should also include a service station, they have rarely agreed among themselves as to the proper nature or extent of the services to be rendered. But such disagreements, like the services themselves, are inescapably political.

For example, long before the Vietnam war made the ROTC such a bone

From *Philosophic Exchange* (Summer 1970): 3–18. Reprinted by permission of the author and the Center for Philosophic Exchange.

of contention on our campuses, many academicians, old as well as young, insisted that this conspicuous tie between the academy and the military be severed. Occasionally, moreover, they prevailed, thereby saving their colleges energies for better ways of showing patriotism. Another example may be mentioned which is more interesting and important. As some of you may recall, it was during the First World War, at Columbia, and during the Second, at Harvard, that programs which now go by the name of General Education were respectively initiated at those distinguished universities where recently there has been so much turmoil. At the outset, the purpose of such programs was undisguisedly political: their function, quite simply, was to awaken the minds of hitherto indifferent or misguided students to the transcendental virtues of our American system and to the wickedness of all systems that oppose it. To be sure, this great awakening should be accomplished in a suitably genteel and roundabout way, by searching out the fountainheads of freedom in the works of such ancient masters as Plato (the greatest of all exponents of the aristocratic ideal who reserved the higher forms of learning for the guardians of his ideal Republic) and Aristotle (the first pragmatist who preferred a mixed polity in which nonetheless some men, being slaves by nature, cannot be allowed to participate since they are unable to grasp the meaning of political obligation). From the beginning, of course, General Education was widely opposed. Some opposed it on the grounds that so obviously politicized an educational venture demeans the university, whose modes of political indoctrination should be less conspicious; others (in their own way perhaps anticipating educationist such as President Abram) opposed it on the ground that any form of politicking on the campus should be excluded since it diverts institutions of higher learning from their proper business, which is advancement and dissemination of learning. Were they consistent, such purists, who do not pause to examine the varieties of human learning, would have to go much further. In America, however, where even purists are pragmatists, few have questioned the prerogatives of established departments of political science and sociology, in which much time and energy are spent in ideological and hence political controversy.

Several lessons may be drawn from this example: one is that politicized activity on the part of the members of the so-called academic community is generally acceptable if it is sufficiently concealed, indirect, learned, and firmly established; it is below the salt only when it becomes open and direct, formally unlearned and boldly innovative. But another and happier lesson may be learned from the example of General Education. For it was through the efforts of highly politicized academic patriots that a great educational movement was launched whose function has been to revive the spirit of what used to be called liberal education in an age of rampant specialism, professionalism, and scientism. The failures of the movement, alas, are all too plain. But in nearly all cases they are owning to the fact that its exponents have been too timid and too concessive, too limited in their demands for educational reform, too conventional in their conception of the forms of education that are necessary for free men in a really free society.

Here it should be emphasized that purists who oppose such existing politically-oriented educational programs as the ROTC or General Education are politicized by the very act of opposing them. In fact, the only way a scholar can avoid the trap of politics is by shutting the door to his study, pulling down the shades, and sticking, despite hell and high water, to his own neutral researches and to courses of instruction related exclusively to them. President Abram's presidential address, whether he realized it or not, was a political act, in the same way that the actions of committed anarchists, who yearn to dispense altogether with politics, employ political means to achieve their post-political ends. The state, as we have learned, never does its own withering away. But of course the depoliticizers (if "depoliticize" is a word then so is "depoliticizer"), like the anarchists, cannot succeed. History, human nature, not to mention existing versions of the American dream, all conspire against them. In one direction, the Pentagon and the great scientific-technological establishments that are themselves so closely intertwined with government, will continue to find their way into the universities and colleges, in part because they have an insatiable need for the products of the "knowledge factory." In the opposite direction, even the most servile university, in bringing together exceptionally lively and imaginative individuals, also brings into existence what I call a "shadow university" where free men find ways of instructing and advising one another about the social and political conditions of a more fully human life. In Russia, in Spain, in Czechoslovakia, and in the United States, the university has always served in spite of itself as a breeding ground for the education of political dissenters, reformers, and revolutionists. The only way to disperse such dissidents, and so to prevent them from enlightening one another, would be to disband the universities. But this is precisely what the state and its functionaries, academic and otherwise, cannot afford to do. Hence, since politics, like nature, abhores a vacuum, the educationally absorbing question is not whether the universities and colleges can be depoliticized, but rather what forms of political activity they may properly encourage or tolerate. And it is to this question that we must presently address ourselves.

Still, granted that efforts to depoliticize the academy are, to put the point least offensively, quixotic, it is an instructive exercise in the philosophy of higher education to perform the imaginative experiment of considering what the educational as well as human results would be, were our colleges actually to succeed in eliminating every form of political activity from the academy.

In the first place, liberal education would disappear. For liberal education is intended by definition for free men, and free men, by definition, are political beings, concerned not with their own self-government only, but with the liberation of all their kind from every form of human bondage, including those forms of bondage by which men in societies enslave one another. Clearly, liberal education is committed from the outset of the study of institutions, including the state, and this not merely as they have been and are, but as they ought or ought not to be. In a word, to depoliticize the university would require the exclusion of all normative social and political studies. But it would also entail the abandonment of ethics, since, as Aristotle long ago pointed out, ethics and politics are ultimately inseparable. And since ethics, broadly conceived, is the heartland of philosophy, it would have to exclude philosophy too, or at least those parts of it that are not purely analytical. Neither Aristotle nor Plato—nor, above all, Socrates—could get a job in the depoliticized academy.

Indeed, as we ponder the matter we are driven to the conclusion that a depoliticized academy could not tolerate any educational program nor any sort of sustained speculation and criticism aimed at the radical reformation of human personality. "Know thyself," said the oracle. But what would be the point of trying to know oneself, with the help of enlightened teachers, unless one were determined to change one's life? And how could one think of undertaking such a task if one were not prepared to entertain the possibility or necessity of actions which, if they succeeded, might revolutionize all our social institutions, including of course the colleges and the state themselves?

I am bound to say also that a fully depoliticized academy could not permit any form of religious study which aimed at something more than the external examination of historical religions, their creeds and rituals, and churchly paraphernalia. For active religious reflection, as Paul Tillich used to say, has to do with matters of ultimate concern to us as human beings, with what is worthy of our profoundest loyalty and love. But the awakened religious consciousness, as all great religious leaders, from the Prophets and Jesus to Gandhi and Pope John XXIII, have demonstrated both in their teachings and in their lives, is always a threat to the established order, including the political order. Indeed, great religious geniuses, like great philosophers, and artists—*by their very existence*—endanger the established orders, and the dominations and obsessions of their governing elites.

What then would be left to the higher learning were all significant political thought and activity excluded from the university? We are driven, I think, to the conclusions that if our academies were systematically depoliticized, many traditional and humanly important parts of the humanities and the so-called social sciences, even in their present-day confused and emasculated forms, would have to be dropped from the curriculum. Moreover, many researches now conducted under the more austere auspices of natural science departments would have to be abandoned, since their results, devoid of theoretical interest, have value only for governments committed to the deadly business of power politics. To be more concrete (and I shall continue to play our little game as even-handedly as possible), one cannot imagine that cathedrals of pure scholarship would tolerate such political activists as Professor Marcuse or (at the other extreme) Professor Sidney Hook; no doubt Chomsky would have to go, but so too would Professors Schlesinger and Galbraith, to say nothing of such eminent newcomers to the academic scene as Professors Humphrey and Johnson. But these are not all. For thousands of indentured technological scientists, along with their multitudes of graduate assistants, would also have to find new jobs in the great industrial laboratories where there is no quibbling about the aims of higher education.

What about the student activists, who are currently such burrs in the saddles of our academic administrators? Surely there would be no place for them, even if they stopped carrying arms and rifling the files of deans of the faculty. For they would still be politicized. So it would be necessary to proscribe such student organizations as the SDS and (were the authorities consistent) the Young Republican Clubs. And if the reply were made, which is not without merit, that one can get an education of sorts by engaging in such extra-curricular political activities, the reply, in this instance, would fail, for a political education is still a part of the political life of men in societies.

Nor have I forgotten here the distinction between forms of political education that are topical and directly activistic and those concerned more abstractly with the critique and formation of general ideological principles which serve their political ends more indirectly. And to those who concede that the higher learning *should* have a place for studies of the latter sort (and I fully agree with them) the reply must be that they are forgetting the game we are playing. I cannot see how an academy, depoliticized in any depth, could tolerate a William James, a John Dewey, or a Bertrand Russell, and any more than it could tolerate a Marcuse. For again, all forms of political reasoning, whether abstractly ideological like Plato's *Republic* and Rousseau's *Social Contract,* or concrete and topical, like the *Declaration of Independence, The Emancipation Proclamation,* or the *Communist Manifesto,* have a practical intention: that is to say, they are aimed, whether for the longer or shorter run, at the modification of active political-social attitudes. In fact, they defeat their own purposes if, when the time is ripe, they fail to move us to action designed to reform or, if necessary, revolutionize the existing order.

In sum, a thoroughly depoliticized academy, were it ever actualized, would not be an institute for all the forms of advanced study necessary to the progressive enlightenment of mature human beings, but instead would be learned mandarins lost finally both to the world and to themselves. No doubt an affluent society like our own, which presumably can afford anything that takes its fancy, could afford such an institution, and for a time at least it might even be willing to tolerate it, just as it now tolerates religious retreats and sanctuaries. What is more doubtful is that the internal purity of the academy could be maintained. How could it make certain that a few whole men—whether students or professors—might not get into it by mistake? And how could it guarantee that such impure spirits, like our own campus rebels, would not in the end become so alienated from it that, despairing of further argument with their uncomprehending superiors, they would not be disposed at last, like all other alienists, to take matters into their own hands? Surely it is not hard to imagine in these troubled times that beginning with teach-ins and sit-ins, they might be tempted to seize the administration building by main force and hold the president and his deans incommunicado until their "non-negotiable" demands for a more liberal conception of higher education were met.

Suppose they did. In such an event, we may well imagine, a depoliticized college president or board of trustees would be exceedingly reluctant to make use of the strong arm of the state. For in so doing they would of course be responding in kind—that is to say, politically—to the actions of the rebels. Still, one must suppose that in the end they would feel obliged, necessarily in uneasy conscience, to call in the police in order to protect the integrity and the freedom of the academy. But what sort of freedom would this be? Not, surely, the freedom to discuss in a critical spirit the nature and limits of science, whithersoever the argument might lead. For anyone who starts asking limiting questions about the proper aims and functions of scientific inquiries may well find that such limits are extremely unclear or else that they are in need of radical revision in an age like our own in which governments, with the indispensable help of scientists, can destroy mankind. No matter how paradoxically, it is doubtful whether a depoliticized academy could tolerate active and open debates about the aims of the higher learning as a whole, since these would almost certainly result in disagreements whose implications are inescapably political. Indeed, the whole problem of academic freedom would become so stylized, so touchy, that discussions of it would be permitted only in cases of specific violations, and then only by safe men who have accepted in advance the ground rules established by academic authorities who understand the limitations of a politicized academy.

Suppose, however, that some overly-conscientious professor raised questions about the wisdom or the good faith of his superiors? Would he not also have to be put down in one way or another, thus further compromising the purity of the guardians of the depoliticized academy? What then? Here plainly the road becomes exceedingly slippery. But compromise, as usual, leads to compromise. And one may as well be hung for a sheep as for a lamb.

In the real world, as Plato himself foretold, intelligent purists must also be realists, and even the depoliticized academy needs guardians who are willing and able to sustain it. Physicists and mathematicians, as well as poets, must eat and their studies and laboratories must be decently provided for. Hence donors must be solicited, foundations appealed to, legislatures and governors of states placated and cajoled, congressmen begged, and presidents of state exhorted. Thus in practice even the purest institutions of advanced study and higher learning require their front men, who know how to wheedle funds from those who possess or control them: lobbyists, public relations men, and sober-sided presidents like Mr. Pusey, who know how to talk to congressional committees that might otherwise not be able to understand the non-political aspirations of the academies. But this is not all. For academicians, no matter how chaste their intentions, are invariably misunderstood by the hoi polloi that live in the slums that surround the precincts of the academy, and in many cases are owned—in trust of course—by the academies for purposes of future expansion and for the housing of their own less affluent members. Let us face it. The hoi polloi do not understand, nor care to understand, the purposes of the academy; what they see are oppressive landlords, indifferent and condescending professors, students who raise hell on Saturday night. So the academy must either maintain its own praetorian guards, which invariably prove inadequate to the demands made upon them, or else be willing to call upon the armed services of the city or the state in order to protect its privacy and its property against intruders who mean harm to the members of its community. Extraterritorial rights are not honored save at a price. And the price, as we may as well recognize, is a price whose name is politics.

Is this picture overdrawn? Then merely by an inch. Does it also ring a bell? I believe it must. Can the deep inconsistencies which it involves be overcome? Short of utopia, I am sure they cannot.The conclusion is inescapable: The managers of our academic establishments, like their allies in our legislatures and state houses, in the congress, and the White House, who tell us that the proper business of the universities and colleges is not with politics but only with the advancement of neutral learning, are either disingenuous and hence guilty of bad faith or else so self-deceived that they are incompetent and deserve to be removed from office.

These, I realize, are harsh terms; nor do I use them lightly. Let me explain. Such men act in bad faith, or else are self-deceived to the point of madness when they invoke the image of the academy as a haven and repository of pure learning, itself completely at variance with the actual practices of their own institutions, and then condemn, or else—as the English put it—send down obstreperous student activists who give them the lie direct and the countercheck quarrelsome. They act in bad faith, or are self-deluded, when they accept government or foundation money, which commonly has political strings attached, yet pretend that they are free, and are outraged when dissident students and faculty members point this out to them and then, in their own turn, take steps, not always genteel, to see that those strings are cut. They are disingenuous when they represent themselves as agents of law and order, yet never raise deep questions about the justice of that law or order, nor acknowledge that there can be no law or order without government and hence politics.

They are particularly disingenuous, let me add, when they argue, as McGeorge Bundy and others do, that university administrations and governing boards possess merely formal power and that the actual power and authority in the academy resides in the faculty, when they know that our faculties are chock full of careerists who have no interest in its governance so long as they themselves are left alone to do their work according to their own flickering lights. As they very well know, faculties are nearly always self-divided and usually incapable of independent and decisive action to rectify either educational wrongs or administrative malpractices. They also know how clever and determined administrators, with their own informal ties to government, industry and business, can and do manipulate their faculties to secure their own frequently political ends. Finally, these apologists for faculty authority cannot fail to know, especially in this time of troubles, that formal power can always be reconverted into actual power by university presidents and by the governing boards at whose pleasure all presidents enjoy their tenure.

They speak and act in bad faith when they pretend to be votaries of reasonableness, yet reserve for themselves the peremptory authority to determine for students and faculty members alike the standards and limits of reasonableness, and times and places where their critics may foregather to present their reasons for opposing existing academic practices and policies. Above all, they are either appallingly naive or again are guilty of bad faith when they angrily condemn those dissidents who, disillusioned by arguments that get them nowhere, resort to force, yet in the clutch react—and over-react—in kind.

But here I myself may have been a bit disingenuous. For I concede that gentlemen like the presidents of universities such as Columbia and Harvard do not react in kind to students who unceremoniously eject academic deans from their offices, occupy administrative buildings, rifle files, and sip presidential sherry in order to quiet their nerves. For as they well know, the force employed by the students is informal, personal, and usually intramural and poorly organized, whereas the force upon which they themselves rely is extramural, highly skilled, well armed, and sublimely confident in the assurance of its constituted authority. Of course such administrators know full well that when the chips are down, as they have so often been of late, this majesterial power is always incomparably greater than that of their youthful opponents, with their obscenities, sticks and stones, pop bottles, their occasional pistols (for we must be fair), most of them unused, and their bare hands and unshielded bodies.

These last comments may be misleading. Let me then emphasize that it is not part of my own argument to condone acts of gross violence, whether on the part of the university authorities and the governments that offer their moral and military support, or on the part of misguided students—black as well as white—that jeopardize the very existence of *liberal* learning (and mind you, I emphasize the word "liberal"). Cowardly arsonists who come in the night to burn books and manuscripts, studies, libraries, are not exponents of freedom, their own included. On the contrary, from the point of view which I defend, the destruction of any constructive and liberating work of the human mind is always appalling. But if a burned book or study is something forever to be grieved over, broken heads or backs are far more lamentable, especially when they are the heads and backs of innocents who are always sacrificed when men in groups resort to violence.

But this is not the place to undertake a general discussion of violence and its legitimate (or illegitimate) issues. It is my conviction that in most situations, thoughtful but sparing use by academic administrators of the legal device of injunction is justified in order to protect scholars and students, as well as the legitimate fruits of their labors, against marauding hoards whose only purpose is to terrorize the academy and to destroy the materials and records necessary to its proper work. This conviction commits me, accordingly, to the view that the university as a corporate body is entitled to perform legal and political acts in its own defense. By the same token, however, I am obliged to consider whether the university, as such, may also be entitled to take other political positions when its own integrity is threatened.

As it happens, Professor Hook and I found ourselves in at least partial agreement some years ago when a number of distinguished colleagues proposed, at a business meeting of the American Philosophical Association, that the association, as a corporate body, condemn the government's policies in Vietnam. And I, for my part, contended that a purely professional organization, concerned exclusively with its own professional business and ends, was not entitled to take political stands not closely germane to that business and those ends. This, so I argued, in no way denied the right of members of our association, speaking not only as private persons but also, if they wished, as individual members of the group, to condemn the Vietnam War (which I myself have always heartily opposed). And I agreed to sign any sensible memorandum or petition deploring the war, not only in my own person but also as a member of the association. (I should add in passing that the American Philosophical Association, if one could judge by its annual programs, seems to me to have long since given up any common concern with the pursuit of wisdom and has become as narrowly specialized and professionalized as, say, the American Association of Morticians.)

The fact is that I am less certain now than I was then of this position. For I now see that even a fairly narrow professional association, dedicated to a small part of the advancement of learning, may find its own work undermined, or even rendered impossible, by policies and actions of the state. However, I shall waive this question here. For the sake of argument, I am prepared to reaffirm the position I took in 1967 regarding the provenance of the American Philosophical Association, viewed simply as a professional society. And I do so because I want to free myself for independent scrutiny of the situation of the university in matters of this sort.

Now, most academicians, including not only students and professors but also administrators, generally agree that the university is not and cannot be understood as a mere galaxy of professional associations. To be sure, its task includes the advancement of learning, by research and teaching, in a wide variety of subjects. And this task has its important professional side, which includes the granting of degrees to student apprentices that will qualify them for more advanced work in particular fields, as well as the creation and maintenance of conditions necessary to the researches of established professional scholars. But the university is much more than an institute for the training of pre-professionals and the support of professional scholars. It is also he great unifying institution of higher learning whose difficult task, above all, includes the education of free men. Because of this, the educational heart of the university is, or should be, its college, not its professional graduate schools.

Thus, unlike the professional society, the university has educational responsibilities which cannot be defined in purely professional terms. As we know, professional societies can sometimes function tolerably well under governments which are repressive and warlike. The university, however, by its nature is threatened by any social or political policy which diminishes the freedom of ordinary citizens. More positively, because the university bears such a heavy responsibility for the full intellectual, moral, and human development of all its members, professors as well as students, it has a corporate obligation to protest, and in some circumstances even to defy or obstruct, social practices or political policies which undermine or constrict its comprehensive educational purposes.

Given the organizational principles which at present obtain in the American university, I for one am loathe to support, without qualification, any and all corporate decisions affecting the relations of the academy to the national society or its government, which the university's existing governing boards and administrative officers may come to. Many such boards and officers lack a clear notion of the extensive freedom necessary to the university. But the faculties and student bodies of the university whose primary concerns are educational, in the wide sense I have here in mind, do seem to me to have the right, after full and open debate, to speak and act against certain social and governmental policies and practices as corporate bodies. Thus, I should argue, the faculties of universities in the South have the right, and perhaps the obligation, to adopt corporate principles and to express corporate attitudes which are at variance with the segregationalist and racist policies of existing state governments. I should also argue, in the same vein, that faculties, perhaps in concert with students, have the right and at times the obligation to condemn, and on occasion to obstruct, policies and practices of the federal government which are inimical to their own educational purposes.

I am not a formalist. Student bodies and faculties, as well as university presidents and boards of trustees, are liable to error and confusion. Indeed, I can imagine circumstances in which wise administrators may be obliged to make decisions at variance with those adopted by their faculties and students. In every institution, in my judgment, no man or group of men is, or should be, sovereign. Yet this does not, I think, affect the point at issue. Universities, and especially their faculties and students, have rights and responsibilities which entitle or indeed require them to make corporate decisions of a political nature when national or state governments adopt policies which undermine the conditions of liberal learning. Of course such decisions should be thoughtfully made, and even when thoughtfully made they may still be mistaken. And it is the duty of minority groups within the university to point out such errors when they occur. Indeed they themselves may be obliged to obstruct or to defy decisions which, in their view, are academically as well as politically unwise. But these qualifications do not impugn the principle: the university, and especially its faculty and students, have the right to take corporate political action when such action is necessary in order to protect the wide and deep aims of higher education.

In bringing this part of my paper to a close, let me emphasize that every institution, if only in its own defense, is involved in politics. The church-state problem, for example, necessarily involved the churches in corporate political action. The same holds, as Leslie Fielder has discovered, even of the family. Politics is an inescapable dimension of every form of institutional activity. And those who refuse to involve themselves in it must, if they are responsible, foreswear participation in every form of institutional life. To my mind, however, this is platitudinous. The great and ineluctable fact is that no institution, given its ends, is more profoundly involved in problems of politics and government than the university.

Thus, as I have tried to show, the question before us is not whether the university can be depoliticized. Rather it is the question of how and to what ends the university should engage in political activity, and what forms of political activity are proper to it.

To this question my answers must be brief. I shall proceed from those problems which are more topical and hence debatable to those that are more enduring.

To begin with, the university must be free to call in question and, on occasion, oppose any form of service to the nation-state designed primarily to enhance the state's military power. Here I have in mind not only such forms of military instruction as are conducted by the ROTC [Reserve Officer Training Corps], but, far more important, research projects supported by federal grants-in-aid whose basic purpose is to increase our national capacity for nuclear warfare. Beyond this, the university is entirely within its rights if it refuses to countenance forms of research designed to explore means of degrading or maiming human beings or of destroying natural resources upon which they are dependent for life. For the university, as an institution of higher learning dedicated to the religious, moral, and political enlightenment, defeats its own ends and undermines the conditions of its own existence when it, or the members of its faculties, engage in such activities as a matter of course. Moreover, the forms of enlightenment fostered by the university are by their very nature public. Hence the university is entitled to deny, and in my judgment should deny, the use of its facilities to academicians involved in the work of such secret governmental services as the CIA and the FBI. And of course the same applies to similar services to industry or other social institutions or societies. In a word, academicians cannot also be secret agents. Finally, the university must be free to criticize, or on occasion actively oppose, both particular public policies and private practices which create an ambience inimical to its own broad educational purposes. And it must make available the use of its facilities to members of the academic community who are concerned to criticize and to oppose such policies and practices.

At the level of ideology, I should deny no member of the academy the right, in the proper circumstances and under proper auspices, to defend any form of thought, religious, ethical, or political, no matter how heterodox, so long as he does so in a manner which is appropriate to it. It is sometimes argued that the only forms of inquiry which are proper to the university as the primary institution of higher learning are those that aim at scientific truth. In another way, it is argued that the only studies which a university should support, or tolerate, are those which are "neutral" or "value free." As I have already suggested, such a principle is educationally pernicious, since, among other things, it precludes the possibility of philosophical investigations whose task is to provide critiques of all forms of putative knowledge. Without begging basic philosophical questions, it simply cannot be assumed that the scientific method is the one and only method of achieving human understanding. A philosopher, not to mention a theologian, a moralist, a literary critic, or an artist, must be free not merely to consider what forms of study are proper to his activity, but also to employ the methods and procedures which upon reflection he deems appropriate. If he is mistaken, then it is the business of his colleagues and students to expose his errors.

What concerns me here, above all, are these pervasive but frequently unformulated philosophies, or ideologies of higher learning, that regard liberal education, which is concerned with the development and enlargement of the whole life of the mind, to be a dispensable or peripheral luxury. On another level, such philosophies are deeply suspicious, or even fearful, of liberal education precisely because it is not and cannot be neutral in the scientific sense. From the latter point of view, liberal education, owing to its active concern not merely with scientific study but also with the appraisal and advocacy of religious, ethical, and political attitudes and institutions, automatically involves the teacher and his students in controversial issues which can and do create an atmosphere of dissension which is inimical to that basic congeniality of mind which a community of scholars seems to require.

In reply I must take the bit in my teeth: liberal education does indeed lead to controversy, and undoubtedly its exponents and participants are given forms of dissension that frequently go very deep. The liberal mind is inherently non-conformist, and nonconformity usually has a political aspect. In my view, however, controversy, dissension, and nonconformity are indispensable to intellectual and hence educational development. Accordingly, the price in terms of conflict, both within the faculty and the student body, simply has to be paid. And if this reduces the sense of community among the members of the university, we must make the best of it. The business of higher education is not to make those engaged in it comfortable with one another, but to advance all the basic forms of human understanding. In short, I do not deplore conflict on the university campus, I applaud it. Nor in saying this do I commit myself to an uncritical or flaccid acquiescence in all the forms of turmoil which now beset our universities. Physical violence on the campus is nearly always to be deplored. And the same holds not only for student "revolutionaries" but also for administrative "reactionaries."

Let me close by making some positive proposals which, if adopted, would greatly reduce the wrong sort of tension which has now become endemic to the contemporary American university. A great part of this tension, which reflects analogous tensions within the wider society, is owing to the obsolete organization of the academy. I do not deplore academic leadership, and certainly such leadership must come, in some part, from the university administration. But this requires that university administrators and, behind them, the governing boards, be educators and not merely arbiters and fund raisers. And they cannot be, or remain, educators unless they also study, teach, and go to school. To this end, I propose a principle of rotation that will close the profound intellectual, moral, and political gaps that presently divide the various academic classes.

Administrators must be given, or obliged to take, leave from time to time so that they may renew, in a more concrete and intimate way, their understanding of the work, the attitudes, and the problems of their faculties and students. They must be obliged in a more-than-ceremonial way to participate in the life and work of both faculties and students. Administration, in short, must no longer be treated as a full-time job, and, again, if we all will have to pay a certain price for the change, then so be it. Faculty members must be enabled to participate fully in the governance of the university. Thus, faculty members should be elected by the governing boards in whose hands, as we have learned, to our sorrow, great actual as well as formal power still resides. In some degree the same holds with respect to students. For example, able and enlightened students must not only be permitted but encouraged to participate in the instruction of their classmates and in the formation and revision of departmental curricula. And, in sum, through these and other entirely practicable changes, actions can and must be taken to convert what is now merely an institution into a truer community of self-respecting and mutually understanding scholars.

Beyond this, valuable forms of educational and political activity that are now conducted exclusively within the shadow university should be encouraged to come out of the shadow and to be recognized, not as extracurricular alternatives to football or Saturday night parties, but as relevant educational activities designed for the improvement of the understanding of all members of the university community. Specifically, dissident and radical groups, whose aim is the reconstruction of the whole society, must not merely be tolerated with a grimace, but invited to meet in the light of day with those who disagree with them so that meaningful and continuous dialogues may be established concerning the problems and jobs of work to be done in our confused and faltering social system.

Nor is this all. More enlightened head-start, upward- and outward-bound programs should be established in order to bring into, and so to enrich, the intellectual life of the academic community, many more gifted but disadvantaged students whose deprivation, real as well as imagined, are owing to poverty, inadequate secondary school education, and racial prejudice. These students must be provided with ample scholarships that may enable them to live and to study on equal terms with their classmates. Further, the colleges and universities must be prepared to invite to the campus, whether on a full or part-time basis, knowledgeable and enlightened laymen who have so much to tell us about the possibilities, educational and otherwise, of reform and reconstruction throughout the national society. And sustained programs of adult education need to be established which are no longer marginal and conducted by disadvantaged professors in need of another honest buck.

But all these, of course, are no more than approach shots. What is necessary, above all, is a massive return to the ideals and practices of liberal education itself, properly updated for contemporary men and women who have something more to do in the world than acquire forms of professional and vocational training that may enable them to move upward in the social and economic hierarchy. These ideals and practices must also be reintroduced into the graduate and professional schools. We need and must have forms of liberal education that are relevant to the lives of human beings in an age of unprecedented social and cultural crisis, in an age in which there are problems of life which human beings have never had to face before: the massive consolidation of power in the hands of elites responsible in practice to no one but themselves, the contests for ideological and political control by great states, all of them, including our own, increasingly repressive ad totalistic, and, most important of all, the uncontrolled employment of weapons of destruction that, in an instant, can convert this planet into a sense of lunar desolation where the life and work of civilized human beings is completely blotted out.

This is the great and difficult work that lies before us. In an era in which as never before the academy is the state's most important institutional auxiliary, we must again make sure that what we call higher education is an education, not for technicians and specialists only, but for autonomous men, enlightened and unafraid. Ours is the responsibility to make certain that the advancement of learning includes the improvement of our understanding of what it means to be a man and a human being. And this task, once again, imposes responsibilities whose meanings are through and through political.

27

From the Platitudinous to the Absurd
(A Response to H. D. Aiken)

Henry Aiken's gush of impassioned rhetoric has carried him from a position that he himself suspects is "platitudinous"—the word is his—to one that will strike others as positively mischievous in its absurdity. How is this remarkable feat achieved? Very simply. First he disregards the specific historical context in which certain campus groups, both students and faculty, are explicitly calling for the politicalization of the university, demanding that the university as a corporate entity become an agency of political, even revolutionary, political change. He then proposes an arbitrary conception of the term "political" so broad that it has no intelligible opposite in human affairs, according to which "to be is to be political"—so that by definition, the university, the church, even the family and kindergarten are political institutions. Thereupon he gradually slides or slips into a more specific, conventional conception of political behavior that in effect would make the political functions and conerns of the university almost coextensive with that of a political party. There is a complete and irresponsible disregard of the overwhelmingly likely consequences of such a program, viz., opening the floodgates to a political reaction that would destroy existing academic freedoms and the relative autonomy of the university which have been so precariously won in the last sixty-odd years against earlier conceptions and practices of politicalization.

On top of all this, he scandalously misstates the position of those whom he is ostensibly criticizing, including President Abrams. He stuffs figures with straw, burns them with gusto, and, sheltered by the resulting thick smoke, charges that those who oppose politicalization *of* the university therefore are, or must be, opposed even to the study of politics *by* or *in* the university,

From *Philosophic Exchange* (Summer 1970):21–28. Reprinted by permission of the Center for Philosophic Exchange.

and that they cannot consistently defend the principles of academic freedom when such defense has political implications. This semantic obscurantism makes it easier to blur the distinction between the study of politics and commitment to political action.

Let me illustrate Aiken's method by a reference to some episodes of American higher education of whose history, to put it most charitably, he is egregiously innocent, for he seems to believe that there was what he calls a golden age of freedom in the American college. (I assure you that those he thinks he is criticizing believe no such thing.) There was a time when American colleges were completely denominational—so much so that no one who was critical of Christianity could teach in them. As Professor Gildersleeve once put it: "The teachers were either clergyman or men who, having failed to make good in foreign missions, were permitted to try their hands on the young barbarians at home." In some colleges no one could teach unless he was a Baptist, and in others unless he subscribed to some specific dogmas and techniques of Baptism. When the proposal was made to de-religionize or secularize the colleges, everyone understood what this meant. It didn't mean that religion wouldn't be studied but only that the college as a corporate institution would take no religious position, that instruction would not be geared to any Christian dogma, that faculty and students would be free to believe or not to believe, and that if they were Baptists the college would not be concerned whether they chose to dip or sprinkle to achieve salvation.

What would we say to some spiritual forbear of Henry Aiken who objected to the proposal that colleges as institutions be neutral in religion, and addressed us in the following words: "It is absurd to demand that the colleges not take a religious position. For our real choice is between one religion and another. The very refusal to take a religious position is itself a religious position. Even those who urge the colleges to reorganize their curriculums to permit students to seek the truth for themselves about religion or anything else—are they not making a religion of the truth?"

What, I ask, would we say to this kind of retort, that parallels Aiken's view that the refusal of a university to take a political position is itself a brand of politics? I think we would say with Charles Peirce that there is such a thing as the ethics of words in given contexts, and that Aiken has manifestly violated it. We would say that he has missed the whole point of the controversy, which is whether it is appropriate for the college to make a *specific* religious or political commitment when its members differ widely in their religious and political views.

The illogic of the retort obfuscates political thinking, too. I believe, for example, that we should tolerate in the political marketplace the expression of any ideas. Consequently, I must also believe that we cannot suffer those who are actively intolerant of the expression of ideas, who prevent those of whom they disapprove from speaking by force. Along comes someone inspired by Henry Aiken's logic who charges me with intolerance, too. "You, too, are intolerant," he says, "just as much as the intolerant Nazi Storm Troopers and Red Guards who break up the classes of their professors. Everyone is intolerant—only about different things. In claiming to be tolerant *you* are guilty of bad faith! For if you were *truly* tolerant, you would tolerate intolerance. Since you are intolerant of intolerance—you are a hypocrite!"

What does it mean when we say that the university should be depoliticalized? Nothing so absurd as Aiken pretends to believe in most of his paper. There are perfectly clear contexts in which we understand and have used the expression without difficulty. I shall give two illustrations, one from this country and one from Germany.

As everyone knows or should know, American higher education has never been free from political controls of the most blatant kind. When I began my academic career, no one who was known as a Socialist and, in many places even as a progressive, could be hired. I could cite instances galore of a political, religious, racial, and social bias that violated the principles of academic freedom. As Council Members of the AAUP [American Association of University Professors] during the thirties, fighting to establish recognition of these principles, we meant by "depoliticalization of the university" that the university was not to penalize faculty members or students for exercising thier rights as citizens, that the universities were not to make allegiances to capitalism or to any other social or political ideology a condition for membership in the academic community. These principles of academic freedom—reversing the whole course of educational history—gradually began to win acceptance. For example, in 1935, together with A. J. Muste and some left-wing labor leaders, I organized the American Workers Party with a militant socialist political program. Whereupon the Hearst Press launched a national campaign demanding my dismissal. To everyone's surprise, New York University refused to yield. That was a great step towards the depoliticalization of the university in America—Roger Baldwin thought it was a turning point!—for other institutions rapidly moved in the same direction. There are, of course, still abuses. But how far acceptance of academic freedom has gone is evident in the failure to unseat Professor Eugene Genovese, a public supporter of the Viet Cong, despite a gubernatorial campaign in which his right to teach was the chief issue. Aiken claims that if the American university were depoliticalized, Marcuse couldn't teach, Chomsky couldn't teach, nor could I. On the contrary: the fact that all of us, and even individuals far more extreme politically, teach is evidence of the degree to which depoliticalization has gone. *The American university is far less politicalized today than at any time in the past.*

Here is the second illustration. In the late years of the Weimar Republic, the Nazis attacked the professional integrity of the German universities because of their failure as corporate bodies to condemn the Versailles *Dictat*—the peace treaty which unfairly asserted that Germany was solely responsible for the First World War. This was denounced as a betrayal of *das deutsche Volk* [*the German people*]. It was charged, with a logic and language much like Aiken's, that the refusal to take a political position, to become politically involved, was itself a political act hostile to the German community, German education, and to German youth who were branded as the offspring of war criminals in the eyes of the world. And when Hitler came to power, his minions purged those who had urged the German universities to remain politically neutral. That action was properly called "politicalizing" the university.

Those of us who oppose politicalization contend that teachers should be free to make whatever political choices or commitments they please as citizens, but that the university as a corporate body should not make partisan political commitments. What Aiken contends is that it is partisan to be nonpartisan. (The same silly logic would prove that there are only nouns in the English language because when I say that " 'And' is a conjunction," " 'From' is a preposition," etc. they are really *nouns* because they are subjects of the sentence.)

In short, the "depoliticalization" of the university means the growth, defense, and vitality of academic freedom. The "politicalization" of the university means threats to and erosion of the principles of academic freedom. By academic freedom is meant the freedom of professionally qualified persons to inquire into, to discover, to publish, and to teach the "truth" as they see it—or reach "conclusions" in fields where the term 'truth' may be inapplicable, as in the fine or practical arts—without interference from ecclesiastical, political, or administrative authorities. The only permissible limits on the academic freedom of any teacher would flow from evidence established by qualified bodies of his peers or profession that he was clearly incompetent or had violated the standards of professional ethics. These are the current rules of the AAUP, which now are almost universally accepted.

Today it is a fact ignored by Professor Aiken that these principles of academic freedom are being threatened more by extremist students than by fundamentalist bishops, economic royalist tycoons, and political demagogues. For these students presume to determine who should speak on campus and who shouldn't, break up meetings of those with whom they disagree, disrupt the classrooms of teachers of whom they disapprove, demand the cessation of research *they* regard as not in the public interest, and clamor for the dismissal of teachers whose views they denounce as racist, reactionary or imperialist. On campus after campus, as the *New York Times* editorially declared when Dr. Hayakawa's meetings were shamelessly disrupted, these students acted just like the Nazi Storm Troopers whose hob-nailed boots and clubs broke up the classes of the Socialist and Jewish professors.

A depoliticalized university is one in which all sorts of political positions may be studied, defended, and criticized, so long as the ethics of inquiry are not violated. It is one in which the university as a corporate body may take a stand on public political issues that threaten the existence and operation of the principles of academic freedom. It is or should be jealous of its relative educational autonomy of the state even when it receives the support of the state. But this does not make it a political institution any more than a church which protests a measure that would restrict its freedom of religious worship therewith becomes a political institution. As an institution, the function of the university is not to exercise political power but to clarify and test ideas.

This conception of the university, as I shall try to make plain, differs from Aiken's not only in degree but in kind. But before developing these differences I want to say something about his descriptions of American higher education, past and present. He tells us he is no formalist. I don't know what he exactly means by this, but if all he means is that he is indifferent to formal logic, it is apparent enough. I am not a formalist either, but I believe that a little respect for formal logic would not be amiss. It would enable him to distinguish more clearly between a contradictory and contrary, which he obviously confuses.

If Aiken is not a formalist, is he an empiricist taking his point of departure from concrete historical fact? Unfortunately not, because on critical matters he makes up his facts as he goes along. Here are three major examples.

1. He states that the programs of General Education introduced at Columbia and Harvard were "quite simply to awaken the minds of students to the transcendental virtues of our American system and the wickedness of all systems that oppose it." This is sheer invention. I know something about the Columbia system and the men who devised and taught it. Almost to a man they were critics of contemporary society. The program grew out of John Erskine's "great books" course in the humanities and was broadened to include social studies which were actually basic critiques of the students' assumptions about the American society. For the first time in the history of American education, Marx and Engels's *Communist Manifesto* was required reading. Many of the teachers and students in that program became the architects of the New Deal. For many years it was a genuine liberating educational experience. It received the approval of John Dewey. The major criticisms of it were not that it was political but that it wasn't specialized enough, and this criticism came from the scientists because of the great difficulties encountered in developing General Education courses in science.

2. Or take Aiken's charge that government and foundation grants have "political strings attached" to them. Just a few years ago, when Aiken was still at Harvard, a Report of a Special Faculty Committee appointed to supervise the operation of grants, declared that no political strings were attached to any grant, that no government or foundation financing had subverted research.

It is interesting that some research grants to Chomsky and other ardent critics of American foreign policy have come from the Navy and other government institutions with absolutely no political strings attached.

The subject is very complex but three things are clear. No one compels a university or a faculty member to undertake any research of which it or he disapproves. The faculty as an educational body has the right to lay down guidelines governing the use of its facilities, the time of its members, the limits of secrecy, et cetera. No accredited university I know of accepts grants to prove a point of view in advance, or to inculcate opinions or conclusions specified by the donor. Subject to these conditions it is perfectly permissible for a person passionately concerned for the education of free men in a free society to accept research bearing on the defense of the free society, without which academic freedom and the free university cannot survive. To leave the free *society* defenseless and vulnerable to totalitarian aggression is to imperil the survival of the free *university,* too. Defense-related research initiated by Einstein in this country and other scientists in England enabled the Western world to turn back the threat of Hitler, whose victory would have meant the end of all basic freedoms—in the academy and out. Neither Aiken nor I would be talking here tonight if universities had been forbidden to engage in any research "designed to enhance the (democratic) state's military power" during the years when totalitarianism threatened to engulf the Western world.

3. Finally, take Aiken's charge that faculties have no real academic authority over curriculum or conditions of tenure, that overnight "the formal powers can always be reconverted by university presidents and governing boards into actual power." This is wrong about things that matter most. Aiken is simply ignorant that in most legal jurisdictions in the United States today, the tenure rules adopted by the AAUP and the AAU [the American Association of Universities] have the force of law. President Abrams holds his post at the will of his board but happily for us Professor Aiken cannot be deprived of his tenure either by the will of President or the Board of Brandeis. And if he doesn't believe that this represents real progress and power for the faculty, I recommend that he read Hofstadter and Metger's *The History of Academic Freedom in American Higher Education* or Upton Sinclair's *Brass Check.*

There are many things wrong with American colleges and universities and you will find my criticisms detailed in my book *Education for Modern Man* and *Academic Freedom and Academic Anarchy.* But Aiken's picture or map of academic reality is way off base. He himself says it is overdrawn by an "inch." But on some maps drawn to scale an inch represents a hundred miles or more. Actually his is the wrong map of the wrong country. It tells us more about him than about the university. It proves that he is not a formalist, not a sober empiricist but—what shall we say?—a fantasist! And although he confesses—in an attempt to disarm criticism—that he may be "a bit disingenuous" he is obviously no judge of size or distance.

Basically, the great and unbridgeable difference between Aiken's position and the view he misrepresents is that, whereas the latter recognizes the right and sometimes the obligation of the university as an *unpolitical corporate body* to take a stand on issues that threaten the integrity of academic freedom, Aiken would convert the university into a political action organization taking corporate decisions on anything which affects "the condition of liberal learning" or "the wide and deep aims of higher education." This takes in the whole range of politics from the income tax, housing programs, interstate commerce, to defense, foreign policy, and disarmament measures.

Listen to this: "The great and ineluctable fact is that no institution, given its ends, is more profoundly involved in problems of politics and government than the university (note: not even our Courts, Congress and Legislatures! S. H.) . . . Ours has become for better or worse a kind of Platonic republic whose crucial institution is the academy."

This gives the whole case away: We are *not* a Platonic republic but a democratic republic whose crucial institutions in political matters are not the academy but a Congress and Executive responsible to the electorate. This is the worst form of elitism, and smacks of Marcuse, not of James or Dewey. This university is founded by the democratic community not to engage in politics or influence legislation but to provide opportunities for the free exploration and critical study of all ideas, political and nonpolitical, in the faith that this quest will lead to clearer ideas, more reliable knowledge, and indirectly to more enlightened policy. The university should be the locus of competent and disinterested investigation of human problems, a source and resource for the entire community, dedicated not only to the teaching and testing of known truths and accepted values but to winning new truths, broaching fresh perspectives and values on the open frontiers of human experience. The community does not look to the university as a political action group or political corporate body engaged in a struggle for political power by influencing legislation or laying down Platonic mandates for the masses of ignorant citizens. It looks to it, to be sure, to *study* political ideas, among others. But to study political ideas does not make the university a political institution, to study religious ideas does not make it a religious institution, any more than to study crime makes it a criminal institution.

To politicalize the university in the manner Aiken suggests is to invite educational disaster. First of all, it would lead to the loss of its tax exemption. Legal actions even now are pending against some universities which officially endorsed the Vietnam Mobilization Day by dismissing classes! Secondly, it would turn faculties into warring political factions, each of which would seek allies not only among students but among outside political groups—at the cost of genuine educational activity. Intellectual controversy, of course, is to be welcomed in the universities. But the kind of political controversies generated by concern with all the political issues that are construed by some faculty members as having a bearing on "the wide and deep aims of higher education" is sure to plunge institutions into educational chaos. The results of such politicalization are evident in some South American and Asian universities, and manifest also on some embattled campuses in this country.

Finally—and this is the greatest danger of all—the attempt to politicalize the university along Aiken's lines is sure to inspire a reaction from the larger political community resentful of the political intrusion of a publicly subsidized educational institution. Political majorities, local, state, and national, will themselves move to politicalize the universities to prevent educational resources and opinions from being mobilized against them. There are some evidences of this at hand already. Colleges and universities will be politicalized with a vengeance. The first casualities of this vengeance will be the principles of academic freedom and tenure themselves, won after such bitter battles, and among the victims will be not only the Aikens—who know not what they do when they needlessly rouse by their provocations the sleeping furies of American vigilantism—but those of us who wish to preserve the autonomy of the educational process at its highest levels.

Aiken is blind or reckless about the educational direction of his policy of politicalization. What he proposes is to set back the clock to the days when the cultural Babbits and the economic Bourbons declared that scholarship and teaching must be kept in leading strings to good citizenship—except that his conception of good citizenship differs from theirs.

The view I oppose to his is that the university does not have to choose between one conception of good citizenship or another, that what makes a man a good citizen is no more the affair of the university than what makes him a good husband, that its primary concern is whether he is a good teacher and scholar. Just as I have no right when I take a political stand as a citizen to commit the university, so the university as a corporate body of which I am a member, except on matters of academic freedom, has no right to take a political stand that in the eyes of the public commits me.

28

Myths and Realities: McCarthyism and Communism

INTRODUCTION

Political passion and prejudice have contributed to developing a false picture of the nature, pervasiveness, and lasting effect of Senator Joseph McCarthy's crusade in the fifties against Communists in government, before he destroyed his credibility by attacks on the United States Army and the officers who wear its uniform. An entire treatise would be necessary to do justice to the multiform aspects of the McCarthy phenomenon. Here I wish to state certain truths that have been lost sight of or denied for partisan purposes by one political side or another.

The first is that McCarthyism was a political and cultural disaster that outlasted the half-decade of its emergence and eclipse. One sign of this is that the term "McCarthyism" has become synonymous with unjustified and unjustifiable criticism. When used and uncontested, the term renders unnecessary any reasoned reply to criticism. It has in consequence become the standard response to any prima facie case directed against individuals falsely alleged to be liberals or radicals or Communists and sometimes by those truthfully identified but who seek to avoid meeting the evidence.

The second truth is that McCarthyism, as a movement dedicated to the exposure and criticism of Communism, was, by virtue of its excesses and exaggerated claims, a positive boon to the Communist movement and particularly to those who were not officially members of the Communist party but who were consciously supporting the political line of the Communist party

---

Originally published as "Communists, McCarthy and American Universities," from *Minerva: A Review of Science, Learning and Policy* 25, No. 3, (Autumn, 1987): 331–48. The author has added a new introduction for this volume.

in a vast number of so-called united front cultural and political associations. They passed themselves off as victims and martyrs of a ruthless demagogue engaged in a "witch hunt." Everyone knew that witches didn't exist. . . .

Third, American public opinion, as measured by the polls, showed overwhelming support for McCarthy and his investigative procedures until the debacle of his attack on the Army.

Fourth, very few discussions of McCarthy and his era give an adequate explanation of the popularity of McCarthy's demagogic approach to the problem of national security, Even President Eisenhower, who personally detested McCarthy, avoided a public showdown with him until McCarthy had alienated the American public and was officially rebuked by the Senate. There are some who have argued that it was President Truman's security program that prepared the way for McCarthy—a view that suffers from serious difficulties. It overlooks the obvious fact that the conditions that gave rise to Truman's security program were also the ones that alarmed the American public about the readiness, and capacity, of our administrative and executive procedures to resist penetration by hostile agents or individuals under the close influence and guidance of Communist organizations. Even more important, this view overlooks—and sometimes contests—the moral and prudential justification of a security program at a time when the threat of war with the Soviet Union was apparent. Of course, there were absurdities and excesses in the security program, particularly by politically unsophisticated types recruited from the Midwest who had difficulty distinguishing between an enthusiastic New Dealer, a follower of Norman Thomas, and a Communist adept in the ways of protective rhetorical coloration. However, it was none other than Roger Baldwin, founder of the American Civil Liberties Union, who declared, before that organization had become transformed to further a political and social agenda, "Anyone who owes a primary allegiance to a foreign government is disqualified from serving his own."

This brings us to the complex events that created the public feelings which McCarthy was able to exploit by his unscrupulous exaggerations. Any knowledgeable person who lived through the period would have to acknowledge the cumulative impact of the following: the Communist *coup d'état* in Democratic Czechoslovakia; the Gouzenko and Hiss cases; the Hiss trials; the Congressional revelation that Communist penetration extended to high places in the American government; the Rosenberg cases; the Judith Coplan case; the victory in China by Communists sometimes referred to as "agrarian reformers"; the success of the Soviet Union in breaking the U.S. monopoly of atomic weapons—widely even if mistakenly believed to be a consequence of violations of security; the trials of the leaders of the American Communist party, who frankly avowed that in the event of a conflict with the Soviet Union, they would not support the United States; the successive crises over

Berlin, culminating in the Berlin airlift; and finally the outbreak of the Korean War, at which time Senator McCarthy had already launched his campaign. It was these events, not listed in historical order, but all occurring within a narrow period of time, that account for the public tolerance McCarthy enjoyed until his act of political suicide. It was *not* President Truman's belated security program that prepared the way for McCarthy's reception.

One other factor could be mentioned. As a long line of respondents summoned to appear before Congressional committees legally authorized to conduct their inquiries resorted to artful deception or refusal to testify or to the invocation of the Fifth Amendment, hitherto the last resort of notorious criminals, an impression was generated that the number, activity, and danger from Communists in American life was much greater than it actually was. Traditionally, socialists and Communists in the past—from the times of Karl Marx to that of Eugene V. Debs—had made proud avowals of their beliefs, disdaining concealment. They acted like heretics, not conspirators. Whatever one thought of the wisdom of Congressional investigations—and liberals had lauded their usefulness in the past—the Communist party was a legal organization; membership in it was not a criminal affair; and acknowledgment of mere membership involved no risk to one's freedom or life. To be sure, truthfulness entailed danger to continued employment, but so did invocation of the Fifth Amendment.

In addition, most of the witnesses summoned had been identified by former members of the Communist party. The Communist party was ostensibly a party of professional revolutionists. It was part of an international revolutionary movement—the Comintern, later the Cominform, both organized by the Soviet Union. The Congressional hearings provided an opportunity for these men and women to proclaim their beliefs openly, to defend them in a principled way. This had been done by their mortal enemies, the Trotskyists in the Socialist Workers party, whose unjust conviction they had enthusiastically approved. Instead of voicing their sincere beliefs, these revolutionists resorted to every stratagem and sometimes to outright perjury to avoid disclosing the truth. Years later, with the help of sympathizers in the media, they tried to pass themselves off as martyrs to their convictions. Sometimes they succeeded. Most of these individuals were teachers or Hollywood figures.

It is often said that the McCarthy years initiated a "reign of terror" in American educational institutions that resulted in a chilling of dissent in universities of the time. The notion still enjoys a wide currency on both sides of the Atlantic. It is symptomatic of the fanastic way history is sometimes rewritten. As a matter of fact, the American universities were the most active centers of opposition to McCarthy and McCarthyism. In a famous study by Paul Lazarsfeld and Wagner Thidens on the impact of McCarthyism on universities—especially on the attitudes of American social scientists when

McCarthy was riding high—they concluded, after a survey of 2,500 individuals, that the academic supporters of McCarthy ran a greater risk of being ostracized and penalized by their colleagues (denied promotion, salary increases, and customary perks) than did those accused of communism. The researchers also discovered that comparatively few confessed to having been less outspoken in their criticisms of the foreign and domestic policies of the nation in consequence of McCarthy's intimidation. Of this group, there was no evidence of any professor who had been a vehement critic of national policy *before* the advent of McCarthy, moderating his voice and views *after* McCarthy appeared on the scene. Those who are customarily silent remained silent. There was no persuasive evidence that the continuation of their silence was induced by fear of McCarthyism.

Those who suffered most from the excesses of McCarthy's crusade against Communists in government were not the teachers but government officials in the State Department and overseas agencies. McCarthy and his lieutenants, Roy Cohen and David Schine, sought to blow up every liberal association of government officials into something politically sinister. In consequence, until McCarthy's debacle, government officials were seriously hampered in the execution of their official duties. They tended to play it safe in order not to call attention to themselves. Cohen and Schine ransacked the libraries of the U.S. information offices and other international agencies to find evidence of deliberate political indoctrination, making themselves appear ridiculous in the pages of the European press and prejudicing the judgment of intelligent Europeans against the nation these uninformed zealots professed to serve.[1]

It was the prolonged television hearings on the U.S. Army, particularly McCarthy's insult to General Zurcher, who had promoted Major Perris, a member of the Communist party, that destroyed McCarthy's credibility. His ratings among public viewers plummeted after he charged that General Zurcher was "a disgrace to the uniform he wore." General Zurcher was blissfully unconscious of the nature of communism and believed that the Communist party as a political party was no different from other political parties. In part this reflected a survival of the attitude among sections of the military developed during the euphoric days when the Soviet Union was being greeted, after Hitler's double-cross of Stalin, as "a democratic ally" rather than a co-belligerent. It also reflected the failure of political education in the armed forces, for which attempts at a remedy were soon made.[2]

General Zurcher's lapse was no warrant for impugning his patriotism and integrity, and indirectly, that of our armed forces. These hearings sealed McCarthy's fate. The official adoption by the United States Senate of a resolution rebuking the Senator from Wisconsin ended his political career—which, oddly enough, had begun on a national scale when he unseated the anti-Communist Progressive Philip LaFollette, with the indirect support of the Communist party.

I have deemed this introductory note to be necessary because of the periodic attempts to picture the period when McCarthy was making his wild accusations and exaggerations as "a reign of terror," in which the United States narrowly escaped losing its freedom. The further removed we are from this period and the less knowledge one possesses of the whole picture, the more embellished is the myth circulated about it by left-wing figures. Not long ago, Leonard Bernstein, the patron and host of the revolutionary Black Panthers of the sixties, declared that the McCarthy incident was "the closest we have come to tyranny."[3] Musical gifts make one no more immune to political absurdity than do artistic or poetic gifts, as the cases of Pablo Picasso and Ezra Pound so aptly show.

The primary point about the reaction of the nation's professional educators to McCarthy is that their strong opposition to him and his tactics was coupled with a principled opposition to communism. McCarthy may have been the precipitating cause of their discovery of the problem of the presence of active members of the Communist party whose official party instructions bid them to indoctrinate "without exposing themselves" for the party line. But the position they took in particular cases—whether regarded as right, wrong, or simply confused—was taken independently, not out of fear of McCarthy or anyone else. Any one familiar with the life, character, and scholarship of men like Arthur O. Lovejoy, Brand Blanshard, John Dewey, or Norman Thomas, and other leading figures in the discussion that raged on the American campuses in the early fifties will testify to that.

If this book, *No Ivory Tower: McCarthyism and the Universities* by Ellen Schrecker,[4] were not offered as a serious study of an important period in American higher education, one would be tempted to characterize it as an extraordinary work of fiction. It is a purportedly objective piece of historical scholarship which tries to establish that the approximately hundred persons dismissed from their posts in American institutions of higher education in the 1940s and 1950s, on the grounds that their membership in the Communist party was incompatible with the fulfilment of their professional academic duties, were innocent victims of the greatest violation of academic freedom in the history of the United States. Further, the book contends that the chief responsibility for these outrageous actions must be attributed not to the reactionary spokesmen of cultural and political vigilantism like Senator McCarthy and Senator McCarran and their committees, but to the liberal establishment itself in the universities, including, for all their fine words, liberal administrators, and especially the liberal professors—among whom I for one am singled out as notably guilty. "The conservative colleagues were probably more antagonistic [to the members of the Communist party] but the liberal ones were more powerful. And it was the latter, those moderate and respectable professors who, as the established leaders of the faculty on most campuses, discouraged strenuous opposition to the witch-hunt and so in that way collaborated in its implementation."[5]

Dr. Schrecker does not go so far as to assert that had the liberals not been so cowardly, especially the American Association of University Professors, there would have been no acts of injustice against the hapless victims identified as members of the Communist party. But she certainly believes that if the liberals had vigorously opposed the "witch-hunt," and the rationalizations for them, the dismissals would have been far fewer. She is very indignant with them for swallowing the—to her—preposterous notion that active and present membership in the Communist party in its Stalinist heyday was no more relevant than membership in any other political party to the performance of one's professional duties and fidelity to the academic ethic.

The author makes other claims, equally extravagant, about related issues, including the Truman security program. To do justice to them would require a volume. Indeed I have already written such a volume bearing on the problem of academic freedom and Communist party membership, *Heresy, Yes—Conspiracy, No,*[6] and I would be content with the judgment of a critical-minded reader in comparing that book with Dr. Schrecker's.

Why, then, do I regard it as justifiable to take the time and energy to assess Dr. Schrecker's extreme claims? First, her book continues a trend initiated by Miss Vivian Gornick's fairy tale, *The Romance of American Communism,* and other volumes to rehabilitate in the eyes of the liberal American public, the American Communist party during the years of its absolute Stalinist vassalage. Thanks to this trend, and despite assumptions to the contrary, students today and a considerable number of their teachers are not well informed about the nature of communism and its history, especially the activities of the Communist party in the 1930s and 1940s and the degree of control exercised over it by the Kremlin.

The second reason for paying attention to Dr. Schrecker's books is that despite the shoddiness of its argument and the vast ignorance—some may charge deceit—displayed about the structure and operations of the Communist party cells during the period in question, the book has been astonishingly well received. With two exceptions, Theodore Draper's devastating criticism in *The New Republic*[7] and Edward Shapiro's review in *The World and I,*[8] Dr. Schrecker's reading of the events has enjoyed a sympathetic and, in places, an enthusiastic reception. Thirdly, the book calls attention to a very difficult problem posed by "New Left" scholarship during recent years in its persistent effort to politicize the universities.

How does Dr. Schrecker go about establishing her case? Primarily by suppressing relevant evidence, and by distorting the relevant evidence where it could not be shrugged off.

Among the interesting omissions is her failure to make even a passing reference to the educational credo of the Graduate Faculty of the New School for Social Research founded in 1934 for German and Italian exiles who at the time, and in the nature of the case, could hardly be denounced as "red-baiters" by Dr. Schrecker and her political allies. Once very well known, and widely quoted during the period she discusses, its credo conveys the key distinction between heresy and conspiracy that I elaborated in my many writings on the theme:

> The New School knows that no man can teach well, nor should he be permitted to teach at all, unless he is prepared "to follow the truth of scholarship wherever it may lead." No inquiry is ever made as to whether a lecturer's private views are conservative, liberal, or radical; orthodox or agnostic; views of the aristocrat or commoner. Jealously safeguarding this precious principle, the New School stoutly affirms that a member of any political party or group which assert the right to dictate in matters of science or scientific opinion is not free to teach the truth and thereby is disqualified as a teacher.

What is the relevance of the statement of the Graduate Faculty to Dr. Schrecker's inquiry? Direct and indirect reference was frequently made to the statement, and specifically to the last sentence. Dr. Schrecker is very well aware that sometimes university committees, wrestling with the problem posed by the existence of Communist party members on their faculties, actually cited the very words of the statement. Had she, too, cited it, readers would naturally ask whether the Communist party was a party which "asserts the right to dictate" to its members whatever their discipline; if so, how that could be squared with the commitment to honest inquiry, and why a considered belief that it could not should be evidence of "witch-hunting" and mindless McCarthyism.

But Dr. Schrecker's sins of omission pale when compared with her sins of distortion. She is quite aware of the explicit instructions to members of the Communist party published in its official organ as integral to their responsibilities. For example, the following:

> Party and YCL [Young Communist League] factions set up within classes and departments must supplement and combat by means of discussions, brochures, etc. bourgeois omissions and distortions in the regular curriculum. . . . Marxist-Leninist analysis must be injected into every class.
>
> Communist teachers must take advantage of their positions, without exposing themselves, to give their students to the best of their ability working-class [i.e., Communist] education. . . .
>
> Only when teachers have really mastered Marxism-Leninism will they be able skilfully to inject it into their teaching at the least risk of exposure and at the same time conduct struggles around the school in a truly Bolshevik manner.[9]

She cites only one sentence from this and dismisses its significance as something written by "a pseudonymous Richard Frank," suddenly unaware that the use of false party names was *de rigueur* for all but a few professional members of the party apparatus, and unaware too of the authoritative character of the publication. She adds that this and other evidence was "out of date" but fails to state where, when, and in what respect these instructions were modified or repealed. Since she complains that great play was made of these and other citations from the Communist official press, nothing could have been easier than for the party to indicate that Richard Frank was guilty of "left deviationism" and that his declaration and comparable citations—like Earl Browder's sworn statement that party members must carry out all party directives, and the Resolution of the Ninth Convention of the Communist party that "All Communists must at all times take a position on every question that is in line with the party"—were no longer binding.

Dr. Schrecker simply ignores wherever she can any declaration of the Communist party that on its face would raise a *prima facie* doubt about the academic fitness of an active Communist party member to live up to his obligations to pursue and teach the truth as he honestly sees it, regardless of whether it agrees with the party line or not. Thus she never mentions William Z. Foster's directive, "In drawing professionals into the Party care should be taken to select only those individuals who show by definite work that they definitely understand the Party line, and are prepared to accept Party discipline."[10] Sometimes Schrecker unwittingly gives her case away by overlooking the significance of a reference in the retrospective account of a disillusioned Communist. She quotes from the recollections of a Communist student leader at Harvard: "I remember being visited by a couple of members of the Control Committee of the Boston Party."[11] This was as late as 1949! She does not seem to understand the implications of the reference to a "control committee"—referred to as a "control commission" by Earl Browder in other testimony; nor of the implications of her reference to another Communist who "was expelled on some far-fetched charges that reflected the Party's desire to rid itself of someone who was becoming increasingly critical of its growing rigidity and sectarianism."[12] Apparently the control commission was working! Dr. Schrecker does not dream of asking whether any doubt could be reasonably entertained about the academic fitness from the university's viewpoint of those present and active members of the Communist party on its teaching staff who had survived the operations of the Communist control commission. Would not a fair-minded, even if politically partisan, inquirer have considered this question legitimate?

Dr. Schrecker refuses to consider these and similar questions because she flatly and repeatedly asserts that the evidence I have cited of the Communist party's desire to promote communism in the classroom constituted no proof.

She then adds "There was no other proof, no doubt [*sic!*] because there was no indoctrination."[13] Whether there was other proof and what would constitute proof, I shall come to in a moment. But if we ask Dr. Schrecker what is the source of her certainty that the Communist party members did not indoctrinate, her answer is that each and every one denied it. In view of her own admissions about the lies, deceptions, and perjuries of those she questions, which in places she herself deplores as unwise strategy, albeit understandable and forgivable, her faith in their veracity on this point is touching.

Dr. Schrecker is not alone in falling back on the retort, which in effect repudiates the credo of the Graduate Faculty of the New School and holds that no matter what members of the Communist party are ordered to do, no matter even what they intended to do, one must prove that they actually carried out their instructions before one is justified in taking any measures against them. This would be a proper retort if they or anyone else were charged with having committed a crime and threatened with deprivation of their life or liberty. But otherwise where a person is under orders to betray a trust or there is good evidence that he is a member of a group which intends to betray a trust, it is not unreasonable to take protective steps to deprive him or her of the opportunity to betray that trust. It is simply a matter of common sense. The situation comes up again in considering the nonlegal applications of the invocation of the Fifth Amendment. A person in my employment as a nurse or secretary or tutor or any post involving trust may legally stay out of jail by invoking the Fifth Amendment in answer to a relevant question by legal authorities bearing on the performance of his or her duties in past or present employment, but a refusal to answer my questions relevant to the performance of their duties in my employment may undermine my confidence in their trustworthiness, and affect their eligibility for holding the position. And this has nothing to do with questioning and punishing them for their political beliefs. There are occasions when a person's beliefs may have a bearing on his eligibility for a post. For example, if a person were a fervent advocate of voluntary euthanasia on demand, this might be held to count against him if he were applying for the post of superintendent of a home for the aged and infirm. I suspect that Schrecker would not approve of barring a person who endorsed the Communist party's denunciation of the Marshall Plan as a means of enslaving Europe from a post supervising its execution, but would applaud barring persons with racist views from the police force. My question concerns their membership in an organization that instructs them to act in a manner that clearly violates the duties or obligations of their post.

I have written many pages, ignored by Dr. Schrecker, showing that although it is quite possible by occasional visits to determine a teacher's technical competence in the classroom, there is no feasible way of detecting systematic and potential indoctrination without continued eavesdropping, or secret surveillance or requesting students to act as informers or spies, and thus demoralizing the whole teaching process. That is why it seems axiomatic that once teachers are certifed as competent, we must have faith in their fidelity to the academic ethic, and forgo harassing them by any kind of ideological supervision. The presuppositions of the pedagogical credo of the Graduate Faculty of the New School are the presuppositions of honest inquiry and teaching, especially on the tertiary level of education.

Dr. Schrecker is also quite mistaken about whether other evidence exists about activities of members of the Communist party within the classroom and without. There is detailed testimony about meetings of Communist party teachers—some of it amusing—in which a member is criticized for the crudity of his propagandistic methods by his more skillful comrades. And far more compelling, because it is material evidence, are the shop-papers published anonymously under the official imprint of the Communist party cell and clandestinely distributed to teachers and students. The papers contained the most scurrilous and defamatory denunciations of colleagues who have run afoul of the Communist party line of the moment.[14] Dr. Schrecker is a trifle embarrassed by these shop-papers, but only a trifle. She refers to their "supposed scurrilousness," calls them "wildly controversial," and admits they were somewhat deficient "in good taste." She carefully refrains, however, from telling her readers some of the detailed charges they levelled at colleagues by name, such as accusing them of defalcation of college funds, charging that some were under surveillance for fraud, and others guilty of gross plagiarism, diversion of college property for home use, falsifying time-cards of workers to deprive them of their earnings, serving as paid informers "who perhaps get paid for taking photographs of students at meetings and demonstrations." Some of these charges were quite serious, particularly the charges of plagiarism and the criminal diversion of public funds. They were always and only directed against persons targeted because of their political views.

Even in retrospect Dr. Schrecker seems to have no notion of how such widely circulated anonymous charges affected those who were named, and their mischievous effect on morale and collegiality in universities and colleges. "Certainly," she confesses, "as some of these papers' editors were later to admit, they were somewhat lacking in gentility [*sic!*] as well as embarrassingly uncritical about the Soviet Union. . . ."[15] Instead of completing the sentence with a recognition of the untenability of such practices in a community of scholars and teachers, she adds, "but they were, nonetheless, the authentic voice of a politically significant segment of the academic community. They were also, apparently, fun to read."[16] These anonymous scurrilities may appeal to Dr. Schrecker's macabre sense of humor but there is reason to believe that the enjoyment was not shared by many readers at the time. Nor were they regarded merely as "shenanigans"—another disarming word she uses to discount their contemptible and libelous character. They are however authentic evidence of conduct unbecoming to teachers and scholars.

Despite all the evidence available, largely unmentioned in Dr. Schrecker's book, yet obviously known to her, of the fidelity with which Comrade Richard Frank's directives were carried out, she unwaveringly insists that interrogations about membership in the Communist party not only by congressional committees but by faculty committees were a crass violation of the rights of citizens who were every whit as loyal to their country as members of other political parties. Never mind the official declarations of the leaders of the Communist party that their primary allegiance was to defend the Soviet Union and to further the victory of communism here and elsewhere, and what that entailed. Never mind the frank avowal of the leaders of the Communist party that in the case of war between the United States and the Soviet Union the Communist party would remain faithful to its public pledge to defend the Soviet Union. The full pitch of Dr. Schrecker's denunciatory fury is directed against the liberal teachers and administrators who did not oppose and publicly protest against the dismissals of the Communist party members, and who often actually voted approval of the policy that present and active membership in the party was incompatible with the presuppositions of honest inquiry and teaching. It was they, Dr. Schrecker insists, who flagrantly violated the principles of academic freedom, not the members of the Communist party.

One is somewhat taken aback by the coolness of Dr. Schrecker's demands on teachers in the American universities at the time. She herself stresses that the issue of Communist party membership became a focus of national interest during the height of the Cold War, after a series of Communist seizures of power in Czechoslovakia, China, Eastern Europe and the threat of Communist victories in Western Europe, after a series of shocking disclosures of Communist penetration in high government offices, when there was popular fear that the Korean War might lead to another world war. Again and again she refers to the widespread and sometimes openly expressed apprehension—seemingly well-justified—that state legislatures and boards of trustees would curtail the budgets of universities if their faculties failed to take action against teachers identified as members of the Communist party and who refused to answer the relevant questions of their colleagues about complicity in the unprofessional conduct advised in the official party directives. Such curtailment of budgets could have led to a far greater loss of posts than the number of actual dismissals of Communists. True, it would not have directly affected anyone's tenure, but a spartan, punitive budget over some years, besides being educationally disastrous, would indirectly have put the tenure and promotion of many at risk.

Dr. Schrecker self-righteously rebukes the liberal teachers of American universities for lacking the courage to espouse a position that might have provoked a radical reduction in state budgets and risked a substantial loss in teaching posts—all in defense of a handful of persons who were actively engaged in a movement that had ruthlessly destroyed academic freedom wherever it came to power—often the very lives and families of its victims—and which if successful in the United States would destroy academic freedom of the teachers whom she censures. This is certainly no modest expectation!

Well, why not? If, as Dr. Schrecker assures us, these individuals had independent minds, were given to question authority, who, as she reads the available evidence, never resorted to indoctrination and who were committed in their inquiries and teaching to recognizable standards of objectivity and fairness, why should they not have been treated and tolerated as heretics, and not as conspirators against academic freedom and the academic ethic? Should not principled believers in academic freedom have been prepared to pay a price for their convictions? (Although Dr. Schrecker does not know it, Arthur O. Lovejoy, the redoubtable critic of Communists, founder with John Dewey of the American Association of University Professors—and together with me regarded by Dr. Schrecker as more villainous than Senator McCarthy because of our professed liberalism—was one of the few men in American academic life to resign a post in protest against the violation of the academic freedom of a colleague.)

But what about the overwhelming evidence—evidence Dr. Schrecker does not contest—that the allegedly objective-minded Communist party members in the universities followed the party line. "True," she admits, "but they did so in large part because it was heading in the same direction they were."[17] In other words, from common premises both the political committee of the Communist party, whether in the United States or the Soviet Union, and the members of the Communist party in American universities, independently reached common conclusions. If true, this goes decisively to the heart of the matter. Dr. Schrecker tells us that as a professional historian she "feels comfortable" with the evidence that it is true.

Here we have an assertion that is easy to check. There have been so many turns and somersaults in the direction of the Communist party on all sorts of questions that surely there must be some sort of evidence that academic members of the Communist party, especially the hundred whom Dr. Schrecker interviewed at length, publicly proclaimed a position critical of the existing direction and program of the Communist party before the change took place.

Let us begin with some local American issues. One day the American Communist party proclaimed as part of its political program the grant of "self-determination for the Black Belt." This was the application of the Soviet nationalities program on paper to the United States. In effect it was a "Jim

Crow policy" still preserving segregation. The effects of the proclamation of the slogan in the South was often pernicious and increased the already great obstacles to liberal progress in the South. The slogan was adopted by the Communist party before the entry of most university teachers into the party. It remained the party's policy throughout the 1930s and 1940s. Did the independent minds in the party's academic membership have any doubts about it? Did Dr. Schrecker ask them if they ever expressed opposition to this absurd, irresponsible, provocative policy that needlessly enhanced the dangers of educational and trade union organization in the South?

The theory of "Social Fascism," according to which Social Democrats were twins, not enemies, of fascism, was discarded by the Kremlin and the American party at the time of the Popular Front. Is there some evidence that somewhere, sometime, the persons of whose independence of mind Dr. Shrecker is convinced, criticized the theory before it was abandoned? She does not supply it.

By 1940 the Trotskyists had become "Trotskyite-Fascists," the Moscow trials of the Trotskyites and Old Bolsheviks had run their course, and the commission of which John Dewey was chairman had established that they were crude frame-ups. Some of the members of the Communist party interviewed and defended by Dr. Schrecker had originally been drawn to the Communist movement by Trotsky's writing on the Russian Revolution. Did any of them ever raise a question about the validity of the trials and the aspersions cast on Trotsky as an agent of Hitler? Among the persons Dr. Schrecker alleges to have independent minds were some who not only defended the Moscow trials but savagely attacked those of us who set out to establish a commission to examine the evidence. Some of them put their signatures to an infamous letter in the *Daily Worker* characterizing the Committee for Cultural Freedom, chief among whose organizers was John Dewey, as "Fascists and allies of Fascism," for referring to the Soviet Union as a totalitarian country.

At the outset of the New Deal, President Roosevelt's National Recovery Act was declared "Fascist" in the Communist Press. After the VIIth Congress of the Comintern, Roosevelt became a great democratic leader; after the Nazi-Soviet Pact he became an arrant warmonger; after Hitler turned on his ally, Stalin, Roosevelt became a greater democratic leader than before. Did any of the independent-minded members of the Communist party anticipate or call for these changes in direction before they took place? They did not. Schrecker admits that all but a very few remained members of the Communist party during the period of the Nazi-Soviet Pact. How then can she be comfortable with the evidence that clearly shows the truth of what she denies: that most followed the party line without any publicly expressed doubts or criticisms.

Most of the Communist party members interviewed by Dr. Schrecker were Jewish. In 1940 they may not have known that Stalin had turned over to Hitler and the Gestapo more than one hundred German-Jewish Communists who had fled to the Soviet Union for refuge, among whom was Margaret Neumann-Buber. Did any one of them protest when it became known? They certainly knew that Alter and Ehrlich, the leaders of the Jewish Bund, had been executed by Stalin despite Eleanor Roosevelt's plea for them, as spies of Hitler. Did they utter one word of protest?

Among the members of the Communist party whose intellectual integrity and independence Dr. Schrecker takes great pains to defend were scientists—some in physics, others in biology and medicine. In the late 1930s, when the reports of the purges and executions among the astronomers at the Pulkovo Observatory were published charging them with the incredible crime of "importing Trotskyite-Fascist ideas into the field of astronomy," did any of the natural scientists among American Communists speak out? When subsequently the purge of the geneticists began, did the members of the party, ostensibly dedicated to objective research, make public protest? Did Dr. Schrecker ask them? If not, why not? Did any of them say, as Lillian Hellman once explained in answer to the question why she never criticized Stalin, "He didn't affect me; after all I was living in the U.S., not the Soviet Union"? And if they did say something like this, did she ask: "Why then did you criticize so often and so strongly scientific repressions in Italy, Germany and Spain, other countries in which you did not live?"

With reference to the purge of Soviet geneticists and the failure of the allegedly independent-minded party members to protest against it, Dr. Schrecker has a typical way of insinuating that, despite appearances, they really were free from party guidance or dictation. They refrained from applauding the purge and upholding Lysenko. She cites the statement of an editor of the party's chief scholarly organ, *Science and Society,* which he claims was founded as "a forum where Marxists and non-Marxists of good will [*sic*] could argue the case for and against . . . over the entire range of scholarship." The editors, she asserts, "prided themselves on keeping their magazine wholly free from guidance or dictation from any quarter."

Dr. Schrecker is inclined to believe them: "And for the most part, they do seem to have kept the CP at a distance." Evidence? "When, in the 1950s, some of the Party's functionaries approached *Science and Society* with the suggestion that it deal sympathetically with Lysenko's genetic theories, they were flatly rejected." What kind of evidence is this to a professional historian? How many of the hundreds of articles and book reviews in *Science and Society* were critical of any position of the Communist party or Kremlin? Was there even one? What does "for the most part" mean here?

Dr. Schrecker does not deal honestly with the appearances, the failure to publish one critical word on the Soviet purges, even if the reality of the origin and operation of *Science and Society* were not clear to her. For a brief period in the mid-1930s there was an effort to publish a theoretical journal of Marxism outside the Communist party. It came to nought because Earl Browder insisted on vetoing as editors those he regarded as "enemies of the party," as Francis Henson of the negotiating committee reported. Because of that, *The Marxist Quarterly* was launched with Lewis Corey, James Burnham, Meyer Schapiro, Bertram Wolfe and myself as chief editors. It was followed by the publication of the organ of the true believers, *Science and Society*. By the 1950s Lysenko and the Soviet purges were a by-word in Western scientific circles.

One final question to Dr. Schrecker since her book covers the period from the early 1930s to the period after the Second World War: Out of the blue, Stalin decided to jettison Earl Browder and signal through the Cominform letter to Jacques Duclos, the leader of the French Communist party, the resumption of the Cold War against the West and the abandonment of the policy of "class collaboration." Not a single member of the cells of the Communist party in universities and colleges spoke up in criticism of Browder's policy before it was disavowed by the Kremlin. Before the receipt of the Duclos letter, Sam Darcy, not a member of any cell of university teachers, had criticized Browder for his excessive adherence to the policy of class collaboration. He was promptly expelled. In due course, to signify the importance of the new line, Browder himself was unceremoniously expelled. Did a single one of the independent minds Dr. Schrecker would have us believe were members of the Communist party come to Browder's defense? Not one. Independent minds! Indeed of all the Communist parties the American Communist party seems to have been the least independent. It was more like the Bulgarian party than the Communist party of Great Britain, the members of which had difficulty at times with the policy of deception, and which permitted J. B. S. Haldane in the pages of its *Daily Worker* to defend the view that life could survive the destruction of the body. Such freedom of thought was not tolerated in the American Communist party; there is no evidence presented by Dr. Schrecker that any of the American academics whom she defends ever attempted such freedom of expression.

I could fill pages with additional evidence that what Dr. Schrecker offers us as objective research in her guise of a professional historian seeking the truth is erroneous and misleading from the first page to the last. She has offered us what some might consider the equivalent of a cooked, "managed" experiment in the natural sciences, or of a report of scientific findings that deliberately omits some essential data and distorts others. When such things are discovered in the sciences the culprits are usually barred from academic life, and those responsible for their presence or who have approved of their work, are severely censured by their peers for violating elementary standards of scholarship.

Could Dr. Schrecker have approached her project with an open mind and a genuine desire to reach "objective" scholarly conclusions? She seems to write as a defense attorney, resolved in advance, regardless of the evidence, to portray her clients as innocent martyrs of a cowardly and sometimes vicious liberal inquisition. At no time does she state fairly the position of those who in troubled times had to deal with the problems of academic integrity within the university or of national security without. Because members of the Communist party were "loyal" American citizens, she holds there was no need of a "security programme" even in governmental research laboratories. The security officers in atomic plants "did not realize that most of the secrets they were zealously guarding belonged to Mother Nature, not Uncle Sam."[18] She caricatures as political persecution the reasonable position of those who argued that the denial of access to positions of trust to members of a tightly disciplined party pledged to the support of the Soviet Union at all costs. Their argument "rested on the explicit [*sic!*] assumption that all Communists followed the Party line all the time. This meant not only the academic Communists would commit illegal acts if ordered to do so by the Kremlin but also that they had surrendered their intelligence to the Party as well."[19] It meant nothing of the sort. One need not defend the excesses and errors of the security policy to recognize that it rested on the reasonable view, grounded in evidence, that members of the Communist party were untrustworthy where matters of trust were involved. Hypothetically, of course, it is not impossible to find a member of the Communist party who remains loyal to his own government rather than to the directives of the party. The best reply to that hypothetical possibility in security measures was made by Clement Attlee, then British Prime Minister, who declared, after a whole herd of valuable horses had been stolen from the stables: "there is no way of distinguishing such people from those who, if opportunity offered, would be prepared to endanger the security of the state in the interests of another power. Therefore it is too risky to employ them." Roger Baldwin, the then head of the American Civil Liberties Union, an organization quite different from the present one that misuses the name, had earlier declared that "a superior loyalty to a foreign government disqualifies a citizen from service to our own."

Teaching in a university, of course, did not involve as a rule national security. But it did involve matters of trust—of professional ethics and integrity. From time to time, Dr. Schrecker quotes members of the Communist party who insist that they held the ideas they did, not because they were members of the Communist party, but were members of the Communist party because of the ideas they held. Very well then. We know the Communist party, in theory and practice, anywhere, did not believe in academic freedom, regarded it as not only legitimate but as a mandatory duty of its members to indoctrinate in classrooms, enroll students wherever possible in Communist youth organizations, rewrite textbooks from the Communist point of view, build cells within the teaching staff of colleges and universities, gain control of departments, and inculcate the Communist line that in case of imperialist war, especially if the United States was at war with the Soviet Union, students should turn their arms against their own government. There was no secret where the Communist party stood on any of these matters. Did any of the persons whom Dr. Schrecker defends ever repudiate these tenets? Could there be any doubt what the Communist party position was on academic freedom, and what the fate of opponents and dissidents would be wherever the Communist party came to power?

To Arthur O. Lovejoy's powerful formulation of the case against appointing members of the Communist party, Dr. Schrecker retorts: "In other words because there is no academic freedom in Russia, American Communists had no right to enjoy it here."[20] The words are certainly "other" but not Arthur Lovejoy's. The point is not that there is no academic freedom in the Soviet Union, or even that members of the American Communist party approve of its absence there. The point is rather that their unfitness to teach is established by their voluntary membership in an organization in the United States that instructs its members to violate the standards of honest inquiry and teaching, an organization devoted among other things to the destruction of academic freedom in the United States. One could differ with Lovejoy on how to carry out a policy to preserve the integrity of teaching, but hardly with his argument.

Running away from the relevant point is evidenced wherever Dr. Schrecker cannot meet the argument. In 1953, before my book on *Common Sense and the Fifth Amendment* appeared, I published an essay in *The New York Times* Sunday magazine on the moral aspects of invoking the Fifth Amendment. This was at a time when the courts were still struggling with the complex legal aspects of the clause against self-incrimination. I was concerned only with the common-sense implication for appointments policy of the refusal of a person to answer a relevant question bearing on his or her fitness for a position of trust, asked by an authorized person or committee of peers. I was not considering the invocation of the Fifth Amendment before a court or government agency of any kind. I argued, to repeat a point already made, that the exercise of a constitutional right which exempts a man from any legal punishment does not necessarily exempt him from some social sanctions. There is an indefinitely large number of things that a person may constitutionally do—from casting aspersions on the paternity of his colleagues or declaring that the world is flat or that *The Protocols of Zion* is an authentic work of scholarship—for which he may justifiably suffer social sanctions or professional condemnation. A question that a member of the Communist party may refuse to answer to a congressional committee or a court may, if relevant to the performance of his trust or post, be legitimately asked of him by his peers, aside from the legal context. The refusal to answer relevant questions bearing on the fulfilment of his duties in the face of some incriminating evidence could justifiably lead to some sanction, including dismissal.

In that article, I discussed a number of hypothetical cases. I argued that if an individual who drives a school bus is asked whether he has attempted to peddle narcotics to school children and refuses to answer the question, parents and school officials would be justified in concluding that he is untrustworthy and in taking sanctions against him, including dismissal. Dr. Schrecker believes that even those identified as members of the Communist party are justified in refusing to answer relevant questions about their actions put to them by university administrators or committees of their teaching staffs. The issue here, as in the case of the bus driver questioned by school authorities, is the validity of the common-sense inference about trustworthiness. Dr. Schrecker runs away from the question by charging that "for Hook [membership in the Communist party is] . . . the academic equivalent of selling drugs to youngsters."[21] I do not know what the academic equivalent of selling drugs to children is. What I was discussing was the academic equivalent of trustworthiness. I held and still hold the common-sense view that even if a person could escape imprisonment by refusing to answer relevant questions about his or her behavior on grounds of fear of self-incrimination, whether that person was a nurse or cook or teacher, we would be justified in refusing to appoint and even in dismissing him or her, if he or she refused to answer our questions.

Dr. Schrecker does a greater injustice to others than she does to me, particularly to Ralph Himstead, the secretary of the American Association of University Professors, who in the 1930s and 1940s was chiefly responsible for building up the organization practically from scratch to a point where in virtue of its influence the observance of academic freedom became the common law of American universities. That is another and highly complex story. One keeps marvelling at Dr. Schrecker's display of synthetic anger and indignation with liberals who would not put the jobs of colleagues on the line by supporting the cause of the academic members of the Communist party who she insists, in the face of evidence to the contrary, were loyal citizens, models of scholarly behavior and never guilty of anything but well-intentioned perjury to keep their posts. Perjury, she suggests, is, of course, bad but members of the Communist party were forced into it by red-baiters and their liberal apologists. It goes without saying that Dr. Schrecker is not convinced by the evidence of the guilt of Alger Hiss or the Rosenbergs.

II

Dr. Schrecker's book raises in an acute way a present-day problem more intractable than the question posed by the existence of cells of the Communist party among university leaders in the 1930s to the 1950s. They no longer exist. There is no evidence of their presence on any campus. They have been replaced by members of the New Left, who are free of allegiance to the Communist party and unburdened by the legacy of Stalin and the Soviet Union, of Khrushchev in Hungary in 1956 and of Brezhnev in Czechoslovakia in 1968. Much more numerous than members of the Communist party were at any time, the New Left is openly and often fiercely tendentious in its effort to politicize the universities, intent on making current American institutions appear to be part of the apparatus of the corporate state, exposing American values as rationalizations of American imperialism, and presenting the saga of American history not so much as a growth of freedom but as a succession of continuing oppression of the Indians, blacks, women, ethnic minorities, and workers. Their efforts to rehabilitate the martyred old Communist Left is designed to reveal the oppressive underside of the myth of American democracy. In every discipline in the humanities and social studies they function as a militant "radical" caucus. Most of them profess to be Marxists of a sort although also committed to doctrines that would hardly pass muster as Marxist, leaving aside their validity from the standpoint of historical materialism.

The members of this New Left make no pretense of objective teaching, sometimes asserting that the very concept of objective truth is a pretense. Far from denying that they engage in indoctrination in their classrooms, they make a virtue of it. They declare that all teaching is indoctrination, and contend that the only significant distinction that can be drawn is between good indoctrination for a classless society and bad indoctrination for American class society. This is an old ploy. Every group that wants to put something over on the public declares that all teaching is propaganda. But the New Left carries on as if they have made a discovery. The opposite of propagandistic teaching in their view would not be nonpropagandistic teaching but no teaching at all.

The fact that someone is a declared radical or a Marxist in a university faculty should of itself be no occasion of intellectual concern for the academic community. There are radicals and radicals, Marxists and Marxists. We can learn from a scholarly radical as much as, or sometimes more than, from a conventional conservative, find as much or more stimulus and insight in the writings of a scholarly Marxist as in the works of one who followers Max Weber or Leo Strauss. But there's the rub! How scholarly are the contributions and the research of those who proudly proclaim themselves members of the New Left, who boast of capturing departments and the official posts of professional associations as if they were political parties? Are the decisions on appointments and promotions in American universities to be made on the basis of the intellectual quality, the level or depth of analysis, the originality and fruitfulness of the published or unpublished work of the candidate, or on the basis of his or her political orientation, on where they stand in the "class struggle" or on some controversial topical issue? There have always been, of course, profound differences on basic issues in all disciplines but, in the past, despite some notorious lapses, a general consensus has developed in the academic world on what was acceptable or unacceptable evidence of intellectual ability and intellectual integrity. By applying its criteria fairly, it was possible to approve the appointment or promotion of individuals with whose views on fundamental issues one disagreed. Those days seem gone in certain fields as far as members of the New Left are concerned. That someone like Dr. Schrecker who crudely plays ducks and drakes with the evidence, who can bring herself to write that members of the Communist party who changed their line with clock-like regularity as the Kremlin did, had in every case performed their doctrinal somersaults independently, could hold a post at Princeton University and be entrusted with teaching her conclusions to unsuspecting students is astonishing. Something seems wrong.

What is wrong is not merely the dubious scholarship of some members of the New Left, but the deliberate way they use the classroom to subvert the standards of honest teaching and the intellectual obligation to attempt to present a balanced analysis of controversial issues—pedagogic ideals to which the Old (Communist) Left for purposes of protective coloration sometimes gave lip-service. Here is Professor Bertell Ollman in a volume co-edited by Dr. Schrecker[22] arguing that the very ideal of academic freedom in American society functions as a "three-tiered mechanism of academic repression." Far from promising a solution of the problems faced by honest teachers and inquiries, "it may be part of the problem . . . because the ideal of academic freedom helps to disguise and distort an essentially repressive practice [which, by definition, academic freedom must be under capitalism. S. H.] by presenting it as an imperfect version of what should be."[23] When, then, can we expect to enjoy genuine academic freedom? Only "in a society that no longer needs its universities to help reproduce and rationalize existing inequalities, that is, a socialist society."[24]

That no existing "socialist" (i.e., communist) society recognizes academic freedom either as an ideal or in practice, that they not only bar dissenters from teaching but sometimes hang them or imprison them in psychiatric institutions, is immaterial and irrelevant to Professor Ollman. He is concerned only with academic freedom in American universities. It is not in their favor that academic conditions are worse in all existing socialist societies. What is in their favor is that, despite the "three-tiered repression" of their ideal of academic freedom, they have also "opened up a little space" for the likes of Professor Ollman. But no thanks to them for that: "the growing crisis in capitalism and the inability of most bourgeois scholarship to explain it" has compelled the universities to open its ranks to Marxists like Ollman in practically every discipline. Yet the repression still goes on, because "At the same time, there are more radical professors not getting hired or tenured."[25]

Now that the Ollmans and Schreckers have been carried by the Zeitgeist of capitalism in decline into university posts, they are free "to contribute to the development of critical thinking in the university." How? "Saved from displays of moral outrage, we are freed to work for academic freedom by helping to build the democratic socialist conditions that are necessary for it to exist. . . . Academic freedom by this interpretation, lives and grows in the conscious struggle for a socialist society."[26]

Now suppose that one's students do not believe this but object that the socialist society for which Professor Ollman propagandizes in the name of Marxism will have even less academic freedom than the academic freedom he enjoys in capitalist society. That shows they have simply misunderstood him. If they truly understood him, Professor Ollman claims, they would know that what he is saying is true. We can now better understand the remarkable contention in his reply to an earlier criticism of his defense of propaganda in the classroom. "If non-Marxists see my concern with such questions as an admission that the purpose of my courses is to convert students to socialism, I can only answer that in my view . . . a correct understanding of Marxism (or any body of scientific truth) leads automatically to its acceptance."[27] In other words if his students do not automatically accept Marxism—in Ollman's caricature of it—they do not understand it, and must accept the consequence of their obtuseness.

What Ollman believes and says and does is believed and said and done by numerous New Left teachers in American colleges and universities today. His words can be matched by similar declarations from one end of the country to another. Most of them are more direct. They scorn the dialectical double-talk used by Professor Ollman to rationalize the brazen effrontery with which he pictures the system of academic freedom that tolerates him as evidence of its repressive practices. More representative as well as more forthright is the denial of academic freedom in the remarks of another academic radical, Alan Wolfe, who tells us what to expect in the university of tomorrow:

> The social university is not primarily concerned with the abstract pursuit of scholarship, but with the utilization of knowledge obtained through scholarship to obtain social change. Therefore it does not recognize the right of its members to do anything they wish under the name of academic freedom: instead it assumes

> that all its members are committed to social change. To give an example, a course in riot control would simply be declared out of place in such a university, while a course in methods of rioting might be perfectly appropriate.[28]

What is even more unfortunate, some of the spokesmen for this position work hand-in-glove with radical agitators among students to disrupt the meetings of invited guests who propound views of which they disapprove. There is less freedom of speech on American campuses today, measured by the tolerance of dissenting views on controversial political issues, than at any other recent period in peacetime in American history.

What can be done about it? Nothing or very little by governmental intervention or even by boards of trustees. The growth of academic self-governance guarantees that any attempt at intervention by any outside institution will unify the academic community in protecting the Ollmans and Schreckers regardless of their violations of the ethics of honest teaching and research. Only the universities and colleges can heal themselves. It is a slow, time-consuming and ungrateful process. It must begin by senior scholars in their respective disciplines subjecting the vaunted contributions of the New Left to unsparing, scholarly criticism, and systematically exposing the shoddiness of much of the research on which their analysis allegedly rests. Contributions that genuinely illumine a problem by members of the New Left should be welcomed, regardless of the point of view from which they are made and contrasted with the far greater number of papers that articulate little except a point of view.

It is not only in the field of scholarship that those who have won their academic spurs must find the courage and time to resist the politicization of their disciplines. The systematic efforts to deny freedom of speech on many campuses, including our most eminent ones, to visiting scholars and other invited guests of students and teachers, to express views disapproved by the New Left, must be vigorously resisted. We must insist that the administrators of colleges and universities enforce the guarantees of free speech, and take disciplinary action against those guilty of disruptions. If administrators persist in their current policy of self-defeating appeasement and refuse to enforce the provisions of the disciplinary codes established on most campuses by joint committees of students and teachers, then concerned teachers should invoke the Civil Rights law. There are other measures to be considered. Now that the American Association of University Professors has abandoned its responsibility for upholding professional standards of conduct in this area, perhaps it is time for some new regional groups of scholars to organize to uphold the banner unfurled by John Dewey and Arthur Lovejoy more than seventy years ago.

NOTES

1. Their attack on perfectly loyal employers of the USIA was the occasion of the publication of my Open Letter in the *New York Times* of May 9, 1953, while McCarthy was still in public favor, calling for the organization of a national movement to retire him from public life.

2. Not all generals were as politically unsophisticated as General Zurcher. General Biddle Smith, whom I got to know through Louis Marx, the toy manufacturer who had taken courses with me at the New School, admitted on several occasions that the political education of army officers, in his time, had left a great deal to be desired. The situation with respect to the training of naval officers seemed no different. Indeed, the talks I heard Admiral Stanfield Turner deliver at Stanford, shortly after he was appointed to head the CIA, showed him to be completely innocent of knowledge about the theory and practices of communism. He gave the impression that he was less anxious and fearful of the activities of the intelligence agencies of the Soviet Union, despite their stupendous successes in penetrating the British MI5 and MI6 intelligence networks, than he was of the behavior of his immediate predecessors and their subordinates. It has been a continuing mystery to many well-informed scholars to determine on the basis of what qualifications Stanfield Turner was appointed to head the CIA, other than that of having been a classmate of Jimmy Carter at the Naval War College.

3. *The New York Times* (October 30, 1988).

4. (New York: Oxford University Press, 1986.)

5. Ibid., p. 309.

6. (London: Greenwood Press; New York: John Day, 1953.)

7. 196 (January 26, 1987).

8. 3 (January 1987):439ff.

9. *The Communist* 14 (May 1937):440, 445.

10. Ibid., 17 (September 1938):808, under the heading of "Selective Recruitment."

11. Ibid., p. 59.

12. Ibid., p. 168.

13. Ibid., p. 108.

14. A sampling of them is contained in my *Heresy, Yes—Conspiracy, No.*

15. *No Ivory Tower,* p. 51.

16. Ibid.

17. Ibid., p. 62.

18. Ibid., p. 132.

19. Ibid., p. 107.

20. Ibid., p. 106.

21. Ibid., p. 191.

22. Craig Kaplan and Ellen Schrecker eds., *Regulating the Intellectuals: Perspectives on Academic Freedom in the 1980s* (New York: Praeger, 1983), pp. 45ff.

23. Ibid., p. 53.

24. Ibid., p. 54.

25. Ibid., p. 56.

26. Ibid., pp. 55-56.

27. Theodore Mills Norton and Bertell Ollman eds., *Studies in Socialist Pedagogy* (New York: Monthly Review Press, 1978), p. 248.

28. Alan Wolfe, "The Myth of a Free Scholar," *The Center Magazine* (July 1969):77.

29

A Philosophical Perspective

Contemporary philosophy has abandoned the quest for an explanatory foundation of our knowledge of the world. It has renounced this grandiose project and returned to the more modest quest for wisdom in pursuing resolutions of the successive problems of mankind. This trend represents a fruitful convergence of interests with those engaged in the policy sciences of today, which by nature tend to be interdisciplinary.

When we speak of a philosophical perspective, we cannot intelligibly speak of a point of view bearing on all the problems of mankind. To be sure, many of them are interrelated and come in clusters, but the clusters are ineradicably pluralistic. Nonetheless, in facing the future we cannot make the bland assumption that all our problems are of equal significance or urgency. Despite foreign policy developments in recent years, the most important problem confronting mankind—as measured by the intrinsic weight of the values involved and by the number of other problems that depend on its resolution—is whether the free and open society of the West, which has blossomed in a comparatively brief period of recorded history, will survive or whether it will be overwhelmed by some form of secular or religious totalitarianism. Although the current threat from communism or secular totalitarianism is far greater than from any forms of religious fundamentalism, it certainly is not the only challenge to the survival of the free society.

What adds to the hazards of any analysis of our current problems and their probable resolution is the danger of an easy extrapolation of the historical and economic tendencies observable in the past and present. In past centuries the prophets of doom and gloom as well as of joy and peace have been

---

From *Thinking About America: The U.S. in the 1990s,* edited by A. Anderson and D. L. Bark (Stanford, Calif.: Hoover Institution Press, 1988).

exposed by unexpected developments in the historical process they relied on to confirm their predictions. There is a sobering moral in the parable of a political prophet in Munich in 1928

> who was asked to prophesy what would be happening to the burghers of his city in five, fifteen, twenty and forty years' time. He began: "I prophesy that in five years' time, in 1933, Munich will be a part of a Germany that has just suffered 5 million unemployed and that is ruled by a dictator with a certifiable mental illness who will proceed to murder 6 million Jews."
>
> His audience said: "Ah, then you must think that in fifteen years' time we will be in a sad plight."
>
> "No," replied the prophet, "I prophesy that in 1943 Munich will be part of a Greater Germany whose flag will fly from the Volga to Bordeaux, from Northern Norway to the Sahara."
>
> "Ah, then you must think that in twenty years' time, we will be mighty indeed."
>
> "No, my guess is that in 1948 Munich will be part of a Germany that stretches only from the Elbe to the Rhine, and whose ruined cities will recently have seen production down to only 10 per cent of the 1928 level."
>
> "So you think we face black ruin in forty years' time?"
>
> "No, by 1968 I prophesy that real income per head in Munich will be four times greater than now, and that in the year after that 90 per cent of German adults will sit looking at a box in a corner of their drawing rooms, which will show live pictures of a man walking upon the moon."
>
> They locked him up as a madman, of course.[1]

The moral is not that anything is possible and that we should give credence to any wild surmise about the future but that the natural assumption that the future will always be inferable from the present is unavoidably risky.

As hazardous as predictions are, I am not venturing much in asserting that during the next few decades free Western society—where the term *Western* is not merely a geographical designation—will face a serious challenge to its survival. Some maintain that its survival is possible only if the external threats from its totalitarian enemies are eliminated. Others assert that these threats no longer exist in virtue of the gradual transformation of communist societies and the abandonment of their program of world domination in favor of genuine peaceful coexistence—once merely proclaimed as a propaganda slogan but now imposed by the stern necessities of economic hardship. I believe that both positions are questionable. The preservation of our free society does not require the elimination of all totalitarian societies, secular or religious. Nor has the threat to the Western would lapsed with the policies of *glasnost* in the Soviet Union and the overthrow of Maoism in China.

What is indisputably true is that socialism as an economic system has failed in our time not only in the fully socialized economies of the communist states and the Third World but also in several of the semisocialized countries of Western Europe. As an economy, socialism in varying degrees has failed to solve the problem of incentive and to find a substitute for the free market to satisfy the needs of the consumer. But it is simplistic to assume that the failure of socialism as an economy necessarily spells the end of communism as a movement. For what is distinctive about communism as a movement in the twentieth century is that it has synthesized an economic program and a political program.

The more accurate designation of communism today is Leninism, not Marxism. The distinction is perhaps best expressed in the profound difference between the way in which Marx and Lenin understood the unfortunate phrase "the dictatorship of the proletariat," which appears peripherally in Marx's writings and centrally in Lenin's. For Marx the Paris Commune, governed by a coalition of political parties whose economic measures were reformist rather than revolutionary, exemplified the dictatorship of the proletariat. For Lenin the dictatorship of the proletariat could only be exercised through the absolute dictatorship of the Communist party *over* society guided by no law or restraint save its own power. Leninism, not Marxism, governs every communist country of the world today. In the life of communist countries everywhere, all lesser figures may be criticized for mistakes or excoriated for crimes; only Lenin remains an icon.

The great historical paradox, beyond the grasp of those unfamiliar with the theory and practice of communism, is that the principles of Marxism as Marx understood them explain the failure of socialism in communist countries. Marx himself declared that any attempt to collectivize society in an economy of scarcity (actually, in economies like those found wherever communism has been introduced in our century) would result not in prosperity but in socializing poverty.[2] On this score Marx's analysis and prediction have been historically confirmed. He believed that the development of the forces of production to their highest available level was a necessary condition for the introduction of socialism. The extent to which countries under communist rule were able to build up the industrial infrastructure required for socialism depended on what they were able to buy or steal from the capitalist economies of the West. On this point, Marx was perfectly justified in predicting the failure of any attempt to skip what he regarded as a necessary phase in social evolution. Where he went wrong was in his failure to predict that the attempt would be made and in the horrendous social and political consequences of the resulting failure for the modern world. Marx's theory of history was refuted by the political victory of Lenin and Leninism even as the economic breakdown of Leninist society testifies to the historical validity of Marx's economic analysis on this point.[3]

The alleged new turn in recent Soviet economic policy represents a departure from Marx's notion of how a socialist economy should function. It does not as yet represent an abandonment of the political philosophy of Leninism and its underlying strategy. It is the most ambitious tactic in a long series of efforts to induce the Western world both to lower its military defense and to share its advanced technology to make the economic life of the Soviet masses more acceptable, at least to the point where the Soviet class system and differential privileges within it become tolerable. That Leninists should make this effort, even if it involves a strategic retreat, is comprehensible and consistent with the history of Leninism since 1918, when it dissolved the Russian Constituent Assembly whose convocation Leninist had called for before seizing power in October 1917. That some credulous Western leaders and distinguished organs of public opinion should regard the adoption of some features of the free-market economy as an abandonment of Leninism is more difficult to explain as anything but a form of wishful thinking.

We need not explain this wishful thinking to recognize the importance of strengthening intelligent allegiance to the democratic faith of the West and its institutions.[4] That faith has been under attack not only from the agitation and propaganda agencies of the Kremlin but from irreconcilably alienated elements within the Western world who, professing an indifference or even hostility to the communist totalitarian states, concentrate their main critical fire against "the so-called free world," especially the United States. When I contrast the democratic faith or allegiance to the free society with the ideology of communism, I use the term *ideology* to mean the set of ideas and ideals that constitute the legitimizing rationale of a society one is prepared to defend, if only as the best of the available alternatives. I am not saying that great historical events and decisions can be explained by these ideological allegiances or that they always override considerations of practical survival or the advantages of compromise. Even during the era of fierce ideological religious wars, dynastic and nationalistic factors disrupted theological and ecclesiastical allegiances. Because ideology or one's fighting faith is not everything, it is not nothing. In some crucial periods of history it may play an important even if not decisive role, and our time is such a period.

When we ask ourselves what intellectual supports we can rely upon to strengthen the free world, we must note with sadness the transformation of the philosophy of American liberalism into the doctrines and practices of illiberalism. The philosophy of American liberalism is rooted in Jefferson and flowered in the philosophy of John Dewey. This philosophical hybrid accepts as its mandate of authority in social affairs the freely given consent of the governed, that such consent cannot be free unless there are guaranteed rights of dissent, that the locus of these rights is the individual (not the class or caste or group), that the arbiter of the inevitable conflict of human rights is the democratic process, that intelligence or the use of reason in social affairs functions best when there is a free market of ideas, and that truth and justice however defined are color-blind and have no gender. In the American liberal philosophy the individual, not individualism, is central and the community, committed to an equal concern for all individuals to achieve the fullest measure of their desirable potential, recognizes its responsibility to adopt measures that will further equality of opportunity, not equality of result.

If this is indeed the historical legacy of American liberalism, then it has been betrayed by those who have donned the mantle of liberalism in our generation. It would require a volume to do justice to the record, but I content myself here with two important manifestations of that betrayal.

The first and most persuasive evidence of the erosion of liberal political traditions is the retreat among professedly liberal individuals and groups from a position of judicial restraint to one of judicial activism. The genuinely liberal tradition in the United States is rooted in the position of Jefferson and Lincoln. Until recently, judicial activism has been associated with the fear of legislative majorities, with a history that began with the Dred Scott decision and continued with the overthrow of the civil rights acts after the Civil War, with *Plessy* v. *Ferguson,* and with the invalidation of New Deal legislation in the 1930s. With the emergence of the Warren court, the power of the Supreme Court has increased immeasurably, aided by the reluctance of congressional authority to exercise its mandate. Indeed, beginning with the Warren court, federal court decisions have had a more profound influence on the daily life of the nation—especially in education, business, and labor relations—than explicit legislation. The judiciary has reinterpreted the text of congressional legislation and presidential executive orders and has disregarded the legislative history of the acts in question.[5] Never in the history of the Supreme Court have defenders of judicial activism made bolder claims for its jurisdiction. Not only do they defend the role of the court as the supreme defender of the basic freedoms of the people (although all branches of government are equally pledged to their defense), but they believe that the court is empowered to invoke rights and freedoms, even by a five-to-four decision, not explicitly recognized either in the text of the Constitution or by any previous court or branch of government.

The extent to which the traditional philosophy of political liberalism, with its faith in the legislative process to educate the people in the meaning of freedom and to preserve the rights of minorities while upholding majority rule, has been transformed into the current view that the courts are the chief defenders of our basic freedoms may be measured by contrasting Henry Steele Commager's position in 1943 with his views today and with those of Professor Laurence Tribe, who under the aegis of present-day liberalism led the attack against the nomination of Judge Robert Bork to the Supreme Court. The flavor of Commager's early book, written in defense of the views of Justice Felix Frankfurter, comes through in these representative citations:

> The real battles of liberalism are not to be won in any court. If we make constitutionality the test of civil-rights legislation we are pretty sure to lose our case. It tends to distract attention from the real issues, places an improper responsibility on the courts, and encourages government by litigation instead of government by political machinery. No, the place to meet, and to defeat, unwise or unconstitutional legislation is in the legislature or in the arena of public opinion. . . .
>
> The impatient liberal, confronted with some example of legislative stupidity or of injustice, is eager for immediate action. The court may nullify the offensive legislation, but would not more be gained if the question were raised and agitated in the political instead of the judicial arena? The tendency to decide issues of personal liberty in the judicial arena alone has the effect of lulling the people into apathy towards issues that are fundamentally their concern, with the comforting notion that the courts will take care of personal and minority rights. It effectively removes these issues from the arena of public discussion. . . .
>
> This is the crucial objection to the judicial nullification of majority will in any field: that "education in the abandonment of foolish legislation is itself a training in liberty."[6]

There is no reason to believe that the justices of the Supreme Court are more qualified to determine the meaning of the basic freedoms on which our democracy rests or to resolve the inescapable conflicts of rights, values, and interests posed by legislative measures than the duly elected representatives of the people. Our nation was founded in a revolution against the actions of the British Crown and the British Parliament that were not responsible to the interests and consent of the American people. To accept the judicial activism of U.S. liberals is to abandon the principles of democracy and both the letter and the spirit of the Constitution.[7]

The second area of contemporary life that reflects the transformation of the liberal philosophy is the systematic perversion by certain administrative government agencies and the courts of the language of the Civil Rights Act of 1964 and of the original text of Presidential Executive Order 11246, which formulated the principles of affirmative action. The plain language of both documents forbids discrimination against any individual on grounds of race, religion, sex, or national origin. This position of traditional liberalism is expressed in Justice Harlan's famous dissent in *Plessy* v. *Ferguson.* His statement "the Constitution is color-blind" became the slogan of the National Association for the Advancement of Colored People (NAACP) when Roy Wilkins was its national secretary. It presupposes that individuals, not groups or classes, are the focus of human rights.

Today, even in situations and institutions with no history of discrimination against minorities and women, the principles of affirmative action have become the instruments of policies of reverse discrimination and preferential hiring.

In practice, the required "numerical goals and time schedules" to guide hiring practices wherever the underutilization of women and minorities is alleged actually result in a quota system. The historical effects of the deplorable discriminatory practices of the past are thus countered not only by remedial measures to increase the numbers of qualified minority and female candidates but by another kind of invidious discrimination.

Professional sports were rampantly discriminatory until Jackie Robinson shattered the immoral color barrier. Today no sensible or fair person argues that numerical goals and time schedules regulating the composition of the teams should replace the principle that open positions should be filled by the best players regardless of the racial percentage distribution on the team compared with the ratios in the general population or the pool of candidates trying out for the position. Why should it be different in any other field, especially in the universities and professions? Obviously the quest for excellence in education cannot survive the perversion of the principles of affirmative action into anything resembling a quota system. Although the term *quota* is carefully eschewed by those who have perverted the original meaning of affirmative action, in every area of public life today, especially in education, race and sex are regarded as relevant criteria in decisions affecting the admission, promotion, and reduction of personnel. How far the departure has gone from the traditional principle of liberalism is indicated by a recent declaration of Roy Wilkins's successor at the NAACP, Benjamin Hooks. Asked what was wrong with a "color-blind" approach to civil rights that would bar all forms of discrimination including reverse discrimination or preferential hiring, he responded, "it's wrong because it's stupid"[8]

Of all the negative effects of the illiberal view of affirmative action, probably the most worrisome is its impact on the prospects for liberal education. It has led in many areas to an abandonment of the quest for excellence on the ground that this leads to an invidious emphasis on the achievement of the elite. Even an equal-opportunity employer's announcement of a competitive scholarship for the study of English literature with the caution "Only the Best Need Apply" has been deemed "inappropriate, insensitive, and inconsistent" with the policies of affirmative action. The assumption that teaching personnel should reflect the proportion of women and minorities in the pool of potentially qualifiable candidates may before long be extended to the subject matter taught. Some university students and faculty have demanded that curricular offerings in standard courses on Western civilization or Western culture eliminate their alleged imperialist racial and sexual bias and reflect the hitherto unrecognized contributions of the cultures of the oppressed.

Our concern with the nature and quality of our educational system is decidedly relevant to the prospects of survival of a free society. Jefferson's conviction that only an educated and enlightened democracy can overcome the weaknesses of the popular rule of the past that succumbed to anarchy or despotism gains strength in the light of events in our century. Both the Old World and the New confirm Madison's observation that democracies "have been as short in their lives as they have been violent in their deaths." We argue that the very survival of our culture is at risk in our increasingly technological age unless we raise the level of general education and enhance the quality of higher education.

The current conditions of both are disquieting. Public education in large U.S. cities now turns out functionally illiterate students unable to cope with modern society. The courts have contributed to undermining the authority of teachers, who can no longer bar disrupters from the classroom. Everyone seems to have a vested interest in concealing the endemic violence in school systems where rape, robbery, and assault often occur. The lack of discipline in the schools is a major reason for the white flight that defeats plans for desegregation in city schools. Parents will endure hardships to avoid the expense and inconvenience of relocation. But once they perceive threats to the safety of their children, inferior educational programs, and disorderly classrooms, they will uproot.

Ironically, uncontrolled permissiveness defeats the aim of democratic education: to teach students to accept the authority of rational method in reaching conclusions. For without recognizing the importance of disciplined habits and the authority of the teacher over the process by which those habits are acquired, the educational experience cannot truly develop. It is nearly libelous to attribute the state of U.S. public education today to progressive education as John Dewey understood it.[9]

When we turn to U.S. higher education, the devastating consequences of the so-called student revolution of the 1960s are still apparent in the curricular chaos of most undergraduate campuses, where the requirements of a liberal education were abolished for a miscellany of unrelated general and vocational courses. But a far more serious development, sedulously concealed by administrative authorities, is that freedom to teach and learn in our major universities has in effect been abolished in certain disciplines. The winds of freedom no longer blow on U.S. campuses where foreign policy, race relations, affirmative action, feminist studies, and allied areas are concerned. Outstanding officials and scholars defending the foreign policy of the U.S. government in recent years, even when officially invited by university bodies, have often been unable to speak without organized disruption by extremist students immune from disciplinary action even when the guidelines of permitted dissent are clearly violated. The contrasting receptions accorded by campus audiences to Angela Davis, the notorious communist agitator, and to Jeane Kirkpatrick, former U.S. ambassador to the United Nations, symbolize the situation.

More serious in its long-term effect is the growing politicalization of the humanities and social sciences, where classrooms have become bully pulpits for anti-American sentiment. The history of the United States in commonly portrayed as the successive oppression of Indians, Chicanos, blacks, Chinese, European immigrants, and women without reference to the liberating aspects of the U.S. experience that attracted millions of the underprivileged and deprived everywhere, who found a better life for themselves and their offspring in the United States. It is perfectly legitimate to develop a critical attitude toward national pieties and complacencies about U.S. foreign and domestic policies. It is not legitimate to employ double standards, to judge the United States by its practices and failure to fulfill its ideals, and to contrast it with the professions and rhetoric of its enemies in a comparative evaluation that draws a moral equation between the free and open society of the United States and totalitarian communist regimes.

Classroom procedures of this kind, whether motivated by a desire to further capitalism or socialism, really violate the responsibilities of honest teaching incorporated in the principles of academic freedom. Academic freedom defends the rights of qualified teachers to investigate, discuss, publish, or teach the truth as they see it in the discipline of their competence, subject to no authority except the standards of professional ethics and inquiry. Academic freedom, the common law of U.S. university life, not only tolerates intellectual heresy but legally supports it. Even more remarkable, it provides complete immunity from institutional sanctions for the exercise of one's constitutional rights—an immunity not enjoyed by other fellow citizens. For example, I share a public platform with my physician, my attorney, my grocer, and my butcher from which we defend some highly controversial position on a burning issue of the moment. My fellow speakers may all pay a high price for the expression of their opinions—the loss of clients or the loss of trade—but only I, as a member of a university where academic freedom obtains, am absolved of the normal costs of unpopularity.

The community directly or indirectly (by tax exemption) underwrites the great costs of university education upholding the institution of academic freedom because it is in the common interest to do so. But clearly the right to academic freedom is correlative to certain duties and responsibilities flagrantly violated by the practices described above. The proper enforcement of these duties and responsibilities must be in the hands of the faculties themselves. Their reluctance to enforce these intellectual standards may undermine public support for higher education. Even private support may be affected. U.S. corporations contribute close to two billion dollars annually in support of higher education. If they refused to appropriate funds to institutions in open violation of the principles of academic freedom, faculties might take the necessary corrective measures. In extreme situations in which university administrations refuse to enforce the provisions of disciplinary codes established by joint student-faculty committees, the Civil Rights Act should be invoked on the ground that those in a position to enforce the laws are violating the civil rights of students and teachers victimized by organized violence or disruption.

The politicalization of our universities relates directly to our basic theme, the defense of the free world against the threats of totalitarianism. Unlike elementary education, where some form of indoctrination is inescapable even while the critical faculties of students are being developed, higher education has no need for it, if by *indoctrination* we mean "the process of teaching through which acceptance of belief is induced by nonrational or irrational means or both."[10] In higher education every position should be open to critical evaluation. Karl Jaspers notwithstanding, there is no need to make propaganda for the truth. Conflicting claims about the achievements of free and totalitarian societies and their costs should be examined as carefully as conflicting claims in any field of knowledge or policy. We need not fear the outcome of honest inquiry—that is, the commitment to an intellectual discipline that examines both sides of an issue and recognizes the difference between historical truth, however incomplete and inadequate, and historical fiction.

No formula or program available can provide reasonable hope for solving the multitude of problems confronting the American people in the coming decade. On the domestic scene it is safe to predict that Americans will settle for a mixed economy but are extremely unlikely to reach a consensus on how wealth is to be created and distributed. A recurrent fear among the philosopher-statesmen who founded the United States was that its citizens would be unable or unwilling to summon up the virtue necessary in times of crisis to subordinate private interest to the public good. The chronic identification of private interest with the public good can only end in chaos and national disaster. There is general agreement that the community must provide a safety net for those who through no fault of their own find themselves living beneath the level of a decent subsistence in a civilized society. But it is impossible literally to provide equality of opportunity for persons of disparate talents and wildly varying parental concern and capacities. All the greater therefore is the necessity for reducing the inequality of opportunity by social action that will provide all groups with a stake in the community and in the democratic process great enough to make them willing to defend it.

Whereas we realize that moral exhortation without institutional reform is empty, we must also recognize that institutional change without the acceptance of moral responsibility for one's individual conduct leaves us with another set of problems. Public outlays that end up with a permanent underclass cannot solve the problems of dependency, misery, and crime. Too much of our social and juridical thinking and the attitude of the victims of misfortune themselves reflect the view that human beings are so completely the creatures of circumstance that they are merely objects to which things happen. Such a view lacks coherence and contributes to the difficulty of resolving problems. It denies human beings responsibility for their own condition, despite the variation in behavior among persons in the same condition. At the same time it blames other human beings for permitting these conditions to exist, assuming in their case that they have moral responsibility, a human status, denied to others. But there is less to be said for this division between human beings, between those who are objects of the social process and those who are subjects, than for any division along national, religious, racial, or sexual lines. In effect such a view wipes out the moral difference between the criminals and their victims.[11]

A liberal jurist has recently protested against those like myself who have pointed out that we give far less attention to the rights of the victims and potential victims of crime than to the rights of the criminal defendants and potential criminal defendants. He regards the question of responsibility as either irrelevant or equally pertinent. "I am astonished," he writes, "by those who point to the docile deprived and say, 'Their conditions do not force them to break the law: why should those connditions force others to?' " Instead of answering the question, he evades it by telling us that we should be as alarmed by those who accept their conditions as by those who engage in criminal violence reacting against them. Strange doctrine for a jurist! We should, of course, be alarmed by both groups, but where those who accept their conditions become the victims of the criminal violence of those who do not, we should certainly be *more* concerned to protect the first group and punish the second. But according to our worthy jurist, the victims are responsible as well as the criminals. "What is amazing is that so many deprived Americans accept their lot without striking out," that is, without engaging in violent crime, too.[12]

Can we abolish crime, reduce poverty, and bring new opportunities by social reorganization alone? We certainly cannot do so without social reorganization, but that is not sufficient without human beings accepting some responsibility for their lives within the organization—a proposition Karl Marx recognized in his scornful contrast between the proletariat and the lumpen proletariat both living in a deprived environment. By all means let us provide those tempted by the easy money available by violence and vice with meaningful job opportunities and with modern housing that makes possible a comfortable family home. But how can we expect them to appear at work on Friday and Monday, to have the proper work ethic on other days, and to take care of their housing without their acceptance of personal—yes, moral—responsibility for their own behavior? The history of social reform and its impact on the statistics of violent crime in the last fifty years demonstrate that any increase in social concern must be accompanied by an increase in personal moral responsibility by encouraging those in need to reduce their social dependency on agencies beyond their own powers of participation and influence.

As long as we are committed as a nation to the defense of free societies, we can live without a consensus on the shifting pressures and conflicts of domestic policy. All the more necessary therefore is a consensus on a foreign policy that puts freedom first. The gravest internal threat to our survival is the danger that out of arrogance or ignorance U.S. foreign policy will be made a football in the struggle for U.S. electoral victory.

A genuinely democratic consensus cannot be established by manipulation but only by discussion, debate, and rational persuasion. The capacity to engage in this process and the quality of thought displayed in the decisions that emerge from it will reflect the character of the education—especially the public education—Americans receive. That is why wherever we are and whatever else we do, we must begin by improving our public education.

NOTES

1. General Sir John Hackett, *The Third World War* (London: Macmillan, 1979), p. 424. I owe this reference to my colleague, Lewis Gann.

2. Karl Marx, *Collected Works* (London: Lawrence & Wishart, 1976), 5:49.

3. See Sidney Hook, "Marxism Versus Communism," in *Marxism and Beyond* (Totowa, N.J.: Rowen & Littlefield, 1982).

4. See Sidney Hook, *Political Power and Personal Freedom* (New York: Criterion Books, 1959), esp. pt. 1.

5. A conspicuous illustration of judicial legislation in the guise of arbitrary reinterpretation of the text of the Civil Rights Act is the case of *Kaiser Aluminum and Chemical Corporation* v. *Brian F. Walker et al.* (1979).

6. Henry Steele Commager, *Majority Rule and Minority Rights* (New York: Oxford University Press, 1943), pp. 72ff.

7. On the general question of the relationship between democracy and judicial review, see Sidney Hook, *The Paradox of Freedom,* 2d ed. (Buffalo, N.Y.: Prometheus Books, 1987).

8. *New York Times* (May 30, 1983).

9. Cf. Thomas Main, "John Dewey and Progressive Education," *American Education* (Fall 1987):24.

10. See Sidney Hook, *Education for Modern Man: A New Perspective* (New York: Alfred Knopf, 1963), pp. 169 ff.

11. I believe I was the first to sound the tocsin in "The Rights of Victims," a 1971 commencement address at the University of Florida, reprinted in Sidney Hook, *Philosophy and Public Policy* (Carbondale: Southern Illinois University Press, 1980).

12. Judge David L. Bazelon, quoted in *New York Times* (January 7, 1988).